Fodor's 98

San Diego

The complete guide, thoroughly up-to-date

Packed with details that will make your trip

The must-see sights, off and on the beaten path

What to see, what to skip

Vacation itineraries, walking tours, day trips

Smart lodging and dining options

Essential local do's and taboos

Transportation tips

Key contacts, savvy travel advice

When to go, what to pack

Clear, accurate, easy-to-use maps

Books to read, videos to watch, background essays

Detailed index

Fodor's Travel Publications, Inc.
New York • Toronto • London • Sydney • Auckland
www.fodors.com/

Fodor's San Diego

EDITOR: Daniel Mangin

Editorial Contributors: Robert Andrews, David Brown, Lori Chamberlain, Kate Deely, Edie Jarolim, Christina Knight, Maribeth Mellin, Cynthia Queen, Heidi Sarna, Helayne Schiff, Kathryn Shevelow, M. T. Schwartzman (Gold Guide editor), Dinah Spritzer, Bobbi Zane

Editorial Production: Tracy Patruno

Maps: David Lindroth, *cartographer*; Steven K. Amsterdam, *map editor*

Design: Fabrizio La Rocca, *creative director*; Guido Caroti, *associate art director*; Jolie Novak, *photo editor*

Production/Manufacturing: Mike Costa

Cover Photograph: Peter Guttman

Copyright

Special Sales

CONTENTS

On the Road with Fodor's *v*

About Our Writers *v*
New This Year *v*
How to Use This Book *vi*
Don't Forget to Write *vi*

The Gold Guide: Smart Travel Tips A to Z *xvi*

1 Destination: San Diego *1*

Warm and Welcoming *2*
New and Noteworthy *4*
What's Where *4*
Pleasures and Pastimes *6*
Great Itineraries *7*
Fodor's Choice *8*
Festivals and Seasonal Events *10*

2 Exploring San Diego *12*

Balboa Park *15*
Downtown *25*
Coronado *33*
Harbor Island, Point Loma, and Shelter Island *36*
La Jolla *39*
Mission Bay and Sea World *45*
Old Town *49*

3 Exploring San Diego with Children *55*

4 Dining *64*

5 Lodging *77*

6 Nightlife and the Arts *93*

7 Outdoor Activities and Sports *103*

8 Shopping *119*

9 Side Trips *125*

10 Tijuana, Rosarito Beach, and Ensenada *147*

11 Portraits of San Diego *171*

"Idylling in San Diego," by Edie Jarolim *172*
Books and Videos *176*

Index *177*

Maps

San Diego *viii–ix*
Southern California *x–xi*
The United States *xii–xiii*
World Time Zones *xiv–xv*
Exploring San Diego *14*
Balboa Park *19*
Central San Diego *28–29*
La Jolla *42*
Mission Bay *47*

Old Town San Diego *52*
San Diego Dining *68–69*
San Diego Lodging *80–81*
San Diego Beaches *105*
San Diego North County *128*
Northwestern Baja *149*
Tijuana *152*
Ensenada *162*

ON THE ROAD WITH FODOR'S

WE'RE ALWAYS THRILLED to get letters from readers, especially one like this:

It took us an hour to decide what book to buy and we now know we picked the best one. Your book was wonderful, easy to follow, very accurate, and good on pointing out eating places, informal as well as formal. When we saw other people using your book, we would look at each other and smile.

Our editors and writers are deeply committed to making every Fodor's guide "the best one"—not only accurate but always charming, brimming with sound recommendations and solid ideas, right on the mark in describing restaurants and hotels, and full of fascinating facts that make you view what you've traveled to see in a rich new light.

About Our Writers

Our success in achieving our goals—and in helping to make your trip the best of all possible vacations—is a credit to the hard work of our extraordinary contributors.

Attorney **Lori Chamberlain** wrote the chapter on traveling in San Diego with kids. Her two small children, Sophie and Ryder, were her research assistants.

Kate Deely, who updated the nightlife and the arts chapter, divides her time between San Diego, San Francisco, and Arizona. A former staffer at *Parenting* magazine, Kate writes for national and local magazines and newspapers. A native San Diegan, she's kept tabs on the city's hot spots and hidden hole-in-the-wall hangouts.

Edie Jarolim was a senior editor at Fodor's before moving to Tucson—which is within easy driving distance of San Diego. She first fell in love with the city while doing dissertation research at the spaceship-shaped library at the University of California at San Diego and now returns yearly for a fix of sand and surf.

Cynthia Queen, who's played tour guide to out-of-town friends for years, enjoyed the chance to share her knowledge "beyond my immediate circle." She updated our Gold Guide and the lodging chapter. The former executive editor of three San Diego community newspapers and the current communications director for a non-profit corporation that supplies computers to San Diego–area schools, Cynthia is a freelance writer for the San Diego Zoological Society's magazine, ZOONOOZ, and several other local publications.

When she's not busy tracking down interesting new restaurants, **Kathryn Shevelow** teaches within the Literature Department of the University of California at San Diego.

Longtime southern Californian **Bobbi Zane,** who revised our Side Trips chapter, will soon make her home in the mountain hamlet of Julian. Bobbi's byline has appeared in the *Los Angeles Times, Los Angeles Daily News, Orange County Register,* and *San Jose Mercury News.* Among the many other Fodor's titles she has contributed to are *California's Best Bed & Breakfasts* and *California '97.* With her husband Gregg she publishes *Yellow Brick Road,* a monthly newsletter about bed-and-breakfast inns.

Fodor's *San Diego '98* editor **Daniel Mangin,** who also worked on the '97 edition, has been visiting San Diego since the mid-1970s, when he was the road manager for a punk-rock band. More recently, he's lectured about the cinema at UCSD and explored the North County scene.

New This Year

This year we've added terrific **Great Itineraries** that will lead you through the best of the city, taking into consideration how long you have to spend.

Bobbi Zane has completely revised the **North County chapter,** adding new sights in Julian, Santa Ysabel, and other towns.

Kathryn Shevelow added more than a dozen **new eating establishments** to the chapter, reflecting the culinary renaissance taking place outside San Diego proper.

And this year, Fodor's joins Rand McNally, the world's largest commercial mapmaker to bring you a **detailed color map** of San Diego.

We're also proud to announce that the American Society of Travel Agents has endorsed Fodor's as its guidebook of choice. ASTA is the world's largest and most influential travel trade association, operating in more than 170 countries, with 27,000 members pledged to adhere to a strict code of ethics reflecting the Society's motto, "Integrity in Travel." ASTA shares Fodor's devotion to providing smart, honest travel information and advice to travelers, and we've long recommended that our readers consult ASTA member agents for the experience and professionalism they bring to the table.

Check out **Fodor's Web site** (www.fodors.com/) for information on major destinations around the world and travel-savvy interactive features. The Web site also lists the 80-plus stations nationwide that carry the **Fodor's Travel Show,** a live radio call-in program that airs every weekend. Tune in to hear guests discuss their adventures—or call in to get answers for your most pressing travel questions.

How to Use This Book

Organization

Up front is the **Gold Guide,** an easy-to-use section divided alphabetically by topic. Under each listing you'll find tips and information that will help you accomplish what you need to in San Diego. You'll also find addresses and telephone numbers of organizations and companies that offer destination-related services and detailed information and publications.

The first chapter in the guide, **Destination: San Diego,** will help get you in the mood for your trip. New and Noteworthy cues you in on trends and happenings, What's Where gets you oriented, Pleasures and Pastimes describes the activities and sights that really make San Diego unique, Great Itineraries includes day-by-day sightseeing plans, Fodor's Choice showcases our top picks, and Festivals and Seasonal Events alerts you to special events throughout the year.

The **Exploring** chapter is subdivided by neighborhood; each subsection recommends a walking or driving tour and lists neighborhood sights alphabetically, including sights that are off the beaten path. The remaining chapters are arranged in alphabetical order by subject: **dining, lodging, nightlife and the arts, outdoor activities and sports, shopping,** and **side trips.**

At the end of the book you'll find **Portraits,** an essay about San Diego, followed by suggestions for any pretrip research you want to do, from recommended reading to movies on tape with San Diego as a backdrop.

Icons and Symbols

★	Our special recommendations
✕	Restaurant
🏨	Lodging establishment
🐥	Good for kids (rubber duckie)
☞	Sends you to another section of the guide for more information
✉	Address
☎	Telephone number
◷	Opening and closing times
💵	Admission prices (those we give apply to adults; substantially reduced fees are almost always available for children, students, and senior citizens)

Numbers in white and black circles that appear on the maps, in the margins, and within the tours correspond to one another.

Hotel Facilities

We always list the facilities that are available—but we don't specify whether they cost extra: When pricing accommodations, always ask what's included. Assume all rooms have private baths unless otherwise noted.

Credit Cards

The following abbreviations are used: **AE,** American Express; **D,** Discover; **DC,** Diners Club; **MC,** MasterCard; and **V,** Visa.

Don't Forget to Write

You can use this book in the confidence that all prices and opening times are based on information supplied to us at press time; Fodor's cannot accept responsibility for any errors. Time inevitably brings changes, so always confirm information when it matters—especially if you're making a detour to visit a specific place. In addition, when making reservations be sure to mention if you have a disability or are traveling with children, if you prefer a private bath or a certain type of bed, or if you have specific dietary needs or other concerns.

Were the restaurants we recommended as described? Did our hotel picks exceed your expectations? Did you find a museum we recommended a waste of time? If you have complaints, we'll look into them and revise our entries when the facts warrant it. If you've discovered a special place that we haven't included, we'll pass the information along to our correspondents and have them check it out. So send us your feedback, positive and negative: email us at editors@fodors.com (specifying the name of the book on the subject line) or write the San Diego editor at Fodor's, 201 East 50th Street, New York, New York 10022. Have a wonderful trip!

Karen Cure
Editorial Director

San Diego

PACIFIC OCEAN

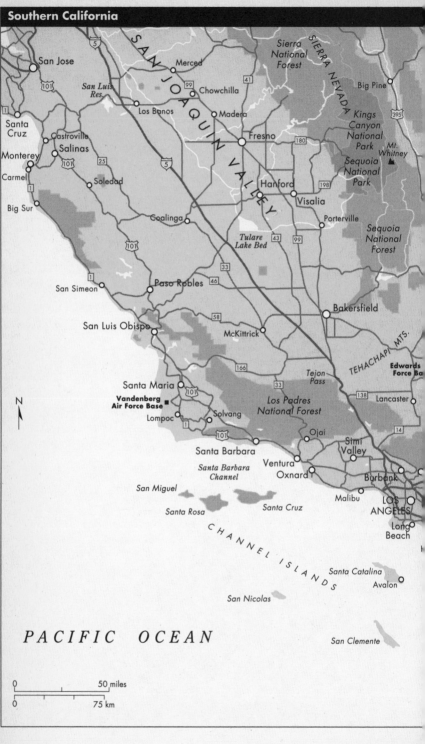

Southern California

PACIFIC OCEAN

N

0 ——— 50 miles

0 ——— 75 km

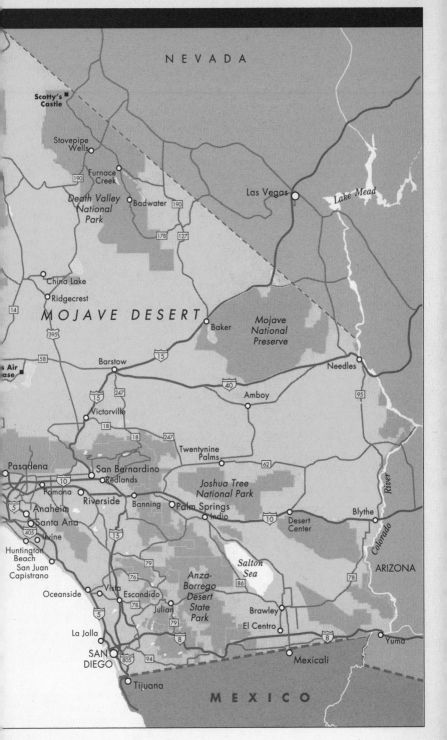

The United States

ONTARIO

CANADA

QUÉBEC

NEW BRUNSWICK

Québec

Fredericton

MINNESOTA

Duluth

Lake Superior

MICHIGAN

Lake Huron

Montréal

MAINE

Augusta

Ottawa

Montpelier

Concord

WISCONSIN

St. Paul

Green Bay

Toronto

Lake Ontario

Buffalo

N.H.

Boston

Minneapolis

Madison

Milwaukee

Lansing

Lake Erie

Albany

Hartford

MASS.

R.I.

Providence

Detroit

Cleveland

NEW YORK

CONN.

New York

IOWA

Des Moines

Chicago

ILLINOIS

Springfield

Pittsburgh

Harrisburg

PENNSYLVANIA

N.J.

Trenton

Philadelphia

Omaha

OHIO

Columbus

Baltimore

MD.

Dover

DEL.

Annapolis

Washington, D.C.

Topeka

Kansas City

Jefferson City

St. Louis

INDIANA

Indianapolis

Cincinnati

Louisville

Frankfort

WEST VIRGINIA

Charleston

Richmond

VIRGINIA

Norfolk

MISSOURI

KENTUCKY

Nashville

Raleigh

Tulsa

ARKANSAS

Memphis

Tennessee R.

TENNESSEE

NORTH CAROLINA

Little Rock

Birmingham

Atlanta

Columbia

SOUTH CAROLINA

Savannah R.

ATLANTIC OCEAN

Jackson

MISSISSIPPI

ALABAMA

GEORGIA

Montgomery

Savannah

Baton Rouge

Mobile

Tallahassee

Jacksonville

Houston

New Orleans

LOUISIANA

FLORIDA

Orlando

Bahama Islands

Gulf of Mexico

Miami

Nassau

N

0   500 miles

0   800 km

World Time Zones

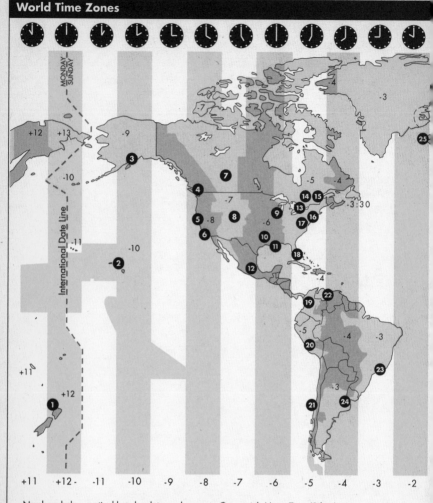

Numbers below vertical bands relate each zone to Greenwich Mean Time (0 hrs.).
Local times frequently differ from these general indications,
as indicated by light-face numbers on map.

Algiers, **29**

Anchorage, **3**

Athens, **41**

Auckland, **1**

Baghdad, **46**

Bangkok, **50**

Beijing, **54**

Berlin, **34**

Bogotá, **19**

Budapest, **37**

Buenos Aires, **24**

Caracas, **22**

Chicago, **9**

Copenhagen, **33**

Dallas, **10**

Delhi, **48**

Denver, **8**

Djakarta, **53**

Dublin, **26**

Edmonton, **7**

Hong Kong, **56**

Honolulu, **2**

Istanbul, **40**

Jerusalem, **42**

Johannesburg, **44**

Lima, **20**

Lisbon, **28**

London
(Greenwich), **27**

Los Angeles, **6**

Madrid, **38**

Manila, **57**

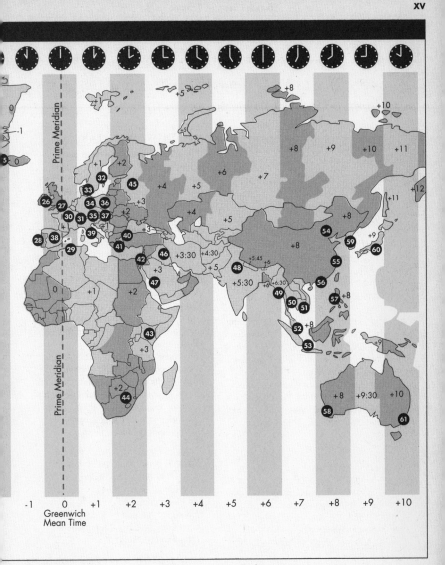

Mecca, **47**
Mexico City, **12**
Miami, **18**
Montréal, **15**
Moscow, **45**
Nairobi, **43**
New Orleans, **11**
New York City, **16**

Ottawa, **14**
Paris, **30**
Perth, **58**
Reykjavík, **25**
Rio de Janeiro, **23**
Rome, **39**
Saigon (Ho Chi Minh City), **51**

San Francisco, **5**
Santiago, **21**
Seoul, **59**
Shanghai, **55**
Singapore, **52**
Stockholm, **32**
Sydney, **61**
Tokyo, **60**

Toronto, **13**
Vancouver, **4**
Vienna, **35**
Warsaw, **36**
Washington, D.C., **17**
Yangon, **49**
Zürich, **31**

SMART TRAVEL TIPS A TO Z

Basic Information on Traveling in San Diego, Savvy Tips to Make Your Trip a Breeze, and Companies and Organizations to Contact

A

AIR TRAVEL

MAJOR AIRLINE OR LOW-COST CARRIER?

Most people choose a flight based on price. Yet there are other issues to consider. Major airlines offer the greatest number of departures; smaller carriers—including regional, low-cost, and no-frill airlines—usually have a more limited number of flights daily. Major airlines have frequent-flyer partners, which allow you to credit mileage earned on one airline to your account with another. Low-cost airlines offer a definite price advantage and fewer restrictions, such as advance-purchase requirements. Safety-wise, low-cost carriers as a group have a good history, but **check the safety record before booking** any low-cost carrier; call the Federal Aviation Administration's Consumer Hotline (☞ Airline Complaints, *below*).

➤ MAJOR AIRLINES: **America West** (☎ 800/235–9292). **American** (☎ 800/433–7300). **British Airways** (☎ 800/247–9297). **Continental** (☎ 800/231–0856). **Delta** (☎ 800/241–4141). **Midwest Express** (☎ 800/452–2022). **Northwest** (☎ 800/225–2525). **Southwest** (☎ 800/435–9792). **TWA** (☎ 800/892–4141). **United** (☎ 800/241–6522). **US Airways** (☎ 800/428–4322).

➤ SMALLER AIRLINES: **Aeromexico** (☎ 800/237–6639). **Alaska Airlines** (☎ 800/426–0333). **American Eagle** (☎ 800/433–7300). **Reno Air** (☎ 800/736–6247).

➤ FROM THE U.K.: **American** (☎ 0345/789–789) via Los Angeles or Chicago. **British Airways** (☎ 0345/222–111) via Phoenix. **Delta** (☎ 0800/414–767) via Atlanta or Los Angeles. **United** (☎ 0800/888–555) via Los Angeles, San Francisco, Washington or Chicago. **Virgin Atlantic** (☎ 01293/747–747) via Los Angeles.

GET THE LOWEST FARE

The least-expensive airfares to San Diego are priced for round-trip travel. Major airlines usually require that you **book in advance and buy the ticket within 24 hours,** and you may have to **stay over a Saturday night.** It's smart to **call a number of airlines, and when you are quoted a good price, book it on the spot**—the same fare may not be available on the same flight the next day. Airlines generally allow you to change your return date for a $25–$50 fee. If you don't use your ticket you can apply the cost toward the purchase of a new ticket, again for a small charge. However, most low-fare tickets are nonrefundable. To get the lowest airfare, **check different routings.** If your destination or home city has more than one gateway, compare prices to and from different airports. Also price off-peak flights, which may be significantly less expensive.

To save money on flights from the United Kingdom and back, **look into an APEX or Super-PEX ticket.** APEX tickets must be booked in advance and have certain restrictions. Super-PEX tickets can be purchased at the airport on the day of departure—subject to availability.

DON'T STOP UNLESS YOU MUST

When you book, **look for nonstop flights** and **remember that "direct" flights stop at least once.** Try to **avoid connecting flights,** which require a change of plane. Two airlines may jointly operate a connecting flight, so ask if your airline operates every segment—you may find that your preferred carrier flies you only part of the way.

USE AN AGENT

Travel agents, especially those who specialize in finding the lowest fares (☞ Discounts & Deals, *below*), can be especially helpful when booking a plane ticket. When you're quoted a price, **ask your agent if the price is**

likely to get any lower. Good agents know the seasonal fluctuations of airfares and can usually anticipate a sale or fare war. However, waiting can be risky: The fare could go *up* as seats become scarce, and you may wait so long that your preferred flight sells out. A wait-and-see strategy works best if your plans are flexible, but if you must arrive and depart on certain dates, don't delay.

AVOID GETTING BUMPED

Airlines routinely overbook planes, knowing that not everyone with a ticket will show up, but sometimes everyone does. When that happens, airlines ask for volunteers to give up their seats. In return these volunteers usually get a certificate for a free flight and are rebooked on the next flight out. If there are not enough volunteers the airline must choose who will be denied boarding. The first to get bumped are passengers who checked in late and those flying on discounted tickets, **so get to the gate and check in as early as possible,** especially during peak periods.

Always **bring a photo ID to the airport.** You may be asked to show it before you are allowed to check in.

ENJOY THE FLIGHT

For better service, **fly smaller or regional carriers,** which often have higher passenger-satisfaction ratings. Sometimes you'll find leather seats, more legroom, and better food.

For more legroom, **request an emergency-aisle seat;** don't however, sit in the row in front of the emergency aisle or in front of a bulkhead, where seats may not recline.

If you don't like airline food, **ask for special meals when booking.** These can be vegetarian, low-cholesterol, or kosher, for example.

To avoid jet lag **drink water (not alcohol), and move about the cabin** to stretch your legs.

COMPLAIN IF NECESSARY

If your baggage goes astray or your flight goes awry, **complain right away.** Most carriers require that you file a claim immediately.

➤ AIRLINE COMPLAINTS: U.S. Department of Transportation **Aviation Consumer Protection Division** (✉ C-75, Washington, DC 20590, ☎ 202/366–2220). **Federal Aviation Administration (FAA) Consumer Hotline** (☎ 800/322–7873).

AIRPORTS & TRANSFERS

Flying time to San Diego is 5 hours from New York, 3½ hours from Chicago, and ¾ hour from Los Angeles.

➤ AIRPORT INFORMATION: **San Diego International Airport Lindbergh Field** (☎ 619/231–2100).

TRANSFERS

San Diego Transit Route 2 buses depart for downtown from the front of East Terminal's US Airways section, daily from 5:30 AM to 1 AM. The fare is $1.50. Cloud 9 Shuttle and Public Shuttle vans will take you directly to your destination, often for less than a taxi would cost.

If you have rented a car at the airport, you can take Harbor Drive, at the perimeter of the airport, to downtown, only about 3 mi away.

Taxi fare is $7–$9 plus tip to most center-city hotels.

➤ BUS INFORMATION: **San Diego Transit** (☎ 619/233–3004). **Cloud 9 Shuttle** (☎ 619/278–8877 or 800/974–8855 in San Diego). **Public Shuttle** (☎ 619/990–8770).

B
BUS TRAVEL

Greyhound operates 26 buses a day between San Diego and Los Angeles, connecting with buses to all major U.S. cities. Many buses are express or nonstop; others make stops at coastal towns en route.

➤ INFORMATION: **Greyhound** (✉ 120 W. Broadway, ☎ 619/239–8082 or 800/231–2222).

WITHIN AND AROUND SAN DIEGO

The biggest link in the Metropolitan Transit System (MTS) is San Diego Transit, whose information line is open daily 5:30 AM–8:30 PM. It can provide details on getting to and from any location. Regional bus companies service areas outside the city.

➤ BUS COMPANIES: **ATC Van Co.** (☎ 619/427–5660), for Coronado, the Silver Strand, and Imperial Beach;

Chula Vista Transit (☎ 619/233–3004), for Bonita and Chula Vista; **National City Transit** (☎ 619/474–7505), for National City; **North County Transit District** (☎ 760/722–6283), for the area bound by the ocean, east to Escondido, north to Camp Pendleton, and south to Del Mar; **Northeast Rural Bus System** (☎ 760/767–4287) or **Southeast Rural Bus System** (☎ 619/478–5875), for access to rural county towns; and **San Diego Transit** (☎ 619/233–3004, TTY/TDD 619/234–5005) for city transit.

DISCOUNT PASSES

A Day Tripper Transit Pass is good for unlimited trips on the same day on San Diego Transit buses and on the trolley and the ferry for $5; there's also a four-day pass for $15. Both passes are available at the Transit Center. One-day passes can be purchased at UCSD, the ferry landing, and at trolley stations.

➤ TRANSIT CENTER: **Transit Store** (✉ 102 Broadway, ☎ 619/234–1060).

C

CAMERAS, CAMCORDERS, & COMPUTERS

Always **keep your film, tape, or computer disks out of the sun.** Carry an extra supply of batteries, and **be prepared to turn on your camera, camcorder, or laptop** to prove to security personnel that the device is real. Always **ask for hand inspection of film,** which becomes clouded after successive exposure to airport X-ray machines, and **keep videotapes and computer disks away from metal detectors.**

➤ PHOTO HELP: **Kodak Information Center** (☎ 800/242–2424). *Kodak Guide to Shooting Great Travel Pictures,* available in bookstores or from Fodor's Travel Publications (☎ 800/533–6478); $16.50 plus $4 shipping.

CAR RENTAL

A car is essential for San Diego's sprawling freeway system and comes in handy for touring Baja California, but one is not necessary in Tijuana.

Rates in San Diego begin at $25 a day and $136 a week for an economy car

with air conditioning, an automatic transmission, and unlimited mileage. This does not include tax on car rentals, which is 8.25%.

➤ MAJOR AGENCIES: **Alamo** (☎ 800/522–9696, 0800/272–2000 in the U.K.). **Avis** (☎ 800/331–1084, 800/879–2847 in Canada). **Budget** (☎ 800/527–0700, 0800/181181 in the U.K.). **Dollar** (☎ 800/800–4000; 0990/565656 in the U.K., where it is known as Eurodollar). **Hertz** (☎ 800/654–3131, 800/263–0600 in Canada, 0345/555888 in the U.K.). **National InterRent** (☎ 800/227–7368; 0345/222525 in the U.K., where it is known as Europcar Inter-Rent).

CUT COSTS

To get the best deal, **book through a travel agent who is willing to shop around.** When pricing cars, **ask about the location of the rental lot.** Some off-airport locations offer lower rates, and their lots are only minutes from the terminal via complimentary shuttle. You also may want to **price local car-rental companies,** whose rates may be lower still, although their service and maintenance may not be as good as those of a name-brand agency. Remember to ask about required deposits, cancellation penalties, and drop-off charges if you're planning to pick up the car in one city and leave it in another.

Also **ask your travel agent about a company's customer-service record.** How has it responded to late plane arrivals and vehicle mishaps? Are there often lines at the rental counter, and, if you're traveling during a holiday period, does a confirmed reservation guarantee you a car?

Be sure to **look into wholesalers,** companies that do not own fleets but rent in bulk from those that do and often offer better rates than traditional car-rental operations. Prices are best during off-peak periods.

➤ RENTAL WHOLESALERS: **Kemwel Group** (☎ 914/835–5555 or 800/678–0678, ℻ 914/835–5126).

NEED INSURANCE?

When driving a rented car you are generally responsible for any damage to or loss of the vehicle. You also are liable for any property damage or personal injury that you may cause while driving. Before you rent, **see what coverage you already have** under the terms of your personal auto-insurance policy and credit cards.

For about $14 a day, rental companies sell protection, known as a collision- or loss-damage waiver (CDW or LDW) that eliminates your liability for damage to the car; it's always optional and should never be auto- matically added to your bill. Some states, including California, have capped the price of CDW and LDW.

In most states you don't need CDW if you have personal auto insurance or other liability insurance. However, **make sure you have enough coverage to pay for the car.** If you do not have auto insurance or an umbrella policy that covers damage to third parties, purchasing CDW or LDW is highly recommended.

BEWARE SURCHARGES

Before you pick up a car in one city and leave it in another, **ask about drop-off charges or one-way service fees,** which can be substantial. Note, too, that some rental agencies charge extra if you return the car before the time specified on your contract. To avoid a hefty refueling fee, **fill the tank just before you turn in the car,** but be aware that gas stations near the rental outlet may overcharge.

MEET THE REQUIREMENTS

In the United States **you must be 21 to rent a car,** and rates may be higher if you're under 25. You'll pay extra for child seats (about $3 per day), which are compulsory for children under five, and for additional drivers (about $2 per day). Residents of the U.K. will need a reservation voucher, a passport, a U.K. driver's license, and a travel policy that covers each driver, in order to pick up a car.

CHILDREN & TRAVEL

CHILDREN IN SAN DIEGO

Be sure to plan ahead and **involve your youngsters** as you outline your trip. When packing, include things to keep them busy en route. On sightsee- ing days try to schedule activities of special interest to your children. If you are renting a car don't forget to **arrange for a car seat when you reserve.** The monthly *San Diego Family Press* is filled with listings of events and resources; it is available by mail for $3.50, which covers postage and handling, or free in San Diego at Longs drugstores, Toys R Us, and local libraries.

➤ LOCAL INFORMATION: *San Diego Family Press* (✉ Box 23960, San Diego 92193, ☎ 619/685–6970). Fodor's by-parents, for-parents *Where Should We Take the Kids? California* (☎ 800/533–6478 or in bookstores); $17.

HOTELS

Most hotels in San Diego allow children under a certain age to stay in their parents' room at no extra charge, but others charge them as extra adults; be sure to **ask about the cutoff age for children's discounts.**

FLYING

As a general rule, infants under two not occupying a seat fly free. If your children are two or older **ask about children's airfares.**

In general the adult baggage allowance applies to children paying half or more of the adult fare.

According to the FAA it's a good idea to use safety seats aloft for children weighing less than 40 pounds. Air- lines, however, can set their own policies: U.S. carriers allow FAA- approved models but usually require that you buy a ticket, even if your child would otherwise ride free, since the seats must be strapped into regu- lar seats. Airline rules vary regarding their use, so it's important to **check your airline's policy about using safety seats during takeoff and land- ing.** Safety seats cannot obstruct any of the other passengers in the row, so get an appropriate seat assignment as early as possible.

When making your reservation, **request children's meals or a free- standing bassinet** if you need them; the latter are available only to those seated at the bulkhead, where there's enough legroom. Remember, however, that bulkhead seats may not have their own overhead bins, and there's no storage space in front of you—a major inconvenience.

CONSUMER PROTECTION

Whenever possible, **pay with a major credit card** so you can cancel payment if there's a problem, provided that you can provide documentation. This is a good practice whether you're buying travel arrangements before your trip or shopping at your destination.

If you're doing business with a particular company for the first time, **contact your local Better Business Bureau and the attorney general's offices** in your state and the company's home state, as well. Have any complaints been filed?

Finally, if you're buying a package or tour, always **consider travel insurance** that includes default coverage (☞ Insurance, *below*).

➤ LOCAL BBBs: **Council of Better Business Bureaus** (✉ 4200 Wilson Blvd., Suite 800, Arlington, VA 22203, ☎ 703/276–0100, FAX 703/525–8277).

CUSTOMS & DUTIES

ENTERING THE U.S.

Visitors age 21 and over may import the following into the United States: 200 cigarettes or 50 cigars or 2 kilograms of tobacco, 1 liter of alcohol, and gifts worth $100. Prohibited items include meat products, seeds, plants, and fruits.

ENTERING CANADA

If you've been out of Canada for at least seven days you may bring in C$500 worth of goods duty-free. If you've been away for fewer than seven days but more than 48 hours, the duty-free allowance drops to C$200; if your trip lasts 24–48 hours, the allowance is C$50. You may not pool allowances with family members. Goods claimed under the C$500 exemption may follow you by mail; those claimed under the lesser exemptions must accompany you.

Alcohol and tobacco products may be included in the seven-day and 48-hour exemptions but not in the 24-hour exemption. If you meet the age requirements of the province or territory through which you reenter Canada you may bring in, duty-free, 1.14 liters (40 imperial ounces) of wine or liquor *or* 24 12-ounce cans or bottles of beer or ale. If you are 16 or older you may bring in, duty-free, 200 cigarettes and 50 cigars; these items must accompany you.

You may send an unlimited number of gifts worth up to C$60 each duty-free to Canada. Label the package UNSOLICITED GIFT—VALUE UNDER $60. Alcohol and tobacco are excluded.

➤ INFORMATION: **Revenue Canada** (✉ 2265 St. Laurent Blvd. S, Ottawa, Ontario K1G 4K3, ☎ 613/993–0534, 800/461–9999 in Canada).

ENTERING THE U.K.

From countries outside the EU, including the United States, you may import, duty-free, 200 cigarettes or 50 cigars; 1 liter of spirits or 2 liters of fortified or sparkling wine or liqueurs; 2 liters of still table wine; 60 milliliters of perfume; 250 milliliters of toilet water; plus £136 worth of other goods, including gifts and souvenirs.

➤ INFORMATION: **HM Customs and Excise** (✉ Dorset House, Stamford St., London SE1 9NG, ☎ 0171/202–4227).

D

DISABILITIES & ACCESSIBILITY

ACCESS IN SAN DIEGO

Most of San Diego is easily accessible to visitors using wheelchairs. Most public buses and trolleys are equipped with lifts. Although the Old Town district has some moderately uneven streets, curb cuts and smooth sidewalks are decidedly the rule rather than the exception for the city as a whole. The extensive network of walkways in Balboa Park affords views that are both lovely and accessible.

The Access Center of San Diego publishes lists of hotels, motels, and restaurants with access for people with disabilities. Accessible San Diego has a visitor information center and telephone hot line, makes hotel referrals, and provides guides to San Diego's attractions for visitors with mobility problems.

About one-third of the bus lines are served by buses with elevator ramps; call San Diego Transit (☞ Bus Travel, *above*) for detailed information. The San Diego Trolley (☞ Trolleys, *below*), which goes as far as the Mexican border, has wheelchair lifts. Round-the-clock wheelchair transportation throughout San Diego is available through MTS Access.

➤ LOCAL RESOURCES: **Access Center of San Diego** (✉ Information and Referrals, 1295 University Ave., Suite 10, San Diego 92103, ☎ 619/293–3500, TDD 619/293–7757). **Accessible San Diego** (✉ Executive Complex, 1010 2nd Ave., Suite 1630, San Diego 92101, ☎ 619/279–0704). **MTS Access** (✉ 4970 Market St., San Diego 92102, ☎ 619/266–9000).

TIPS AND HINTS

When discussing accessibility with an operator or reservations agent, **ask hard questions.** Are there any stairs, inside *or* out? Are there grab bars next to the toilet *and* in the shower/tub? How wide is the doorway to the room? To the bathroom? For the most extensive facilities meeting the latest legal specifications, **opt for newer accommodations,** which are more likely to have been designed with access in mind. Older buildings or ships may offer more limited facilities. Be sure to **discuss your needs before booking.**

➤ COMPLAINTS: **Disability Rights Section** (✉ U.S. Department of Justice, Box 66738, Washington, DC 20035–6738, ☎ 202/514–0301 or 800/514–0301, ☏ 202/307–1198, TTY 202/514–0383 or 800/514–0383) for general complaints. **Aviation Consumer Protection Division** (☞ Air Travel, *above*) for airline-related problems. **Civil Rights Office** (✉ U.S. Department of Transportation, Departmental Office of Civil Rights, S-30, 400 7th St. SW, Room 10215, Washington, DC, 20590, ☎ 202/366–4648) for problems with surface transportation.

TRAVEL AGENCIES & TOUR OPERATORS

The Americans with Disabilities Act requires that travel firms serve the needs of all travelers. That said, you should note that some agencies and operators specialize in making travel arrangements for individuals and groups with disabilities.

➤ TRAVELERS WITH MOBILITY PROBLEMS: **Access Adventures** (✉ 206 Chestnut Ridge Rd., Rochester, NY 14624, ☎ 716/889–9096), run by a former physical-rehabilitation counselor. **Hinsdale Travel Service** (✉ 201 E. Ogden Ave., Suite 100, Hinsdale, IL 60521, ☎ 630/325–1335), a travel agency that benefits from the advice of wheelchair traveler Janice Perkins. **Wheelchair Journeys** (✉ 16979 Redmond Way, Redmond, WA 98052, ☎ 425/885–2210 or 800/313–4751), for general travel arrangements.

➤ TRAVELERS WITH DEVELOPMENTAL DISABILITIES: **New Directions** (✉ 5276 Hollister Ave., Suite 207, Santa Barbara, CA 93111, ☎ 805/967–2841, ☏ 805/964–7344). **Sprout** (✉ 893 Amsterdam Ave., New York, NY 10025, ☎ 212/222–9575 or 888/222–9575, ☏ 212/222–9768).

DISCOUNTS & DEALS

Be a smart shopper and **compare all your options before making a choice.** A plane ticket bought with a promotional coupon may not be cheaper than the least expensive fare from a discount ticket agency. For high-price travel purchases, such as packages or tours, keep in mind that what you get is just as important as what you save. Just because something is cheap doesn't mean it's a bargain.

LOOK IN YOUR WALLET

When you use your credit card to make travel purchases you may get free travel-accident insurance, collision-damage insurance, and medical or legal assistance, depending on the card and the bank that issued it. American Express, MasterCard, and Visa provide one or more of these services, so **get a copy of your credit card's travel-benefits policy.** If you are a member of the American Automobile Association (AAA) or an oil-company-sponsored road-assistance plan, always **ask hotel or car-rental reservations agents about auto-club discounts.** Some clubs offer additional discounts on tours, cruises, or admission to attractions. And don't forget that auto-club membership entitles you to free maps and trip-planning services.

DIAL FOR DOLLARS

To save money, **look into "1-800" discount reservations services,** which use their buying power to get a better price on hotels, airline tickets, even car rentals. When booking a room, always **call the hotel's local toll-free number** (if one is available) rather than the central reservations number—you'll often get a better price. Always ask about special packages or corporate rates.

➤ AIRLINE TICKETS: ☎ 800/FLY–4–LESS. ☎ 800/FLY–ASAP.

➤ HOTEL ROOMS: **Hotel Reservations Network (HRN; ☎ 800/964–6835). RMC Travel (☎ 800/245–5738).**

SAVE ON COMBOS

Packages and guided tours can both save you money, but don't confuse the two. When you buy a package your travel remains independent, just as though you had planned and booked the trip yourself. Fly/drive packages, which combine airfare and car rental, are often a good deal. In cities, ask the local visitors bureau about hotel packages. These often include tickets to major museum exhibits and other special events.

JOIN A CLUB?

Many companies sell discounts in the form of travel clubs and coupon books, but these cost money. You must use participating advertisers to get a deal, and only after you recoup the initial membership cost or book price do you begin to save. If you plan to use the club or coupons frequently you may save considerably. Before signing up, find out what discounts you get for free.

➤ DISCOUNT CLUBS: **Entertainment Travel Editions** (✉ Box 1068, Trumbull, CT 06611, ☎ 800/445–4137); $28–$53, depending on destination. **Great American Traveler** (✉ Box 27965, Salt Lake City, UT 84127, ☎ 800/548–2812); $49.95 per year. **Moment's Notice Discount Travel Club** (✉ 7301 New Utrecht Ave., Brooklyn, NY 11204, ☎ 718/234–6295); $25 per year, single or family. **Privilege Card International** (✉ 201 E. Commerce St., Suite 198, Youngstown, OH 44503, ☎ 330/746–5211 or 800/236–9732); $74.95 per year. **Sears's Mature Outlook** (✉ Box 9390, Des Moines, IA 50306, ☎ 800/336–6330); $14.95 per year. **Travelers Advantage** (✉ CUC Travel Service, 3033 S. Parker Rd., Suite 1000, Aurora, CO 80014,

☎ 800/548–1116 or 800/648–4037); $49 per year, single or family. **Worldwide Discount Travel Club** (✉ 1674 Meridian Ave., Miami Beach, FL 33139, ☎ 305/534–2082); $50 per year family, $40 single.

DRIVING

Interstate 5 stretches from Canada to the Mexican border and bisects San Diego. Interstate 8 provides access from Yuma, Arizona, and points east. Drivers coming from Nevada and the mountain regions beyond can reach San Diego on I–15. To avoid traffic, **steer clear of rush-hour periods.** Parking around town is generally easy.

E

EMERGENCIES

Dial 911 for police, ambulance, and fire departments.

➤ HOSPITALS/DOCTORS: **Hotel Doctors** (☎ 619/275–2663 or 800/468–3537). **Mercy Hospital and Medical Center** (✉ 4077 5th Ave., ☎ 619/294–8111). **Scripps Memorial Hospital** (✉ 9888 Genesee Ave., La Jolla, ☎ 619/457–4123). **UCSD Medical Center** (✉ 200 W. Arbor Dr., Hillcrest, ☎ 619/543–6222). **Veterans Administration Hospital** (✉ 3350 La Jolla Village Dr., La Jolla, ☎ 619/552–8585).

➤ DENTISTS: **San Diego County Dental Society** (☎ 619/275–0244). **Hotel Doctors** (☎ 619/275–2663 or 800/468–3537).

F

FERRY TRAVEL

The ferry to Coronado leaves from the Broadway Pier daily, every hour on the hour, Sunday–Thursday 9–9, until 10 PM Friday and Saturday. The fare is $2 each way and 50¢ for each bicycle.

➤ SAN DIEGO–CORONADO FERRY: **Information Line (☎ 619/234–4111).**

G

GAY & LESBIAN TRAVEL

San Diego has a large and fairly visible gay community. Hillcrest is the gayest part of town, but lesbians and gay men have settled all over.

➤ LOCAL RESOURCES: *Fodor's Gay Guide to Los Angeles and Southern California* (*Fodor's Travel Publications*, ☎ 800/533–6478 or in bookstores); $11. *The Lesbian and Gay Men's Community Center* (✉ 3916 Normal St., San Diego 92103, ☎ 619/692–4297). **Update** (☎ 619/299–0500), a weekly gay paper.

➤ GAY- AND LESBIAN-FRIENDLY TRAVEL AGENCIES: **Advance Damron** (✉ 1 Greenway Plaza, Suite 800, Houston, TX 77046, ☎ 713/682–2002 or 800/695–0880, FAX 713/888–1010). **Club Travel** (✉ 8739 Santa Monica Blvd., West Hollywood, CA 90069, ☎ 310/358–2200 or 800/429–8747, FAX 310/358–2222). **Islanders/Kennedy Travel** (✉ 183 W. 10th St., New York, NY 10014, ☎ 212/242–3222 or 800/988–1181, FAX 212/929–8530). **Now Voyager** (✉ 4406 18th St., San Francisco, CA 94114, ☎ 415/626–1169 or 800/255–6951, FAX 415/626–8626). **Yellowbrick Road** (✉ 1500 W. Balmoral Ave., Chicago, IL 60640, ☎ 773/561–1800 or 800/642–2488, FAX 773/561–4497). **Skylink Women's Travel** (✉ 3577 Moorland Ave., Santa Rosa, CA 95407, ☎ 707/585–8355 or 800/225–5759, FAX 707/584–5637), serving lesbian travelers.

I

INSURANCE

Travel insurance is the best way to **protect yourself against financial loss.** The most useful policies are trip-cancellation-and-interruption, default, medical, and comprehensive insurance.

Without insurance you will lose all or most of your money if you cancel your trip, regardless of the reason. It's essential that you **buy trip-cancellation-and-interruption insurance,** particularly if your airline ticket, cruise, or package tour is nonrefundable and cannot be changed. When considering how much coverage you need, look for a policy that will cover the cost of your trip plus the nondiscounted price of a one-way airline ticket, should you need to return home early. Also **consider default or bankruptcy insurance,** which protects you against a supplier's failure to deliver.

Citizens of the United Kingdom can buy an annual travel-insurance policy valid for most vacations during the year in which it's purchased. If you are pregnant or have a preexisting medical condition, make sure you're covered. According to the Association of British Insurers, a trade association representing 450 insurance companies, it's wise to buy extra medical coverage when you visit the United States.

If you have purchased an expensive vacation, comprehensive insurance is a must. **Look for comprehensive policies that include trip-delay insurance,** which will protect you in the event that weather problems cause you to miss your flight, tour, or cruise. A few insurers sell waivers for preexisting medical conditions. Companies that offer both features include Access America, Carefree Travel, Travel Insured International, and Travel Guard (☞ *below*).

Always **buy travel insurance directly from the insurance company;** if you buy it from a travel agency or tour operator that goes out of business you probably will not be covered for the agency or operator's default, a major risk. Before you make any purchase, **review your existing health and home-owner's policies** to find out whether they cover expenses incurred while traveling.

➤ TRAVEL INSURERS: In the U.S., **Access America** (✉ 6600 W. Broad St., Richmond, VA 23230, ☎ 804/285–3300 or 800/284–8300), **Carefree Travel Insurance** (✉ Box 9366, 100 Garden City Plaza, Garden City, NY 11530, ☎ 516/294–0220 or 800/323–3149), **Near Travel Services** (✉ Box 1339, Calumet City, IL 60409, ☎ 708/868–6700 or 800/654–6700), **Travel Guard International** (✉ 1145 Clark St., Stevens Point, WI 54481, ☎ 715/345–0505 or 800/826–1300), **Travel Insured International** (✉ Box 280568, East Hartford, CT 06128–0568, ☎ 860/528–7663 or 800/243–3174), **Travelex Insurance Services** (✉ 11717 Burt St., Suite 202, Omaha, NE 68154-1500, ☎ 402/445–8637 or 800/228–9792, FAX 800/867–9531), **Wallach & Company** (✉ 107 W. Federal St., Box 480, Middleburg, VA 20118, ☎ 540/687–3166 or 800/

237–6615). In Canada, **Mutual of Omaha** (✉ Travel Division, 500 University Ave., Toronto, Ontario M5G 1V8, ☎ 416/598–4083, 800/268–8825 in Canada). In the U.K., **Association of British Insurers** (✉ 51 Gresham St., London EC2V 7HQ, ☎ 0171/600–3333).

L

LIMOUSINES

Limousine companies operate airport shuttles and customized tours. Rates vary and are per hour, per mile, or both, with some minimums established.

➤ LIMO COMPANIES: **Advantage Limousine Service** (☎ 619/563–1651). **La Jolla Limousines** (☎ 619/459–5891). **Limousines by Linda** (☎ 619/234–9145). **Olde English Livery** (☎ 619/232–6533).

LODGING

APARTMENT & VILLA RENTALS

If you want a home base that's roomy enough for a family and comes with cooking facilities, **consider a furnished rental.** These can save you money, however some rentals are luxury properties, economical only when your party is large. Home-exchange directories list rentals (often second homes owned by prospective house swappers), and some services search for a house or apartment for you (even a castle if that's your fancy) and handle the paperwork. Some send an illustrated catalog; others send photographs only of specific properties, sometimes at a charge. Up-front registration fees may apply.

➤ RENTAL AGENTS: **Europa-Let/Tropical Inn-Let** (✉ 92 N. Main St., Ashland, OR 97520, ☎ 541/482–5806 or 800/462–4486, ℻ 541/482–0660). **Property Rentals International** (✉ 1008 Mansfield Crossing Rd., Richmond, VA 23236, ☎ 804/378–6054 or 800/220–3332, ℻ 804/379–2073). **Rent-a-Home International** (✉ 7200 34th Ave. NW, Seattle, WA 98117, ☎ 206/789–9377 or 800/488–7368, ℻ 206/789–9379). **Hideaways International** (✉ 767 Islington St., Portsmouth, NH 03801, ☎ 603/430–4433 or 800/843–4433, ℻ 603/430–4444) is a

travel club whose members arrange rentals among themselves; yearly membership is $99.

HOME EXCHANGES

If you would like to exchange your home for someone else's, **join a home-exchange organization,** which will send you its updated listings of available exchanges for a year and will include your own listing in at least one of them. Making the arrangements is up to you.

➤ EXCHANGE CLUBS: **HomeLink International** (✉ Box 650, Key West, FL 33041, ☎ 305/294–7766 or 800/638–3841, ℻ 305/294–1148) charges $83 per year.

M

MONEY

ATMS

Before leaving home, **make sure that your credit cards have been programmed for ATM use.**

➤ ATM LOCATIONS: **Cirrus** (☎ 800/424–7787). **Plus** (☎ 800/843–7587).

N

NATIONAL PARKS

You may be able to **save money on park entrance fees** by getting a discount pass. The Golden Eagle Pass ($50) gets you and your companions free admission to all parks for one year. (Camping and parking are extra). Both the Golden Age Passport, for U.S. citizens or permanent residents age 62 and older, and the Golden Access Passport, for travelers with disabilities, entitle holders to free entry to all national parks plus 50% off fees for the use of many park facilities and services. Both passports are free; you must show proof of age and U.S. citizenship or permanent residency (such as a U.S. passport, driver's license, or birth certificate) or proof of disability. All three passes are available at all national park entrances. Golden Eagle and Golden Access passes are also available by mail.

➤ PASSES BY MAIL: **National Park Service** (✉ Department of the Interior, Washington, DC 20240).

P

PACKING FOR SAN DIEGO

San Diego's casual lifestyle and year-round mild climate set the parameters for what you'll want to pack. You can **leave formal clothes and cold-weather gear behind.**

Plan on warm weather at any time of the year. Cottons, walking shorts, jeans, and T-shirts are the norm at tourist attractions. **Pack bathing suits and shorts regardless of the season.** Casual attire is generally acceptable; only a few restaurants require a jacket and tie for men. Women may want to bring something a little dressier than their sightseeing garb.

Evenings are cool, even in summer, so be sure to **bring a sweater or a light jacket.** Rainfall in San Diego is not usually heavy; you won't need a raincoat except during the winter months, and even then, an umbrella may be sufficient protection. Be sure you **take proved, comfortable walking shoes** with you. Even if you don't walk much at home, you'll find yourself covering miles while sightseeing on your vacation.

Sunglasses are a must in San Diego. Binoculars can also come in handy, especially if you're in town during whale-watching season.

Bring an extra pair of eyeglasses or contact lenses in your carry-on luggage, and if you have a health problem, **pack enough medication** to last the entire trip. It's important that you **don't put prescription drugs or valuables in luggage to be checked**: it might go astray.

LUGGAGE

In general you are entitled to check two bags on flights within the United States. A third piece may be brought on board, but it must fit easily under the seat in front of you or in the overhead compartment.

Airline liability for baggage is limited to $1,250 per person on flights within the United States. On international flights it amounts to $9.07 per pound or $20 per kilogram for checked baggage (roughly $640 per 70-pound bag) and $400 per passenger for unchecked baggage. Insurance for losses exceeding these amounts can be bought from the airline at check-in for about $10 per $1,000 of coverage; note that this coverage excludes a rather extensive list of items, which is shown on your airline ticket.

Before departure, **itemize your bags' contents** and their worth, and label the bags with your name, address, and phone number. (If you use your home address, cover it so that potential thieves can't see it readily.) Inside each bag, **pack a copy of your itinerary.** At check-in, **make sure that each bag is correctly tagged** with the destination airport's three-letter code. If your bags arrive damaged or fail to arrive at all, file a written report with the airline before leaving the airport.

PASSPORTS & VISAS

CANADIANS

A passport is not required to enter the United States.

U.K. CITIZENS

British citizens need a valid passport to enter the United States. If you are staying for fewer than 90 days on vacation, with a return or onward ticket, you probably will not need a visa. However, you will need to fill out the Visa Waiver Form, 1-94W, supplied by the airline.

➤ INFORMATION: **London Passport Office** (☎ 0990/21010) for fees and documentation requirements and to request an emergency passport. **U.S. Embassy Visa Information Line** (☎ 01891/200–290) for U.S. visa information; calls cost 49p per minute or 39p per minute cheap rate. **U.S. Embassy Visa Branch** (⊠ 5 Upper Grosvenor St., London W1A 2JB) for U.S. visa information; send a self-addressed, stamped envelope. Write the **U.S. Consulate General** (⊠ Queen's House, Queen St., Belfast BTI 6EO) if you live in Northern Ireland.

S

SENIOR-CITIZEN TRAVEL

Many discounts are available to older travelers: Meals, lodging, entry to various attractions, car rentals, tickets for buses and trains, and campsites are among the prime examples. Some discounts are given solely on the basis of age, without membership requirement; others require membership in an organization. In California, the state park system, which includes more than 200 locations, provides a $2 discount on campsites for anyone 62 or over and others in the same private vehicle; ask for this discount when you make reservations.

If you are 50 or older, **ask about senior discounts even if there is no posted notice.** A 10% cut on a bus ticket and $2 off a pizza may not seem like major savings, but they add up, and you can cut the cost of a trip appreciably if you remember to take advantage of these options.

To qualify for age-related discounts, **mention your senior-citizen status up front** when booking hotel reservations (not when checking out) and before you're seated in restaurants (not when paying the bill). Note that discounts may be limited to certain menus, days, or hours. When renting a car, **ask about promotional car-rental discounts,** which can be cheaper than senior-citizen rates.

➤ EDUCATIONAL TRAVEL PROGRAMS: **Elderhostel** (✉ 75 Federal St., 3rd floor, Boston, MA 02110, ☎ 617/426–7788).

SIGHTSEEING

Weather permitting, **hot-air balloons** lift off from San Diego's North County; the average cost is $130 per person. Most flights float at sunrise or sunset and are followed by a champagne celebration.

Free two-hour **trolley tours** of the downtown redevelopment area, including the Gaslamp Quarter, are hosted by Centre City Development Corporation Downtown Information Center. Groups of 35 passengers leave from 225 Broadway, Suite 160, downtown, the first and third Saturday of each month at 10 AM. Reservations are necessary. The tour may be canceled if there aren't enough passengers.

The Old Town Trolley travels to almost every attraction and shopping area on open-air trackless trolleys. Drivers double as tour guides. You can take the full two-hour, narrated city tour or get on and off as you please at any of the nine stops. An all-day pass costs $20 for adults, $8 for children 6–12; under 5 free. The trolley, which leaves every 30 minutes, operates daily 9–5 in summer, 9–4 in winter.

Two companies operate one- and two-hour **harbor cruises.** San Diego Harbor Excursion and Hornblower Invader Cruises boats depart from the Broadway Pier. No reservations are necessary for the $12–$17 voyages, and both vessels have snack bars on board. Classic Sailing Adventures has morning and afternoon tours of the harbor and San Diego Bay and nighttime in summer cruises for $45 per person.

Several fine **walking tours** are available on weekdays or weekends. On weekends, the California State Park System gives free walking tours of Old Town. Groups leave from 4002 Wallace Street at 2 PM daily, weather permitting. The Gaslamp Quarter Historical Foundation leads two-hour historical walking tours of the restored downtown historic district on Saturday at 11 AM ($5). The foundation operates a museum at its 410 Island Ave. headquarters. Hours vary, so call ahead. Walkabout conducts several free walking tours throughout the city each week.

Great views of land and sea can be had on a **whale-watching cruise.** As many as 200 gray whales pass the San Diego coast each day during their migration, south to Mexico and then back north, from mid-December to mid-March.

➤ BALLOON TOURS: **Pacific Horizon** (☎ 619/756–1790 or 800/244–1790). **Skysurfer** (☎ 619/481–6800 or 800/660–6809 in CA).

➤ BUS AND TROLLEY TOURS: **Centre City Development Corporation's Downtown Information Center** (☎ 619/235–2222). **Gray Line Tours** (☎ 619/491–0011 or 800/331–5077 outside CA). **San Diego Mini Tours** (☎ 619/477–8687). **Old Town Trolley** (☎ 619/298–8687).

➤ CRUISES: **Classic Sailing Adventures** (☎ 619/224–0800). **Hornblower Invader Cruises** (☎ 619/234–8687). **San Diego Harbor Excursion** (☎ 619/234–4111).

➤ HELICOPTER TOURS: **Civic Helicopters** (☎ 619/438–8424 or 800/438–4354); tours start at $69 per person per half hour.

➤ WALKING TOURS: **California State Park System** (☎ 619/220–5422). **The Gaslamp Quarter Historical Foundation** (☎ 619/233–4692). **Walkabout** (☎ 619/231–7463).

➤ WHALE-WATCHING: **Classic Sailing Adventures** (☎ 619/224–0800) tailors whale-watching expeditions for up to six people. **H&M Landing** (☎ 619/222–1144), **Seaforth Sportfishing** (☎ 619/224–3383), and **San Diego Harbor Excursions** (☎ 619/234–4111) have daily whale-watching trips in large boats.

STUDENTS

To save money, **look into deals available through student-oriented travel agencies.** To qualify you'll need a bona fide student ID card. Members of international student groups are also eligible.

➤ STUDENT IDS AND SERVICES: **Council on International Educational Exchange** (CIEE; ⊠ 205 E. 42nd St., 14th floor, New York, NY 10017, ☎ 212/822–2600 or 888/268–6245, ℻ 212/822–2699), for mail orders only, in the United States. **Travel Cuts** (⊠ 187 College St., Toronto, Ontario M5T 1P7, ☎ 416/979–2406 or 800/667–2887) in Canada.

➤ HOSTELING: **Hostelling International—American Youth Hostels** (⊠ 733 15th St. NW, Suite 840, Washington, DC 20005, ☎ 202/783–6161, ℻ 202/783–6171). **Hostelling International—Canada** (⊠ 400-205 Catherine St., Ottawa, Ontario K2P 1C3, ☎ 613/237–7884, ℻ 613/237–7868). **Youth Hostel Association of England and Wales** (⊠ Trevelyan House, 8 St. Stephen's Hill, St. Albans, Hertfordshire AL1 2DY, ☎ 01727/855215 or 01727/845047, ℻ 01727/844126). Membership in the U.S., $25; in Canada, C$26.75; in the U.K., £9.30.

➤ STUDENT TOURS: **Contiki Holidays** (⊠ 300 Plaza Alicante, Suite 900, Garden Grove, CA 92840, ☎ 714/740–0808 or 800/266–8454, ℻ 714/740–0818).

T

TAXIS

Taxi fares are regulated at the airport—all companies charge the same rate (generally $1.80 for the first mile, $1.20 for each additional mile). Fares vary among companies on other routes, however, including the ride back to the airport. If you call ahead and ask for the flat rate ($7) you'll get it, otherwise you'll be charged by the mile (which works out to $9 or so).

➤ CAB COMPANIES: **Co-op Silver Cabs** (☎ 619/280–5555). **Coronado Cab** (☎ 619/435–6211). **La Jolla Cab** (☎ 619/453–4222). **Orange Cab** (☎ 619/291–3333). **Yellow Cab** (☎ 619/234–6161).

TELEPHONES

CALLING HOME

AT&T, MCI, and Sprint long-distance services make calling home relatively convenient and let you avoid hotel surcharges. Typically you dial an 800 number.

➤ TO OBTAIN ACCESS CODES: **AT&T USADirect** (☎ 800/874–4000). **MCI Call USA** (☎ 800/444–4444). **Sprint Express** (☎ 800/793–1153).

TOUR OPERATORS

Buying a prepackaged tour or independent vacation can make your trip to San Diego less expensive and more hassle-free. Because everything is prearranged you'll spend less time planning.

Operators that handle several hundred thousand travelers per year can use their purchasing power to give you a good price. Their high volume may also indicate financial stability. But some small companies provide more personalized service; because they tend to specialize, they may also be more knowledgeable about a given area.

A GOOD DEAL?

The more your package or tour includes, the better you can predict the ultimate cost of your vacation. Make sure you know exactly what is covered, and **beware of hidden costs.** Are taxes, tips, and service charges included? Transfers and baggage handling? Entertainment and excursions? These can add up.

If the package or tour you are considering is priced lower than in your wildest dreams, **be skeptical.** Also, **make sure your travel agent knows the accommodations** and other services. Ask about the hotel's location, room size, beds, and whether it has a pool, room service, or programs for children, if you care about these. Has your agent been there in person or sent others you can contact?

BUYER BEWARE

Each year consumers are stranded or lose their money when tour operators—even very large ones with excellent reputations—go out of business. So **check out the operator.** Find out how long the company has been in business, and ask several agents about its reputation. **Don't book unless the firm has a consumer-protection program.**

Members of the National Tour Association and United States Tour Operators Association are required to set aside funds to cover your payments and travel arrangements in case the company defaults. Nonmembers may carry insurance instead. Look for the details, and for the name of an underwriter with a solid reputation, in the operator's brochure. Note: When it comes to tour operators, **don't trust escrow accounts.** Although there are laws governing charter-flight operators, no governmental body prevents tour operators from raiding the till. For more information, *see* Consumer Protection, *above.*

➤ TOUR-OPERATOR RECOMMENDATIONS: **National Tour Association** (NTA; ✉ 546 E. Main St., Lexington, KY 40508, ☎ 606/226–4444 or 800/755–8687). **United States Tour Operators Association** (USTOA; ✉ 342 Madison Ave., Suite 1522, New York, NY 10173, ☎ 212/599–6599, FAX 212/599–6744). **American Society of Travel Agents** (☞ Travel Agencies, *below*).

USING AN AGENT

Travel agents are excellent resources. When shopping for an agent, however, you should **collect brochures from several sources**; some agents' suggestions may be skewed by promotional relationships with tour and package firms that reward them for volume sales. If you have a special interest, **find an agent with expertise in that area** (☞ Travel Agencies, *below*). Don't rely solely on your agent, who may be unaware of small-niche operators. Note that some special-interest travel companies only sell directly to the public and that

some large operators only accept bookings made through travel agents.

SINGLE TRAVELERS

Prices for packages and tours are usually quoted per person, based on two sharing a room. If traveling solo, you may be required to pay the full double-occupancy rate. Some operators eliminate this surcharge if you agree to be matched with a roommate of the same sex, even if one is not found by departure time.

GROUP TOURS

Among companies that sell tours to San Diego, the following are nationally known, have a proven reputation, and offer plenty of options. The classifications below represent different price categories, and you'll probably encounter these terms when talking to a travel agent or tour operator. The key difference is usually in accommodations, which run from budget to better, and better-yet to best.

➤ DELUXE: **Globus** (✉ 5301 S. Federal Circle, Littleton, CO 80123-2980, ☎ 303/797–2800 or 800/221–0090, FAX 303/347–2080). **Maupintour** (✉ 1515 St. Andrews Dr., Lawrence, KS 66047, ☎ 913/843–1211 or 800/255–4266, FAX 913/843–8351). **Tauck Tours** (✉ Box 5027, 276 Post Rd. W, Westport, CT 06881-5027, ☎ 203/226–6911 or 800/468–2825, FAX 203/221–6828).

➤ FIRST-CLASS: **Collette Tours** (✉ 162 Middle St., Pawtucket, RI 02860, ☎ 401/728–3805 or 800/832–4656, FAX 401/728–1380).

➤ BUDGET: **Cosmos** (☞ Globus, *above*).

PACKAGES

Like group tours, independent vacation packages are available from major tour operators and airlines. The companies listed below offer vacation packages in a broad price range.

➤ AIR/HOTEL/CAR: **American Airlines Fly AAway Vacations** (☎ 800/321–2121). **Continental Vacations** (☎ 800/634–5555). **Delta Dream Vacations** (☎ 800/872–7786). **United Vacations** (☎ 800/328–6877). **US Airways Vacations** (☎ 800/455–0123).

➤ HOTEL ONLY: **SuperCities** (✉ 139 Main St., Cambridge, MA 02142, ☎ 800/333–1234).

➤ CUSTOM PACKAGES: **Amtrak's Great American Vacations** (☎ 800/321–8684). **Budget WorldClass Drive** (☎ 800/527–0700, 0800/181181 in the U.K.) for self-drive itineraries.

➤ FROM THE U.K.: **British Airways Holidays** (✉ Astral Towers, Betts Way, London Rd., Crawley, West Sussex RH10 2XA, ☎ 01293/723–121). **Jetsave** (✉ Sussex House, London Rd., East Grinstead, West Sussex RH19 1LD, ☎ 01342/312–033). **Key to America** (✉ 1–3 Station Rd., Ashford, Middlesex TW15 2UW, ☎ 01784/248–777). **Kuoni Travel Ltd.** (✉ Kuoni House, Dorking, Surrey RH5 4AZ, ☎ 01306/742–222). **Premier Holidays** (✉ Premier Travel Center, Westbrook, Milton Rd., Cambridge CB4 1YG, ☎ 01223/516–688). **Trailfinders** (✉ 42–50 Earls Court Rd., London W8 6FT, ☎ 0171/937–5400; ✉ 58 Deansgate, Manchester, M3 2FF, ☎ 0161/839–6969).

THEME TRIPS

➤ BICYCLING: **Imagine Tours** (✉ Box 475, Davis, CA 95617, ☎ 916/758–8782).

➤ GOLF: **Golf Pacific Coast** (✉ 1267 Saratoga Ave., Ventura, CA 93003, ☎ 800/335–3534).

➤ HORSEBACK RIDING: **Equitour FITS Equestrian** (✉ Box 807, Dubois, WY 82513, ☎ 307/455–3363 or 800/545–0019, FAX 307/455–2354).

➤ WHALE-WATCHING: **Natural Habitat Adventures** (✉ 2945 Center Green Ct., Boulder, CO 80301, ☎ 303/449–3711 or 800/543–8917, FAX 303/449–3712). **Oceanic Society Expeditions** (✉ Fort Mason Center, Bldg. E, San Francisco, CA 94124, ☎ 415/441–1106 or 800/326–7491). **Pacific Sea Fari Tours** (✉ 2803 Emerson St., San Diego, CA 92106, ☎ 619/226–8224).

TRAIN TRAVEL

Amtrak services downtown San Diego's Santa Fe Depot from Los Angeles. Amtrak stops in San Diego North County at Solana Beach and Oceanside.

➤ TRAINS: **Amtrak** (☎ 800/872–7245). **Oceanside train station** (☎ 760/722–4622). **Santa Fe Depot** (✉ 1050 Kettner Blvd., ☎ 619/239–9021). **Solana Beach train station** (☎ 619/259–2697).

TROLLEYS

The San Diego Trolley travels from downtown to within 100 ft of the U.S.–Mexican border, stopping at 21 suburban stations en route. The basic fare is $1.75 one way, 75¢ for senior citizens. The trolley also travels from downtown to Encanto, Lemon Grove, La Mesa, El Cajon, and Santee in East County. **Purchase tickets just before boarding**; ticket-vending machines are located at each station. Trolleys operate daily, approximately every 15 minutes, 5 AM–9 PM, then every 30 minutes until 1 AM. The Bayside line serves the Convention Center and Seaport Village. Another line travels from downtown to Old Town; one to Mission Valley is slated to begin operations in 1998.

➤ TROLLEYS: **San Diego Trolley** (☎ 619/233–3004).

TRAVEL AGENCIES

A good travel agent puts your needs first. Look for an agency that has been in business at least five years, emphasizes customer service, and has someone on staff who specializes in your destination. In addition, **make sure the agency belongs to the American Society of Travel Agents** (ASTA). If your travel agency is also acting as your tour operator, *see* Tour Operators, *above*.

➤ LOCAL AGENT REFERRALS: American Society of Travel Agents (ASTA; 800/965–2782 for 24-hr hot line, FAX 703/684–8319). **Alliance of Canadian Travel Associations** (✉ Suite 201, 1729 Bank St., Ottawa, Ontario K1V 7Z5, ☎ 613/521–0474, FAX 613/521–0805). **Association of British Travel Agents** (✉ 55–57 Newman St., London W1P 4AH, ☎ 0171/637–2444, FAX 0171/637–0713).

TRAVEL GEAR

Travel catalogs specialize in useful items, such as compact alarm clocks and travel irons, that can **save space when packing.**

➤ MAIL-ORDER CATALOGS: **Magellan's** (☎ 800/962–4943, FAX 805/568–5406). **Orvis Travel** (☎ 800/541–3541, FAX 540/343–7053). **TravelSmith** (☎ 800/950–1600, FAX 800/950–1656).

U

U.S. GOVERNMENT

The U.S. government can be an excellent source of inexpensive travel information. When planning your trip, **find out what government materials are available.**

➤ ADVISORIES: **U.S. Department of State American Citizens Services Office** (✉ Room 4811, Washington, DC 20520); enclose a self-addressed, stamped envelope. **Interactive hot line** (☎ 202/647–5225, FAX 202/647–3000). **Computer bulletin board** (☎ 202/647–9225).

➤ PAMPHLETS: **Consumer Information Center** (✉ Consumer Information Catalogue, Pueblo, CO 81009, ☎ 719/948–3334) for a free catalog that includes travel titles.

V

VISITOR INFORMATION

For general information and brochures before you go, contact the city, regional, and state tourism bureaus; the convention and visitors bureau publishes the helpful *San Diego Official Visitors Guide*. When you arrive, stop by one of the local visitors centers for general information.

➤ CITY-WIDE: **San Diego Convention & Visitors Bureau** (✉ 401 B St., Suite 1400, San Diego, 92101, ☎ 619/232–3101).

➤ LOCAL INFORMATION: **Balboa Park Visitors Center** (✉ 1549 El Prado, ☎ 619/239–0512), open daily 9–4. **International Visitor Information Center** (✉ 11 Horton Plaza, at 1st Ave. and F St., ☎ 619/236–1212), open Monday–Saturday 8:30–5. **San Diego Visitor Information Center** (✉ 2688 E. Mission Bay Dr., off I–5 at the Mission Bay Dr. exit (☎ 619/276–8200), open Monday–Saturday 9–5, Sunday 9:30–4:30.

➤ METRO AREA: **Borrego Springs** (✉ 622 Palm Canyon Dr., 92004, ☎ 760/767–5555). **Carlsbad** (✉ Box 1246, 92018, ☎ 760/434–6093). **Coronado** (✉ 1047 B Ave., 92118, ☎ 619/437–8788 or 800/622–8300). **Del Mar** (✉ 1104 Camino del Mar, 92014, ☎ 619/755–4844). **Escondido** (✉ San Diego North County Convention & Visitors Bureau, 720 N. Broadway, 92025, ☎ 760/745–4741 or 800/848–3336). **Julian** (✉ 2129 Main St., 92036, ☎ 760/765–1857). **La Jolla** (✉ 7734 Herschel Ave., 92038, ☎ 619/454–1444). **Oceanside** (✉ 928 N. Coast Hwy., 92054, ☎ 760/722–1534 or 800/350–7873).

➤ STATE-WIDE: **California Office of Tourism** (✉ 801 K St., Suite 1600, Sacramento, CA 95814, ☎ 916/322–2882 or ☎ 800/862–2543).

➤ IN THE U.K.: **California Tourist Office** (✉ ABC California, Box 35, Abingdon, Oxfordshire OX14 4TB, ☎ 0891/200–278). Calls cost 50p per minute peak rate or 45p per minute cheap rate; send check for £3 for brochures.

W

WHEN TO GO

For the most part, **any time of the year is the right time** for a trip to San Diego. The climate is generally close to perfect. Typical days are sunny and mild, with low humidity—ideal for sightseeing and for almost any sport that does not require snow and ice. From mid-December through mid-March, gray whales can be seen migrating along the coast. And in early spring, wildflowers transform the desert into a rainbow of colors.

CLIMATE

The annual high temperature averages 70°F with a low of 55°F, and the annual rainfall is usually less than 10 inches. Most of the rain occurs in January and February, but precipitation usually lasts for only part of the day or for a day or two at most.

➤ FORECASTS: **Weather Channel Connection** (☎ 900/932–8437), 95¢ per minute from a Touch-Tone phone.

Climate in San Diego

The following are average maximum and minimum temperatures for San Diego.

Jan.	62F	17C	May	66F	19C	Sept.	73F	23C
	46	8		55	13		62	17
Feb.	62F	17C	June	69F	21C	Oct.	71F	22C
	48	9		59	15		57	14
Mar.	64F	18C	July	73F	23C	Nov.	69F	21C
	50	10		62	17		51	11
Apr.	66F	19C	Aug.	73F	23C	Dec.	64F	18C
	53	12		64	18		48	9

THE GOLD GUIDE / SMART TRAVEL TIPS

1 Destination: San Diego

WARM AND WELCOMING

ACH YEAR, San Diego absorbs thousands of visitors who are drawn by the climate: sunny, dry, and warm nearly year-round. They swim, surf, and sunbathe on long beaches facing the turquoise Pacific, where whales, seals, and dolphins swim offshore. They tour oases of tropical palms, sheltered bays fringed by golden pampas grass, and far-ranging parklands blossoming with brilliant bougainvillea, jasmine, ice plant, and birds-of-paradise.

They run, bike, and stroll down wide streets and paths planned for the recreation of the natives, who thrive on San Diego's varied health, fitness, and sports scenes. They drive by Mission Bay, a 4,600-acre aquatic park, where dozens of colorful, intricate kites fly above hundreds of picnickers lounging in the sun. They wander through the streets of downtown, where the fanciful Horton Plaza shopping center serves as a vibrant hub, with theaters, restaurants, and shops drawing crowds from nearby steel-and-glass office towers.

San Diego County is the nation's sixth largest—larger than nearly a dozen U.S. states—with a population of more than 2.5 million. It sprawls east from the Pacific Ocean through dense urban neighborhoods to outlying suburban communities that seem to sprout on canyons and cliffs overnight. Its eastern boundaries are the Cleveland National Forest, where the pines and manzanita are covered with snow in the winter, and the Anza-Borrego Desert, where delicate pink and yellow cactus blooms herald the coming of spring. San Diegans visit these vast wildernesses for their annual doses of seasonal splendor, then return to the city, where flowers blossom year-round and the streets are dry and clean. One of the busiest international borders in the United States marks the county's southern line, where approximately 60 million people a year legally cross between Mexico's Baja California peninsula and San Diego. To the north, the marines at Camp Pendleton practice land, sea, and air maneuvers in southern California's largest coastal

greenbelt, marking the demarcation zone between the congestion of Orange and Los Angeles counties and the more relaxed expansiveness of San Diego.

The city of San Diego is the state's second largest, after Los Angeles. It serves as a base for the U.S. Navy's 11th Naval District and a port for ships from many nations. A considerable number of its residents were stationed here in the service and decided to stay put. Others either passed through on vacation or saw the city on TV or movie screens and became enamored of this prosperous Sunbelt playground. From its founding San Diego has attracted a steady stream of prospectors, drawn to the nation's farthest southwest frontier. Nearly 10,000 new residents arrive in San Diego each year.

Tourism is San Diego's third-largest industry, after manufacturing and the military. In the past few years, the San Diego Convention and Visitors Bureau and other local boosters have courted and won internationally important events that have brought uncalculated tourism benefits to the city. Worldwide media events, such as the America's Cup race, and in early 1998 (assuming that the expansion of Qualcomm Stadium, formerly San Diego Jack Murphy Stadium, is completed in time), the Super Bowl football game, keep San Diego visible as a vacation option.

The waterfront has assumed a completely new look and ambience since the 1990 opening of the 760,000-square-ft San Diego Convention Center at the foot of 5th Avenue, its sail-like rooftop thrust before downtown's skyline. The convention center's completion spurred development of the area at an unprecedented rate, and the thousands of conventioneers who visit San Diego are boosting the downtown business climate and image as never before. Hotel development has peaked after a spate of building on what seemed every patch of available land, but San Diego's politicians, business leaders, and developers have set the city's course toward a steadily increasing influx of visitors—which gives residents pleasant attractions as well as not-so-enjoyable distractions. With growth comes congestion, even in San Diego's vast expanse.

Fortunately, there are many reminders of the city's more peaceful times. In Old Town, San Diego's original city center, the courthouse, newspaper offices, and haciendas are historical adobe buildings covered with ancient twisted vines. The village of La Jolla, often compared with Monte Carlo, has retained its gentle charm despite continual development. And Balboa Park, the city's centerpiece, is a permanent testimonial to the Spanish architecture and natural ecology that give San Diego its unique character and charisma.

If San Diego sounds just a bit too laid-back and serene, consider its proximity to Mexico. Tijuana, a typically colorful and frenetic border town, is only 30 minutes away. San Diegans think of Tijuana and all the Baja peninsula as their backyard playground.

During Prohibition, Americans drove down dusty, rutted roads to the spectacular gambling halls of Tijuana, Rosarito Beach, and Ensenada, where unbridled hedonism was not only tolerated but encouraged. Hollywood stars settled in for the duration, waiting out the dry days north of the border in lavish grandeur and investing their dollars in Mexican real estate. Some of Baja's grandest hotels were built during this era, when U.S. financiers recognized the value of the peninsula's rugged coastal wilderness.

THOSE PLEASURE PALACES of the past have since crumbled, but Baja is undergoing a new surge of development now that the Mexican government has targeted the area as a tourist destination. The coastline from Tijuana through Rosarito Beach to Ensenada is rapidly being transformed from an isolated hideaway with a few resorts and vacation-home communities into a major holiday destination with elegant condominium and time-share developments, full-scale RV parks that have more amenities than most hotels, and enough restaurants, artisans' markets, and bars to keep the onslaught of weekend travelers content. Tijuana's main Avenida Revolución continues to attract shoppers and those looking for the border city's wild side, but such cultural attractions as Mexit-

lan, the outdoor museum–entertainment center, are gaining in popularity as well.

Visiting Baja is easier than ever, thanks to the San Diego–Tijuana trolley, which runs from the Santa Fe Depot in downtown San Diego to the international border in San Ysidro. The trolley travels south through the suburbs of National City and Chula Vista, where giant shipyards and fish canneries have been replaced by fancy marinas. Near San Ysidro, the trackside billboards display Spanish ads for Tijuana's shopping centers, highlighting bargains in brand-name clothing from Ralph Lauren and Guess?. Still, for all its familiarity, Tijuana could never be mistaken for an American town. Therein lies its appeal.

If you prefer more organized attractions, San Diego has its share of theme parks and specialized museums. Sea World, on the shores of Mission Bay, highlights San Diego's proximity to the sea with spectacular aquariums, whale shows, shark exhibits, and penguin habitats. The San Diego Zoo, often called the country's finest zoological-botanical park, is a must-see attraction. The Wild Animal Park, 30 minutes east of downtown, preserves the natural wonders of San Diego's chaparral country while protecting endangered wildlife from around the world. Balboa Park, site of the 1915 Panama-California International Exposition, houses not only the zoo but the city's finest museums in historic Spanish-Moorish palaces set amid lush lawns and rocky canyons.

San Diego has always been recognized as an environmental paradise. As the city grows, its cultural base expands to meet more sophisticated demands. Today San Diego retains its sense of a western frontier as it develops into a major cosmopolitan centerpiece for the nation. No wonder visitors from all over the world come for vacations and decide to stay for life.

— Maribeth Mellin

A longtime resident of San Diego, travel writer and photographer Maribeth Mellin is a former senior editor at *San Diego Magazine* and a contributor to several magazines and newspapers.

NEW AND NOTEWORTHY

With its biotechnology companies luring business from around the world, San Diego is angling for a leadership role as the new millennium approaches. Visitors to the area in 1998 will find that several future-oriented projects have already come to fruition.

Those who arrive by air will notice dramatic upgrades to **San Diego International Airport Lindbergh Field,** the most eye-catching improvement being the addition of a $1.5 million public-art project. The sculptures, paintings, and installations range from a depiction of weary passengers to more abstract pieces (one involves seaweed), all purchased by the San Diego Unified Port District, the governing body responsible for maintaining the city's harbor area. A new commuter terminal, scheduled for completion in November 1997, will service Alaska Commuter, American Eagle, Continental Connection, Delta Connection, Northwest Airlink, and US Airways Express. The airport's main terminals have been dressed up with a brighter color scheme.

In the continuing effort to make San Diego easier to get around once you're in town, the **San Diego Trolley,** a light rail transit system, laid more track. The Mission Valley Line, with access to plentiful shopping and entertainment, was scheduled to open in late 1997. The Mission Valley Line starts at the Old Town Transit Center and connects with the trolley's North Line, the Coaster commuter rail line, and major bus routes. It serves six stations east of Mission Valley. Sports fans and shoppers will cheer for the stops at Fashion Valley and Qualcomm Stadium. The **Fashion Valley** stop is part of an extensive overhaul at this Mission Valley shopping mall. A new upper level and the addition of 100 shops and a theater complex have increased Fashion Valley's size from 1.4 million to 1.6 million square ft.

On the wilder side, the Zoological Society of San Diego's second campus, the **Wild Animal Park** in the San Pasqual Valley, completed a new walking exhibit in summer 1997. The sprawling park, which visitors usually view on a monorail ride through four huge field areas inhabited by a mix of exotic hoofstock, now welcomes visitors to walk through the heart of its East Africa exhibit. Following a stream to an African waterhole, a path winds past Okapi, giraffe, and cheetahs. A floating walkway leads to a working research station. Discount passes can be purchased for those who would like to see both the Wild Animal Park and the **San Diego Zoo,** where, after a two-year delay, two pandas on an extended loan from China have finally arrived. The zoo is in **Balboa Park,** which also holds the **Reuben H. Fleet Theater and Science Center.** A multimillion-dollar expansion will double the facility's size by May 1998, in time for the center's 25th anniversary. Among the new exhibits will be one that allows visitors to participate in simulated scientific missions.

A new mile-long bicycle, skating, and pedestrian path in **Mission Bay Park** has made walking in the city even more pleasurable. The path hugs Bahia Point, in front of the Bahia Hotel, and connects to many other bike paths in the coastal area.

WHAT'S WHERE

Balboa Park

Straddling two mesas overlooking downtown and the Pacific Ocean, Balboa Park is set on 1,400 beautifully landscaped acres. Home to the majority of San Diego's museums and a world-famous zoo, the park serves as the cultural center of the city, as well as a recreational paradise for animal lovers and folks who want to spend a day picnicking or strolling in a lush green space. Most of the museums are grouped around El Prado, the park's central pedestrian mall; many are housed in Spanish-Moorish buildings that were built for the Panama–California International Exposition of 1915. Most of the downtown thoroughfares lead north to the park (it's hard to miss). From the west side of downtown, take any east–west street until you hit Park Boulevard, and drive north into the park. From Old Town, take I–8 east to Highway 163 south into the park. From I–5, take any of the well-marked exits.

Coronado

Across the water from the Embarcadero, Coronado Island is a combination of wealthy suburban enclave and naval air base. Visible from downtown and Point Loma and accessible from the San Diego–Coronado Bridge, Coronado, in reality a peninsula, has wide, graceful streets, well-manicured neighborhood parks, and grand Victorian homes. The community grew up around the ornate Hotel Del Coronado, a celebrity hangout from the late 19th century and now a National Historic Site. Those who aren't interested in Victorian architecture come to Coronado to catch some rays and splash in the surf at Silver Strand Beach State Park and Imperial Beach, which extend in a long arc to the south from the body of the island.

Downtown

Downtown San Diego's main arteries are Harbor Drive, which runs along the Embarcadero; Broadway, which cuts through the center of downtown; and 6th Avenue as far as Balboa Park. Numbered streets run roughly north–south; the lettered and named streets (Broadway, Market, Island, and Ash) run east–west. San Diego's downtown and waterfront came back to life in the mid-'80s as a bustling, colorful jumble of hotels, restaurants, shopping centers, floating gift shops, and seagoing vessels of every size and shape. The centerpiece of the area is Horton Plaza, a shopping, dining, and entertainment mall that fronts Broadway and G Street from 1st to 4th avenues and covers more than six city blocks. Surrounding Horton Plaza is the Gaslamp Quarter, an area with art galleries, antiques, and specialty shops housed in Victorian buildings and renovated warehouses. Another of downtown's main attractions is the Embarcadero, the section of waterfront that follows Harbor Drive along the curve of San Diego Bay. This is the best spot to linger for views of the bay and its docked boats, ranging from huge cruise ships to old sailing vessels. South of the Embarcadero on Harbor Drive is Seaport Village, 14 acres of shopping plazas designed to reflect the architectural styles of early California.

La Jolla

Spanish for "the jewel," La Jolla lives up to its name in both beauty and expense with its dramatic beachfront, spectacular views, and huge designer homes. Boutiques and restaurants cater to the affluent local gentry, but the largely unspoiled scenery of its coast, coves, and verdant hill-sides is still free. North of Mission Bay, La Jolla can be approached by the meandering coastal road (Mission and La Jolla boulevards) or via the speedier I–5.

Mission Bay and Sea World

The coastal Mission Bay area is San Diego's monument to sports and fitness, where locals and visitors interested in boating, running, sunning, or jet skiing spend their days. Some parts of the amorphous 4,600-acre aquatic park, which has numerous coves and inlets and 27 mi of bayfront beach, are specifically designated for swimming, waterskiing, and sailing. Terrestrial types can jog, play basketball, toss a Frisbee, or fly a kite on the bay's peninsulas and two main islands, Vacation Island and Fiesta Island. Easily the most popular attraction in Mission Bay (and for some, in all of San Diego), Sea World displays fish and captive marine mammals, including sea otters, dolphins, seals, and the trademark killer whales.

Old Town

A few miles north of downtown off I–5, Old Town is essentially a collection of remnants from the original San Diego, the first European settlement in California (the first Spanish mission, which preceded the town, was established by Father Junípero Serra on a hill north of Old Town now known as Presidio Park). The former pueblo of San Diego is now preserved as a state historic park and contains several original and reconstructed buildings. The historic sites are clustered around Old Town Plaza, which is bounded by Wallace Street, Calhoun Street, Mason Street, and San Diego Avenue.

Point Loma

Acting as a buffer against the temperamental Pacific, Point Loma curves along San Diego Bay and extends south into the sea. Beyond its main streets—which are cluttered with fast-food restaurants and motels—Point Loma is made up of well-to-do neighborhoods and bayside estates (it's a favorite retirement spot for naval officers). From the bay side you can enjoy a terrific view of downtown San Diego, and for an incomparable view of the Pacific, head to Sunset Cliffs, between Point Loma and Ocean Beach, among the most dramatic places in San Diego to watch the sunset.

San Diego North County and Beyond

San Diego County sprawls from the Pacific Ocean through dense urban neighborhoods to outlying suburban communities that seem to sprout overnight on canyons and cliffs. The Cleveland National Forest and Anza-Borrego Desert mark the county's eastern boundaries; the busiest international border in the United States is its southern line.

The seaside towns north of La Jolla developed separately from San Diego, and from each other. Del Mar, which actually lies within the limits of the city of San Diego, is a seaside preserve with inordinately expensive lodging and exclusive boutiques. Small Solana Beach has a mellow ambience and acres of sand. Encinitas is justly famous for its fabulous fields of flowers and gardens, which extend inland from excellent surfing waters. Carlsbad flaunts its history as a spa town to visitors lured by package tours, and Oceanside shows off its harbor and Mission San Luis Rey. The coastal portion of North County is best accessed via I–5, but traveling along Route S21 (old Highway 101) once you reach the area will give you a better feel for the differences among the settlements.

Even though the coast is only a short drive away, the North County beach communities seem far removed from the resort town of Rancho Bernardo, the quiet lakes of Escondido, the avocado-growing country surrounding Fallbrook, the former gold-mining town of Julian, or the vineyards of Temecula. Home to old missions, San Diego Wild Animal Park, the Welk Resort Center, and innumerable three-generation California families, the inland area of North County is the quiet, rural sister to the rest of San Diego County.

Tijuana, Rosarito Beach, and Ensenada

If you've ventured this far south in California, you ought to consider at least a day-trip across the border to Baja California. Just 23 mi south of San Diego, Tijuana has grown over the last 20 years from a border town of 700,000 to a city of approximately 2 million inhabitants; it continues to attract hordes of "yanquis" with its souvenir shops, sports events, and great Mexican dining. Eighteen miles farther south, laid-back Playas de Rosarito (Rosarito Beach) has become something of a week-end hangout for southern Californians. And another 40 mi down the coast is the port city of Ensenada.

PLEASURES AND PASTIMES

Beaches

The coastline in and around San Diego encompasses some of the best beaches on the West Coast. Some are wide and sandy, others narrow and rocky; some are almost always crowded with athletes and sun-worshipers, others seem created for solitary beachcombers and romantic pairs. Among the standouts are Imperial Beach, a classic southern California beach favored by surfers, swimmers, and Frisbee maniacs; Silver Strand State Beach, a relatively calm, family-friendly beach on the isthmus of Coronado; Ocean Beach, a.k.a. Dog Beach because of the number of canines found romping next to volleyball players and sunbathers; Mission Beach, which has a boardwalk popular with walkers, roller skaters, and bicyclists; La Jolla Cove, where tidal pools and cliff coves provide exciting diversions for explorers; and Torrey Pines State Beach in Del Mar, one of the easiest and most comfortable beaches to visit in the area.

Outdoor Activities and Sports

At least one stereotype of San Diego is true—it is an active, outdoors-oriented community. People recreate here more than they spectate, and as a visitor, it's hard not to join in. As you would expect, the emphasis is on fun in the sun and surf—sailing, swimming, surfing, diving, and fishing head the list. Here is a sampling of favorite activities and best place to enjoy them: scuba diving off La Jolla Cove, surfing at almost any of the beaches, golfing at Torrey Pines, roller skating at Mission Bay, jogging along the Embarcadero, playing volleyball on Ocean Beach, windsurfing on Mission Bay, and jet-skiing at the Snug Harbor Marina.

Shopping

San Diego's many shopping districts are a mélange of self-contained megamalls, historic districts, homey villages, funky neighborhoods, and chic suburbs. Horton Plaza, in the heart of center city, is the place to go for department stores and one-of-a-kind shops; the adjoining Gaslamp Quarter is chock full of art galleries, antiques shops, and specialty stores. The Paladion, also adjoining Horton Plaza, is a posh grouping of upscale boutiques. Seaport Village on the waterfront is thick with theme shops and arts-and-crafts galleries. Coronado Island has a few blocks of fancy boutiques and galleries as well as Ferry Landing Marketplace, a waterfront shopping center. The historic Old Town district has what resembles a colorful Mexican marketplace, where you can browse in shops selling international goods, toys, souvenirs, and arts and crafts. Hillcrest is the place to go for vintage clothing, furnishings, and accessories. La Jolla has been hopping since some exciting shops and galleries opened around Prospect Street and Girard Avenue.

GREAT ITINERARIES

Many folks spend their time in San Diego just lazing away on a beach—if you're thus inclined, you'll enjoy some of the best sand and surf in the country. But the more energetic will find sufficient outlets to satisfy their sightseeing urges. The following suggested itineraries will help you structure your visit efficiently. See the neighborhood exploring tours in Chapter 2 for more information about individual sights.

If You Have 3 Days

Head over to the **San Diego Zoo** in **Balboa Park** on the morning of your first day. It would be easy to spend your entire visit to the park here—and if you're traveling with kids, you may have little choice in the matter—but it would be a shame to miss **El Prado** and its rows of architecturally interesting museums, a five-minute drive south of the zoo on Park Boulevard.

Start your second day downtown at **Seaport Village;** after browsing the shops, catch a ferry from the Convention Center to **Coronado.** From Coronado's **Ferry Landing Marketplace,** board a bus going down Orange Avenue to tour the town's Victorian extravaganza, the **Hotel Del**

Coronado. Back in San Diego, stroll north on the **Embarcadero** Street; if you've gotten back early from Coronado, you can view the **Maritime Museum.** If it's whale-watching season, skip the trip to Coronado, tour the Embarcadero in the late morning, have lunch, and book an afternoon excursion boat from the B Street Pier.

If you set out early enough on the third morning, you might get a parking spot near **La Jolla Cove.** Enjoy the beach for a bit and then head inland one block to Prospect Street, where you'll see the pink **La Valencia** hotel and rows of tony shops; this is also a good spot for a oceanview lunch. Walk east on Prospect for a spin through the **Museum of Contemporary Art,** and then retrieve your car and head back into town on I–5 to the **Gaslamp Quarter,** where you can tour the historic streets, perhaps stop by the adjacent **Horton Plaza** shopping mall, and stay for dinner.

If You Have 5 Days

Follow the three-day itinerary above, and begin your fourth day with a morning visit to **Cabrillo National Monument.** Have lunch at one of the seafood restaurants on **Scott Street,** and then head over to **Old Town** (take Rosecrans Street north to San Diego Avenue). If the daily schedule lists low tide for the afternoon, reverse the order to catch the tide pools at Cabrillo.

En route to North County on day five, stop off at **Torrey Pines State Park.** Then get on I–5 and head up to **Del Mar** for lunch, shopping, and sea views. Continue north on S21 to other coastal towns such as **Encinitas** and **Carlsbad.** A visit to **Mission San Luis Rey,** slightly inland from **Oceanside** on Highway 76, will infuse some history and culture into the tour.

If You Have 7 Days or More

Get an early start on day six and tour the **Wild Animal Park.** Then head east to **Julian,** where you can overnight. Or tour Julian and continue on to the town of Borrego Springs. Spend day seven (except in summer) at **Anza-Borrego Desert State Park.**

Another option would be to return to San Diego on evening six and head to Mexico on day seven. If you'll only be visiting for the day, take the San Diego Trolley to **Tijuana.** If you're going to extend your stay in Mexico, take a car rather than

visit Tijuana, con-
...to Beach or Ense-
... have overnight
...great places to sip
...

FODOR'S CHOICE

Special Moments

★ **Driving across the San Diego–Coronado Bridge.** The view of the harbor, downtown, and Coronado Island from this landmark is breathtaking, day or night.

★ **A morning stroll about La Jolla Cove.** Palm-tree-lined Ellen Browning Scripps Park on the cliffs overlooking the cove is one of the prettiest spots in the world. Try breakfast on the patio at Brockton Villa with a fantastic view of the cove.

★ **Spotting a gray whale spouting during the winter migration.** As many as 200 whales pass the San Diego coast each day on their way south to Mexico (starting in mid-December) or back north (until mid-March).

★ **Hiking at Cabrillo National Monument on Point Loma.** Perched at the end of the peninsula, this 144-acre preserve of rugged cliffs and shores and outstanding overlooks was set aside as a National Park Service site to commemorate Portuguese explorer Juan Rodríguez Cabrillo.

★ **A Sunday picnic in Balboa Park.** Forget about the park's museums (for one day, anyway) and settle down to your own custom-made meal on a grassy spot near one of the park's many landscaped gardens.

★ **Winter stargazing in Anza-Borrego Desert State Park.** The exceptionally black winter sky provides a backdrop for a veritable cascade of stars, planets, constellations, and comets.

Restaurants

★ **Anthony's Star of the Sea Room.** This spot on the Embarcadero is one of San Diego's top seafood restaurants. A new terrace takes great advantage of its choice waterfront location. $$$–$$$$

★ **Dobson's.** Local movers and shakers come to this clubby eatery to see and be seen. That aside, Dobson's has one of the most innovative and consistent kitchens in the city. $$$

★ **George's at the Cove.** It's hard to say what's better here: the stunning view overlooking La Jolla Cove or the superb cooking. $$$

★ **Laurel.** The culinary philosophy at this wildly successful French and Mediterranean restaurant is straightforward: the best fresh ingredients prepared simply, *con gusto*. $$$

★ **Bella Luna.** The menu at this small, stylish downtown restaurant includes dishes from all over Italy. Pastas are particularly recommended. $$–$$$

★ **Cafe Pacifica.** At this Old Town favorite you'll find eclectic California cuisine with an emphasis on seafood. The restaurant's crème brûlée is worth blowing any diet for. $$–$$$

★ **Alizé.** The menu at this comfortable, moderately priced French West Indies restaurant balances the exotic and the more familiar. Seafood reigns supreme at dinner; lunch options include salads, sandwiches, and light entrées. $$

★ **California Cuisine.** Innovative nouvelle-American cuisine in a minimalist dining room is what you'll encounter at this outstanding Uptown restaurant. The grilled items are especially tasty. $$

★ **Piatti Ristorante.** A wood-burning oven turns out excellent pizzas and imaginative pastas at this country-style Italian restaurant. Dine indoors or on a tree-shaded patio. $$

★ **Palenque.** Come to this family-run Pacific Beach restaurant for an introduction to regional Mexican cooking. $–$$

Lodging

★ **Hyatt Regency San Diego.** This Hyatt receives high marks from business and leisure travelers. Right next to Seaport Village, it has an unbeatable location. $$$$

★ **Le Meridien San Diego at Coronado.** Lushly landscaped grounds and flamingos set the scene for the deluxe accommodations you'll find indoors. The top-of-the-line spa facilities are an added draw. $$$$

★ **La Valencia.** An art deco landmark near the shops and restaurants of La Jolla

Village, the venerable La Valencia is still in great shape and continues to attract repeat visitors enchanted by its setting. *$$$–$$$$*

★ **Westgate Hotel.** Just across the street from Horton Plaza, this opulent high rise has fantastic views from the ninth floor up. *$$$–$$$$*

★ **The Lodge at Torrey Pines.** It may be a bit off the beaten path—on a bluff between La Jolla and Del Mar—but the Lodge's proximity to scenic beaches, pristine coastline, a nature reserve, and one of the best golf courses in the country have made it a perennial favorite. *$$*

★ **Gaslamp Plaza Suites.** This Gaslamp district hotel, San Diego's first skyscraper, has comfortable European-style accommodations and complimentary Continental breakfast on the rooftop terrace. *$–$$*

FESTIVALS AND SEASONAL EVENTS

WINTER

➤ JAN.: The **Mercedes Championships** (☎ 800/918–4653 for tickets; 760/438–9111, ext. 4612, for information) brings PGA tour winners from the previous year for competition at La Costa Resort and Spa.

➤ FEB.: The **Buick Invitational Golf Tournament** (☎ 800/888–2842) attracts more than 100,000 people, including local and national celebrities, to the Torrey Pines Golf Course.

SPRING

➤ FEB.–APR.: **Wildflowers in the desert** bloom during a two- to six-week period during these months. The span is determined by the winter rainfall. Phone the Anza-Borrego Desert State Park visitor center (☎ 760/767–4684) for information.

➤ MAR.: The **Ocean Beach Kite Festival** (☎ 619/531–1527) is a kite-decorating and -flying contest for all ages.

➤ MAR. OR APR.: The **La Jolla Easter Hat Parade** (☎ 619/454–2600) finds La Jollans and others parading in their Easter finest for prizes.

➤ APR.: The **San Diego Crew Classic** (☎ 619/488–0700) brings together more than 2,600

high school, college, and masters athletes from across the United States for a rowing competition at Crown Point Shores in Mission Bay.

➤ APR.–MAY: The **Del Mar National Horse Show** (☎ 619/792–4288) at the Del Mar Fairgrounds presents thousands of show horses in competition.

➤ MAY: The **Downtown ArtWalk** (☎ 619/232–4395), an open house for downtown's art galleries, has become a weekend-long festival in the G Street neighborhood. **Fiesta Cinco de Mayo** (☎ 619/299–6055) brings entertainment and booths to Old Town San Diego State Historic Park and the Bazaar del Mundo. The **Pacific Beach Block Party** (☎ 619/272–7282) is a street fair with live music, food stands, and arts-and-crafts vendors.

SUMMER

➤ JUNE: **Fiesta del Sol** (☎ 619/755–4775), a Solana Beach event that includes crafts booths, musical entertainment, games for kids, and a surfing competition, opens the North County summer season. The **Indian Fair** (☎ 619/239–2001) attracts Native Americans from throughout the Southwest for arts, crafts, ethnic foods, and dances at the Museum of Man in Balboa Park. Pungent aromas and wacky goings-on characterize the **Annual**

Ocean Beach Street Fair and Chili Cook-Off (☎ 619/226–2193), usually held the last weekend in June.

➤ JUNE–JULY: The **Del Mar Fair** (☎ 619/793–5555) is a classic county fair, with live entertainment, flower and garden shows, a carnival, livestock shows, and Fourth of July fireworks.

➤ JUNE–AUG.: During the **Summer Organ Festival** (☎ 619/226–0819), free Monday concerts take place at 8 PM at Balboa Park's Spreckels Organ Pavilion.

➤ JUNE–SEPT.: The **Nighttime Zoo** at the San Diego Zoo (☎ 619/234–3153) and **The Park at Dark** at Wild Animal Park (☎ 619/234–6541) are wild ways to spend the evening, with extended evening hours and additional entertainment through the beginning of September.

➤ JULY: The **Over-the-Line Tournament** (☎ 619/688–0817) is a rowdy party, with more than 1,000 three-person teams competing in a sport that's a cross between softball and stickball; it takes place over two weekends on Fiesta Island in Mission Bay. **Sand Castle Days** (☎ 619/424–6663) at Imperial Beach Pier, brings together sand sculptors of all ages for one of the largest castle-building events in the United States.

➤ JULY–SEPT.: The **Old Globe Festival** (☎ 619/239–2255) features works of Shakespeare in repertory with other classic and contemporary plays at the Old Globe Theatre in Balboa Park. Free outdoor **La Jolla Concerts by the Sea** (☎ 619/645–8115) are held every Sunday through Labor Day weekend, 2 PM–4 PM, in Scripps Park at La Jolla Cove. Top-name jazz and other performers participate in the outdoor **Humphrey's Concerts by the Bay** (☎ 619/523–1010 or 619/220–8497).

➤ AUG.: **America's Finest City Week** (☎ 619/645–8594) gives San Diegans a chance to proclaim their pride with a half-marathon, parades, and concerts. During the **Annual Hillcrest Cityfest Street Fair** (☎ 619/299–3330), 5th Avenue is blocked off for a fun day of local arts and crafts, displays, live entertainment, a beer garden, and food. **Body Surfing Contests** (☎ 760/434–2828) pit more than 200 of California's top competitors against each other at Carlsbad State Beach. Mexican arts and crafts, food booths, and lively music and dancing are all on the agenda of the **Las Californias/Tijuana Fair** (☎ 619/298–4105; 66/84–05–37 in Tijuana) a south-of-the-border event. The outdoor **Red, White & Blues Fest** (☎ 619/282–7329) brings good music and food to San Diego's Normal Heights neighborhood. The **Summerfest** (☎ 619/459–3728)

chamber music festival at Sherwood Auditorium includes concerts, lectures, master classes, and open rehearsals.

➤ SEPT.: The two-day **Free Fall Festival** (☎ 619/282–7329) hosts nearly five dozen musical acts (rock, folk, and other genres), plus street clothiers and arts-and-crafts vendors. **Street Scene** (☎ 619/557–8490) transforms the historic Gaslamp Quarter into a rollicking three-day food and music festival, with 10 stages showcasing more than 100 bands from around the world. The **Thunderboats Unlimited Hydroplane Championships** (☎ 619/268–1250) draws thunderboat enthusiasts to Mission Bay for an exhilarating, deafening weekend of racing.

➤ OCT.: **Lego Construction Zone** (☎ 619/239–8180) allows visitors to participate in the Horton Plaza Sports Deck competition or just watch. All patrons of the San Diego Zoo (☎ 619/231–1515) are admitted free on **Founders Day,** the first Monday in October, and children get in free the entire month.

➤ NOV.: The **Dixieland Jazz Festival** (☎ 619/

297–5277) presents a weekend filled with performances by well-known bands at the Town & Country Hotel. El Cajon's **Mother Goose Parade** (☎ 619/444–8712) is a two-hour nationally televised spectacular with 200 floats, bands, horses, and clowns.

➤ DEC.: **Christmas on the Prado** (☎ 619/239–0512) is sponsored by the museums in Balboa Park on the first Friday and Saturday of December; attractions include carolers and a candlelight procession, and admission is free to all the museums. **Old Town Holiday in the Park** (☎ 619/220–5422) includes tours of historic homes and other buildings in Old Town by costumed docents. **San Diego Harbor Parade of Lights** (☎ 619/236–1212) brings colorfully lit boats through the downtown harbor. The **Wild Animal Park Festival of Lights** (☎ 760/747–8702, ext. 5140) includes free kid-oriented activities, Christmas caroling, live-animal presentations, and real snow. The **Annual Ocean Beach Parade and Tree Festival** (☎ 619/225–1080) takes place on Newport Avenue, generally the second weekend in December. The Ocean Beach Geriatric Surf Club tops any entry in any parade, anywhere.

2 Exploring San Diego

Exploring San Diego is an endless adventure. To visitors the city and county may seem like a conglomeration of theme parks: Old Town and the Gaslamp Quarter historically oriented ones, the wharf area a maritime playground, La Jolla a throwback to southern California elegance, Balboa Park a convergence of the town's cerebral and action-oriented personae. There are, of course, real theme parks—Sea World and the San Diego Zoo—but the great outdoors, in the form of forests, landscaped urban areas, and sandy beaches, is the biggest of them all.

EXPLORING SAN DIEGO may be an endless adventure,
but there are limitations, especially if you don't have
a car. San Diego is more a chain of separate communities than a cohesive city. Many of the major attractions are sep-
arated by some distance from one another. The streets are fun for getting
an up-close look at how San Diegans live, but true southern Californians use the freeways, which crisscross the county in a sensible fashion. Interstate 5 runs a direct north–south route through the county's
coastal communities to the Mexican border. Interstates 805 and 15 do
much the same inland, with I–8 as the main east–west route. High-
ways 163, 52, and 94 act as connectors.

By Edie Jarolim

If you are going to drive around San Diego, study your maps before
you hit the road. The freeways are convenient and fast most of the time,
but if you miss your turnoff or get caught in commuter traffic, you'll
experience a none-too-pleasurable hallmark of southern California
living—freeway madness. Southern California drivers rush around on
a complex freeway system with the same fervor they use for jogging
scores of marathons each year. They particularly enjoy speeding up at
interchanges and entrance and exit ramps. Be sure you know where
you're going before you join the chase.

Downtown, Balboa Park, Sea World, Cabrillo National Monument,
and Mission Bay all have huge parking lots, and it is rare not to find a
space, though it may seem as if you've parked miles away from your destination. Parking is more of a problem in Old Town, where the free lots
fill up quickly, and in La Jolla and Coronado, where you generally need
to rely on hard-to-find street spots or expensive by-the-hour parking lots.

If you stick with public transportation, plan on taking your time. San
Diego's trolley line has expanded into Old Town; a light-rail line called
the *Coaster* runs from Oceanside into downtown; and the bus system
covers almost all the county—but making the connections necessary
to see the various sights is time consuming. Fashion Valley Shopping
Center in Mission Valley is one of the two major bus transfer points—
downtown is the other—but since many of the city's major attractions
are clustered along the coast, you'll be best off staying there. Some buses
have bicycle racks in the back. A bike is a great mode of transportation here; the bike-path system is extensive and well marked. With the
large distances between sights, taxis can be expensive and are best used
for getting around once you're in a given area.

San Diego County's dry climate nurtures some amazing flora. Golden
stalks of pampas grass grow in wild patches near Sea World. Bougainvillea covers roofs and hillsides in La Jolla, spreading magenta blankets
over whitewashed adobe walls. Towering palms and twisted junipers
are far more common than maples or oaks, and fields of wild daisies
and chamomile cover dry, dusty lots. Red and white poinsettias pro-
liferate at Christmas, and candy-colored pink and yellow flowered ice
plants edge the roads year-round. Jasmine blooms on bushes and vines
in front yards and parking lots; birds-of-paradise poke up straight and
tall, tropical testimonials to San Diego's temperate ways. Citrus groves
pop up in unlikely places, along the freeways and back roads. When
the orange, lemon, and lime trees blossom in spring, the fragrance of
their tiny white blossoms is nearly overpowering. Be sure to drive with
your windows down—you'll be amazed at the sweet, hypnotic scent.

Unless you're on the freeway, it's hard *not* to find a scenic drive in San
Diego, but an officially designated 52-mi Scenic Drive over much of

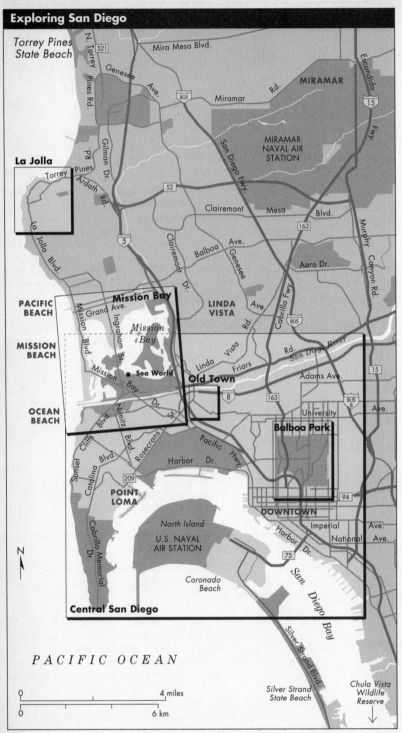

Torrey Pines
State Beach

La Jolla

MIRAMAR

MIRAMAR
NAVAL AIR
STATION

Clairemont   Mesa   Blvd.

PACIFIC
BEACH

Mission Bay

LINDA
VISTA

MISSION
BEACH

Mission
Bay

Sea World   Old Town

OCEAN
BEACH

Balboa Park

POINT
LOMA

North Island
U.S. NAVAL
AIR STATION

DOWNTOWN

Coronado
Beach

San Diego Bay

Central San Diego

Silver Strand
State Beach

Chula Vista
Wildlife
Reserve

N

PACIFIC OCEAN

0   4 miles

0   6 km

central San Diego begins at the foot of Broadway. Road signs with a white seagull on a yellow-and-blue background direct the way through the Embarcadero to Harbor and Shelter islands, Point Loma and Cabrillo Monument, Mission Bay, Old Town, Balboa Park, Mount Soledad, and La Jolla. It's best to take this three-hour drive, outlined on some local maps, on the weekend, when the commuters are off the road.

BALBOA PARK

Straddling two mesas overlooking downtown and the Pacific Ocean, Balboa Park is set on 1,400 beautifully landscaped acres. Hosting the majority of San Diego's museums and a world-famous zoo, the park serves as the cultural center of the city, as well as a recreational paradise for animal lovers and folks who want to spend a day picnicking or strolling in a lush green space.

Many of the park's Spanish-Moorish buildings were intended to be temporary structures housing exhibits for the Panama–California International Exposition of 1915, which celebrated the opening of the Panama Canal. Fortunately, city leaders realized the buildings' value and incorporated them in their plans for Balboa Park's acreage, which had been set aside by the city founders in 1868. The Spanish theme first instituted in the early 1900s was in part carried through in new buildings designed for the California Pacific International Exposition of 1935–36, but architectural details from the temples of the Maya and other indigenous peoples of the Americas were added. In an attempt to unify and beautify the museum complex, many of the buildings on El Prado—the courtyard and walkway created for the 1915 exposition—-are currently undergoing restoration to recapture their 1935–36 look.

The Laurel Street Bridge, also known as Cabrillo Bridge, is the park's official gateway; it leads over a vast canyon, filled with downtown commuter traffic on Highway 163, to El Prado, which, beyond the art museum, becomes the park's central pedestrian mall. The 100-bell carillon in the California Tower, El Prado's highest structure, tolls the hour; figures of California's historic personages decorate the base of the 200-ft spire, and a magnificent blue-tiled dome shines in the sun. On fine days mimes, jugglers, and musicians perform on the long lawns beside the Lily Pond in front of the Botanical Building.

The parkland across the Cabrillo Bridge, at the west end of El Prado, has been set aside for picnics and athletics. Roller skaters perform along Balboa Drive, leading to the highest spot in the park, Marston Point, overlooking downtown. Ladies and gents in spotless white outfits meet regularly on summer afternoons for lawn-bowling tournaments at the green beside the bridge. Dirt trails lead into pine groves with secluded picnic areas. In the southwest portion of the park, along Park Boulevard—the park's main north–south thoroughfare—Pepper Grove has lots of picnic tables and a playground.

Most first-time visitors come to see the museums and the animals, but Balboa Park is really a series of botanical gardens, with a verdant, tropical oasis in its midst at the San Diego Zoo. Cultivated and wild gardens are an integral part of all Balboa Park, thanks to the "Mother of Balboa Park," Kate Sessions, who made sure both the park's developed and undeveloped acreage bloomed with the purple blossoms of the jacaranda tree and planted thousands of palms and other trees throughout. Left alone, Balboa Park would look like Florida Canyon, which lies between the main park and Morley Field, along Park Boulevard.

On its eastern side, El Prado ends in a bridge that crosses over Park Boulevard to the perfectly tended Rose Garden, which has more than 2,000 rose plants. In the adjacent Cactus Garden, trails wind around prickly cacti and soft green succulents, many indigenous to the area. The Palm Arboretum, near the Spreckels Organ Pavilion, has more than 60 varieties of palm trees along a shady bridge. Three more of Balboa Park's verdant spots are detailed in the Sights to See section, *below.*

Parking near Balboa Park's museums is no small accomplishment, especially on sunny summer days, when lots fill up quickly. If you're driving in via the Laurel Street Bridge, the first parking area you'll come to is off the Prado to the left, going toward Pan American Plaza. Don't despair if there are no spaces here; you'll see more lots as you continue down along the same road. If you end up parking a bit far from your destination, consider the stroll back through the greenery part of the day's recreational activities.

On the other hand, if all that culture has tired you, the free trams that operate around the park provide an alternative way to get back to your car or bus. Trams run every 20 minutes April–October 9:30–5:30, and the rest of the year 11–5.

Numbers in the text correspond to numbers in the margin and on the Balboa Park map.

Two Good Walks

It's impossible to cover all the park's museums in one day, so choose your focus before you head out. If your interests run to the aesthetic, the Museum of Photographic Arts, the San Diego Museum of Art, the Mingei International Museum of folk art, and the Timken Museum of Art should be on your list; architecture buffs will want to add the Marston House. Those with a penchant for natural and cultural history shouldn't miss the San Diego Natural History Museum and the Museum of Man; folks oriented toward space and technology should see the Reuben H. Fleet Space Theater and Science Center, the San Diego Aerospace Museum, and the San Diego Automotive Museum.

On a day when the weather is nice, you might just want to stroll and enjoy the unique architecture of the museum complex. A walk along El Prado, where you'll be treated to the Spanish and Mexican designs of the 1915 exposition, is about 1 mi round-trip. More details about the buildings with numbers next to them can be found in the Sights to See section, *below.*

Enter via Cabrillo Bridge through the West Gate, which depicts the Panama Canal's linkage of the Atlantic and Pacific oceans. Park just south of the **Alcazar Garden** ①. It's a short stretch north across El Prado to the landmark **California Building,** modeled on a cathedral in Mexico and now home to the **San Diego Museum of Man** ②. Look up to see busts and statues of heroes of the early days of the state. Next door is the **Simon Edison Centre for the Performing Arts** ③, which adjoins the sculpture garden of the **San Diego Museum of Art** ④, a Plateresque-style structure built to resemble the 17th-century University of Salamanca in Spain.

Continuing east, you'll come to the **Timken Museum of Art** ⑤, the **Botanical Building** ⑥, and the Spanish colonial–style **Casa del Prado,** where the San Diego Floral Association has its offices and a gift shop. At the end of the row is the **San Diego Natural History Museum** ⑦; you'll have to detour a block north to visit the **Spanish Village Art Center** ⑧. If you were to continue north, you would come to the **carousel** ⑨, the **miniature railroad** ⑩, and, finally, the entrance to the **San Diego Zoo** ⑪.

Return to the history museum and cross Plaza de Balboa—its large central fountain is a popular meeting spot—to reach the **Reuben H. Fleet Space Theater and Science Center** ⑫. (Beyond the parking lot to the south lies the **Centro Cultural de la Raza** ⑬.) You're now on the opposite side of the Prado and heading west. You'll next pass **Casa de Balboa** ⑭, home to history, model-railroad, photography, and sports museums. Next door in the newly restored **House of Hospitality** ⑮ is the **Balboa Park Visitors Center.** Just across the Plaza de Panama, the **Mingei International Museum** ⑯ resides in a recently constructed Spanish-style building that blends well with older park architecture. Your starting point, the Alcazar Garden, is just west of the Mingei.

Another option is to walk south from the Plaza de Panama, which doubles as a parking lot. Just as most of the buildings along El Prado were created for the 1915 exposition, the majority of those along this route date to the 1935 fair, when the architecture of the Maya and native peoples of the Southwest was highlighted. The first building you'll pass is the **Japanese Friendship Garden** ⑰. Next comes the ornate, crown-like **Spreckels Organ Pavilion** ⑱. The round seating area forms the base, with the stage as its diadem. The road forks here; veer to the left to reach the **House of Pacific Relations** ⑲, a Spanish Mission–style cluster of cottages and one of the few structures on this route built for the earlier exposition. Another is the Balboa Park Club, which you'll pass next. Now used for park receptions and banquets, the building resembles a mission church on the New Mexico Pueblo of Acoma; you might want to step inside to see the huge WPA mural. Continue on beyond the Palisades Building, which hosts the Marie Hitchcock Puppet Theater, to reach the **San Diego Automotive Museum** ⑳, appropriately housed in the building that served as the Palace of Transportation in the 1935–36 exposition.

The road loops back at the space ship–like **San Diego Aerospace Museum and International Aerospace Hall of Fame** ㉑. As you head north again, you'll notice the Starlight Bowl on your right. It sits in the flight path to Lindbergh Field; during the live musicals presented in the summer on its outdoor stage, actors freeze in their places when planes roar overhead. The Gymnasium Building—slated to become the home of the sports museum in a few years—follows. Perhaps the most impressive structure on this tour, the **Federal Building,** used for indoor sports these days, is next: its main entrance was modeled after the Palace of Governors in the ancient Maya city of Uxmal, Mexico. You'll be back at the Spreckels Organ Pavilion after this, having walked a total of a little less than a mile.

TIMING

Unless you're pressed for time, you'll want to devote an entire day to the perpetually expanding zoo; there are more than enough exhibits to keep you occupied for five or more hours, and you're likely to be too tired for museum hopping when you're through. The zoo is free for kids the entire month of October.

Most of the park's museums are open daily 10–4; during the summer, a number have extended hours—phone ahead to ask. On Tuesday, the museums have free admission on a rotating basis; call the Balboa Park Visitors Center (☞ House of Hospitality, *below*) for a schedule. Free concerts take place Sunday afternoons and summer Monday evenings at the Spreckels Organ Pavilion, and the House of Pacific Relations hosts Sunday afternoon folk-dance performances. Christmas on the Prado, celebrated the first Friday and Saturday in December, is not to be missed.

Sights to See

① Alcazar Garden. The gardens surrounding the Alcazar Castle in Seville were the model for the landscaping here; you'll feel like royalty resting on the benches by the tiled fountains. The flower beds are ever-changing horticultural exhibits, with bright orange and yellow poppies blooming in the spring and deep rust and crimson chrysanthemums appearing in the fall. The park's horticulturists have been working in recent years to restore it to its 1935 appearance. The garden is off El Prado, next to the Mingei International Museum and across from the Museum of Man.

⑥ Botanical Building. The graceful redwood-lathed structure built for the 1915 exposition houses more than 500 types of tropical and subtropical plants. Ceiling-high tree ferns shade fragile orchids and feathery bamboo. There are benches beside miniature waterfalls for resting in the shade. The Lily Pond, filled with giant koi fish and blooming water lilies, is popular with photographers. ⊠ *1550 El Prado,* ☎ *619/235–1110.* ⊠ *Free.* ⊙ *Fri.–Wed. 10–4.*

⑨ Carousel. Riders on this antique merry-go-round stretch from their seats to grab the brass rings suspended an arm's-length away and earn a free ride. Hand-carved in 1910, the bobbing animals include zebras, giraffes, and dragons; real horse hair was used for the tails. ⊠ *1889 Zoo Pl. (behind zoo parking lot).* ⊠ *$1.25.* ⊙ *Daily 11:30–5:30 during extended summer vacation; during school yr, only school holidays and weekends.*

⑭ Casa de Balboa. This building on El Prado's southeast corner houses four museums, the Museum of Photographic Arts, the Museum of San Diego History, the San Diego Hall of Champions–Sports Museum, and the San Diego Model Railroad Museum. *See* individual museum descriptions, *below.* ⊠ *1649 El Prado.*

⑬ Centro Cultural de la Raza. An old water tower was converted into this center for Mexican, Native American, and Chicano arts. Attractions include a gallery with rotating exhibits and a theater, as well as a permanent collection of mural art, a fine example of which may be seen on the tower's exterior. ⊠ *2004 Park Blvd.,* ☎ *619/235–6135.* ⊠ *Free.* ⊙ *Wed.–Sun. noon–5.*

⑮ House of Hospitality. At the refurbished home of the **Balboa Park Visitors Center** you can pick up schedules and route maps for the free trams that operate around the park. You can also purchase the Passport to Balboa Park, which affords entry to nine museums for $19; it's worthwhile if you want to visit more than a few and aren't entitled to the discounts that most give to children, senior citizens, and military personnel. The **Terrace on the Prado** (☎ 619/236–1935) restaurant's Spanish and early-California menu includes recipes from the gold-rush days; there's also a tapas bar here. ⊠ *1549 El Prado,* ☎ *619/239–0512.* ⊠ *Free.* ⊙ *Daily 9–4.*

⑲ House of Pacific Relations. This is not really a house but a cluster of red tile–roof, stucco cottages representing more than 25 foreign countries. And the word "pacific" refers not to the ocean—most of the nations represented are European, not Asian—but to the goal of maintaining peace. The cottages, decorated with crafts and pictures, hold open houses each Sunday, during which you can chat with transplanted natives and try out different ethnic foods. From March through October, they take turns presenting folk song and dance performances on the outdoor stage at around 2 PM—check the schedule at the park information center. Across the road from the cottages but not affili-

Balboa Park

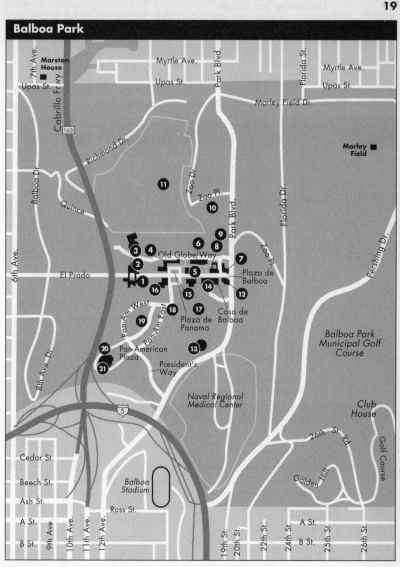

Alcazar Garden, **1**

Botanical Building, **6**

Casa de Balboa, **14**

Carousel, **9**

Centro Cultural de la Raza, **13**

House of Hospitality, **15**

House of Pacific Relations, **19**

Japanese Friendship Garden, **17**

Mingei International Museum, **16**

Miniature Railroad, **10**

Museum of Photographic Arts, **14**

Museum of San Diego History, **14**

Reuben H. Fleet Space Theater and Science Center, **12**

San Diego Aerospace Museum and International Aerospace Hall of Fame, **21**

San Diego Automotive Museum, **20**

San Diego Hall of Champions–Sports Museum, **14**

San Diego Model Railroad Museum, **14**

San Diego Museum of Art, **4**

San Diego Museum of Man, **2**

San Diego Natural History Museum, **7**

San Diego Zoo, **11**

Simon Edison Centre for the Performing Arts, **3**

Spanish Village Art Center, **8**

Spreckels Organ Pavilion, **18**

Timken Museum of Art, **5**

ated with them, the Spanish colonial–style **United Nations Building** is home to the United Nations Association's International Gift Shop, open daily, which has reasonably priced crafts, cards, and books. ✉ *2160 Pan American Rd. W,* ☎ *619/292–8592.* 🎫 *Free.* ☉ *Sun. 12:30– 4:30; hrs may vary with season.*

⓱ **Japanese Friendship Garden.** The rocks and trees are arranged to inspire contemplation in the park's Eastern-style garden, which is still being developed. It currently includes an exhibit house where such arts as origami and flower arranging are taught, a traditional sand-and-stone garden, a picnic area with a view of the canyon below, a snack bar, and a small gift shop. ✉ *2215 Pan American Rd. E,* ☎ *619/232–2780.* 🎫 *$2.* ☉ *Fri.–Sun. and Tues. 10–4.*

The Marston House. The residence of businessman George W. Marston, a San Diego pioneer and philanthropist who financed the architectural landscaping of Balboa Park, was visited by Teddy Roosevelt and Booker T. Washington, among other prominent people. Marston's 16-room home at the northwest edge of the park is now maintained by the San Diego Historical Society. Built in 1905 by San Diego architects Irving Gill and William Hebbard, it's a classic example of the American Arts and Crafts style, which emphasizes simplicity and functionality of form. The furnishings, which include pieces by Roycroft and Gustav Stickley, are also prime products of this important design movement. The 5-acre grounds are landscaped in the English Romantic tradition as interpreted in California. ✉ *3525 7th Ave.,* ☎ *619/232–6203.* 🎫 *$3.* ☉ *Weekends noon–4:30.*

★ **⓰** **Mingei International Museum.** All ages will enjoy the colorful and creative exhibits of toys, pottery, textiles, costumes, and gadgets from around the globe at the Mingei. You'll find everything from antique American carousel horses to the latest in Japanese ceramics in the light-filled museum. ✉ *1439 El Prado,* ☎ *619/239–0003.* 🎫 *$5.* ☉ *Tues.–Sun. 10–4.*

⓾ **Miniature railroad.** Adjacent to the zoo parking lot, a pint-size 48-passenger train runs a ½-mi loop through eucalyptus groves. The engine is a small-scale version of the General Motors F-3 locomotive. ✉ *2885 Zoo Pl.,* ☎ *619/239–4748.* 🎫 *$1.25.* ☉ *Weekends and school holidays 11:30–4:30 (daily during school summer break).*

Morley Field Sports Complex. The park's athletic center has a Frisbee Golf Course, with challenging "holes"—wire baskets hung from metal poles—where players toss their Frisbees over canyons and treetops to reach their goal. Morley Field also has a public pool, a velodrome, an archery range, playgrounds, and boccie, badminton, and tennis courts. The complex is at the far east end of Balboa Park, across Park Boulevard and Florida Canyon. ✉ *2221 Morley Field Dr.,* ☎ *619/692–4919.*

⓮ **Museum of Photographic Arts.** World-renowned photographers such as Ansel Adams, Imogen Cunningham, Henri Cartier-Bresson, and Edward Weston are represented in the museum's collection, along with lesser-known contemporary artists. Gallery tours and talks by artists are often given on the weekends; call ahead to find out if anything is going on. ✉ *Casa de Balboa, 1649 El Prado,* ☎ *619/239–5262.* 🎫 *$3.50.* ☉ *Daily 10–5; closed some holidays and for installations.*

⓮ **Museum of San Diego History.** The San Diego Historical Society maintains its research library in the Casa de Balboa's basement and organizes shows on the first floor. Permanent and rotating exhibits survey local urban history after 1850, when California became part of the United States. The museum has a 100-seat theater for public lectures, workshops, and educational programs. A gift shop sells books and amusing historical posters. ⊠ *Casa de Balboa, 1649 El Prado,* ☎ *619/232–6203.* ☜ *$6.* ☉ *Wed.–Sun. 10–4:30.*

★ ⑫ **Reuben H. Fleet Space Theater and Science Center.** Children and adults alike enjoy the Fleet Center's clever interactive exhibits that teach scientific principles. The IMAX Dome Theater screens exhilarating nature and science films shot to make viewers feel as though they're part of an expedition. The gift shop is akin to a museum, with toys and gadgets that inspire the imagination. A multimillion-dollar expansion program that will double the facility's size is scheduled for completion by May 1998. ⊠ *1875 El Prado,* ☎ *619/238–1233 or 619/232–6866 for advance tickets.* ☜ *Science Center $2.50, or included with price of theater ticket; Space Theater tickets $6.50; planetarium show $3.* ☉ *Mon.–Tues. 9:30–6, Wed.–Sun. 9:30–9 (hrs change seasonally; call ahead).*

㉑ **San Diego Aerospace Museum and International Aerospace Hall of Fame.** The streamlined edifice commissioned by the Ford Motor Company for the 1935–36 exposition looks unlike any other structure in the park; at night, with a line of blue neon outlining it, the round building appears—appropriately enough—to be a landlocked UFO. Every available inch of space in the rotunda is filled with exhibits about aviation and aerospace pioneers, including examples of enemy planes during the world wars. A collection of real and replicated aircraft fills the central courtyard. ⊠ *2001 Pan American Plaza,* ☎ *619/234–8291.* ☜ *$6, active military personnel free.* ☉ *Daily 10–4:30.*

⑳ **San Diego Automotive Museum.** Even if you don't know a choke from a chassis, you're bound to admire the sleek designs you'll see here. The museum maintains a core collection of vintage motorcycles and cars, ranging from an 1886 Benz to a De Lorean, as well as a series of rotating exhibits from collections around the world. There's an ongoing automobile restoration program, and the museum sponsors many outdoor automotive events; call to find out about any rallies or concours that might be scheduled. ⊠ *2080 Pan American Plaza,* ☎ *619/231–2886.* ☜ *$6.* ☉ *Daily 10–5.*

⑭ **San Diego Hall of Champions–Sports Museum.** Celebrate local jock heroes via a vast collection of memorabilia, uniforms, paintings, photographs, and computer and video displays. An amusing bloopers film is screened at the Sports Theater. ⊠ *Casa de Balboa, 1649 El Prado,* ☎ *619/234–2544.* ☜ *$3.* ☉ *Daily 10–4:30.*

⑭ **San Diego Model Railroad Museum.** When the six model-train exhibits are in operation, you'll hear the sounds of chugging engines, screeching brakes, and shrill whistles. And if you come in on Tuesday and Friday evenings, 7:30–11, there's no admission charge to watch the model-train layouts being created. ⊠ *Casa de Balboa, 1649 El Prado,* ☎ *619/696–0199.* ☜ *$3.* ☉ *Tues.–Fri. 11–4, weekends 11–5.*

★ ❹ **San Diego Museum of Art.** Known primarily for its Spanish Baroque and Renaissance paintings, including works by El Greco, Goya, Rubens, and Van Ruisdale, San Diego's most comprehensive art museum also has strong holdings of Southeast Asian art, Indian miniatures, and contemporary California paintings. The Baldwin M. Baldwin wing displays more than 100 pieces by Toulouse-Lautrec. If traveling shows from other cities come to San Diego, you can expect to see them here. An outdoor Sculpture Garden exhibits both traditional and modern pieces in a striking natural setting. The IMAGE (Interactive Multimedia Art Gallery Explorer) system allows visitors to locate the highlights of the museum's collection on a computer screen and custom-design a tour, call up his-

torical information on the works and artists, and print color repro-
ductions ($5 per print for adults, $3 for students). ⊠ *Casa de Balboa,
1450 El Prado,* ☎ *619/232–7931.* ☎ *$7 Tues.–Thurs., $8 Fri.–Sun.*
☉ *Tues.–Sun. 10–4:30.*

NEED A
BREAK?   Take a respite from museum-hopping with a cup of coffee or a glass of
California chardonnay in the San Diego Museum of Art's **Sculpture Gar-
den Café** (☎ 619/696–1990), which also has a small selection of
tasty—if somewhat costly—gourmet lunches from 11 AM to 2 PM
Tuesday–Sunday.

❷ **San Diego Museum of Man.** Exhibits at this highly respected anthro-
pological museum focus on southwestern, Mexican, and South American cultures. Carved monuments from the Maya city of Quirigua in
Guatemala, cast from the originals in 1914, are particularly impressive. Rotating shows might include intricate examples of beadwork from
across the Americas, and demonstrations of such skills as weaving and
tortilla-making are regularly held. Among the museum's more recent
additions is a hands-on Children's Discovery Center. ⊠ *California Building, 1350 El Prado,* ☎ *619/239–2001.* ☎ *$4.* ☉ *Daily 10–4:30.*

❼ **San Diego Natural History Museum.** You'll be struck, but not literally,
when you enter by a 185-pound brass Foucault pendulum, suspended
on a 43-ft cable and designed to demonstrate the earth's rotation. The
Hall of Mineralogy hosts an impressive collection of gems, but children tend to be most interested in the dinosaur bones and the live-in-
sect zoo. The museum focuses on the plants and animals of southern
California and Mexico; it frequently schedules free guided nature
walks on the weekends, as well as films and lectures throughout the
week. An $18 million expansion program began in 1997. ⊠ *1788 El
Prado,* ☎ *619/232–3821.* ☎ *$6.* ☉ *Sun.–Wed. and Fri.–Sat. 9:30–
5:30, Thurs. 9:30–6:30.*

★ ⓫ **San Diego Zoo.** Balboa Park's—and perhaps the city's—most famous
attraction is its 100-acre zoo. Nearly 4,000 animals of some 800 diverse species roam in expertly crafted habitats that spread down into,
around, and above the natural canyons. The zoo's charm and fame come
from its tradition of creating hospitable environments that replicate
natural habitats as closely as possible: The flora and the fauna in the
zoo, including many rare species, are even more costly than the animals.

From the moment you walk through the entrance, you know you've
entered a rare pocket of natural harmony. Exploring the zoo fully requires the stamina of a healthy hiker, but open-air trams that run
throughout the day allow visitors to see 80% of the exhibits on their
3-mi tour. The animals are attuned to the buses and many like to show
off; the bears are particularly fine performers, waving and bowing to
their admirers. The Kangaroo bus tours include the same informed and
amusing narrations as the others, but for a few dollars more you can
get on and off as you like at eight different stops. The Skyfari ride, which
soars 170 ft above ground, gives a good overview of the zoo's layout
and, on clear days, a panorama of the park, downtown San Diego, the
bay, and the ocean, far past the Coronado Bridge.

Still, the zoo is at its best when you wander the paths that climb
through the huge, enclosed **Scripps Aviary,** where brightly colored
tropical birds swoop between branches just inches from your face. **Gorilla Tropics,** beside the aviary, is among the zoo's latest ventures into
bioclimatic zone exhibits, where animals live in enclosed environments

modeled on their native habitats. These zones may look natural, but they're helped a lot by modern technology: The sounds of the tropical rain forest emerge from 144 speakers that play 20 CDs recorded on location in Africa.

Throughout the zoo, walkways wind over bridges and past waterfalls ringed with tropical ferns; giant elephants in a sandy plateau roam so close you're tempted to pet them. The San Diego Zoo houses the only koalas outside Australia, and three rare golden monkeys number among its impressive collection of endangered species.

The zoo's simulated Asian rain forest, **Tiger River,** brings together 10 exhibits with more than 35 species of animals. As spectacular as the tigers, pythons, and water dragons are, they seem almost inconsequential among the $500,000 collection of exotic trees and plants. The mist-shrouded trails winding down a canyon into Tiger River pass by fragrant jasmine, ginger lilies, and orchids, giving the visitor the feeling of descending into a South American jungle. In **Sun Bear Forest,** playful cubs constantly claw apart the trees and shrubs that serve as a natural playground for climbing, jumping, and general merrymaking. At **Hippo Canyon**—a 2-acre African rain forest at the base of Tiger River—you can watch the huge but surprisingly graceful beasts frolicking underwater. Four frisky polar bears plunge into a chilly pool at a popular exhibit where Siberian reindeer, white foxes, and other Arctic creatures are separated from the predatory bears by a series of camouflaged moats.

But these and other zoo locals are being overshadowed by the hoopla surrounding two glamorous overseas visitors: Shi Shi and Bai Yun, a pair of giant pandas on loan for 12 years from the People's Republic of China. Seeing them is certainly a not-to-be-missed experience, but if you're traveling with children, it's best not to raise their expectations too high: The pandas are kept apart because they don't get along very well, and the one you see may be sleeping—both like to snooze during the day. Since the pandas are here for conservation research purposes, there's also a chance that they won't be on display when you visit.

Goats and sheep at the **Children's Zoo** beg to be petted and are particularly adept at snatching bag lunches; bunnies and guinea pigs seem willing to be fondled endlessly. In the nursery windows, you can see baby lemurs and spider monkeys playing with Cabbage Patch kids, looking much like the human babies peering from strollers through the glass. The exhibits are designed in size and style for four-year-olds, but that doesn't deter children of all ages from having fun. The **Wedgeforth Bowl,** a 3,000-seat amphitheater, holds various animal shows throughout the day.

In many ways also a self-sustaining habitat for humans, the zoo rents strollers, wheelchairs, and cameras; it also has a first-aid office, a lost-and-found, and an ATM. It's best to avert your eyes from the zoo's two main gift shops until the end of your visit; you can spend a half-day just poking through the wonderful animal-related posters, crafts, dishes, clothing, and toys. One guilt-alleviating fact if you buy too much: Half the profits of your purchases go to zoo programs. Behind-the-scenes tours, walking tours, tours in Spanish, and tours for people with hearing or vision impairments are available; inquire at the entrance.

✉ *2920 Zoo Dr.,* ☎ *619/234–3153.* 🎟 *$15 includes zoo, Children's Zoo, and animal shows; $21 includes above, plus 35-min guided bus tour and Skyfari ride; Kangaroo bus tour $8 additional; zoo free for children under 12 in Oct. and for all on Founder's Day (Oct. 3). AE,*

D, MC, V. ☉ *Fall–spring, daily 9–4 (visitors may remain until 5); summer, daily 9–9 (visitors may remain until 10); Children's Zoo and Skyfari ride close earlier.*

NEED A
BREAK?
There are plenty of food stands selling popcorn, pizza, and enormous ice-cream cones. If you want to eat among strolling peacocks—who will try to cadge your food—consider the **Peacock and Raven,** just inside the main entrance, serving sandwiches, salads, and light meals. Of the zoo's various indoor restaurants, the best is **Albert's,** part of a three-tiered dining complex near Gorilla Tropics. Grilled fish, homemade pizza, and fresh pasta are among the offerings, and this is the only place where wine and beer are sold. The Rhino Chaser American Ale is a good microbrew.

❸ Simon Edison Centre for the Performing Arts. Even if you're not attending a play, the complex, comprising the Cassius Carter Centre Stage, the Lowell Davies Festival Theatre, and the Old Globe Theatre, is a pleasant place to relax between museum visits. The theaters, done in a California version of Tudor style, sit between the Sculpture Garden of the San Diego Museum of Art and the California Tower. A gift shop sells theater-related wares, including posters, cards, and brightly colored puppets. ⊠ *1363 Old Globe Way,* ☎ *619/239–2255 or 619/234–5623.*

❽ Spanish Village Art Center. Glassblowers, enamel workers, woodcarvers, sculptors, painters, jewelers, photographers, and other artists rent space in the 35 little red tile–roof studio–galleries that were set up for the 1935–36 exposition in the style of an ancient Spanish village. The artists give demonstrations of their work on a rotating basis, aware, no doubt, that it's fun to buy wares that you've watched being created. ⊠ *1770 Village Pl.,* ☎ *619/233–9050.* ⊡ *Free.* ☉ *Daily 11–4.*

⑱ Spreckels Organ Pavilion. The 2,000-seat pavilion, dedicated in 1915 by sugar magnates John D. and Adolph B. Spreckels, holds the 4,445-pipe Spreckels Organ, believed to be the largest outdoor pipe organ in the world. You can hear this impressive instrument at one of the year-round, 2 PM Sunday concerts. On summer evenings, local military bands, gospel groups, and barbershop quartets hold concerts, and at Christmas, the park's Christmas tree and life-size nativity display turn the pavilion into a seasonal wonderland. ⊠ *2211 Pan American Rd. E,* ☎ *619/226–0819.*

❺ Timken Museum of Art. This modern structure is made of travertine marble imported from Italy. The small museum houses a selection of minor works by major European and American artists as well as a superb collection of Russian icons. ⊠ *1500 El Prado,* ☎ *619/239–5548.* ⊡ *Free.* ☉ *Oct.–Aug., Tues.–Sat. 10–4:30, Sun. 1:30–4:30.*

OFF THE
BEATEN PATH
UPTOWN DISTRICT AND HILLCREST – Northwest of Balboa Park, Hillcrest is San Diego's center for the gay community and artists of all types. University, 4th, and 5th avenues are filled with cafés, boutiques, and excellent bookstores. The Guild Theater and the Ken, both on 5th Avenue, show first-run foreign films. The Blue Door, next to the Guild, is one of San Diego's best small bookstores. Like most of San Diego, Hillcrest has been undergoing redevelopment. The largest project is the Uptown District, on University Avenue at 8th Avenue. This self-contained residential-commercial center was built to resemble an inner-city neighborhood, with shops and restaurants within easy walking distance of high-priced town houses. To the northeast, Adams Avenue, reached via Park Boulevard heading north off Washington Street, has many antiques stores.

Adams Avenue leads east into Kensington and Talmadge, two handsome old neighborhoods that overlook Mission Valley.

DOWNTOWN

Thanks to a redevelopment effort started in the late 1970s, elegant hotels, upscale condominium complexes, and swank, trendy cafés now attract newcomers and natives to a newly developed city center that has retained an outdoor character. Mirrored office and banking towers reflect the nearly constant blue skies and sunshine.

Downtown's natural attributes were easily evident to its original booster, Alonzo Horton, who arrived in San Diego in 1867. Horton looked at the bay and the acres of flatland surrounded by hills and canyons and knew he had found San Diego's heart. Though Old Town, under the Spanish fort at the Presidio, had been settled for years, Horton understood that it was too far away from the water to take hold as the commercial center of San Diego. He bought 960 acres along the bay at 27½¢ per acre and gave away the land to those who would develop it or build houses. Within months, he had sold or given away 226 city blocks; settlers camped on their land in tents as their houses and businesses rose.

The transcontinental train arrived in 1885, and the land boom was on. Although the railroad's status as a cross-country route was short-lived, the population soared from 5,000 to 35,000 in less than a decade—a foreshadowing of San Diego's future. In 1887, the Santa Fe Depot was constructed at the foot of Broadway, two blocks from the water. Freighters chugged in and out of the harbor, and by the early 1900s, the navy had moved in.

As downtown grew into San Diego's transportation and commercial hub, residential neighborhoods blossomed along the beaches and inland valleys. The business district gradually moved farther away from the original heart of downtown, at 5th Avenue and Market Street, past Broadway, up toward Balboa Park. Downtown's waterfront fell into bad times during World War I, when sailors, gamblers, and prostitutes were drawn to one another and the waterfront bars.

But Alonzo Horton's modern-day followers, city leaders intent on prospering while preserving San Diego's natural beauty, have reclaimed the downtown area. Replacing old shipyards and canneries are hotel towers and waterfront parks. The Martin Luther King Jr. Promenade project, which will cost an estimated $25 million by the time it's completed, has put 12 acres of greenery along Harbor Drive from Seaport Village to the convention center. It includes a pedestrian walkway with benches, space for joggers and bicyclists, and assorted artwork; a recent addition is the Children's Park, across the street from the Children's Museum (☞ Sights to See *in* Chapter 3). The San Diego Convention Center, which hosted its first events in 1990, is thriving; spurred by its success in hosting the Republican National Convention in 1996, the administrators of the 760,000-square-ft facility have plans to double its size. A few blocks inland, the hugely successful Horton Plaza shopping center led the way for the hotels, restaurants, shopping centers, and housing developments that are now rising on every square inch of available space in downtown San Diego.

Downtown's main thoroughfares are Harbor Drive, running along the waterfront; Broadway, through the center of downtown; and 6th Avenue, to Balboa Park. The numbered streets run roughly north–south; the lettered and named streets—Broadway, Market, Island, and Ash—

run east–west. Only Broadway, Market Street, and Island Avenue have two-way traffic. The rest alternate one-way directions.

There are reasonably priced ($3–$7 per day) parking lots along Harbor Drive, Pacific Highway, and lower Broadway and Market Street. The price of many downtown parking meters is $1 per hour, with a maximum stay of three hours; unless you know for sure that your stay in the area will be short, you're better off with a lot. If you're planning to tour the Embarcadero, the lot on the Cruise Ship pier, which costs only $1 an hour with a maximum of $3 a day, is a bargain.

Numbers in the text correspond to numbers in the margin and on the Central San Diego map.

Two Good Walks

Most people do a lot of parking-lot hopping when visiting downtown, but for the energetic, two distinct areas may be explored on foot.

Those who want to stay near the water might start a walk of the **Embarcadero** ① at the foot of Ash Street on Harbor Drive, where the *Berkeley,* headquarters of the **Maritime Museum** ②, is moored. A cement pathway runs south from the *Star of India* along the waterfront to the pastel B Street Pier. Another two blocks south on Harbor Drive are Broadway and the Broadway Pier, where you can catch the ferry to Coronado. Continue south past Tuna Harbor to **Seaport Village** ③. Six blocks north of Seaport Village on Kettner Boulevard is the **Transit Center** ④; you'll see the mosaic-domed Santa Fe Depot and the tracks for the Tijuana Trolley out front. Right next door is the downtown annex of the **Museum of Contemporary Art, San Diego** ⑤.

A tour of the working heart of downtown might begin at the corner of 1st Avenue and Broadway, near Spreckels Theatre, a grand old stage that presents pop concerts and touring plays these days. A block east and across the street sits the historic **U.S. Grant Hotel** ⑥. If you cross Broadway, you'll be able to enter **Horton Plaza** ⑦, San Diego's favorite retail playland. Fourth Avenue, the eastern boundary of Horton Plaza, doubles as the western boundary of the 16-block **Gaslamp Quarter** ⑧. Head south to Island Avenue and the William Heath Davis House, where you can get a touring map of the district.

TIMING
The above walks take about an hour each, though there's enough to do in downtown San Diego to keep you busy for at least two days— or three if you really like to shop or if you decide to take a side trip to Coronado or Tijuana. Weather is a determining factor in any Embarcadero stroll, which is pretty much an outdoors endeavor, but San Diego rarely presents any problems along that line. In January and February, when the gray whales migrate from the Pacific Northwest to southern Baja, it's a must to book a whale-watching excursion at the Broadway pier. For a guided tour of the Gaslamp Quarter, plan to visit the area on Saturday.

Sights to See

① **Embarcadero.** The bustle along Harbor Drive's waterfront walkway comes less these days from the activities of tuna and other fishing folk, but it remains the nautical soul of San Diego. People here still make a living from the sea: restaurants line the piers, as do sea vessels of every variety—cruise ships, ferries, tour boats, houseboats, and naval destroyers. Many boats along the Embarcadero have been converted into floating gift shops, and others are awaiting restoration.

On the north end of the Embarcadero, at Ash Street, you'll find the Maritime Museum (☞ *below*). Just south of it, the pastel **B Street Pier** is used by ships from major cruise lines as both a port of call and a departure point. The cavernous pier building has a cruise-information center and a small, cool bar and gift shop.

Day-trippers getting ready to set sail gather at the **Broadway Pier,** also known as the excursion pier. Tickets for the harbor tours and whale-watching trips are sold here.

The navy's Eleventh Naval District has control of the next few waterfront blocks to the south—destroyers, submarines, and carriers cruise in and out, some staying for weeks at a time. On weekends, the navy usually conducts tours of these floating cities (☎ 619/532–1430 for information on hours and types of ships, or 619/545–2427 for the U.S.S. *Constellation*). **Tuna Harbor** is the former hub of one of San Diego's earliest and most successful industries, commercial tuna fishing. These days, you'll see only a few boats that continue in this trade tied up at the docks.

Kite fliers, roller-skaters, and picnickers hang out in **Embarcadero Marina Park North,** an 8-acre extension into the harbor from the center of Seaport Village (☞ *below*). Seasonal celebrations are held here and at the similar **Embarcadero Marina Park South** throughout the year.

The **San Diego Convention Center,** on Harbor Drive between 1st and 5th avenues, was designed by Arthur Erickson. The backdrop of blue sky and sea complements the building's nautical lines. The center often holds trade shows that are open to the public, and tours of the building are available.

NEED A
BREAK?   Those waiting for their boats at the Broadway Pier can enjoy some New England–style clam chowder in an edible sourdough bowl at the **Bay Cafe** (✉ 1050 N. Harbor Dr., ☎ 619/595–1083).

❽ **Gaslamp Quarter.** The 16-block National Historic District centered on 5th and 4th avenues from Broadway to Market Street contains most of San Diego's Victorian-style commercial buildings from the late 1800s, when Market Street was the center of early downtown. In the latter part of the 19th century, businesses thrived in this area, but at the turn of the century, downtown's commercial district moved west toward Broadway, and many of San Diego's first buildings fell into disrepair. During the early 1900s, the quarter became known as the Stingaree district. Prostitutes picked up sailors in lively area taverns, and dance halls and crime flourished here; the blocks between Market Street and the waterfront were best avoided.

As the move for downtown redevelopment emerged, there was talk of destroying the buildings in the quarter, bulldozing them and starting from scratch. In 1974, history buffs, developers, architects, and artists formed the Gaslamp Quarter Council. Bent on preserving the district, they gathered funds from the government and private benefactors and began cleaning up the quarter, restoring the finest old buildings, and attracting businesses and the public back to the heart of New Town. Their efforts have paid off. Former flophouses have become choice office buildings, and the area is dotted with shops and restaurants.

The **William Heath Davis House** (✉ 410 Island Ave., at 4th Ave., ☎ 619/233–4692), one of the first residences in town, now serves as the information center for the Gaslamp Quarter. Davis was a San Franciscan whose ill-fated attempt to develop the waterfront area preceded the more successful one of Alonzo Horton. In 1850, Davis had this prefab saltbox-style house shipped around Cape Horn and assembled in San Diego (it was originally located at State and Market streets).

28

Cabrillo National
Monument, **15**

Coronado Beach
Historical Museum, **13**

Embarcadero, **1**

Ferry Landing
Marketplace, **9**

Fort Rosecrans
National Cemetery, **16**

Gaslamp Quarter, **8**

Glorietta Bay Inn, **12**

Harbor Island, **20**

Horton Plaza, **7**

Hotel Del
Coronado, **11**

Maritime Museum, **2**

Museum of
Contemporary Art, San
Diego, **5**

Orange Avenue, **10**

Scott Street, **18**

Seaport Village, **3**

Shelter Island, **19**

Silver Strand Beach
State Park, **14**

Sunset Cliffs, **17**

Transit Center, **4**

U.S. Grant Hotel, **6**

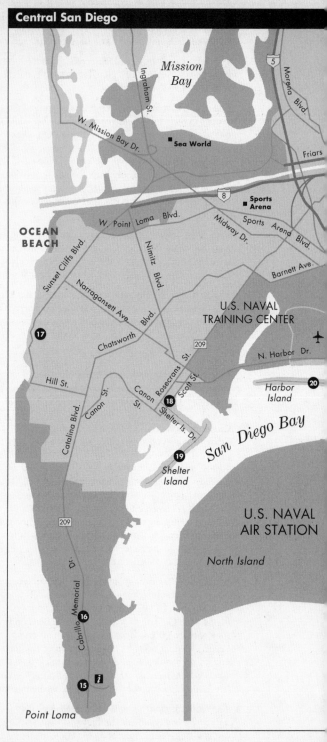

Central San Diego

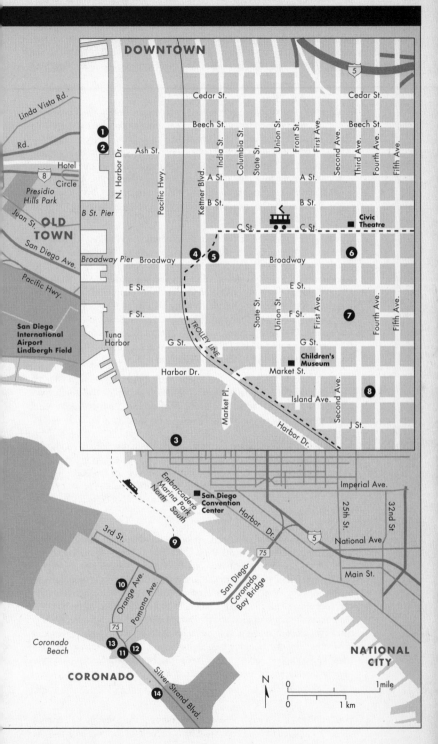

Docents give tours ($2) of the house during museum hours—weekdays from 10 to 2, Saturday from 10 to 4, and Sunday from noon to 4. Two-hour walking tours of the historic district leave from the house on Saturday at 11; the cost for these or a self-guided audio tour (phone ahead to reserve a headset) is $5. The museum also has a detailed map of the district.

The Victorian **Horton Grand Hotel** (✉ 311 Island Ave.) was created in the mid-1980s by joining together two historic hotels, the Kahle Saddlery and the Grand Hotel, built in the boom days of the 1880s; Wyatt Earp stayed at the Kahle Saddlery—then called the Brooklyn Hotel—while he was in town speculating on real estate ventures and opening gambling halls. The two hotels were dismantled and reconstructed on a new site, about four blocks from their original locations. A small Chinese Museum serves as a tribute to the surrounding Chinatown district, a collection of modest structures that once housed Chinese laborers and their families.

The majority of the quarter's landmark buildings are on 4th and 5th avenues, between Island Avenue and Broadway. If you don't have much time, just stroll down 5th Avenue, where highlights include the Backesto Building (No. 614), the Mercantile Building (No. 822), the Louis Bank of Commerce (No. 835), and the Watts-Robinson Building (No. 903). The Tudor-style Keating Building (✉ 432 F St., at 5th Ave.) was designed by the same firm that created the famous Hotel Del Coronado. Peer into Johnny M's 801, at the corner of 4th Avenue and F Street, a restored turn-of-the-century tavern with a 12-ft mahogany bar and a spectacular stained-glass domed ceiling.

The section of G Street between 6th and 9th avenues has become a haven for galleries; stop in one of them to pick up a map of the downtown arts district. For information about openings and other current events in the district, call the **Gaslamp Quarter Hot Line** (☎ 619/233–4691).

NEED A
BREAK?

Fifth Avenue between F and G streets is lined with restaurants, many with outdoor patios. Hip coffeehouses have also sprung up in the Gaslamp Quarter; you can nurse a double espresso at **Café LuLu** (✉ 419 F St., ☎ 619/238–0114) for hours. At **Café Bessom** (✉ 401 Market St., ☎ 619/557–0173), which doubles as a tobacco shop, the non-smokers sit outside.

★ ❼ **Horton Plaza.** Downtown's centerpiece is the shopping, dining, and entertainment mall that fronts Broadway and G Street from 1st to 4th avenues and covers more than six city blocks. Designed by Jon Jerde and completed in 1985, Horton Plaza is far from what one would imagine a shopping center—or city center—to be. A collage of pastels with elaborate, colorful tile work on benches and stairways, cloth banners waving in the air, and modern sculptures marking the entrances, Horton Plaza rises in uneven, staggered levels to six floors; great views of downtown from the harbor to Balboa Park and beyond can be had here. The complex's architecture has strongly affected the rest of downtown's development—new apartment and condominium complexes along G and Market streets mimic its brightly colored towers and cupolas.

Horton Plaza has a multilevel parking garage; the long lines of cars in search of a place to land show just how successful the complex has become. The first three hours of parking are free with validation; after that, it's $1 for every half hour. If you use this notoriously confusing garage, be sure to remember where you leave your car.

Macy's, Nordstrom, and Mervyn's department stores anchor the shopping sections, with an eclectic assortment of nearly 150 clothing, sporting-goods, jewelry, book, and gift shops flanking them. Other attractions include the country's largest Sam Goody's music store and a Hard Rock Cafe. A movie complex, restaurants, and a long row of take-out ethnic food shops and dining patios line the uppermost tier. On the lowest level, facing 1st Avenue, is the Farmers Market, an upscale grocery with fresh gourmet meats, seafood, and produce. The respected San Diego Repertory Theatre has two stages below ground level. Most stores are open from 10 to 9 weekdays, from 10 to 6 Saturday, and from 11 to 6 Sunday, but during the winter holidays and the summer, many places stay open longer (☎ 619/238–1596 for up-to-the-minute information).

The **International Visitor Information Center,** operated in the complex by the San Diego Convention and Visitors Bureau, is the best resource for information on the city. The staff members and volunteers who run the center speak many languages and are acquainted with the myriad needs and requests of tourists. They dispense information on hotels, restaurants, and tourist attractions, including Tijuana. ⊠ *Visitor center: 11 Horton Plaza, street level at corner of 1st Ave. and F St.,* ☎ *619/236–1212.* ☉ *Mon.–Sat. 8:30–5; June–Aug. also Sun. 11–5.*

NEED A
BREAK?

Nice days see hungry shoppers seated at the counters and tables outside the informal eateries on Horton Plaza's top level, where you can get everything from fresh hot cinnamon rolls to pizza and sushi. Just want a caffeine recharge? Coffee carts include the **Expresso Bar,** outside Nordstrom on level 3. **Starbucks** fans can get their favorite fix inside a store on level 1.

② **Maritime Museum.** A collection of three restored ships that may be toured for one admission price, the museum affords a glimpse of San Diego during its heyday as a commercial seaport. Its headquarters are the *Berkeley,* an 1898 ferryboat moored at the foot of Ash Street. The steam-driven ship, which served the Southern Pacific Railroad at San Francisco Bay until 1958, played its most important role during the great earthquake of 1906, when it carried thousands of passengers across San Francisco Bay to Oakland. Its carved-wood paneling, stained-glass windows, and plate-glass mirrors have been restored, and its main deck serves as a floating museum, with exhibits on oceanography, naval history, and the America's Cup Race. Anchored next to the *Berkeley,* the small Scottish steam yacht *Medea,* launched in 1904, may be boarded but has no interpretive displays.

The most interesting of the three ships is the *Star of India,* a windjammer built in 1863. The ship's high wooden masts and white sails flapping in the wind have been a harbor landmark since 1927. The *Star of India* made 21 trips around the world in the late 1800s, when it traveled the East Indian trade route, shuttled immigrants from England to New Zealand, and served the Alaskan salmon trade. The ship languished after being retired to San Diego Harbor, virtually ignored until 1959, when volunteers organized by the Maritime Museum began the laborious task of stripping the wooden decks, polishing the figurehead, and mending the sails. The oldest active iron sailing ship in the world makes rare short excursions but for the most part stays moored at the pier and open to visitors. ⊠ *1306 N. Harbor Dr.,* ☎ *619/234–9153.* 🎟 *$5.* ☉ *Ships daily 9–8.*

⑤ **Museum of Contemporary Art, San Diego.** The downtown branch of the city's modern art museum, which opened in 1993 while the main facility in La Jolla was undergoing renovation, has taken on its own personality. The two-story building has four small galleries that host rotating shows. It's fronted by a Sculpture Plaza. ⊠ *1001 Kettner Blvd.,* ☎ *619/234–1172 or 619/454–3541 for exhibition information.* ⊡ *$4; free 1st Tues. of month.* ☉ *Tues.–Thurs. and Sat. 10–5, Fri. 10–8, Sun. noon–5.*

★ ❸ **Seaport Village.** A wise developer saw the potential in the stretch of prime waterfront that spreads out across 14 acres and connects the harbor with the hotel towers and the convention center. The village's three shopping plazas are designed to reflect the architectural styles of early California, especially New England clapboard and Spanish Mission. A ¼-mi wooden boardwalk that runs along the bay and 4 mi of simulated dirt-road and cobblestone paths, lead to specialty shops, snack bars, and restaurants—about 75 in all. You can browse through a kite store, a rubber-stamp emporium, and a shop devoted to left-handed people and nosh to your heart's delight on everything from fast Greek, Mexican, and Italian fare to seafood in nautical-style indoor restaurants. Seaport Village's shops are open daily 10–9 (10–10 in summer); a few eateries open early for breakfast, and many have extended nighttime hours, especially in summer.

Charles I. D. Looff crafted the the hand-carved, hand-painted steeds on the **Broadway Flying Horses Carousel,** for the Coney Island amusement park in 1890. The ride was moved from its next home, Salisbury Beach in Massachusetts, and faithfully restored for Seaport Village's West Plaza; tickets are $1. Strolling clowns, mimes, musicians, and magicians are also on hand throughout the village to entertain kids; those not impressed by such pretechnological displays can duck into the Time Out entertainment center near the carousel and play video games. ☎ *619/235–4014 or 619/235–4013 for events hot line.*

NEED A BREAK? **Upstart Crow & Co.** (⊠ Seaport Village, Central Plaza, ☎ 619/232–4855), a combination bookstore and coffeehouse, serves good cappuccino and espresso with great pastries and cakes.

❹ **Transit Center.** The Mission Revival–style **Santa Fe Depot,** which replaced the original 1887 station on this site, serves north- and southbound Amtrak passengers. A booth at the graceful, tile-domed depot has bus schedules, maps, and tourist brochures. Formerly an easily spotted area landmark, it's now overshadowed by **1 America Plaza** across the street. At the base of this 34-story office tower, designed by architect Helmut Jahn, is a center that links the train, trolley, and city bus systems. The building's signature crescent-shape glass-and-steel canopy arches out over the trolley tracks. The Greyhound bus station (⊠ 120 West Broadway) is just a few blocks away. ⊠ *Broadway and Kettner Blvd.*

❻ **U.S. Grant Hotel.** Far more formal than most other hotels in San Diego, the doyenne of downtown lodgings has a marble lobby, gleaming chandeliers, white-gloved doormen, and other touches that hark back to the more gracious era when it was built (1910). Funded in part by the son of the president for whom it was named, the hotel was extremely opulent; 350 rooms out of 437 had private baths, highly unusual for that time. Over the years, it became noted for its famous guests—U.S. presidents from Woodrow Wilson to George Bush have stayed here— but it got a different kind of press in 1969, when the old-boy's-clubby Grant's Grill became the site of a sit-in by eight local women who objected to its policy of allowing only males to enter before 3 PM. Taking up a city block—it's bounded by 3rd and 4th avenues, C Street, and Broadway—the hotel occupies the site of San Diego's first hotel, constructed by Alonzo Horton in 1870. Appropriately enough, Horton Plaza is now across the street. ⊠ *326 Broadway.*

OFF THE BEATEN PATH	**VILLA MONTEZUMA** – The former residence of Jesse Shepard, a pianist, spiritualist, and novelist, adapts the elements of high Queen Anne style to Shepard's unique aesthetic interests. The 1887 house is filled with fascinating period and personal details: Stained-glass windows depicting Shakespeare, Beethoven, Mozart, Sappho, and Goethe; redwood panels; tiled fireplaces; family portraits; and tributes from Shepard's famous admirers. Villa Montezuma was restored by the San Diego Historical Society, whose docents give continuous tours. Architecture buffs will enjoy combining a visit to this house, which is in a rather seedy area just east of I–5, with one to the Marston House in Balboa Park, 10 minutes to the north and also operated by the Historical Society. A dual admission ticket will save you $1. ⊠ *1925 K St.,* ☎ *619/239-2211.* ☞ *$3.* ☉ *Weekends noon–4:30 (last tour at 3:45).*

CORONADO

Although it's actually an isthmus, easily reached from the mainland if you head north from Imperial Beach, Coronado has always seemed like an island—and is always referred to as such. The Spaniards called it Los Coronados, or "the Crowned Ones," in the late 1500s and the name stuck. Today's residents, many of whom live in grand Victorian homes handed down for generations, tend to consider their community to be a sort of royal encampment, safe from the hassles and hustle of San Diego proper.

North Island Naval Air Station was established in 1911 on Coronado's north end, across from Point Loma, and was the site of Charles Lindbergh's departure on the transcontinental flight that preceded his famous transatlantic voyage (a San Diego–area company manufactured the *Spirit of St. Louis*). Today high-tech air- and seacraft arrive and depart continually from North Island, providing a real-life education in military armament. Coronado's long relationship with the navy has made it an enclave of sorts for retired military personnel.

The streets of Coronado are wide, quiet, and friendly, with lots of neighborhood parks where young families mingle with the area's many senior citizens. Grand old homes face the waterfront and the Coronado Municipal Golf Course, with its setting under the bridge, at the north end of Glorietta Bay; it's the site of the annual Fourth of July fireworks. Community celebrations and concerts take place in Spreckels Park on Orange Avenue.

Coronado is visible from downtown and Point Loma and accessible via the arching blue 2.2-mi-long San Diego–Coronado Bridge, a landmark just beyond downtown's skyline. There is a $1 toll for crossing the bridge into Coronado, but cars carrying two or more passengers may enter through the free car-pool lane. The bridge handles more than 67,000 cars each day, and rush hour tends to be slow, which is fine, since the view of the harbor, downtown, and the island is breathtaking, day and night.

Until the bridge was completed in 1969, visitors and residents relied on the Coronado Ferry, which ran across the harbor from downtown. When the bridge was opened, the ferry closed down, much to the chagrin of those who were fond of traveling at a leisurely pace. In 1987, the ferry returned, and with it came the island's most ambitious development in decades. Coronado's residents and commuting workers have quickly adapted to this traditional mode of transportation, and the ferry has become quite popular with bicyclists, who shuttle their bikes across the harbor and ride the island's wide, flat boulevards for hours.

You can board the ferry, operated by San Diego Harbor Excursion (☎ 619/234–4111 or 800/442–7847 in CA), at downtown San Diego's Embarcadero from the Broadway Pier at Broadway and Harbor Drive, or from a new stop at the Convention Center; you'll arrive at the Ferry Landing Marketplace. Boats depart every hour on the hour from the Embarcadero and every hour at 42 minutes after the hour from Coronado, Sunday through Thursday from 9 AM to 9:42 PM, Friday and Saturday until 10:42 PM; the fare is $2 each way, 50¢ extra for bicycles. San Diego Harbor Excursion (☎ 619/235–8294 for reservations and schedules) also offers water-taxi service from Seaport Village to Ferry Landing Marketplace, Le Meridien Resort, and the Hotel Del Coronado. The fare is $5.

Numbers in the text correspond to numbers in the margin and on the Central San Diego map.

A Good Tour

Coronado is easy to navigate without a car. When you depart the ferry, you can explore the shops at the **Ferry Landing Marketplace** ⑨ and, from there, catch the shuttle (50¢ fare) that runs down **Orange Avenue** ⑩, Coronado's main tourist drag. You might get off near the tourist information office and pick up a map, or just disembark at an appealing spot and keep strolling along the boutiques-filled promenade until you reach the **Hotel Del Coronado** ⑪ at the end of Orange Avenue. Right across the street from the Del is the **Glorietta Bay Inn** ⑫, another of the island's outstanding early structures. A bit northwest of the hotel is the **Coronado Beach Historical Museum** ⑬. If you've brought your swimsuit, you might continue on to **Silver Strand Beach State Park** ⑭—just past the Hotel Del, Orange Avenue turns into Silver Strand Boulevard, which soon becomes Highway 75.

TIMING

A leisurely stroll through Coronado takes an hour or so, more if you shop or walk along the beach. If you're a history buff, you might want to visit on Thursday or Saturday, when you can combine the tour of Coronado's historic homes that departs from the Glorietta Bay Inn at 11 AM with a visit to the Coronado Beach Historical Museum, open Wednesday through Sunday afternoons. Whenever you come, if you're not staying on the island, remember to get back to the dock in time to catch the final ferry out. The last shuttle to the Ferry Landing Marketplace leaves from the Loews Coronado Bay Resort at 5:57.

Sights to See

 Coronado Beach Historical Museum. An East Coast family built this Cape Cod–style cottage in 1898. The restored building now houses a museum that celebrates the island's history with photographs and displays of its formative events and major sites: the Hotel Del Coronado, including an original chamber pot from one of the rooms; Tent City, a summer resort just south of the Del developed by John Spreckels at the turn of the century; the early ferry boats; and the North Island Naval Air Station. ⊠ *1126 Loma Ave.,* ☎ *619/435–7242.* 🖾 *Free; donations accepted.* ☉ *Wed.–Sat. 10–4, Sun. noon–4.*

 Ferry Landing Marketplace. The aptly named point of disembarkation for the ferry, this collection of shops is actually a new development on an old site. Its buildings resemble the gingerbread domes of the Hotel

Del Coronado, long the area's main attraction. On a smaller—and generally less interesting—scale, the Ferry Landing Marketplace is similar to downtown's Seaport Village, with little shops and restaurants and lots of benches facing the water. ⊠ *1201 1st St. at B Ave.,* ☎ *619/ 435–8895.*

⑫ Glorietta Bay Inn. The former residence of John Spreckels, the original owner of North Island and the property on which the Hotel Del Coronado stands, is now a popular hotel. On Tuesday, Thursday, and Saturday morning at 11, it's the departure point for a fun and informative 1½-hour walking tour of a few of the area's 86 officially designated historical homes. Sponsored by the Coronado Historical Association, the tour focuses on the Glorietta Bay Inn and the Hotel Del Coronado across the street. In addition, it includes—from the outside only—some spectacular mansions and the Meade House, where L. Frank Baum wrote *The Wizard of Oz* (some claim that Coronado is the model for Baum's Emerald City). ⊠ *1630 Glorietta Blvd.,* ☎ *619/435–5892 or 619/435–5444 for tour information.* ☜ *$6 for historical tour.*

★ ⑪ Hotel Del Coronado. The island's most prominent landmark, selected as a National Historic Site in 1977, the Del, as natives call it, has a colorful history, integrally connected with that of Coronado itself. The hotel was the brainchild of financiers Elisha Spurr Babcock Jr. and H. L. Story, who saw the potential of the island's virgin beaches and its view of San Diego's emerging harbor. They purchased a 4,100-acre parcel of land in 1885 for $110,000 and threw a lavish Fourth of July bash for prospective investors in their hunting and fishing resort. By the end of the year, they had roused public interest—and had an ample return on their investment. The hotel was completed in 1888. Thomas Edison himself threw the switch as the Del became the world's first electrically lighted hotel. It has been a dazzler ever since.

The Del's ornate Victorian gingerbread architecture is recognized all over the world because the hotel has served as a set for many movies, political meetings, and extravagant social happenings. It is said that the Duke of Windsor first met Wallis Simpson here. Fourteen presidents have been guests of the Del, and the film *Some Like It Hot,* starring Marilyn Monroe, was filmed at the hotel. Historic photos from the Del's early days line the lower-level corridors.

A red carpet leads up the front stairs to the main lobby, with its grand oak pillars and ceiling, and out to the central courtyard and gazebo. To the right is the cavernous **Crown Room,** whose arched ceiling of notched sugar pine was constructed without nails. You can tell by looking at this space that the hotel's architect, James Reed, had previously designed railroad stations. A lavish Sunday brunch is served here from 9 AM to 2 PM.

The **Grand Ballroom** overlooks the ocean and the hotel's long white beach. The patio surrounding the sky-blue swimming pool is a great place for just sitting back and imagining what the bathers looked like during the '20s, when the hotel rocked with the good times. More rooms have been added in high-rise towers beside the original 400-room building. ⊠ *1500 Orange Ave.,* ☎ *619/435–6611.* ☜ *$10 for guided tour, $5 for headsets for self-guided tour.* ☉ *1-hr guided tours (from lobby) Thurs.–Sat. at 10 and 11.*

⑩ Orange Avenue. It's easy to imagine you're on a street in Cape Cod when you stroll along this thoroughfare, Coronado's version of a downtown: The clapboard houses, small restaurants, and boutiques—many of them selling nautical paraphernalia—are in some ways more characteristic of New England than they are of California. But the East Coast illusion tends to dissipate as quickly as a winter fog when you catch sight of one of the avenue's many citrus trees—or realize it's February and the sun is warming your face. Just off Orange Avenue is the **Coronado Visitors Bureau** (✉ 1047 B Ave., ☎ 619/437–8788 or 800/ 622–8300).

⑭ **Silver Strand Beach State Park.** The stretch of sand that runs along Silver Strand Boulevard from the Hotel Del Coronado to Imperial Beach dispels the illusion that Coronado is an island. The clean beach is a perfect family gathering spot, with rest rooms and lifeguards. Don't be surprised if you see groups exercising in military style along the beach; this is a training area for the navy's underwater Seals. Across from the strand is the Coronado Cays, an exclusive community popular with yacht owners and celebrities, and the Loews Coronado Bay Resort. *See* Beaches *in* Chapter 7 for additional information on this state park.

En Route San Diego's Mexican-American community is centered in Barrio Logan, under the Coronado Bridge on the downtown side. **Chicano Park,** spread along National Avenue from Dewey to Crosby streets, is the barrio's recreational hub. It's worth taking a short detour to see the huge murals of Mexican history painted on the bridge supports at National Avenue and Dewey Street; they're among the best examples of folk art in the city.

HARBOR ISLAND, POINT LOMA, AND SHELTER ISLAND

Point Loma curves around the San Diego Bay west of downtown and the airport, protecting the center city from the Pacific's tides and waves. Although military installations are based here and some main streets are cluttered with motels and fast-food shacks, Point Loma is an old and wealthy enclave of stately family homes. Its bayside shores front huge estates, with sailboats and yachts packed tightly in private marinas. Nearby Harbor and Shelter islands, both created out of detritus from the San Diego Bay in the second half of this century, have become tourist hubs, their high-rise hotels, seafood restaurants, and boat-rental centers looking as solid as those anywhere else in the city.

Numbers in the text correspond to numbers in the margin and on the Central San Diego map.

A Good Tour

Take Catalina Drive all the way south to the tip of Point Loma to reach **Cabrillo National Monument** ⑮; you'll be retracing the steps of the earliest European explorers if you use this as a jumping-off point for a tour. Just north of the monument as you head back into the neighborhoods of Point Loma, you'll see the white headstones of **Fort Rosecrans National Cemetery** ⑯. Continue north on Catalina Boulevard to Hill Street and turn left to reach the dramatic **Sunset Cliffs** ⑰, at the western side of Point Loma near Ocean Beach. Return to Catalina Boulevard and backtrack south for a few blocks to find Canon Street, which leads toward the peninsula's eastern (bay) side. Almost at the shore, you'll see **Scott Street** ⑱, the main commercial drag of Point Loma. Scott Street is bisected by Shelter Island Drive, which leads to **Shelter Island** ⑲, a most impressive product of landfill. For another example of what can be done with tons of dirt dredged from a bay, go back up Shelter Island Drive, turn right on Rosecrans Street, and make another right on North Harbor Drive to get to **Harbor Island** ⑳.

TIMING

If you're interested in seeing the tidal pools at Cabrillo National Monument, you'll need to call ahead to find out when low tide will occur. Scott Street, with its Point Loma Seafoods, is a good place to find yourself at lunchtime, and Sunset Cliffs Park is where you might want to be when the daylight starts to wane. This drive takes about an hour if you stop briefly at each sight.

Sights to See

★ ⑮ **Cabrillo National Monument.** This 144-acre preserve marks the site of the first European visit to San Diego, made by Portuguese explorer Juan Rodríguez Cabrillo—his real name was João Rodrigues Cabrilho, but it was later Hispanicized. Cabrillo, who had earlier gone on voyages with Hernán Cortés, came to this spot, which he called San Miguel, in 1542. Government grounds were set aside to commemorate his discovery in 1913 and today the monument, with its rugged cliffs and shores and outstanding overlooks, is one of the most frequently visited of all National Park Service sites.

The **visitor center** presents films and lectures about Cabrillo's voyage, the sea-level tidal pools, and the gray whales migrating offshore. The center has an excellent shop with books about nature, San Diego, and the sea. Maps of the region, posters of whales, flowers, shells, and the requisite postcards, slides, and film are also on sale. Rest rooms and water fountains are plentiful along the paths that climb to the monument's various viewpoints, but, except for a few vending machines at the visitor center, there are no food facilities. Exploring the grounds consumes time and calories; bring a picnic and rest on a bench overlooking the sailboats headed to sea.

Interpretive stations with recorded information in six languages—including, appropriately enough, Portuguese—have been installed along the walkways that edge the cliffs. Signs explain the views and posters depict the various navy, fishing, and pleasure craft that sail into and fly over the bay. Directly south across the bay from the visitor center is the North Island Naval Air Station on the west end of Coronado Island. Just to the left on the shores of Point Loma is the Naval Research and Development (NRAD) Center and Ballast Point; nuclear-powered submarines are now docked where Cabrillo's small ships anchored in 1542.

A **statue of Cabrillo** overlooks downtown from the next windy promontory, where visitors gather to admire the stunning panorama over the bay, from the snowcapped San Bernardino Mountains, 130 mi north, to the hills surrounding Tijuana to the south. The stone figure standing on the bluff looks rugged and dashing, but he is a creation of an artist's imagination—no portraits of Cabrillo are known to exist. The statue was donated by the Portuguese Navy in 1957.

The moderately steep 2-mi **Bayside Trail** winds through coastal sage scrub, curving under the clifftop lookouts and bringing you ever closer to the bayfront scenery. You cannot reach the beach from this trail and must stick to the path to protect the cliffs from erosion and yourself from thorny plants and snakes—including rattlers. Along the way, you'll see prickly pear cactus and yucca, black-eyed Susans, fragrant sage, and maybe a lizard or a hummingbird. The climb back is long but gradual, leading up to the old lighthouse.

The oil lamp of the **Old Point Loma Lighthouse** was first lit in 1855. The light, sitting in a brass-and-iron housing above a white wooden house, shone through a state-of-the-art lens from France and was visible from the sea for 25 mi. Unfortunately, it was too high above the cliffs to guide navigators trapped in southern California's thick offshore fog and low clouds. In 1891, a new lighthouse was built 400 ft below. The old lighthouse, recently refitted with furnishings more accurate to the era when it was erected, is open to visitors. The coast guard still uses the newer lighthouse and a mighty foghorn to guide boaters through the narrow channel leading into the bay.

The western and southern cliffs of Cabrillo National Monument are prime whale-watching territory. A sheltered viewing station has a tape-recorded lecture describing the great gray whales' migration from the Bering and Chukchi seas to Baja, and high-powered telescopes help you focus on the whales' water spouts. The whales are visible on clear days in January and February, mostly in early morning.

More accessible sea creatures can be seen in the **tidal pools** at the foot of the monument's western cliffs. Drive north from the visitor center to the first road on the left, which winds down to the coast guard station and the shore. When the tide is low, you can walk on the rocks around saltwater pools filled with starfish, crabs, anemones, octopuses, and hundreds of other sea creatures and plants.

✉ *1800 Cabrillo Memorial Dr.,* ☎ *619/557–5450.* ⌦ *$4 per car, $2 per person entering on foot or by bicycle; free for Golden Age, Golden Access, and Golden Eagle passport holders, and children under 17.* ☉ *Park daily 9–5:15, Old Lighthouse 9–5, Bayside Trail 9–4, tidal-pool areas 9–4:30.*

16 **Fort Rosecrans National Cemetery.** In 1934, 8 acres out of the 1,000 set aside for a military reserve in 1852 were designated as a burial site. About 65,000 people are now interred here; it's impressive to see the rows upon rows of white headstones that overlook both sides of Point Loma just north of the Cabrillo National Monument. Many of those laid to rest at this place were killed in battles that predate California's statehood; the graves of the 17 men and one civilian who died in the 1874 Battle of San Pasqual between the Mexicans and Americans are marked by a large bronze plaque. Perhaps the most impressive structure in the cemetery is the 75-ft granite obelisk called the Bennington Monument, which commemorates the 66 crew members who died from a boiler explosion and fire on board the U.S.S. *Bennington* in 1905. The cemetery, visited by many veterans, is still used for burials. ☎ 619/553–2084. ☉ *Weekdays 8–5, weekends 9–5, Memorial Day 8–7.*

20 **Harbor Island.** Following the success of nearby Shelter Island, the navy decided to use the residue that resulted from digging berths deep enough to accommodate aircraft carriers to build another recreational island. In 1961, a 1½-mi-long peninsula was created adjacent to San Diego International Airport out of 12 million cubic yards of sand and mud dredged from San Diego Bay. Restaurants and high-rise hotels now line the inner shores of Harbor Island. The bay shore has pathways, gardens, and picnic spots for sightseeing or working off the calories from the island restaurants' fine meals. On the west point, Tom Ham's Lighthouse restaurant has a coast guard–approved beacon shining from its tower.

Across from the western end of Harbor Island, at the mainland's **Spanish Landing Park,** a bronze plaque marks the arrival in 1769 of a party from Spain that headed north from San Diego to conquer California. The group was a merger of the crew of two ships, the *San Carlos* and the *San Antonio,* and of a contingent that came overland from Baja California. No one knows exactly where the men landed and camped; we can only be certain it wasn't Harbor Island.

18 Scott Street. Running along Point Loma's waterfront from Shelter Island to the Marine Corps Recruiting Center on Harbor Drive, this thoroughfare is lined with deep-sea fishing charters and whale-watching boats. It's a good spot from which to watch fishermen (and women) haul marlin, tuna, and puny mackerel off their boats.

NEED A BREAK? The freshest and tastiest fish to be found along Point Loma's shores comes from **Point Loma Sea Foods** (✉ 2805 Emerson St., ☎ 619/223–1109), off Scott Street behind the Vagabond Inn. A fish market sells specialties fresh from the boat. Patrons crowd the adjacent take-out counter for seafood cocktails and salads, seviche, and crab and shrimp sandwiches made with freshly baked sourdough bread. Outdoor and indoor seating makes this a good choice in any weather.

19 Shelter Island. In 1950, San Diego's port director thought there should be some use for the soil dredged to deepen the ship channel in the 1930s and '40s. He decided it might be a good idea to raise the shoal that lay off the eastern shore of Point Loma above sea level, landscape it, and add a 2,000-ft causeway to make it accessible.

His hunch paid off. Shelter Island—actually a peninsula—now supports towering mature palms, a cluster of mid-range resorts, restaurants, and side-by-side marinas. It is the center of San Diego's yacht-building industry, and boats in every stage of construction are visible in the yacht yards. A long sidewalk runs from the landscaped lawns of the **San Diego Yacht Club** (tucked down Anchorage Street off Shelter Island Drive), past boat brokerages to the hotels and marinas, which line the inner shore, facing Point Loma. On the bay side, fishermen launch their boats or simply stand on shore and cast. Families relax at picnic tables along the grass, where there are fire rings and permanent barbecue grills, while strollers wander to the huge Friendship Bell, given to San Diegans by the people of Yokohama in 1960.

17 Sunset Cliffs. As their name suggests, the 60-ft-high bluffs on the western side of Point Loma just south of Ocean Beach are a perfect place to watch the sun descend over the sea. To view the tidal pools along the shore, you can descend a staircase on Sunset Cliffs Boulevard at the foot of Laredo Street.

The dramatic coastline here seems to have been carved out of ancient rock. The impact of the waves is very clear: Each year more sections of the cliffs sport caution signs. Don't ignore these warnings—it's easy to lose your footing and slip in the crumbling sandstone, and the surf can become extremely rough. Small coves and beaches dot the coastline and are popular with surfers drawn to the pounding waves and locals from the neighborhood who name and claim their special spots. Needle's Eye is considered especially challenging; it's said that the chain-link fence surrounding a space between the rock is there because a surfer rode his board into it. The homes along the boulevard are fine examples of southern California luxury, with pink stucco mansions beside shingled Cape Cod–style cottages.

LA JOLLA

La Jollans have long considered their village to be the Monte Carlo of California, and with good cause. Its coastline curves into natural coves backed by verdant hillsides and covered with homes worth millions. Though La Jolla is considered part of San Diego, it has its own postal zone and a coveted sense of class; old-monied residents mingle here with visiting film stars and royalty who frequent established hotels and vate clubs. If development and construction have radically altered the once serene and private character of the village, it has gained a cosmopolitan air that makes it a popular vacation resort.

The Native Americans called the site La Hoya, meaning "the cave," referring to the grottos dotting the shoreline. The Spaniards changed the name to La Jolla, "the jewel," and its residents have cherished the name and its allusions ever since.

To reach La Jolla from I–5 if you're traveling north, take the Ardath Road exit and drive slowly down Prospect Street so you can appreciate the breathtaking view. If you're heading south, get off at the La Jolla Village Drive exit, which will lead into Torrey Pines Road.

For those who enjoy meandering, the best way to approach La Jolla from the south is to drive through Mission and Pacific beaches on Mission Boulevard, past the crowds of roller skaters, bicyclists, and sunbathers. The clutter and congestion ease up as the street becomes La Jolla Boulevard. Road signs along La Jolla Boulevard and Camino de la Costa direct drivers and bicyclists past homes designed by such famous architects as Frank Lloyd Wright and Irving Gill. As you approach the village, La Jolla Boulevard turns into Prospect Street.

Prospect Street and Girard Avenue, the village's main drags, are lined with expensive shops and office buildings. Girard holds the village's only movie house, which tends to show nonmainstream films. Over the years, the shopping and dining district has spread to Pearl and other side streets.

Wall Street, a quiet tree-lined boulevard off Girard Avenue, was once the financial heart of La Jolla, but banks and investment houses can now be found throughout the village. The La Jolla nightlife scene is an active one, with jazz clubs, piano bars, and watering holes for the elite younger set coming and going with the trends.

Numbers in the text correspond to numbers in the margin and on the La Jolla map.

A Good Tour

At the intersection of La Jolla Boulevard and Nautilus Street, turn toward the sea to reach **Windansea Beach** ①, one of the best surfing spots in town. **Mount Soledad** ②, about 1½-mi east on Nautilus Street, is La Jolla's highest spot. In the village itself, you'll find the town's cultural center, the **Museum of Contemporary Art, San Diego** ③, on the less trafficked southern end of Prospect. A bit farther north, at the intersection of Prospect and Girard Avenue, sits the pretty-in-pink **La Valencia Hotel** ④. The hotel looks out onto the village's great natural attraction, **La Jolla Cove** ⑤, which can be accessed from Coast Boulevard, one block to the west. Just past the far northern point of the cove, in front of the La Jolla Cave and Shell Shop, a trail leads down to **La Jolla Caves** ⑥.

The beaches along La Jolla Shores Drive north of the caves are some of the finest in San Diego, with long stretches allotted to surfers or swimmers. Just beyond the beaches is the campus of the Scripps Institution of Oceanography. The institution's **Stephen Birch Aquarium-Museum** ⑦ is inland a bit.

La Jolla Shores Drive eventually curves onto Torrey Pines Road, off which you'll soon glimpse the world-famous **Salk Institute** ⑧, designed by Louis I. Kahn. The same road that leads to the institute ends at the cliffs used as the **Torrey Pines Glider Port** ⑨. The hard-to-reach stretch of sand at the foot of the cliffs is officially named **Torrey Pines City Park Beach** ⑩, but locals call it Black's Beach. At the intersection of Torrey

Pines Road and Genesee Avenue you'll come to the northern entrance of the huge campus of the **University of California at San Diego** ⑪ and, a bit farther north, to the stretch of wilderness that marks the end of what most locals consider San Diego proper, **Torrey Pines State Reserve** ⑫.

TIMING

This tour makes for a leisurely day, though it can be driven in about a couple of hours, including stops to take in the views and explore the village of La Jolla. The Museum of Contemporary Art is closed Monday.

Sights to See

The Golden Triangle. La Jolla's newest enclave spreads through the Sorrento Valley east of I–5, a far cry from the beach communities with which the name La Jolla has long been associated. High-tech research-and-development companies, attracted to the area in part by the facilities of the University of California at San Diego, the Scripps Institution of Oceanography, and the Salk Institute, have developed huge state-of-the-art compounds in areas that were populated solely by coyotes and jays not so long ago. The area along La Jolla Village Drive and Genesee Avenue has become an architectural wonderland full of futuristic buildings. The most striking are those in the Michael Graves–designed Aventine complex, visible from I–5 at the La Jolla Village Drive exit. A bit south, just off the Nobel exit, and equally eye-catching, the huge, white Mormon Temple is reminiscent of a medieval castle; completed in 1993, it still startles drivers heading up the freeway.

❻ **La Jolla Caves.** It's a walk down 145 sometimes slippery steps to Sunny Jim Cave, the largest of the grottoes in La Jolla Cove; they may be entered behind the La Jolla Cave and Shell Shop. Claustrophobic types can stay behind and look at the photos of the caves in the shop, and browse a good selection of shells and coral jewelry. ✉ *1325 Coast Blvd.,* ☎ *619/454–6080.* 🎫 *$1.50.* ☉ *Mon.–Sat. 10–5, Sun. 11–5, sometimes later in summer.*

★ ❺ **La Jolla Cove.** The wooded spread that looks out over a shimmering blue inlet is what first attracted everyone from the Native Americans to the glitterati to La Jolla; it remains the reason for the village's continuing cachet. You'll find the cove—as locals always refer to it, as though it were the only one in San Diego—beyond where Girard Avenue dead-ends into Coast Boulevard, marked by towering palms that line a promenade where people strolling in evening dress are as common as Frisbee throwers.

Smaller beaches appear and disappear with the tides, which carve small private coves in cliffs covered with ice plants. Some of these cliffs are unstable, but pathways lead down to the beaches. Keep an eye on the tide to keep from getting trapped once the waves come in. A long layer of sandstone stretching out above the waves provides a perfect sunset-watching spot, with plenty of tiny tide pools formed in eroded pockets in the rocks; starfish, sea anemones, and hermit crabs cluster here when the tide is in. Again, keep an eye on the waves because these rocks can get slippery.

At the north end of La Jolla Cove, an underwater preserve makes the adjoining beach the most popular one in the area. On summer days, when the water visibility reaches 20 ft deep or so, the sea seems almost to disappear under the mass of bodies floating face down, snorkels poking up out of the water. The small beach becomes literally covered with blankets, towels, and umbrellas, and the lawns at the top of the stairs leading down to the cove are staked out by groups of scuba divers

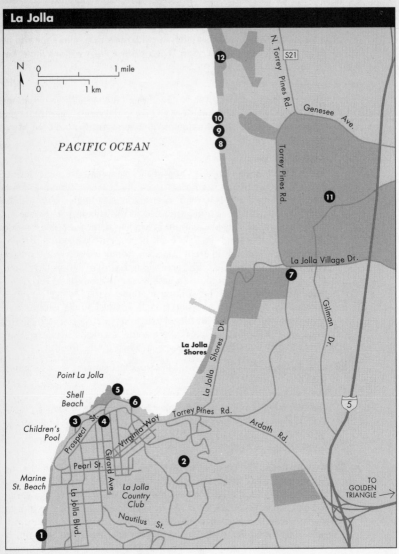

N

0   1 mile

0   1 km

PACIFIC OCEAN

N. Torrey Pines Rd.

S21

Genesee Ave.

Torrey Pines Rd.

12

10
9
8

11

La Jolla Village Dr.

7

Gilman Dr.

Point La Jolla

Shell Beach

5

6

La Jolla Shores Dr.

La Jolla Shores

Children's Pool

3

Prospect St.

4

Virginia Way

Torrey Pines Rd.

Ardath Rd.

5

Marine St. Beach

Pearl St.

Girard Ave.

2

La Jolla Blvd.

La Jolla Country Club

Nautilus St.

1

TO GOLDEN TRIANGLE →

La Jolla Caves, **6**
La Jolla Cove, **5**
La Valencia Hotel, **4**
Mount Soledad, **2**
Museum of Contemporary Art, San Diego, **3**
Salk Institute, **8**
Stephen Birch Aquarium-Museum, **7**

Torrey Pines City Park Beach, **10**
Torrey Pines Glider Port, **9**
Torrey Pines State Reserve, **12**
University of California at San Diego, **11**
Windansea Beach, **1**

putting on wet suits and tanks. The **Children's Pool,** at the south end of the park, is aptly named for its curving beach and shallow waters, protected by a sea wall from strong currents and waves.

If you're not here by noon, forget about finding a parking spot or a small square of sand for your towel. But no matter what time you arrive, walk through **Ellen Browning Scripps Park,** past the groves of twisted junipers to the cliff's edge. Perhaps one of the open-air shelters overlooking the sea will be free, and you can spread your picnic out on a table and watch the scene and the scenery.

❹ La Valencia Hotel. The art deco–style La Valencia, which has operated as a luxury hotel since 1928, has long been a gathering spot for Hollywood celebrities; in the 1940s, Gregory Peck would invite friends to La Valencia's Whaling Bar to try to persuade them to participate in one of his favorite projects, the La Jolla Theater. Today, the hotel's grand lobby, with floor-to-ceiling windows overlooking La Jolla Cove, is a popular wedding spot, and the Whaling Bar is still a favorite meeting place for La Jolla's power brokers. ⊠ *1132 Prospect St.,* ☎ *619/454–0771.*

❷ Mount Soledad. La Jolla's highest spot can be reached by taking Nautilus Street all the way east. The top of the mountain, on which there's a large white cross, is an excellent vantage point from which to get a sense of San Diego's geography: Looking down from here, you can see the coast from the county's northern border to the south far beyond downtown—barring smog and haze. Sunrise services are held here on Easter Sunday.

★ **❸ Museum of Contemporary Art, San Diego.** The oldest section of San Diego's modern art museum was a residence designed by Irving Gill for philanthropist Ellen Browning Scripps in 1916. Robert Venturi and his colleagues at Venturi, Scott Brown and Associates updated and expanded the compound in the mid-1990s. The architects respected Gill's original geometric structure and clean, Mission-style lines while adding their own distinctive touches. The result is a striking contemporary building that looks as though it's always been here.

The light-filled Axlined Court serves as the new entrance to the museum; it does triple duty as reception area, exhibition hall, and forum for special events. A patterned terrazzo floor leads to galleries where the museum's permanent collection and rotating exhibits are on display. The artwork inside gets major competition from the setting: You can look out from the top of a grand stairway onto a garden that contains rare 100-year-old California plant specimens and, beyond that, to the Pacific Ocean. A landscaped garden contains permanent and temporary sculpture exhibits. The bookstore and the refurbished Sherwood Auditorium have separate outside entrances, so you don't have to enter the museum to browse the modern-art volumes and gifts or attend the auditorium's programs.

MOCASD's permanent collection of post-1950s art naturally has a strong representation of California artists but also includes examples of every major art movement of the past half century—works by Andy Warhol, Robert Rauschenberg, Frank Stella, Joseph Cornell, and Jenny Holtzer, to name a few. Important pieces by San Diego and Tijuana artists were acquired in the 1990s. ⊠ *700 Prospect St.,* ☎ *619/454–3541.* ☑ *$4; free 1st Tues. of month.* ☉ *Tues. and Thurs.–Sat. 10–5, Wed. 10–8, Sun. noon–5.*

NEED A BREAK? Along with gourmet soups, salads, and sandwiches—grilled eggplant and goat cheese on focaccia, Pacific Rim chicken salad, and the like—

the **Museum Cafe** serves coffee, tea, beer, and wine. Brownies and cookies are made on the premises.

8 **Salk Institute.** The world-famous biological-research facility founded by polio vaccine inventor Jonas Salk sits on 26 clifftop acres in La Jolla. Architecture buffs will appreciate the original 1965 structures designed by modernist architect Louis I. Kahn in consultation with Dr. Salk. Kahn used concrete and other low-maintenance materials to clever effect. The thrust of the laboratory–office complex is outward toward the Pacific Ocean, an orientation that is accentuated by a foot-wide "Stream of Life" that flows through the center of a travertine marble courtyard between the buildings. The courtyard and stream of water were inspired by architect Louis Barragán. ⊠ *10010 N. Torrey Pines Rd.,* ☎ *619/453–4100.* ⊒ *Free.* ☉ *Grounds 7–6; guided tours weekdays at 11 and 12 (sometimes 10).*

7 **Stephen Birch Aquarium-Museum.** The largest oceanographic exhibit in the United States, a program of the Scripps Institution of Oceanography, sits at the end of a signed drive leading off North Torrey Pines Road just south of La Jolla Village Drive. More than 30 huge tanks are filled with colorful saltwater fish, and a 70,000-gallon tank simulates a La Jolla kelp forest. Next to the fish themselves, the most interesting attraction is the 12-minute simulated submarine ride. Children under three are discouraged; the ocean noises and marine-life visuals are realistic almost to the point of inducing seasickness. A concession at the site sells food, and there are outdoor picnic tables. ⊠ *2300 Expedition Way,* ☎ *619/534–3474.* ⊒ *$6.50, active military free, parking $3.* ☉ *Daily 9–5.*

10 **Torrey Pines City Park Beach.** Black's Beach—as locals call it—is one of the most beautiful and secluded stretches of sand in San Diego, backed by cliffs whose colors change with the light from the sun. There are no rest rooms, showers, or snack shops, though some hardy entrepreneurs lug ice chests filled with sodas and beer down the cliffs to sell to the unprepared. The paths leading down to the beach are steep, and the cliffs are unstable—pay attention to the safety signs and stick to the well-traveled trails. Black's Beach was clothing-optional for many years; although nudity is now prohibited by law, it is practiced whenever the authorities are out of sight. *See* Beaches *in* Chapter 7 for additional details and directions.

9 **Torrey Pines Glider Port.** On days when the winds are just right, gliders line the clifftops, waiting for the perfect gust to carry them into the sky. Seasoned hang gliders with a good command of the current can soar over the sea for hours, then ride the winds back to the cliffs. Less experienced fliers sometimes land on the beach below, to the cheers and applause of the sunbathers who scoot out of their way. If you're coming via the freeway, take the Genesee Avenue exit west from I–5 and follow the signs when you approach the coast.

12 **Torrey Pines State Reserve.** Pinus torreyana, the United States' rarest native pine tree, enjoys a 1,750-acre sanctuary at the northern edge of La Jolla. About 6,000 of these unusual trees, some as tall as 60 ft, grow on the clifftops here. The park is one of only two places where the torrey pine grows naturally. The reserve has several hiking trails leading to the cliffs, 300 ft above the ocean; trail maps are available at the park station. Wildflowers grow profusely in the spring, and the ocean panoramas are always spectacular. When in this upper part of the park, respect the various restrictions: No picnicking, smoking, leaving the trails, or collecting plant specimens is permitted.

You can unwrap your sandwiches, however, at Torrey Pines State Beach, just below the reserve. Walk south past the lifeguard towers and you can find a secluded spot under the golden brown cliffs—you'll feel as though there is no one on the beach but you. When the tide is out, it's possible to walk south all the way to Black's Beach over rocky promontories carved by the waves. **Los Penasquitos Lagoon** at the north end of the reserve is one of the many natural estuaries that flow inland between Del Mar and Oceanside. It's a good place to watch shorebirds. Most weekends, volunteers lead guided nature walks at 11:30 AM and 1:30 PM. ⊠ *North Torrey Pines Rd. (also known as Old Hwy. 101),* ☎ *619/755–2063. From I–5, take Carmel Valley Rd. west exit, then turn left (south) on Old Hwy. 101.* ⌒ *Parking $4 (2 large parking lots on both sides of Los Penasquitos Lagoon; another up the hill by park visitor center).* ☉ *Daily 8–sunset.*

⓫ University of California at San Diego. The campus of San Diego's most prestigious university spreads over canyons and eucalyptus groves, where students and faculty jog, bike, and roller-skate to class. If you're interested in contemporary art, ask at one of the two information booths for a map of the Stuart Collection, a thought-provoking group of sculptures at different points around campus; Nam June Paik and Jenny Holtzer are among the artists whose works are displayed. UCSD's Price Center has a well-stocked two-level bookstore and a good coffeehouse, Roma. Look for the postmodern Geisel Library (named for "Dr. Seuss" and his wife), which resembles a large spaceship. ⊠ *Exit I–5 onto La Jolla Village Dr. going west; take the Gilman Dr. off-ramp to the right and continue on to the information kiosk at the campus entrance.* ☎ *619/534–2230 or 619/534–1935 for campus tour information.* ☉ *Campus tours Mon.–Sat. at 11 AM from Student Center Building B (Gilman Dr. and Mandeville Rd.).*

❶ Windansea Beach. Fans of pop satirist Tom Wolfe may recall *The Pump House Gang,* which pokes fun at the So-Cal surfing culture. Wolfe drew many of his barbs from observations he made at Windansea, the surfing beach just west of La Jolla Boulevard near Nautilus Street. The wave action here is said to be as good as that in Hawaii.

NEED A BREAK?   A breakfast of the excellent buttery croissants or brioches at the **French Pastry Shop** (⊠ 5550 La Jolla Blvd., ☎ 619/454-9094) will fortify you for some serious tanning at Windansea Beach.

MISSION BAY AND SEA WORLD

The 4,600-acre Mission Bay aquatic park is San Diego's monument to sports and fitness. Admission to its 27 mi of bayshore beaches and 17 mi of ocean frontage is free. All you need for a perfect day is a bathing suit, shorts, and the right selection of playthings.

When explorer Juan Rodríguez Cabrillo first spotted the bay in 1542, he called it Baja Falso (False Bay) because the ocean-facing inlet led to acres of swampland inhospitable to boats and inhabitants. In the 1960s the city planners decided to dredge the swamp and build a bay with acres of beaches and lawns for play. Only 25% of the land was permitted to be commercially developed, and as a result, only a handful of resort hotels break up the striking natural landscape.

You don't have to go far from the freeway to experience the beach-party atmosphere of Mission Bay. A 5-mi-long pathway runs through this section of the bay from a trailer park and miniature golf course, south past the high-rise Hilton Hotel to Sea World Drive. Above the lawns facing I–5, the sky is flooded with the bright colors of huge, intricately made kites: the San Diego Kite Club meets on East Mission Bay Drive just south of the Hilton, and on the weekends they set loose their amazing creations.

Playgrounds and picnic areas abound on the beach and low grassy hills of the park. Here, group gatherings, company picnics, and birthday parties are common; huge parking lots seem to expand to serve the swelling crowds on sunny days. On weekday evenings, joggers, bikers, and skaters line the path. In the daytime, swimmers, water-skiers, fishers, and boaters—some in single-person kayaks, others in crowded powerboats—vie for space in the water. The San Diego Crew Classic, which takes place in late March or April, fills this area of the bay with teams from all over the country and college reunions, complete with flying school colors and keg beer.

North of Belmont Park until Pacific Beach, Mission Boulevard runs along a narrow strip embraced by the Pacific Ocean on the west, called Mission Beach, and the bay on the east. The pathways in this area are lined with vacation homes, many of which can be rented by the month. Those who are fortunate enough to live here year-round have the bay as their front yard, with wide sandy beaches, volleyball courts, and—less of an advantage—an endless stream of sightseers on the sidewalk.

One Mission Bay caveat: Swimmers should note signs warning about water pollution; certain areas of the bay are chronically polluted, and bathing is strongly discouraged.

Numbers in the text correspond to numbers in the margin and on the Mission Bay map.

A Good Tour

If you're coming from I–5, the **Visitor Information Center** ① is just about at the end of the Clairemont Drive–East Mission Bay Drive exit (you'll see the prominent sign). At the point where East Mission Bay Drive turns into Sea World Drive you can detour left to **Fiesta Island** ②, popular with jet skiers and speedboat racers. Those who continue around the curve to the west will soon see the turnoff sign for **Sea World** ③, the area's best-known attraction.

You'll next come to Ingraham Street, the central north–south drag through the bay. If you take it north, you'll shortly spot Vacation Road, which leads into the focal point of this part of the bay, the waterskiing mecca of **Vacation Isle** ④. At Ingraham, Sea World Drive turns into Sunset Cliffs Boulevard and intersects with West Mission Bay Drive. Just past this intersection, Quivira Way leads west toward **Hospitality Point** ⑤, where there are nice, quiet places to have a picnic.

If, instead, you continue west on West Mission Bay Drive, just before it meets Mission Boulevard, you'll come to the Bahia Hotel, where you can catch the ***Bahia Belle*** ⑥ and cruise around the bay. Ventura Cove, opposite the Bahia Hotel, is another good spot to unpack your cooler. Almost immediately south of where West Mission Bay Drive turns into Mission Boulevard is the resurrected **Belmont Park** ⑦.

TIMING

It would take less than an hour to drive this tour. You may not find a visit to Sea World fulfilling unless you spend at least a half day. The park is open daily, but not all its attractions are open year-round.

Sights to See

❻ ***Bahia Belle.*** At the dock of the Bahia Hotel, on the eastern shores of West Mission Bay Drive, you can board a restored sternwheeler for a sun-

Bahia Belle, **6**
Belmont Park, **7**
Fiesta Island, **2**
Hospitality Point, **5**
Sea World, **3**
Vacation Isle, **4**
Visitor Information Center, **1**

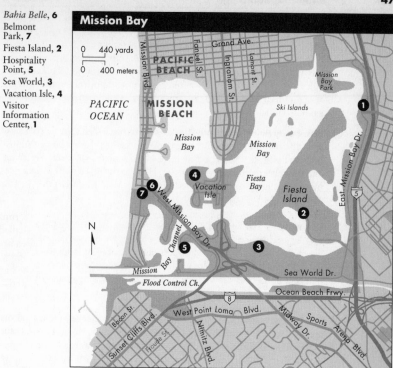

Mission Bay

set cruise of the bay. Owned and operated by the hotel, the boat is free for guests of the Bahia or its sister hotel, the Catamaran. The *Bahia Belle* also stops at the Princess Resort to pick up passengers. ⊠ *998 W. Mission Bay Dr.,* ☎ *619/488–0551.* ✉ *$5 for unlimited cruising (9:30 PM or later, cruisers must be at least 21).* ☉ *Sept.–Nov. and Jan.– June, Fri.–Sat. 7:30 PM–1:30 AM, departures every hr on the ½ hr; July– Aug., Wed.–Sun. on same schedule.*

❼ **Belmont Park.** The once-abandoned amusement park between the bay and Mission Beach boardwalk is now a shopping, dining, and recreation area. Twinkling lights outline the refurbished **roller coaster** on which screaming thrill-seekers ride. Created as the Giant Dipper in 1925, this is one of the few old-time roller coasters left in the United States and is listed on the National Register of Historic Places. **The Plunge,** an indoor swimming pool, also opened in 1925 as the largest—60 by 125 ft—saltwater pool in the world. It's had fresh water since 1951. Johnny Weismuller and Esther Williams are among the stars who were captured on celluloid swimming across Belmont Park's favorite body of water. Other attractions include an indoor fun-world, a video arcade, a submarine ride, bumper cars, an antique carousel, and a trampoline. This is also the place to pick up your neon surf suit, or the latest volleyball equipment. ⊠ *3146 Mission Blvd.,* ☎ *619/491–2988 or 619/ 642–0220 for park, 619/488–1549 for roller coaster, 619/488–3110 for pool.*

❷ **Fiesta Island.** The most undeveloped area of Mission Bay Park is popular with bird-watchers (there's a large protected nesting site for the California tern at the northern tip of the island) as well as with dog owners—it's the only place in the park where their pets can run free. Jet skiers and speedboat racers come here, too. At Christmas, it provides an excellent vantage point for viewing for the bay's Parade of Lights. In July, the annual Over-the-Line Tournament, a competition involving a local variety of softball, attracts thousands of players and oglers, drawn by the teams' raunchy names and outrageous behavior. When you drive onto Fiesta Island, you can't immediately turn back, as the road leads one way around the perimeter.

⑤ Hospitality Point. Enjoy lunch in this pretty, secluded spot, with a view of sailboats and yachts entering the open sea. At the entrance to Hospitality Point, the Mission Bay Park Headquarters supplies area maps and other recreational information. It's also the place to pick up a permit if you decide to throw a wedding in the park. ⊠ *2581 Quivira Ct.,* ☎ *619/221–8900.* ☉ *Weekdays 8–5.*

NEED A
BREAK?
> **Sportsmen's Sea Foods** (⊠ 1617 Quivira Rd., ☎ 619/224-3551) serves good fish-and-chips to eat on the inelegant but scenic patio—by the marina, where sportfishing boats depart daily—or to take out to your chosen picnic spot. Many folks prefer to bring their own food: Picnics and barbecues are popular at the bay, where many picnic areas have stationary barbecue grills.

❸ Sea World. One of the world's largest marine-life amusement parks is spread over 100 tropically landscaped bayfront acres, where a cool breeze always seems to rise from the water. The traditional favorite exhibit at Sea World is the **Shamu show,** with giant killer whales entertaining the crowds, but performing dolphins, sea lions, and otters at other shows also delight audiences. **Shamu Backstage** lets guests watch trainers interact with the killer whales behind the scenes—and even help feed the frisky animals on occasion.

At another popular exhibit, the **Penguin Encounter,** a moving sidewalk passes through a glass-enclosed Arctic environment, in which hundreds of emperor penguins slide over glaciers into icy waters. The penguins like it cold, so consider bringing a light sweater along for this one.

Youngsters are especially fond of the **Shark Encounter,** where they encounter a variety of species of the fierce-looking predators. The hands-on **California Tide Pool** exhibit gives visitors a chance to explore San Diego's indigenous marine life with a guide well versed in the habits of these creatures. At **Forbidden Reef,** you can feed bat rays and come nose-to-nose with creepy moray eels. Visitors to **Rocky Point Preserve** can interact with bottlenose dolphins and Alaskan sea otters that were treated after the 1989 *Exxon Valdez* oil spill. **Mission: Bermuda Triangle** replicates the thrills of a submersible dive to the ocean bottom via a sophisticated motion-based film. **Shamu's Happy Harbor** keeps kids entertained in a hands-on fun zone. Attractions include a two-story ship, where pretend pirates can aim water cannons at each other. Fresh- and salt-water aquariums hold underwater creatures from around the world.

Not all the exhibits are water oriented. **Cap'n Kids' World,** an enclosed playground, has trampolines, swinging wood bridges, towers for climbing, and giant tubs filled with plastic balls. The **Wings of the World** show incorporates a large assemblage of free-flying exotic birds. Those who want to head aloft themselves may consider the **Southwest Airlines Skytower,** a glass elevator that ascends 320 ft; the views of San Diego County from the ocean to the mountains are especially pleasing in early morning and late evening. A six-minute **sky-tram ride** that leaves from the same spot travels between Sea World and the Atlantis Hotel across Mission Bay. Admission for the Skytower and the tram is $2 apiece or $3 for both.

Sea World is filled with souvenir shops and refreshment stands; it's difficult to come away from here without spending a lot of money on top of the hefty entrance fee (the children's admission is $22.95) and parking tab. Many hotels, especially those in the Mission Bay area, have Sea World specials. Some include price reductions, and others allow two days of entry for a single admission price—a good way to spread out what can otherwise be a very full day of activities.

✉ *1720 South Shores Rd., near the west end of I–8,* ☎ *619/226–3815 or 619/226–3901 for recorded information.* ☞ *$30.95; parking $5 cars, $2 motorcycles, $7 RVs and campers; 90-min behind-the-scenes walking tours $6 additional. D, MC, V.* ⊙ *Daily 10–dusk; extended hrs during summer; call ahead for park hrs on day of your visit.*

❹ **Vacation Isle.** Ingraham Street bisects this Mission Bay island, which provides two distinct experiences to visitors. The west side is taken up by the Princess Resort, but you don't have to be a guest to enjoy the hotel's lushly landscaped grounds and bayfront restaurants. The water-ski clubs congregate at **Ski Beach** on the east side of the island, where there's a parking lot as well as picnic and rest room facilities. Ski Beach is the site of the Thunderboats Unlimited Hydroplane Championships, held in September.

❶ **Visitor Information Center.** In addition to being an excellent resource for San Diego tourists, the center is also a gathering spot for runners, walkers, and exercisers. It's the place to pick up a list of rules for playing in the water at Mission Bay Park, or a self-guided tour map of the park's environmental resources, including the Kendall-Frost Reserve & Northern Wildlife Preserve. There's a snack bar and a small gift shop. ✉ *2688 E. Mission Bay Dr.,* ☎ *619/276–8200.* ⊙ *Mon.–Sat. 9–5 (until 6 in summer), Sun. 9:30–4:30 (until 5:30 in summer).*

OLD TOWN

San Diego's Spanish and Mexican history and heritage are most evident in Old Town, just north of downtown at Juan Street, near the intersection of I–5 and I–8. Old Town didn't become a state historic park until 1968, but private efforts kept the area's history alive until then, and a number of San Diego's oldest structures remain in good shape.

Although Old Town is often credited as being the first European settlement in southern California, the true beginnings took place overlooking Old Town from atop Presidio Park. There, Father Junípero Serra established the first of California's missions, San Diego de Alcalá, in 1769. Some of San Diego's Native Americans, called the San Diegueños by the Spaniards, were forced to abandon their seminomadic lifestyle and live at the mission. They were expected to follow Spanish customs and adopt Christianity as their religion, but they resisted these impositions fiercely; of all the California missions, San Diego de Alcalá was the least successful in carrying out conversions. For security reasons, the mission was built on a hill, but it didn't have an adequate water supply, and food became scarce as the number of Native Americans and Spanish soldiers occupying the site increased.

In 1774, the hilltop was declared a Royal Presidio, or fortress, and the mission was moved to its current location along the San Diego River, 6 mi west of the original. Native Americans, responding to the loss of their land as the mission expanded along the riverbed, attacked and burned it in 1775. A later assault on the presidio was less successful, and their revolt was short-lived. By 1800, about 1,500 Native Americans were living on the mission's grounds, receiving religious instruction and adapting to Spanish ways.

The pioneers living within the presidio's walls were mostly Spanish soldiers, poor Mexicans, and mestizos of Spanish and Native American ancestry, many of whom were unaccustomed to farming San Diego's arid land. They existed marginally until 1821, when Mexico gained independence from Spain, claimed its lands in California, and flew the Mexican flag over the presidio. The Mexican government, centered some 2,000 mi away in Monterrey, stripped the missions of their landholdings, and an aristocracy of landholders began to emerge. At the same time, settlers were beginning to move down from the presidio to what is now called Old Town.

A rectangular plaza was laid out along today's San Diego Avenue to serve as the settlement's center. In 1846, during the war between Mexico and the United States, a detachment of marines raised the U.S. flag over the plaza on a pole said to have been a mainmast. The flag was torn down once or twice, but by early 1848, Mexico had surrendered California, and the U.S. flag remained. In 1850, San Diego became an incorporated city, with Old Town as its center.

On San Diego Avenue, the district's main drag, art galleries and expensive gift shops are interspersed with curio shops, restaurants, and open-air stands selling inexpensive Mexican pottery, jewelry, and blankets. The Old Town Esplanade between Harney and Conde streets is best of several mall-like affairs constructed in mock Mexican-plaza style. Shops and restaurants also line Juan and Congress streets.

Numbers in the text correspond to numbers in the margin and on the Old Town San Diego map.

A Good Tour

It's possible to trek around Old Town and see all its sights in one day, but unless you regularly hike the Himalayas, we recommend making this a walking-driving combination.

Visit the information center at Wallace Street and San Diego Avenue in Old Town Plaza to orient yourself to the various sights in **Old Town San Diego State Historic Park** ①. When you've had enough history, cross north on the west side of the plaza to **Bazaar del Mundo** ②, where you can shop or enjoy some nachos on the terrace of a Mexican restaurant. Walk down San Diego Avenue, which flanks the south side of Old Town's historic plaza, east to Harney Street and the **Thomas Whaley Museum** ③. Then continue east 2½ blocks on San Diego Avenue just beyond Arista Street to the **El Campo Santo** ④ cemetery. **Heritage Park** ⑤ is perched on a hill above Juan Street, north of the museum and cemetery. Drive west on Juan Street and north on Taylor Street to Presidio Drive, which will lead you up the hill on which **Presidio Park** ⑥ and the **Junípero Serra Museum** ⑦ sit.

TIMING

Try to time your visit to coincide with the free daily tours of Old Town given at 2 PM by costumed volunteers at the Robinson-Rose House; they vary depending on the guide, but they're always interesting. If possible, avoid coming here on weekends as the parking lots are even fuller than usual when San Diegans are off work (this won't be a problem if you opt to take the San Diego Trolley). It takes about two hours to walk through Old Town. If you drive to Presidio Park, allot another hour to explore the grounds and museum.

Sights to See

② **Bazaar del Mundo.** North of San Diego's Old Town Plaza lies the area's unofficial center, built to represent a colonial Mexican square. The central courtyard is always in blossom, with magenta bougainvillea, scarlet hibiscus, and irises, poppies, and petunias in season. Ballet Folklorico and flamenco dancers perform on weekend afternoons, and the bazaar frequently hosts arts-and-crafts exhibits and Mexican festivals. Colorful shops specializing in Latin American crafts and unusual gift items border the square. Although many of the shops here have high-quality wares, prices can be considerably higher than those at shops on the other side of Old Town Plaza; it's a good idea to do some comparative shopping before you make any purchases. ⊠ 2754 Calhoun St., ☎ 619/296–3161. ⊙ Shops daily 10–9.

NEED A BREAK?

La Panadería bakery (⊠ Bazaar del Mundo, southeast corner, ☎ 619/ 291-7662) sells hot *churros*—long sticks of fried dough coated with cinnamon and powdered sugar. Get some to go and sit out on one of the benches to enjoy the live music at the bandstand (weekends only).

④ **El Campo Santo.** The old adobe-walled cemetery established in 1849 was the burial place for many members of Old Town's founding families, as well as for some gamblers and bandits who passed through town until 1880. Antonio Garra, a chief who led an uprising of the San Luis Rey Indians, was executed at El Campo Santo in front of the open grave he was forced to dig for himself. These days the small cemetery is a peaceful stop for visitors to Old Town. Most of the markers give only approximations of where the people named on them are buried; some of early settlers laid to rest at El Campo Santo really reside under San Diego Avenue. ⊠ North side of San Diego Ave. S, between Arista and Ampudia Sts.

⑤ **Heritage Park.** Save Our Heritage Organization moved and restored a number of San Diego's important Victorian buildings—they're now the focus of this park, up the Juan Street hill near Harney Street. Among them is southern California's first synagogue, a one-room Classic Revival–style structure built in 1889 for Congregation Beth Israel. The most interesting of the six former residences might be the Sherman Gilbert House, which has a widow's walk and intricate carving on its decorative trim. It was built for real estate dealer John Sherman in 1887 at the then-exorbitant cost of $20,000—indicating just how profitable the booming housing market could be. Bronze plaques detail the history of all the houses, some of which may seem surprisingly colorful; they are in fact accurate representations of the bright tones of the era. The homes are now used for offices, shops, restaurants, and, in one case, a bed-and-breakfast inn. The climb up to the park is a little steep, but the view of the harbor is great. ⊠ 2455 Heritage Park Row (park office), ☎ 619/694–3306.

⑦ **Junípero Serra Museum.** The original Spanish presidio and California's first mission were perched atop the 160-ft hill overlooking Mission Valley; it's now the domain of a museum devoted to the history of the Spanish and Mexican periods. Built in 1929 and run by the San Diego Historical Society, the museum houses an interesting collection of artifacts from San Diego's earliest days, including housewares, clothing, and military equipment. Ascend the tower to compare the view you'd have gotten in 1929 with the one you have today. The museum is at the north end of Presidio Park, near Taylor Street. ⊠ 2727 Presidio Dr., ☎ 619/297–3258. 🖾 $3. ⊙ Tues.–Sat. 10–4:30, Sun. noon–4:30.

Bazaar del
Mundo, **2**

El Campo
Santo, **4**

Heritage
Park, **5**

Junípero Serra
Museum, **7**

Old Town
San Diego
State Historic
Park, **1**

Presidio
Park, **6**

Thomas
Whaley
Museum, **3**

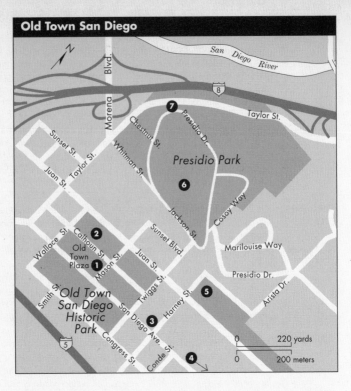

Old Town San Diego

OFF THE
BEATEN PATH

MISSION SAN DIEGO DE ALCALÁ – It's hard to imagine how remote California's earliest mission must once have been; these days, it's accessible by a major freeway (I–15), and close to a busy industrial area on the city's east side. Mission San Diego de Alcalá, the first of a chain of 21 stretching northward along the California coast, was established by Father Junípero Serra in 1769 on Presidio Hill and moved to its present location in 1774. Although the water supply was better, there was no greater security from enemy attack here: Padre Luis Jayme, California's first Christian martyr, was clubbed to death by Native Americans in 1775. The present church is the fifth to be built on the site; it was reconstructed in 1931 following the outlines of the 1813 church. It's 150 ft long but only 35 ft wide because, without easy means of joining beams, the mission buildings were only as wide as the trees that served as their ceiling supports. Father Jayme is buried in the mission sanctuary and a small museum named for him documents the history of the mission, exhibiting tools and artifacts from the early days. From the peaceful palm-bedecked gardens out back, you can gaze at the 46-ft-high *campanario*, the mission's most distinctive feature; one of its five bells was cast in 1822. ✉ *10818 San Diego Mission Rd. (from I–15, take Friars Rd. east and Rancho Mission Rd. south)*, ☎ *619/281–8449.* ✇ *$2.* ⊙ *Daily 9–5.*

★ ❶ **Old Town San Diego State Historic Park.** The six square blocks on the site of San Diego's original pueblo are the heart of Old Town. Most of the 20 historic buildings preserved or re-created by the park cluster around **Old Town Plaza**, bounded by Wallace Street on the west, Calhoun Street on the north, Mason Street on the east, and San Diego

Avenue on the south; you can see the presidio from behind the cannon by the flagpole. These days, the plaza is a pleasant place for resting and regrouping as you plan your tour of the park and watch other visitors stroll by; art shows often fill the lawns between the historic district and Bazaar del Mundo (☞ *above*) on Calhoun Street across from the plaza. San Diego Avenue is closed to traffic here.

Many of Old Town's buildings were destroyed in a huge fire in 1872, but after the site became a state historic park in 1968, efforts were begun to reconstruct or restore the structures that remained. Seven of the original adobes are still intact. The tour map available at the Robinson-Rose House gives details on all of the historic houses on the plaza and in its vicinity; a few of the more interesting ones are noted below. All the houses are open to visitors daily 10–5 (winter hours, which start in November, are shorter); currently none charge admission, though donations are appreciated.

The **Robinson-Rose House** (⊠ 4002 Wallace St., ☎ 619/220–5422), on the west end of Old Town Plaza, serves as the park office. This was the original commercial center of old San Diego, housing railroad offices, law offices, and the first newspaper press. One room has been restored and outfitted with period furnishings; park rangers distribute information from the living room. An excellent free walking tour of the park leaves from here daily at 2 PM, weather permitting. From 10 to 1 every Wednesday and the first Saturday of the month, park staff and volunteers in period costume give cooking and crafts demonstrations at the Machado y Stewart adobe; adjacent to the Bandini House near Juan Street, you can watch a blacksmith hammering away at his anvil, starting at 10 every Wednesday and Saturday.

On San Diego Avenue, beside the state park headquarters, **Dodson's Corner** is a modern retailer in a mid-19th-century setting; two of the shops in the complex, which sell everything from quilts and western clothing to pottery and jewelry, are reconstructions of homes that stood on the spot in 1848.

On Mason Street, at the corner of Calhoun Street, **La Casa de Bandini** is one of the prettiest haciendas in San Diego. Built in 1829 by a Peruvian, Juan Bandini, the house served as Old Town's social center during Mexican rule. Albert Seeley, a stagecoach entrepreneur, purchased the home in 1869, built a second story, and turned it into the Cosmopolitan Hotel, a comfortable way station for travelers on the day-long trip south from Los Angeles. These days, Casa Bandini's colorful gardens and main-floor dining rooms house a popular Mexican restaurant.

Seeley Stable, next door to La Casa de Bandini on Calhoun Street, became San Diego's stagecoach stop in 1867 and was the transportation hub of Old Town until near the turn of the century, when the Southern Pacific Railroad became the favored mode of travel. The stable now houses a collection of horse-drawn vehicles, some so elaborate that you can see where the term "carriage trade" came from. Also inside are western memorabilia, including an exhibit on the California *vaquero*, the original American cowboy, and an array of Native American artifacts.

La Casa de Estudillo was built on Mason Street in 1827 by the commander of the San Diego Presidio, Jose Maria Estudillo. The largest and most elaborate of the original adobe homes, it was occupied by members of the Estudillo family until 1887. After being left to deteriorate for some time, it was purchased and restored in 1910 by sugar magnate and developer John D. Spreckels, who advertised it in bold lettering on the side as "Ramona's Marriage Place." The small chapel in the house was believed to be the setting for the wedding in Helen Hunt Jackson's popular novel.

The **San Diego Union Newspaper Historical Museum** (⊠ Twigg St. and San Diego Ave.) is in a New England–style wood-frame house pre-fabricated in Maine and shipped around Cape Horn in 1851. The building has been restored to replicate the newspaper's offices of 1868, when the first edition of the *San Diego Union* was printed.

Also worth exploring in the plaza area are the **Dental Museum, Mason Street School, Wells Fargo Museum,** and the **San Diego Courthouse.** Ask at the visitor center for locations.

❻ Presidio Park. The rolling hillsides of the 40-acre green space overlooking Old Town from the north end of Taylor Street are popular with pic-nickers, and many couples have taken their wedding vows on the park's long stretches of lawn, some of the greenest in San Diego. You may encounter enthusiasts of a new sport, grass skiing, gliding over the grass and down the hills on wheels. It's a nice walk to the summit from Old Town if you're in good shape and wearing the right shoes—it should take about half an hour. You can also drive to the top of the park via Presidio Drive, off Taylor Street, and then wander around on foot. Presidio Park has a private canyon surrounded by palms at the bottom of the hill, off Taylor Street just before it intersects with I–8.

If you do decide to walk, look in at the Presidio Hills Golf Course on Mason Street, which has an unusual clubhouse: It incorporates the ruins of Casa de Carrillo, the town's oldest adobe, constructed in 1820. At the end of Mason Street, veer left on Jackson Street to reach the **Presidio Ruins,** where adobe walls and a bastion have been built above the foundations of the original fortress and chapel. Archaeology students from San Diego State University who excavated the area have marked off the early chapel outlines. Also on the site are the 28-ft-high Serra Cross, built in 1913 out of brick tiles found in the ruins, and a bronze statue of Father Serra. Before you do much poking around here, however, it's a good idea to get some historical perspective at the Junípero Serra Museum just to the east. Take Presidio Drive southeast of the museum and you'll come to the site of Fort Stockton, built to protect Old Town and abandoned by the United States in 1848. Plaques and statues also commemorate the Mormon Battalion, which enlisted here to fight in the battle against Mexico.

❸ Thomas Whaley Museum. Thomas Whaley was a New York entrepreneur who came to California during the gold rush. He wanted to provide his East Coast wife with all the comforts of home, so in 1856 he had southern California's first two-story brick structure built. The house, which served as the county courthouse and government seat during the 1870s, stands in strong contrast to the Spanish-style adobe residences that surround the nearby historic plaza and marks an early stage of San Diego's "Americanization."

Period furnishings in the living quarters include a miniature dress dummy designed to look like Mary Todd Lincoln, a sofa from Andrew Jackson's White House, and a piano that belonged to singer Jenny Lind. Among the historical artifacts in the reconstructed courtroom is one of the six life masks that exist of Abraham Lincoln. A garden out back includes rosebushes from a pre-hybrid era. The place is perhaps most famed, however, for the ghost that is said to inhabit it; this is one of the few houses authenticated by the United States Department of Commerce as being haunted. ⊠ *2482 San Diego Ave.,* ☎ *619/298–2482.* ☞ *$4.* ☉ *Daily 10–5; shorter winter hours (call ahead).*

3 Exploring San Diego with Children

It's hard to overstate San Diego's qualifications as a kid-friendly place to visit. For starters, it has an abundance of natural playgrounds for children of all ages: beaches. But if the weather is not cooperative or you've always found beaches to be just too filled with sand, San Diego also has one of the world's great zoos, a splashy marine park, train rides, ships, indoor fun zones, the famous Palomar Observatory, and museums that survey everything from ancient civilization to outer space.

By Lori
Chamberlain

IN KEEPING WITH SOUTHERN CALIFORNIA'S relaxed culture, San Diego is an easy place to be with kids. Few
restaurants, for example, make children unwelcome—
and some are specifically designed for those traveling with children.
In addition, intense competition by hotels for the lucrative family market means low rates or special programs for youngsters at many places.
There are also many sources in town for kiddie supplies, including some
great stores for toys and clothing, as well as a number of arts venues
specifically geared toward children.

EXPLORING

The well-known sights in San Diego live up to their reputations and
shouldn't be missed. But consider, too, some of the lower-key attractions, which may prove less crowded and equally well suited to your
children's interests.

Sights to See

Major Attractions

Tidal pools in their natural setting may be seen at **Cabrillo National
Monument** (☞ Point Loma *in* Chapter 2), where kids can also climb
up into an old lighthouse and, outside the visitor center, look through
viewers at the surrounding cityscape and naval installations.

You can follow a visit to the San Diego Maritime Museum (☞ *below*)
with a **harbor excursion** or a **ferry trip to Coronado** (☞ Sightseeing *in*
The Gold Guide for both).

The San Diego Zoological Society maintains two excellent zoos in the
San Diego area. If you have time, visit both; otherwise, you'll have to
make a tough choice. The **San Diego Zoo** (☞ Balboa Park *in* Chapter
2) has an extensive Children's Zoo, with exhibits at kid height and a
petting area with well-behaved goats and sheep. For the rest of the zoo,
use the Skyfari ride to save on walking; some kids will enjoy the ride
as much as they do seeing the animals. The 50-minute monorail ride
through Africa and Asia at the **Wild Animal Park** (☞ Inland North
County *in* Chapter 9), about 45 minutes from town in Escondido, is
best for kids old enough to sit for that period of time. Younger ones
should enjoy stroking the exotic animals in the Petting Kraal or feeding the ducks and other waterfowl in the lagoon surrounding Nairobi
Village, near the entrance to the park. Both the San Diego Zoo and
the Wild Animal Park hold excellent informational presentations about
animals, including sea lion shows at the zoo and bird and elephant shows
at the Wild Animal Park.

Sea World (☞ Mission Bay and Sea World *in* Chapter 2) is another
popular place for kids, although for the price of entry you'll want to
be sure your children are old enough (at least three) to enjoy it. Not
to be missed here are the **Shamu show** (sit up front if you *want* to get
very wet), the dolphin exhibit (they'll eat little fish tidbits right out of
your hand), the bat-ray exhibit (you can pet them as they swim by),
and the **Penguin Encounter** (no touching, but these guys are endlessly
amusing). **Cap'n Kids' World**, an imaginative, no-holds-barred playground, will captivate youngsters and focus their energy for hours. The
play equipment is designed for a variety of ages—the younger ones like
tumbling in huge pools of plastic balls, and older children enjoy racing all over the rope swings and balconies. You may want to bring bathing
suits, as some of the "really" fun play structures involve water.

The **Stephen Birch Aquarium-Museum** (☞ La Jolla *in* Chapter 2) provides another marine experience. Kids five and older should enjoy the simulated submarine ride—the cutoff age is three, but the experience may be a bit scary for little ones—and a tidal pool gives younger children a chance to look at and learn about starfish and sea anemones.

At **Seaport Village** (☞ Downtown *in* Chapter 2), the Flying Horses Carousel should temporarily divert kids who are less keen on shopping than their parents.

Museums

Many of **Balboa Park's museums** (☞ Chapter 2) are geared toward, or have exhibits designed for, children. The Omnimax theater at the **Reuben H. Fleet Space Theater and Science Center,** for example, screens first-rate nature and science films, and the science center has a wide variety of imaginative hands-on exhibits illustrating the laws of physics in ways you'll wish you'd learned in school. The **Natural History Museum** has a solid collection that includes a large dinosaur skeleton, as well as excellent seasonal shows: a recent elephant exhibit included full-scale models and live animal demonstrations. The **Model Railroad Museum,** also a winner, houses one of the world's largest collections of minigauge trains. The **San Diego Museum of Art** has special programs for artistically oriented children. The **Mingei International Museum** has colorful folk art exhibits from all parts of the world—often more interesting to kids than "high art."

The **Children's Museum of San Diego,** in the downtown area near the Convention Center and Seaport Village, has approximately 30,000 square ft of space devoted to interactive, experiential environments for kids. Included are an art zone, where children can work on group projects or their own projects to take home, and a toddler area. Past exhibits have included "If I Had a Hammer," which allowed children over the age of eight to build an 8′ by 11′ house and "Virtual Hoops," in which children could play virtual basketball. "Mi Casa Es Tu Casa/My House is Your House," a 1997 binational virtual-reality installation that should be up for at least part of 1998, links children in San Diego with children at the Centro Nacional de las Artes in Mexico City. ⊠ *200 W. Island Ave.,* ☎ *619/233–5437.* ⊠ *$5, children under 2 free.* ☉ *Tues.–Sun. 10–5.*

Fire-fighting artifacts of all sorts fill the **Firehouse Museum:** motorized and horse- and hand-drawn fire engines, extinguishers, an extensive collection of helmets, and other memorabilia. ⊠ *1572 Columbia St.,* ☎ *619/232–3473.* ⊠ *Free; $1 donation requested.* ☉ *Thurs.–Fri. 10– 2, weekends 10–4.*

At the **San Diego Maritime Museum** (☞ Downtown *in* Chapter 2), you can climb aboard the 1863 *Star of India* windjammer, as well as an 1898 ferryboat and a World War I–vintage steam yacht.

Parks

Kids can pet bat rays at the **Chula Vista Nature Interpretive Center,** a low-key wetland preserve about 15 minutes south of downtown. Hands-on exhibits focus on marine life as well as other animal life typical of salt marshes. Take I–5 south to E Street and park in the lot at E Street and Bay Boulevard; a shuttle will take you across the salt marsh to the museum. ⊠ *1000 Gunpowder Point Dr., Chula Vista,* ☎ *619/ 422–2481.* ⊠ *$3.50, $1 children 6–17; includes round-trip shuttle.* ☉ *Tues.–Sun. 10–5.*

If you're in San Diego in June or early July, don't miss the **Del Mar Fair** (☞ Festivals and Seasonal Events *in* Chapter 1), a *big* exposition with rides, livestock, hundreds of exhibits, food, entertainment, and contests.

The **Solid Rock Gym,** an indoor rock climbing facility, provides a fun way to channel that energy when you or your kids literally want to climb the walls. Professional instructors are available to help participants of all abilities, including the first-time climber. Though kids are welcome anytime, there is a drop-in Kids Climb program on Saturday mornings and Sunday afternoons. Parents of climbers under 8 years must stay with their children. ⊠ 2074 Hancock St., ☎ 619/299–1124. 🖾 Prices vary. ☉ Weekdays 11–10, Sat. 9–9, Sun. 11–7.

The state-of the art **Wave Water Park** has a variety of attractions for those not attracted to the waves at the beach. The fun includes four water slides, the "Flow Rider" (a continuous wave for bodyboarding), and a play structure with a tunnel slide, a crawl tunnel, water jets, and a waterfall. The facilities also include picnic areas, a children's pool, a shallow-depth pool, a pool for lap-swimming, and a grass volleyball court. There's a family night on Sunday evenings during the summer. To get to the park from San Diego, take I–5 north, head east on Hwy. 78, exit on West Vista Way and turn right, head three blocks to Recreation Drive, and turn left. ⊠ 161 Recreation Dr., Vista, ☎ 760/940–9283. 🖾 $8.75, children under 2 free. ☉ Daily 1st weekend in June–Labor Day.

The **Family Fun Center** has miniature-golf courses, batting cages, boats, go-carts, and video-game rooms. ⊠ 6999 Clairemont Mesa Blvd., ☎ 619/560–4211. 🖾 Rates for attractions vary. ☉ Mon.–Thurs. and Sun. 9 AM–midnight, Fri.–Sat. 9 AM–2 AM; outside attractions may close earlier.

The classic **Giant Dipper Roller Coaster,** with more than 2,600 ft of tracks and 13 hills, is the jewel in the crown of Belmont Park (☞ Mission Bay in Chapter 2). Riders must be at least 4'2". ☎ 619/488–1549. 🖾 $2.50. ☉ Sun.–Thurs. 11–6, Fri.–Sat. 11–10.

For a well-rounded day trip with children, consider heading out to the **Palomar Observatory,** an hour or so outside San Diego. You can't actually look through the 200-inch Hale telescope, but there are exhibits here on stars and the universe. Then visit the **Palomar Mountain State Park** or the **Cuyamaca Rancho State Park,** where you can hike and picnic. Top this off with a drive through the mountains to the old mining town of **Julian** to visit a gold mine and get some excellent apple pie. See Inland North County and The Backcountry and Julian in Chapter 9, for details on these attractions.

Pirate's Cove in Belmont Park (☞ Mission Bay in Chapter 2) provides a fantastic maze of brightly colored tunnels, slides, an obstacle course, and more, all with a pirate theme. Socks are required. ☎ 619/539–7474. 🖾 Children 3–18, $6.50 weekdays; children under 3, $4.50; up to 2 chaperones free. ☉ Sun.–Thurs. 10–6, Fri.–Sat. 10–8; extended hrs on holidays, winter hrs may vary.

Under the aegis of the **San Diego Railroad Museum,** the Campo Depot, built in 1915, operates a scenic half-hour train trip through the San Diego backcountry on weekends. Included is an optional walking tour of the museum's approximately 90 pieces of vintage railroad equipment, in various stages of restoration. ⊠ 50 mi east of San Diego (take I–8 east, exit at Buckman Springs Rd., and follow signs), ☎ 619/595–3030 for general information or 619/478–9937 for Campo Depot. 🖾 Depot free; train ride $10 adults, $3 children 6–12. ☉ Trains depart at 12:01 PM and 2:30 PM on weekends only.

DINING

Most San Diego restaurants make at least some accommodation for kids: child-size portions, seats for children, or, at a minimum, friendliness. Generally, the only places you may wish to avoid are upscale restaurants listed in Chapter 4 in the expensive ($$$) and very expensive ($$$$) price ranges.

Restaurants

Of the places reviewed in Chapter 4, the bustling **Piatti Ristorante, Fish Market, Hob Nob Hill, Hard Rock Cafe, Old Town Mexico Cafe, Sam-Son's,** and **El Indio** are particularly suited for families; your children's din will blend right in.

California Pizza Kitchen (⊠ 3363 Nobel, La Jolla, ☎ 619/457–4222) serves a variety of kid-pleasing pizzas and pastas in a busy atmosphere. **Chevy's** (⊠ Flower Hill Mall, 2730 Via De La Valle, Del Mar, ☎ 619/793–8893) dishes up tasty Southwest cooking in an informal atmosphere; the tortilla-making machine will entertain your kids. The **Old Spaghetti Factory** (⊠ 275 5th Ave., downtown, ☎ 619/233–4323), which plays on a railroad-car theme, serves pasta, pasta, pasta—if you can't find one your kids like, then they don't like pasta. If your children are not restaurant-trained, or if you want takeout for a nice picnic, try the terrific chicken at **Saffron Chicken** (⊠ 3731 India St., downtown, ☎ 619/574–0177).

Fast-Food Outlets

Chuck E Cheese (⊠ 3146 Sports Arena Blvd., Point Loma, ☎ 619/523–4385; other locations) serves mediocre food in an environment given over to kids, including toys, games, and those big ball enclosures. In Del Mar, **McDonald's** (⊠ 2705 Via de la Valle, ☎ 619/481–8595) and **Burger King** (⊠ 12847 El Camino Real, ☎ 619/792–4011) both have playgrounds on the premises.

Sweets and Treats

There are plenty of good ice cream parlors in town, but for the full-on experience, try **Farrell's** (⊠ 10606 Camino Ruiz, ☎ 619/578–9895), a lively sit-down place with more ice cream delights than you can eat comfortably.

LODGING

Virtually all tourist-oriented sections of San Diego have lodgings suited to a family's pocketbook and/or recreational needs. The top area for all-around child appeal, however, would have to be Mission Bay, near beaches, parks, the Belmont roller coaster, and Sea World. Many Mission Bay hotels offer Sea World packages or discounts. Accommodations in the lively Embarcadero section downtown are also recommended.

Some of the more expensive hotels and resorts in San Diego have special activity programs and camps to keep their guests' offspring occupied; many places provide family discounts, and a number of lodgings are well suited to those traveling with children because they have kitchen and laundry facilities. Full reviews of most of the following hotels are found in Chapter 5.

Children's Programs

During the summer, the **Hotel Del Coronado** sponsors activities such as sand-castle building, scavenger hunting, and paddle boating. There's a youth tennis program for ages 3 and up during the summer and, for children ages 12 and up, instruction in surfing and sailing. Prices for the programs vary.

At the **Hyatt Islandia** children ages 3 through 15 can take part in 4–10 PM programs Friday and Saturday evenings from Memorial Day through Labor Day; the cost for supervised activities, such as games, videos, and arts and crafts, is $5 per child per hour, with a discount for the second child in the same family. Parents must stay on the hotel property.

Loews Coronado Bay Resort has year-round day and evening programs for children ages 4–12. Programs depend on the age of the children enrolled and include arts and crafts as well as outdoor activities. Prices are $25 per child for half-day programs, $25 for evening programs, and $40 for a full day of events (all prices include meals). There is a discount for the second child enrolled.

Rancho Bernardo Inn (☞ Inland North County *in* Chapter 9) has full- and half-day programs for kids ages 5–17 that include swimming, arts and crafts, and, for kids over 12, golf and tennis. The programs run during the major spring and summer holidays and the month of August. Prices vary.

From Memorial Day through Labor Day, **San Diego Hilton Beach and Tennis Resort** organizes daytime and evening activities designed for children ages 6–12, including indoor and outdoor games, arts and crafts, and movies. Those under 6 may participate, but they must be accompanied by an adult. The program is free, but parents must stay on the property. There's also a small playground on the premises and one close by with play equipment for children with disabilities.

The **San Diego Princess Resort** runs a Kid Camp for children ages 3–12 from June through Labor Day weekend and organizes activities for children during spring break, as well as during the Memorial Day weekend. There is also a teen program. The programs were being updated and revised as we went to press in the summer of 1997. Prices vary.

Family Rates

Many hotels and motels run family specials or allow children to stay free in the same room with their parents, with nominal charges for cribs and $5–$10 charges for extra beds; inquire when making reservations. For example, at the sister Catamaran and Bahia hotels in Mission Bay, there's no charge for children 18 and under; at the Hotel Del Coronado, children 18 and under also stay in their parents' room gratis. Some of the Days Inn hotels (☎ 800/325–2525; six locations in San Diego) charge only a small fee for children under 18; all allow children 12 and under to stay in their parents' room at no extra charge. Children of any age stay free with their parents at the San Diego Mission Valley Hilton. Children also stay free at the Holiday Inn on the Bay in the Embarcadero area.

Facilities

Although cooking and doing laundry don't play a large part in most parents' dream vacations, many like to know that the option for those activities is there—if only to ignore it. **La Jolla Cove Suites** has kitchenettes and laundry facilities, as well as lower room rates than at most other hotels in the La Jolla Cove area. The **Holiday Inn Express** in La Jolla has even lower rates and many remarkably large rooms with huge closets; some rooms have kitchenettes, and three suites have separate eat-in kitchens.

Embassy Suites San Diego Bay in the Embarcadero area has in-room refrigerators, microwaves, and separate sleeping areas. At the **Best Western Island Palms Hotel & Marina,** you can book reasonably priced two-bedroom suites with eat-in kitchens. Full or partial kitchens are available at the **Bahia** and **Catamaran** hotels in Mission Beach. Along the Embarcadero, the **Holiday Inn on the Bay** has laundry facilities.

Baby-Sitting

Many concierges at San Diego hotels recommend **Marion's Child Care** (☎ 619/582–5029) for baby-sitting services.

MUSIC AND THEATER

San Diego provides cultural entertainment for all types of kids. By picking up a free copy of either *San Diego Parent* or *San Diego Family Press,* you can obtain a daily calendar of arts and other related activities.

Music

Budding musicians will enjoy the Discovery series for rising stars put on at 3 PM on select Sundays by the **La Jolla Chamber Music Society** (☎ 619/459–3728); concerts are held at the Sherwood Auditorium (☞ Music *in* Chapter 6) throughout the regular season.

Theater

Christian Youth Theater (☎ 619/588–0206), a nondenominational theater program, presents many productions by and for youths in various locations around San Diego County. Past performances have included *The Secret Garden, Willy Wonka and the Chocolate Factory,* and *Tom Sawyer.* It also runs classes and camps for children 6–18.

For the younger set, the San Diego Guild of Puppetry operates a **Puppetry Hotline** (☎ 619/685–5045). Most performances are staged at the Marie Hitchcock Puppet Theater (✉ Balboa Park, Palisades Building), which is celebrating more than 30 years of puppetry.

The **San Diego Actors Theatre** (☎ 619/268–4494) sponsors the Children's Classics series of fairy tales and children's stories adapted for the stage at L'Auberge Del Mar Garden Amphitheater (✉ 1540 Camino Del Mar, ☎ 619/259–1515). Performances of such stories as *The Mad Hatter's Tea Party, Little Red Riding Hood,* and *Rapunzel* are held on various Saturday mornings throughout the year (call ahead for schedules).

San Diego Children's Theatre (☎ 619/675–0463) stages a few musicals each year at the Poway Center for the Performing Arts (✉ 15500 Espola Rd., Poway, ☎ 619/748–0505), starring children four years of age and up.

San Diego Junior Theatre (✉ Casa del Prado, Balboa Park, ☎ 619/239–1311) puts on five productions each year, featuring student actors ages 4–18, under the direction of theater professionals.

The oldest theater in San Diego, the downtown **Spreckels Theater** (☞ Music *in* Chapter 6), has a Children's Series that includes major productions by the National Theatre for Children, the San Diego Children's Theatre, and the American Ballet Ensemble.

OUTDOOR ACTIVITIES AND SPORTS

Baseball

If baseball is your kids' passion, there are batting cages available at **Family Fun Center** (☞ Parks *in* Exploring, *above*).

For the really serious baseball fanatic, try **J.P. Longball,** an indoor batting center that gives private hitting and pitching lessons. ⊠ *5232 Riley St.,* ☏ *619/299–4487.* 🎫 *Prices vary.* ☉ *Weekdays 2–9, Sat. 9–5, Sun. 10–4.*

Beaches

A number of the San Diego beaches described in Chapter 7 are particularly attractive for children. Try the **Children's Pool** in La Jolla. **La Jolla Cove** has tidal pools and a large grassy area for picnicking. Wide and well-guarded **La Jolla Shores** beach is nicely suited for families. The waves at **Silver Strand State Beach** in Coronado are usually mild. **Del Mar Beach,** a guarded spread of sand, is near a playground, shops, and restaurants. If you're visiting in July, you may want to visit the Imperial Beach Pier to admire the sand castles built during Sand Castle Days (☞ Festivals and Seasonal Events *in* Chapter 1).

Miniature Golf

The most elaborate courses in San Diego are at the **Family Fun Center** (☞ Parks *in* Exploring, *above*), which has two courses organized around different themes, one western and one storybook. The cost is $5.50 for adults, $3.50 for children under 13 and for senior citizens.

Surf & Turf Miniature Golf across from the Del Mar Fairgrounds has a modest course (as well as a practice range right next door). ⊠ *5555 Jimmy Durante Blvd., Del Mar,* ☏ *619/481–0363.* 🎫 *$4.* ☉ *Daily 8–9; hrs may be extended during the summer.*

Parks

Balboa Park (☞ Chapter 2) is a must-see for those traveling with children of any age. In addition to the San Diego Zoo and museums, noted above, the park has a restored wooden carousel, a miniature train ride, a somewhat old-fashioned playground, *plenty* of grass, and, on weekends, an interesting variety of street performers.

Mission Bay Park (☞ Chapter 2) is another sure thing for those toting tots and young kids. The east side of the park has well-equipped playgrounds and good space for flying kites. For those with older children, the sidewalks around the bay are perfect for rollerblading. Belmont Park, which borders Mission Bay Park on the west, has a restored giant roller coaster (☞ Parks *in* Exploring, *above*) and the city's most beautiful swimming pool. In addition to the sand, there's plenty of grass for lounging and picnicking. And, of course, there's the water. Don't venture here on a sunny Saturday, however, unless you're willing to fight the crowds for a parking spot.

Playgrounds

The high price of real estate in San Diego means that not everyone has a house with a huge backyard; in addition, as in most other places, parents here use playgrounds as a guilt-free way to socialize with other parents. There are a number of well-equipped, well-maintained playgrounds in town; the **Community Parks and Recreation Department** (☎ 619/685–1300) can tell you which one is nearest your hotel.

Though there are some playgrounds in the downtown area, better ones can be found close by on the west side of Mission Bay. **Doyle Community Park** (⊠ Regents Rd., at Berino Ct.) near University Towne Centre has an impressive collection of new and progressive playground equipment. The playground at **Kate O. Sessions Memorial Park** (⊠ Soledad Rd. and Loring St.) in Pacific Beach is small, but there's lots of grass for flying kites and some great views of the city and bay. The **La Jolla Recreation Center** (⊠ 615 Prospect St.) has both new and traditional playground equipment within smelling distance of the ocean. In **Del Mar,** you can push your child on the swings and watch the waves breaking down below at a small playground at the foot of 15th Street; adjacent to the park is a grassy area suitable for picnicking.

SHOPPING

If you've brought the wrong clothes for your kids or find yourself without enough toys or other amusements, no problem: San Diego is an easy place to get any supplies that you may need—or that your children decide they have to have. *See* Chapter 8 for mall locations.

Clothing

Gap Kids, in Horton Plaza, University Town Centre, and La Jolla (⊠ 7835 Girard Ave., ☎ 619/454–2052), is probably the best bet for children's togs. **Nordstrom,** in several of the area shopping malls, carries good-quality lines of kids' clothing and shoes. For reasonably priced kids' clothing, try the **Mervyn's** department store in Horton Plaza. **Gymboree,** in the Horton Plaza and the Fashion Valley malls, is good for baby gear.

Toys and Gadgets

Whistle Stop Model Trains (⊠ 3834 4th Ave., downtown, ☎ 619/295–7340) carries books on trains and railroads, in addition to model trains. **Brad Burt's Magic Shop** (⊠ 4690 Convoy, Clairemont Mesa, ☎ 619/571–4749) has a good selection of tricks and clown supplies. If you want to join the fun at Mission Beach, you can pick up a kite at **Kite Country** in Horton Plaza (☎ 619/233–9495). The **Nature Company** (⊠ 7840 Girard Ave., La Jolla, ☎ 619/459–0871; branches in Horton Plaza and Fashion Valley) carries books and gizmos of interest to kids of all ages and also sponsors nature programs for children.

4 Dining

Until the Sunbelt Boom of the late '70s,
San Diego was a relatively slow-paced,
provincial place. Its mild climate and
splendid beaches fostered an open-air,
daytime-oriented culture that did little
to encourage a sophisticated dining
scene. But no longer. Its fine weather
and abundant recreational oppor-
tunities will always ensure a focus
on outdoor activities. But today, an
"outdoor activity" might just as easily
be alfresco dining in a trendy café as
volleyball on the beach.

By Kathryn
Shevelow

IN THE RECENT PAST, a "good San Diego restaurant" u
ally resembled the bland Chamber of Commerce eatery
humorist Calvin Trillin dubs "La Maison de la Casa
House," but these days fine new restaurants appear on the scene with
dizzying rapidity. Redevelopment in the downtown area has created a
vigorous nightlife scene, with a proliferation of clubs and stylish restaurants, especially in the Gaslamp Quarter. A stroll down 5th Avenue will
provide ample evidence of San Diego's love affair with Italian cuisine,
echoed in other parts of the city, but the cooking of Spain and France,
as well as the various cuisines of Latin America, Asia, the Middle
East—and even the United States—are well represented. Of course, San
Diego has numerous palaces of California cuisine, which borrows
from all these culinary traditions. Another hybrid is Pacific Rim cuisine, a mélange of North American, Latin American, and Asian influ-
ences and ingredients.

In addition to downtown, other areas of San Diego share in the new
sense of energy, fueled by a collective "caffeine high" acquired in the
coffeehouses (some of which are listed in Chapter 6) springing up
everywhere from the Gaslamp Quarter to the gas station on the corner. The "Uptown" neighborhood of Hillcrest reminds many people
of San Francisco, partly because of its large gay population, partly because of its culinary sophistication. It's no accident that the best new
restaurant to open in San Diego in recent memory, Laurel, is on the
border of Hillcrest and downtown. And once sleepy La Jolla is now
bursting with restaurants.

The guide that follows introduces some of San Diego's most accom-
plished eateries. Because many of its best practitioners are outside the
areas of the city commonly visited by tourists, we've included fewer
examples of Asian cooking than of other cuisines. But it's worth a pil-
grimage to the Vietnamese restaurants that, along with their Chinese,
Korean, Japanese, and Thai counterparts, can be found along Convoy
Street and Linda Vista Road in Clairemont–Kearny Mesa. **Phuong Trang**
(⊠ 4170 Convoy St., ☎ 619/565–6750) and **Pho Hoa** (⊠ 6921 Linda
Vista Rd., ☎ 619/492–9108) are just two of several excellent Vietnamese establishments. Particularly recommended at either are the
noodle soups called *pho,* beef grilled in grape leaves, and the several
other dishes that diners wrap in lettuce or rice paper. Two area Chinese restaurants are widely considered to be the best in the city: **Emerald Chinese Seafood Restaurant** (⊠ 3709 Convoy St., ☎ 619/565–6888)
and **Jasmine** (⊠ 4609 Convoy St., ☎ 619/268–0888). San Diegans
like to argue about which is better. Try their memorable (but not inexpensive) Hong Kong–style dinners or their daily noontime dim sum,
and decide for yourself.

Coronado has recently begun to establish a reputation for fine dining,
though the area still has less variety than elsewhere in San Diego. The
best restaurants, which are often in hotels, tend to serve elaborate and
pricey Continental cuisine. If you wish to eat well in Coronado and
money is no object, your first choice should be **Marius** (☞ French cuisine, *below*). If you wish to eat elsewhere in Coronado, here are some
of your best bets, listed in descending order from expensive ($$$–$$$$)
to moderate ($$): **Azzura Point** (⊠ Loews Coronado Bay Resort, 4000
Coronado Bay Rd., ☎ 619/424–4000), serving a mixed menu of Con-
tinental and California cuisine with an emphasis upon seafood; **Peohe's**
(⊠ Ferry Landing Marketplace, 1201 1st St., ☎ 619/437–4474), a lav-
ishly decorated seafood restaurant; the **Prince of Wales Room** (⊠ Hotel
Del Coronado, 1500 Orange Ave., ☎ 619/435–6611, ext. 8818),

focuses on grilled food and American regional cuisine; **Chez Loma**
(132 Loma Ave., ☎ 619/435–0661), a Continental restaurant in
toric Coronado house; and **Primavera Ristorante** (✉ 932 Orange
, ☎ 619/435–0454), specializing in northern Italian cuisine.

ether you are visiting San Diego for business or pleasure, there will
inevitably arise times when you need fast food. Besides **KC's Tandoor**
(☞ Indian cuisine, *below*), highly recommended restaurant chains
with locations around the city are the **La Salsa** Mexican eateries, whose
tasty tacos and burritos manage to lower the fat while heightening the
flavor; **Saffron Chicken** (☞ Thai cuisine, *below*); and **Chick's** and **Koo
Koo Roo,** which specialize in spit-roasted chicken with health-conscious
side dishes. Although not a fast-food restaurant, **Pizza Nova** efficiently
serves good designer pizzas as well as enormous salads, pasta dishes,
and sandwiches.

San Diego is an informal city. The advised attire at most of the restaurants listed below is casual: only Anthony's Star of the Sea Room requires men to wear jackets. Reservations are always a good idea,
especially on weekends; we note when they are essential or not accepted.

Restaurants are grouped first by type of cuisine, then by neighborhood.

CATEGORY	COST*
$$$$	over $50
$$$	$30–$50
$$	$20–$30
$	under $20

*per person for a three-course meal, excluding drinks, service, and 7.75%
sales tax*

American

Beaches

$ ✕ **Mission Cafe and Coffeehouse.** Large and slightly shabby, this Mis-
sion Beach café contradicts its appearance by serving stylishly presented
American, Latino, and "Chino-Latino" cuisine. Breakfast dishes are
served throughout the day. Try the French toast—slices of homemade
cinnamon bread arranged over a drizzle of blackberry puree—or the
tamales with eggs and green-chili salsa. For dinner try one of the fu-
sion dishes, such as the Pacific Rim risotto. All menu items may be made
vegetarian. The café serves good beer on tap, specialty coffee drinks,
and shakes and smoothies. This Mission ministers to its community
by opening early in the morning and then, after food service stops at
10 PM, staying open as a coffeehouse until the wee hours. ✉ *3795 Mission Blvd.,* ☎ *619/488–9060. AE, MC, V.*

Downtown

$$$ ✕ **Rainwater's.** Classy Rainwater's is as well known for the size of its
★ portions as for the quality of its cuisine. The menu includes meat and
fish dishes, but this is really the place to come if you crave a perfectly
done, thick and tender steak. All the entrées are accompanied by such
tasty side dishes as shoestring potatoes, onion rings, and creamed
corn. ✉ *1202 Kettner Blvd., 2nd floor,* ☎ *619/233–5757. AE, MC,
V. No lunch weekends.*

La Jolla

$–$$ ✕ **Brockton Villa Restaurant.** This informal restaurant in a restored beach
cottage overlooks La Jolla Cove and the ocean. Come for breakfast or
lunch to take advantage of the fabulous daytime view, but don't overlook dinner, whether you're in the mood for a turkey burger or rack
of lamb. The extensive menu has something for everyone, and there's

a good range of coffee drinks. You'll have to fight the brunch crowd on sunny weekends. ⊠ *1235 Coast Blvd.,* ☎ *619/454–7393. AE, D, MC, V. Call ahead for dinner hrs.*

$ ✕ **Hard Rock Cafe.** The high-energy shrine to rock-and-roll and American food cranks its music up to ear-shattering decibels and hangs rock memorabilia on every available inch of wall space. This is not a place to come for intimate—or audible—conversation, but the burgers are fine. You don't have to be accompanied by a teenager, although it helps. ⊠ *909 Prospect St.,* ☎ *619/454–5101. Reservations not accepted. AE, D, DC, MC, V.*

$ ✕ **Mission Coffee Cup Cafe.** This sibling of the Mission Cafe (☞ Beaches, *above*) serves a similar menu, but it's less funky and open only for breakfast and lunch. ⊠ *1109 Wall St.,* ☎ *619/454–2819. AE, MC, V.*

Uptown

$$ ✕ **Montanas American Grill.** One of Hillcrest's most popular restaurants serves hearty California-American food in a sleek, trendy setting. Stick with the least complicated dishes such as the pastas, barbecued meats, chicken, and salmon, or try the venison chili accompanied by jalapeño cornbread. The appetizer duck cakes are tasty and rich. Wash down your barbecue with one of the interesting microbrewery beers on tap. ⊠ *1421 University Ave.,* ☎ *619/297–0722. AE, DC, MC, V. No lunch weekends.*

$ ✕ **Crest Cafe.** Often jammed with locals, this Hillcrest institution specializes in good renditions of basic American café food. You can't go wrong with old favorites such as pancakes, burgers, onion rings, salads, and the homemade desserts. ⊠ *425 Robinson Ave.,* ☎ *619/295–2510. Reservations not accepted. AE, D, MC, V.*

$ ✕ **Hob Nob Hill.** The type of place where regulars arrive on the same day of the week at the same time and order the same meal they've been ordering for 20 years, this comforting restaurant is still under the same ownership and management as it was when it started in 1944. With its dark wood booths and patterned carpets, Hob Nob Hill seems suspended in the '50s, but you don't need to be a nostalgia buff to appreciate the bargain-price American home cooking—dishes such as pot roast, fried chicken, and corned beef like your mother never really made. Reservations are suggested for Sunday's copious breakfasts. ⊠ *2271 1st Ave.,* ☎ *619/239–8176. AE, D, MC, V.*

Belgian

Beaches

$$–$$$ ✕ **Belgian Lion.** Discerning diners come here for hearty Belgian fare. One of the signature dishes is the cassoulet, a wonderful rich stew of white beans, lamb, pork, sausage, and duck that makes you feel protected from the elements (even in San Diego, where there aren't that many elements). Lighter meals include braised sea scallops with leeks or poached salmon with fresh vegetables. An impressive selection of wines complements the food. ⊠ *2265 Bacon St., Ocean Beach,* ☎ *619/223–2700. Reservations essential. AE, D, DC, MC, V. No lunch. Closed Sun.–Wed.*

Cajun and Creole

Downtown

$–$$ ✕ **Bayou Bar and Grill.** Ceiling fans, dark-green wainscoting, and light-pink walls help create a New Orleans atmosphere for spicy Cajun and Creole specialties. You might start with a bowl of superb seafood gumbo and then move on to the sausage, red beans, and rice, or any of the fresh Louisiana Gulf seafood dishes. Rich Louisiana desserts in-

Anthony's Star of the Sea Room, **20**

Athens Market, **44**

Bayou Bar and Grill, **42**

Belgian Lion, **17**

Bella Luna, **38**

Berta's Latin American Restaurant, **16**

Blue Point Coastal Cuisine, **43**

Brockton Villa Restaurant, **3**

Cafe Japengo, **9**

Cafe Pacifica, **19**

California Cuisine, **30**

Chilango's Mexico City Grill, **22**

Cindy Black's, **11**

Crest Cafe, **23**

Dobson's, **35**

El Indio Shop, **31, 39**

El Tecolote, **27**

Fio's, **40**

The Fish Market, **33**

George's at the Cove, **1**

Hard Rock Cafe, **5**

Hob Nob Hill, **21**

KC's Tandoor, **13, 26**

Laurel, **24**

The Marine Room, **6**

Marius, **28**

Mission Cafe and Coffeehouse, **14**

Mission Coffee Cup Cafe, **4**

Montanas American Grill, **29**

Old Town Mexican Café, **18**

Palenque, **12**

Panda Inn, **36**

Piatti Ristorante, **8**

Rainwater's, **34**

Saffron Chicken, **32**

Sally's, **41**

SamSon's, **7**

Taste of Thai, **25**

Top O' the Cove, **2**

Tosca's, **15**

Trattoria Mamma Anna, **37**

Triangles, **10**

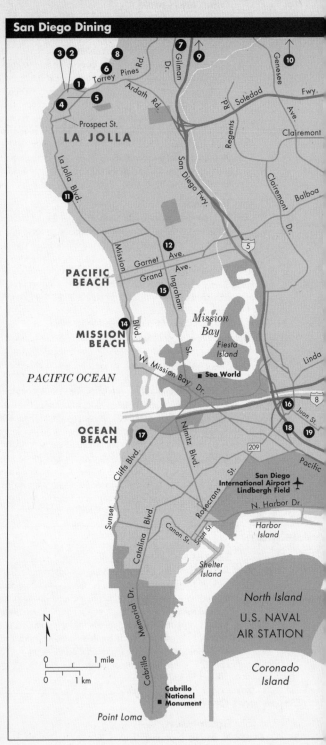

San Diego Dining

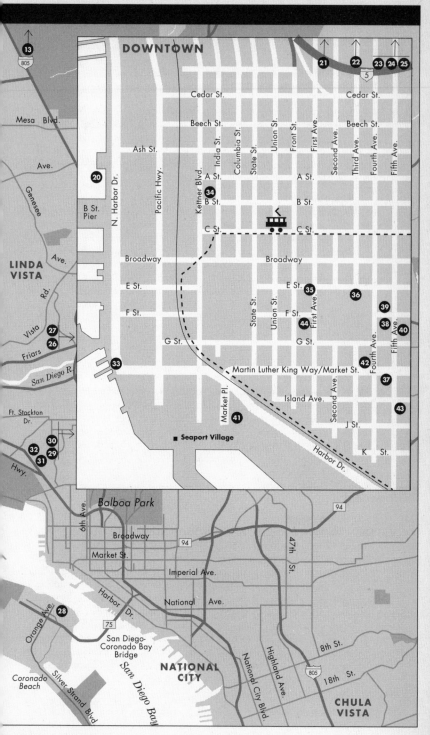

clude a praline cheesecake and an award-winning bread pudding. ⊠ *329 Market St.,* ☎ *619/696–8747. AE, D, DC, MC, V.*

California

La Jolla

$$–$$$ ✕ **Triangles.** In a handsome if slightly stiff setting, this bar and grill in the Golden Triangle area strives for variety. The "California-Continental" menu, which changes seasonally, includes fresh fish (try the ahi tuna) and grilled meats. Along with rich dishes, you'll find lighter meat and vegetarian preparations, as well as some dazzling salads. The wine list here is comprehensive. The small enclosed patio is pleasant at lunch. ⊠ *Northern Trust Bldg., 4370 La Jolla Village Dr.,* ☎ *619/453–6650. AE, DC, MC, V. No lunch Sat. Closed Sun.*

Uptown

$$ ✕ **California Cuisine.** The menu at this minimalist-chic dining room—

★   gray carpet, white walls, and changing displays of locally created artworks—is consistently innovative. Daily selections might include grilled fresh venison and a succulent seared ahi; the tasty warm chicken salad entrée is a regular feature. You can count on whatever you order to be carefully prepared and elegantly presented. The staff is knowledgeable and attentive, the wine list is good, and the desserts are mighty tempting. Heat lamps make the back patio a romantic year-round option. ⊠ *1027 University Ave.,* ☎ *619/543–0790. AE, D, DC, MC, V. No lunch weekends. Closed Mon.*

Chinese

Downtown

$–$$ ✕ **Panda Inn.** One of the better Chinese restaurants in town, this dining room at the top of Horton Plaza serves subtly seasoned Mandarin ★   and Szechuan dishes in an elegant setting that feels far removed from the rush of commerce below. The fresh seafood dishes are noteworthy, as are the Peking duck, the spicy Szechuan bean curd, and the twice-cooked pork. ⊠ *506 Horton Plaza,* ☎ *619/233–7800. AE, D, DC, MC, V.*

Continental

Downtown

$$–$$$ ✕ **Dobson's.** At lunchtime, local politicos and media types rub elbows ★   at the long polished bar of this highly regarded restaurant; evening patrons include many theatergoers. Although the small two-tier building is suggestive of an earlier era—the lower level looks like a men's club and the upper level has a wrought-iron balcony, elegant woodwork, and gilt cornices—there's nothing outdated about the cuisine. Among the carefully prepared entrées, which change daily, might be roasted quail with fig sauce or chicken risotto. The tasty house salad is laced with fennel and goat cheese, and Dobson's signature dish, a superb mussel bisque, comes topped with a crown of puff pastry. The wine list is excellent. ⊠ *956 Broadway Circle,* ☎ *619/231–6771. Reservations essential on weekends. AE, DC, MC, V. No lunch Sat. Closed Sun.*

La Jolla

$$$–$$$$ ✕ **The Marine Room.** Popular young chef Bernard Guillas has updated the menu at this venerable La Jolla Shores institution, where diners can gaze at the ocean immediately outside the windows and, if they're lucky, watch the grunion run or the waves beat against the glass. Even if the ocean isn't producing any special effects at the moment, this restaurant is worth a visit for its genteel beachfront dining-and-dancing and its inventive American and Continental cuisine with accents from around the world. Appetizers include steamed oysters wrapped in spinach with scallops and shiitake mushrooms, and a foie gras and smoked duck breast terrine. Representative entrées include a roasted salmon in a pecan sesame-curry crust served on a couscous red-lentil cake with a blood-orange lavender sauce. Sunday brunch is lavish. ⊠ *2000 Spindrift Dr.,* ☎ *619/459–7222. AE, D, DC, MC, V.*

$$$–$$$$ ✕ **Top O' the Cove.** Although glitzier newcomers now rival this once peerless La Jolla institution, the cozy Top O' the Cove still receives high marks from San Diego diners for its romantic ocean view. Abalone and ostrich are among the unusual items on the highly regarded menu; the less adventuresome might try the filet mignon or the roasted rack of lamb. The service is attentive but not overbearing, and the award-winning wine list is enormous. ⊠ *1216 Prospect St.,* ☎ *619/454–7779. AE, DC, MC, V.*

Deli

La Jolla

$ ✕ **SamSon's.** About as close as you'll come to a real Jewish deli in San Diego, SamSon's serves enormous portions. You can't go wrong with a lox plate for breakfast or a triple-decker sandwich or one of the soup-and-sandwich specials (especially the whitefish when it's available) for lunch. ⊠ *8861 Villa La Jolla Dr.,* ☎ *619/455–1462. AE, D, DC, MC, V.*

French

Coronado

$$$–$$$$ ✕ **Marius.** On any given evening, half the patrons in Le Meridien's highly touted restaurant seem to be celebrating a birthday. But even if it's not a special occasion, you will appreciate the refined, high-ceiling dining room and the impressive menu of French dishes ranging from Parisian haute cuisine to Provençal country cooking. The food and presentation are top-notch, the service attentive and professional. The wine-tasting menu is particularly recommended. ⊠ *2000 2nd St.,* ☎ *619/ 435–3000. Reservations essential on weekends. AE, D, DC, MC, V. No lunch. Closed Sun.–Mon.*

La Jolla

$$–$$$ ✕ **Cindy Black's.** This quietly elegant restaurant in La Jolla's Bird Rock neighborhood serves modern interpretations of French cuisine, subtle, stylishly presented dishes, often with a Mediterranean touch. The menu changes seasonally, but possibilities include an arugula and red-pepper salad, a hearty spaghetti with white beans in a Chianti sauce, tender grilled salmon on caramelized onions, and some seductive desserts: a house soufflé and a beyond-decadent Belgian-chocolate "brownie" with homemade caramel ice cream. Reasonable prix-fixe meals are served all Sunday evening and during the early-bird hours on weeknights. ⊠ *5721 La Jolla Blvd.,* ☎ *619/456–6299. AE, D, DC, MC, V. No lunch.*

French and Mediterranean

Uptown

$$$ ✕ **Laurel.** Chef Douglas Organ's acclaimed restaurant spotlights the cook-
★ ing of southern France and the Mediterranean. Its culinary philosophy is straightforward: the best fresh ingredients prepared simply, but with flair. The flavorful duck or guinea-hen confit, for example, is served on a bed of garlic mashed potatoes, accompanied by seasonal greens. The menu changes daily, but many favorite dishes appear regularly. For starters,

try the red-pepper-and-seafood soup, the grilled quail on a bed of warm red-cabbage slaw, or the lightly smoked trout served with warm potato salad. Among the entrées, roasted fish and risotto (especially when it's made with wild mushrooms) are always good. The wine list is renowned; desserts include a rich *pot au chocolat*. ⊠ *505 Laurel St., at 5th Ave.,* ☎ *619/239–2222. AE, D, DC, MC, V. No lunch weekends.*

Greek

Downtown

$ ✕ **Athens Market.** This cheerful eatery bustles with downtown office workers and members of San Diego's small but active Greek community. Appetizers such as *taramousalata* (fish roe dip), hummus, and stuffed grape leaves are particularly tasty—make a meal of an assortment. Greek music and belly dancers add to the festive atmosphere on weekend evenings. The adjacent Victorian-style coffeehouse, under the same ownership, is open from early morning into the evening, when many patrons switch from coffee to drinks and cigars. ⊠ *109 W. F St.,* ☎ *619/234–1955. AE, D, DC, MC, V. No lunch weekends.*

Indian

Mission Valley

$ ✕ **KC's Tandoor.** Think "food court," and you imagine Styrofoam-packaged starch washed down with liquid sugar: food to be swallowed rather than savored. But KC's Tandoor defies expectations by serving some of the best Indian food in San Diego. True, it is a fast-food restaurant, in one of the city's ubiquitous minimalls, with a few plain tables indoors and several more outside on the patio adjoining the parking lot. If you're looking for atmosphere, forget it. But if it's good Indian food you're after, the tandoori chicken is flavorful, the nan bread is rich and chewy, and the curries are truly impressive. Hearty appetites will find a bargain in the all-you-can-eat buffet brunch (Mission Center location only) on Sundays. A second KC's is northeast of the University of California off I–805. ⊠ *Friars Mission Center, 5608 Mission Center Rd.,* ☎ *619/497–0751;* ⊠ *9450 Scranton Rd.,* ☎ *619/535–1941. MC, V.*

Italian

Beaches

$ ✕ **Tosca's.** With its fluorescent lighting and red-checkered vinyl tablecloths, this eatery is in some ways typical of pizza restaurants everywhere. But you are, after all, in California, which means you can opt for wheat or semolina crusts for your individually sized pizzas or calzones; choose toppings or fillings that include artichokes, pesto, and feta cheese; and wash it all down with a microbrew. ⊠ *3780 Ingraham St., Pacific Beach,* ☎ *619/274–2408. No lunch weekdays. AE, D, DC, MC, V.*

Downtown

$$–$$$ ✗ **Bella Luna.** This small restaurant whose owner hails from the island of Capri has developed a loyal following among diners who prefer good cuisine to being seen. Paintings of "beautiful moons" in many shapes and sizes adorn the walls, and the service is gracious and attentive. The menu includes dishes from all over Italy: For an appetizer, try the rolled mozzarella or the stuffed eggplant. Linguine with clams, fettuccine with salmon, and black squid-ink linguine served with a spicy seafood sauce are among the many fine pastas; if you still have room for an entrée, consider the rack of lamb. ⊠ *748 5th Ave.,* ☎ *619/239–3222. Reservations essential on weekends. No lunch Sun. AE, DC, MC, V.*

$$–$$$ ✗ **Trattoria Mamma Anna.** If, in comparison to its glitzier 5th Avenue
★ rivals, the ambience of this café seems a little subdued, all the better to focus your attention where it belongs: on the food. A few examples of the owners' native Sicilian cuisine show up on the menu, such as the tasty *fagottini di melanzane* appetizer, eggplant stuffed with bread crumbs, peppers, pine nuts, and raisins. But the fare here ventures into the rest of Italy as well: the ravioli *con salsa di funghi* (spinach and ri-cotta ravioli with cream and mushroom sauce) is exquisite, as is the deceptively simple fettuccine *montanari* (homemade pasta with garlic, tomatoes, and wild mushrooms). Be forewarned: portions are gener-ous. If you can get as far as the second courses, try the *pollo campag-nola* (chicken breast with vegetables and olives) or the simple grilled swordfish served with lemon. The menu includes pizzas and excellent focaccia. This is one of the few good 5th Avenue restaurants open on weekends for lunch as well as dinner. ⊠ *644 5th Ave.,* ☎ *619/235–8144. Reservations essential on weekends. AE, D, DC, MC, V.*

$$ ✗ **Fio's.** Glitzy young singles mingle with staid business-suit types in this lively Gaslamp Quarter restaurant. Contemporary variations on traditional northern Italian cuisine are served in a high-ceiling brick-and-wood dining room overlooking the 5th Avenue street scene. The menu includes imaginative pizzas baked in the wood-fire oven and good appetizers and pastas. ⊠ *801 5th Ave.,* ☎ *619/234–3467. Reserva-tions essential on weekends. AE, D, DC, MC, V. No lunch weekends.*

La Jolla

$$ ✗ **Piatti Ristorante.** On weekends, this trattoria is filled to overflow-
★ ing with singles and local families. A wood-burning oven turns out fla-vorful pizzas; pastas include the *pappardelle fantasia* (wide saffron noodles with shrimp, fresh tomatoes, and arugula) and a garlicky spaghetti *alle vongole* (served with clams in the shell). Among the *sec-ondi* are good versions of roast chicken and Italian sausage with po-lenta. The weekday lunch menu includes salads and *panini* (sandwiches); brunch is served weekends. A fountain splashes softly on the tree-shaded patio, where heat lamps allow diners to sit out even on chilly evenings. ⊠ *2182 Avenida de la Playa,* ☎ *619/454–1589. AE, DC, MC, V.*

Latin American

Old Town

$ ✗ **Berta's Latin American Restaurant.** A San Diego rarity—and a sur-prise in a section of town where the food leans toward the safe and touristy—Berta's serves excellent Latin American dishes. The wines are largely Chilean, but the food manages to be tasty and health-conscious at the same time. Try the Brazilian seafood *vatapa* (shrimp, scallops, and fish served in a sauce flavored with ginger, coconut, and chilies) or the Peruvian *pollo a la huancaina* (chicken with chilies and a feta-cheese sauce). The simple dining room is small, but there's also a patio. ⊠ *3928 Twiggs St.,* ☎ *619/295–2343. AE, MC, V.*

Mexican

Beaches

$–$$ ✕ **Palenque.** A welcome alternative to the standard Sonoran-style
★ café, this family-run restaurant in Pacific Beach serves regional Mexican dishes. Recommendations include the chicken with *mole*, in the chocolate-based or green-chili version, and the mouth-watering *camarones en chipotle,* large shrimp cooked in a chili-and-tequila cream sauce (an old family recipe of the proprietor). Piñatas and paper birds dangle from the thatched ceiling, and seating is in comfortable round-back leather chairs; in warm weather you can dine on a small deck in front. Palenque is a bit hard to spot from the street and service is often slow, but the food is worth your vigilance and patience. ⊠ *1653 Garnet Ave., Pacific Beach,* ☎ *619/272–7816. AE, D, DC, MC, V. No lunch Mon.*

Mission Valley

$ ✕ **El Tecolote.** There are few oases in the culinary desert of Mission Valley, unfortunately for the many visitors who stay in its hotels. But one good watering hole is the long-established El Tecolote (The Owl). The restaurant does a good job with the usual taco-burrito fare, but come here also to sample Mexican regional specialties—the enchiladas in *mole* sauce, the fish fillet Ensenada style, or the rich Aztec layered cake (tortillas stacked with cheese, chilies, enchilada sauce, guacamole, and sour cream). ⊠ *6110 Friars Rd. W,* ☎ *619/295–2087. AE, D, DC, MC, V. No lunch Sun.*

Old Town

$ ✕ **Old Town Mexican Café.** Singles congregate at the bar and families crowd into the wooden booths of this boisterous San Diego favorite, decked out with plants and colorful piñatas; an enclosed patio takes the overflow from both groups. You'll find all the Mexican standards here, along with specialties such as *carnitas,* chunks of roast pork served with fresh tortillas and condiments. The enchiladas with spicy ranchero or green-chili sauce are delectable variations on an old theme. You can watch the corn tortillas being handmade on the premises and pick up a dozen to take home with you. The Café opens at 7 AM for breakfast. ⊠ *2489 San Diego Ave.,* ☎ *619/297–4330. AE, D, MC, V.*

Uptown

$ ✕ **Chilango's Mexico City Grill.** Proof positive that good things come in small packages is this tiny but cheerful storefront restaurant. The burritos and *tortas* (sandwiches) are like no others in the city; daily specials might include enchiladas in *mole verde* (green chili sauce) and the fabulous chicken *mole poblano* (a sauce made with chilies and bittersweet chocolate). This much-loved restaurant quickly fills to overflowing, so consider coming in off-hours or ordering takeout. ⊠ *142 University Ave.,* ☎ *619/294–8646. Open for breakfast Fri.–Sun. No credit cards.*

$ ✕ **El Indio Shop.** India Street's landmark taqueria has been serving some of the city's best Mexican fast food since 1940. The menu is extensive; try the large burritos, the *tacquitos* (fried rolled tacos) with guacamole, or the giant quesadillas. Low on atmosphere both at the tables inside and on the patio across the street, El Indio is perfect for beach-bound takeout. There's a branch downtown, and one in Pacific Beach, too. ⊠ *3695 India St. (take I–5 to Washington St. exit),* ☎ *619/299–0333;* ⊠ *409 F St.,* ☎ *619/239–8151. MC, V.*

Pacific Rim

La Jolla

$$$ ✕ **Cafe Japengo.** In one of the most stylish dining rooms in town, framed by elegant marbled walls accented with leafy bamboo trees and unusual black-iron sculptures, Cafe Japengo serves Asian-inspired cuisine with many North and South American touches. There's a selection of grilled, wood-roasted, and wok-fried entrées for dinner; try the 10-ingredient fried rice, the shrimp and scallops with dragon noodles, or the grilled swordfish with red-bean miso stew. The curry fried calamari and the Japengo pot stickers appetizers are guaranteed to wake up your mouth. You can also order very fresh sushi from your table or from a seat at the sushi bar. Keep in mind that the service can be slow here. ⊠ *Aventine Center, 8960 University Center La.,* ☎ *619/ 450–3355. AE, D, DC, MC, V. No lunch weekends.*

Seafood

Downtown

$$$–$$$$ ✕ **Anthony's Star of the Sea Room.** The flagship of Anthony's local ★ fleet of seafood restaurants ensconces its patrons in a formal dining room whose vaguely marine decor got a much-needed facelift in 1997. The house-smoked salmon, sliced at the table, melts in the mouth; the delicious "lobster cappuccino" soup resembles coffee only in name; and the various grilled and roasted seafood entrées are splendidly prepared. A terrace scheduled for completion by fall 1997 will take greater advantage of the choice waterfront location of one of San Diego's premier seafood restaurants. ⊠ *1360 N. Harbor Dr.,* ☎ *619/232–7408. Jacket required. AE, D, DC, MC, V. No lunch.*

$$$ ✕ **Blue Point Coastal Cuisine.** High ceilings, gleaming woodwork, ample booths, and expansive windows give this seafood establishment an urbane air. The extensive selection of home brews and house martinis contributes to the atmosphere of East Coast sophistication. But Blue Point situates its cuisine firmly on the Pacific Rim, incorporating Asian accents and south-of-the-border flavors. Go for the appetizers and seafood entrées here—the pasta dishes are disappointing. Try the griddled oysters or crab cakes, and follow them with the grilled swordfish, the mustard catfish, or the sesame-crusted salmon with sake butter. Meat-eaters needn't despair—the menu includes chicken, pork, steak, and lamb, too. The wine list is serious, and the service is efficient, friendly, and informed. The poached pear with chocolate sauce is one of several well-crafted desserts. ⊠ *565 5th Ave.,* ☎ *619/233–6623. AE, D, DC, MC, V. No lunch.*

$$$ ✕ **Sally's.** The dining room is très chic postmodern, all curves and glass and exposed pipes, and similarly stylish is the cuisine: pan-Mediterranean with a light French accent. Seafood is the star here, although the menu has something for carnivores and vegetarians as well. Order the light, greaseless crab cakes, the best in town, and bite into chunks of fresh crab. Recommended entrées include a seafood paella studded with pieces of fish and shellfish, a rich bouillabaisse, and an unusually moist and tender grilled swordfish. The three-course prix-fixe daily special at dinner is often irresistible. Desserts range from concoctions made with fresh fruit to a sinfully rich chocolate cake. The wine list and beer selection here are both quite good. At the Sunday "jazz

brunch," from 11 to 3:30, you can listen to music while you enjoy an appetizer, an entrée, and unlimited champagne and orange juice for the bargain price of $16. Outdoor dining is available. ⊠ *Hyatt Regency San Diego, 1 Market Pl.,* ☎ *619/687–6080. AE, D, DC, MC, V.*

$–$$$ ✕ **The Fish Market.** Diners at this informal restaurant may choose from a large variety of fresh fish, mesquite grilled and served with lemon and tartar sauce. Also good are shellfish dishes, such as steamed clams or mussels, and the extremely fresh sushi. Most of what is served here has lived in the water, but even dedicated fish-avoiders may think it worth their while to trade selection for the stunning view: Enormous plate-glass windows look directly out onto the harbor, and if you're lucky enough to get a windowside table, you can practically taste the salt spray. This is one of those rare places where families with young children can feel comfortable without sacrificing their taste buds. A more formal restaurant upstairs, the Top of the Market, has a distinctive menu of exquisitely prepared seafood and another fabulous view. It's expensive but worth the splurge. ⊠ *750 N. Harbor Dr.,* ☎ *619/232–3474 for the Fish Market, 619/234–4867 for the Top of the Market. AE, D, DC, MC, V.*

La Jolla

$$$ ✕ **George's at the Cove.** At most restaurants you get either good food
★ or good views; at George's, you don't have to choose. The elegant main dining room, with a wall-length window overlooking La Jolla Cove, is renowned for its daily fresh seafood specials; the menu also includes several good chicken and meat dishes. The soups and the fresh pasta entrées are highly recommended. Desserts are uniformly excellent. For more informal dining, try the Cafe ($–$$) on the second floor. The rooftop Ocean Terrace ($–$$) has a sweeping view of the coast. Wonderful for breakfast, lunch, or brunch on a fine day, the Terrace (like the Cafe) does not take reservations, so you may have a wait. ⊠ *1250 Prospect St.,* ☎ *619/454–4244. Reservations essential for main dining room on weekends. AE, D, DC, MC, V.*

Old Town

$$–$$$ ✕ **Cafe Pacifica.** The airy Cafe Pacifica serves eclectic California cui-
★ sine with an emphasis on seafood. You can't go wrong with any of the fresh fish preparations. Other good bets include the pan-fried catfish, greaseless fish tacos, and superb crab cakes. The crème brûlée is worth blowing any diet for. Cafe Pacifica's wine list has received kudos from *Wine Spectator* magazine. ⊠ *2414 San Diego Ave.,* ☎ *619/291–6666. AE, D, DC, MC, V. No lunch.*

Thai

Uptown

$ ✕ **Saffron Chicken.** The specialty at this take-out restaurant is chicken spit-roasted over a wood fire and served with a choice of sauces: try the peanut or chili. Among the accompanying side dishes, the Cambodian salad is fresh and crunchy. There's limited outdoor seating, but this is an ideal place to pick up a meal to take to Mission Bay or the beach. ⊠ *3731B India St. (from downtown, take I–5 to Washington St. exit),* ☎ *619/574–0177. Reservations not accepted. MC, V.*

$ ✕ **Taste of Thai.** Almost always packed with value-minded diners, this modest café serves up yummy Thai and vegetarian cuisine at reasonable prices. Try the seafood noodles, the red or yellow curry, and the meat or tofu with basil and hot peppers. ⊠ *527 University Ave.,* ☎ *619/291–7525. AE, MC, V.*

5 Lodging

San Diego has a surplus of rooms, which means lower prices for those who shop around. Several properties in Hotel Circle frequently offer special rates and free tickets to local attractions, and many hotels promote lower-priced weekend packages to fill rooms after the week's convention and business customers have departed. When you make reservations, find out about any specials. Book well in advance, especially during the summer.

SAN DIEGO IS SPREAD OUT, so the first thing to consider when selecting lodgings is location. If you choose one of the many hotels with a waterfront location and extensive outdoor sports facilities, you need never leave the premises. But if you plan to do a lot of sightseeing, take into account a hotel's proximity to the attractions you most want to visit. In general, price need not be a major factor in your decision: Even the most expensive areas have some reasonably priced rooms.

By Sharon K.
Gillenwater
and Edie
Jarolim

Updated by
Cynthia Queen

If you are planning an extended stay in San Diego or need lodgings for four or more people, consider an apartment rental. **Oakwood Apartments** (⊠ 3866 Ingraham St., 92109, ☎ 619/490–2100) rents comfortable furnished apartments in the Mission Bay area with maid service and linens; there's a minimum 30-day stay. A bus station is right out front, and you're within walking distance of Pacific Beach hot spots. The complex has a heated pool and tennis and basketball courts. Oakwood also has a smaller establishment in Mission Valley (⊠ 425 Camino del Rio South, 92108, ☎ 619/497–6900), close to downtown, Old Town, Qualcomm Stadium, and shopping. Furnished units are available, and there's only a 3-night minimum stay.

The **Bed & Breakfast Guild of San Diego** (☎ 619/523–1300) lists a number of high-quality member inns. The **Bed & Breakfast Directory for San Diego** (⊠ Box 3292, 92163, ☎ 619/297–3130 or 800/619–7666) covers San Diego County.

CATEGORY	COST*
$$$$	over $175
$$$	$120–$175
$$	$80–$120
$	under $80

*for a double room in high (summer) season, excluding 10.5% San Diego room tax

Coronado

Quiet, out-of-the-way Coronado feels like something out of an earlier, more gracious era. With boutiques and restaurants lining Orange Avenue, the main street, and its fine beaches, Coronado is great for a getaway, but if you plan to see many of San Diego's attractions you'll probably spend a lot of time commuting across the bridge or riding the ferry.

$$$$ 🏨 **Hotel Del Coronado.** "The Del" is a social and historic landmark (☞ Coronado *in* Chapter 2). The rooms and suites in the ornate 1888 building are charmingly quirky. Some have sleeping areas that seem smaller than the baths. Other rooms are downright palatial; two are even said to come with a resident ghost. The public areas are grand, if a bit dark for modern tastes. More standardized accommodations are available in the newer high-rise. ⊠ *1500 Orange Ave., 92118,* ☎ *619/435–6611 for hotel, 619/522–8000 or 800/468–3533 for reservations,* 📠 *619/522–8262. 692 rooms. 3 restaurants, deli, in-room modem lines, room service, 2 pools, barbershop, beauty salon, outdoor hot tub, massage, sauna, steam room, 6 tennis courts, croquet, exercise room, beach, boating, bicycles, shops, video games, concierge, business services, convention center, parking (fee). AE, D, DC, MC, V.*

$$$$ 🏨 **Le Meridien San Diego at Coronado.** Flamingos greet you at the entrance to this 16-acre landscaped resort. Large rooms and suites in low-slung buildings are done in a cheerful California–country French fashion, with colorful Impressionist prints; all rooms have separate show-
★

ers and tubs and come with plush robes. The spa facilities are top-notch, as is the award-winning Marius restaurant (☞ Chapter 4), which serves innovative Provençal cuisine. ⊠ *2000 2nd St., 92118, ☎ 619/ 435–3000 or 800/543–4300 for central reservations,* FAX *619/435–3032. 265 rooms, 7 suites, 28 villa units. 2 restaurants, bar, in-room modem lines, room service, 3 pools, barbershop, beauty salon, 2 outdoor hot tubs, massage, sauna, spa, 6 tennis courts, aerobics, health club, beach, snorkeling, windsurfing, bicycles, pro shop, shops, children's programs, laundry service, concierge, business services, convention center, parking (fee). AE, D, DC, MC, V.*

$$$$ 🏨 **Loews Coronado Bay Resort.** You can park your boat at the 80-slip marina of this elegant resort set on a secluded 15-acre peninsula on the Silver Strand. Rooms are formally but tastefully decorated, and all have furnished balconies with views of water—either bay, ocean, or marina. The Commodore Kids Club has programs for children ages 4–12, and the hotel lounge has nightly entertainment. The Azzura Point restaurant, which specializes in Pacific seafood, has won numerous awards. ⊠ *4000 Coronado Bay Rd., 92118, ☎ 619/424–4000 or 800/ 815–6397,* FAX *619/424–4400. 403 rooms, 37 suites. 2 restaurants, bar, deli, in-room modem lines, room service, 3 pools, barbershop, beauty salon, 3 hot tubs, 5 tennis courts, health club, beach, windsurfing, boating, jet skiing, waterskiing, bicycles, pro shop, children's programs, laundry service, concierge, business services, convention center, parking (fee). AE, D, DC, MC, V.*

$$–$$$ 🏨 **Glorietta Bay Inn.** The main building of this property—across the street from the Hotel Del, adjacent to the Coronado harbor, and near many restaurants and shops—was built in 1908 for sugar baron John D. Spreckels, who once owned most of downtown San Diego. Rooms in this Edwardian-style mansion and in the newer motel-style buildings are attractively furnished. The well-appointed inn is much smaller than the Hotel Del; its clients experience a quieter and less expensive stay. Tours ($6) of the island's historical buildings depart from the inn's lobby three mornings a week. ⊠ *1630 Glorietta Blvd., 92118, ☎ 619/ 435–3101 or 800/283–9383,* FAX *619/435–6182. 98 rooms. In-room modem lines, refrigerators, pool, outdoor hot tub, bicycles, coin laundry, business services, free parking. AE, D, DC, MC, V.*

Downtown

Much to see is within walking distance of downtown accommodations—Seaport Village, the Embarcadero, the historic Gaslamp Quarter, theaters and night spots, and the Horton Plaza shopping center. The zoo and Balboa Park are also nearby. In addition, a number of good restaurants have opened in this part of town in the past few years.

$$$$ 🏨 **Hyatt Regency San Diego.** This high-rise adjacent to Seaport Vil-
★ lage successfully combines Old World opulence with California airiness. Palm trees pose next to ornate tapestry couches in the light-filled lobby, and all of the British Regency–style guest rooms have views of the water. The hotel's proximity to the convention center attracts a large business trade. The "Business Plan" includes access to an area with desks and office supplies; each room on the special business floor has a fax machine. Sally's Restaurant (☞ Seafood *in* Chapter 4) serves inventive cuisine, and the 40th-floor lounge has 360-degree sunset views. ⊠ *1 Market Pl., ☎ 619/232–1234 or 800/233–1234 for central reservations,* FAX *619/233–6464. 820 rooms, 55 suites and Regency Club rooms. 2 restaurants, in-room modem lines, room service, bar, lobby lounge, piano bar, pool, outdoor hot tub, sauna, steam room, 3 tennis courts, health club, boating, bicycles, shops, laundry service, business services, convention center, parking (fee). AE, D, DC, MC, V.*

80

Bahia Hotel, **20**

Balboa Park Inn, **56**

Bay Club Hotel & Marina, **27**

Bed & Breakfast Inn at La Jolla, **3**

Best Western Blue Sea Lodge, **18**

Best Western Hacienda Hotel Old Town, **35**

Best Western Hanalei Hotel, **38**

Best Western Inn by the Sea, **2**

Best Western Island Palms Hotel & Marina, **26**

Best Western Posada Inn, **32**

Catamaran Resort Hotel, **16**

Colonial Inn, **5**

Crystal Pier Motel, **14**

Dana Inn & Marina, **23**

Days Inn Hotel Circle, **57**

Embassy Suites San Diego Bay, **50**

Gaslamp Plaza Suites, **51**

Glorietta Bay Inn, **42**

Heritage Park Bed & Breakfast Inn, **23**

Holiday Inn Express, **1**

Holiday Inn on the Bay, **46**

Horton Grand Hotel, **47**

Hotel Del Coronado, **43**

Humphrey's Half Moon Inn, **28**

Hyatt Islandia, **22**

Hyatt Regency La Jolla, **10**

Hyatt Regency San Diego, **45**

Kona Kai Continental Plaza Resort and Marina, **25**

La Jolla Bed & Breakfast Inn, **3**

La Jolla Cove Suites, **8**

La Pensione, **53**

La Valencia, **7**

Le Meridien San Diego at Coronado, **41**

Lodge at Torrey Pines, **11**

Loews Coronado Bay Resort, **44**

Mission Bay Motel, **17**

Ocean Manor Apartment Hotel, **24**

San Diego Lodging

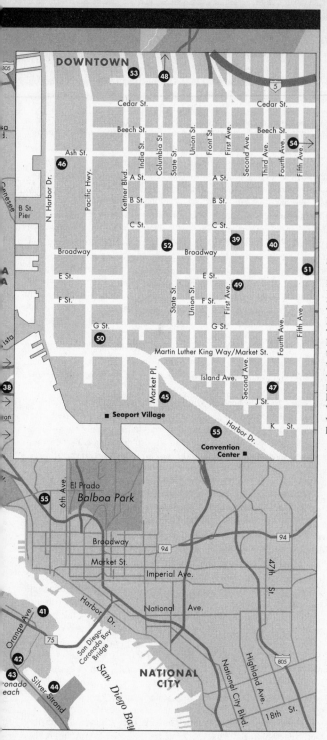

Outrigger Motel, **30**
Pacific Shores Inn, **15**
Prospect Park Inn, **6**
Ramada Limited Point Loma, **29**
Ramada Plaza Old Town, **36**
Red Lion Hotel, **58**
Rodeway Inn, **54**
San Diego Hilton Beach and Tennis Resort, **13**
San Diego Marriott Hotel and Marina, **55**
San Diego Marriott Mission Valley, **59**
San Diego Mission Valley Hilton, **60**
San Diego Princess Resort, **21**
Scripps Inn, **4**
Sea Lodge, **9**
Sheraton Grande Torrey Pines, **12**
Sheraton San Diego Hotel & Marina, **34**
Super 8 Bayview, **48**
Travelodge Point Loma, **31**
Travelodge Hotel Harbor Island, **33**
U.S. Grant Hotel, **40**
Vacation Inn, **37**
Westin Hotel San Diego–Horton Plaza, **49**
Westgate Hotel, **39**
Wyndham Emerald Plaza Hotel, **52**

$$$$ 🖼 **San Diego Marriott Hotel and Marina.** This twin-towers high-rise next to the San Diego Convention Center has everything a businessperson could want, not to mention a superb view of the bay and city from the upper floors. A major site for conventions and conventioneers, the complex can be hectic and impersonal but has such intriguing features as lagoon-style pools nestled between cascading waterfalls. Vacationers will appreciate the location right on the San Diego Bay boardwalk. Be aware that standard rooms are smallish. The hallways can be noisy at night. ⊠ *333 W. Harbor Dr., 92101, ☎ 619/234–1500 or 800/228–9290 for central reservations, ℻ 619/234–8678. 1,299 rooms, 56 suites. 4 restaurants, bar, in-room modem lines, room service, 2 pools, barbershop, beauty salon, outdoor hot tub, sauna, 6 tennis courts, aerobics, basketball, health club, jogging, bicycles, shops, recreation room, coin laundry, concierge, business services, convention center, car rental, parking (fee). AE, D, DC, MC, V.*

$$$–$$$$ 🖼 **Embassy Suites San Diego Bay.** It's a short walk to the convention center, the Embarcadero, and Seaport Village from one of downtown's most popular hotels. The front door of each spacious suite opens out onto the 12-story atrium. The contemporary decor is pleasant, and the views from rooms facing the harbor are spectacular. Business travelers will find it easy to set up shop here; the hotel provides a 24-hour fax and photocopy service. Families can make good use of the in-room refrigerators, microwaves, and separate sleeping areas. A cooked-to-order breakfast and afternoon cocktails are complimentary, as are airport transfers. ⊠ *601 Pacific Hwy., 92101, ☎ 619/239–2400 or 800/ 362–2779 for central reservations, ℻ 619/239–1520. 337 suites. Restaurant, bar, pool, barbershop, beauty salon, sauna, health club, shops, bicycles, coin laundry, business services, meeting rooms, airport shuttle, parking (fee). AE, D, DC, MC, V.*

$$$–$$$$ 🖼 **U.S. Grant Hotel.** This San Diego classic built in 1910 sits across the street from Horton Plaza. Crystal chandeliers and polished marble floors in the lobby and Queen Anne–style mahogany furnishings in the stately and spacious rooms recall a more gracious era when such dignitaries as Charles Lindbergh and Franklin D. Roosevelt stayed here. These days, high-power business types still gather at the hotel's clubby Grant Grill, and English "high tea" is served in the lobby from 3 to 6. ⊠ *326 Broadway, 92101, ☎ 619/232–3121 or 800/237–5029, ℻ 619/ 232–3626. 220 rooms, 60 suites. Restaurant, bar, café, piano bar, room service, exercise room, bicycles, concierge, business services, shops, airport shuttle, parking (fee). AE, D, DC, MC, V.*

$$$–$$$$ 🖼 **Westgate Hotel.** A nondescript modern high-rise across from Hor-
★ ton Plaza hides what must be the most opulent hotel in San Diego. The lobby, modeled after the anteroom at Versailles, has hand-cut Baccarat chandeliers; rooms are individually furnished with antiques, Italian marble counters, and bath fixtures with 24-karat-gold overlays. From the ninth floor up, the views of the harbor and city are breathtaking. Afternoon high tea is served in the lobby to the accompaniment of piano music. The Tijuana trolley stops right outside the door. ⊠ *1055 2nd Ave., 92101, ☎ 619/238–1818 or 800/221–3802, 800/522–1564 in CA, ℻ 619/557–3737. 223 rooms. 2 restaurants, bar, deli, in-room modem lines, room service, barbershop, exercise room, bicycles, concierge, business services, meeting rooms, airport shuttle, parking (fee). AE, D, DC, MC, V.*

$$$–$$$$ 🖼 **Wyndham Emerald Plaza Hotel.** This property's office and conference facilities draw many business travelers. Still, the Wyndham is also fine for vacationers who want to be near downtown shopping and restaurants. Many of the upper-floor accommodations have panoramic views. The green prismlike sculpture that hangs from the 100-ft central atrium

is a bit overwhelming, and the bland beige-dominated standard rooms are not overly large. The health club is quite good. ✉ *400 W. Broadway, 92101,* ☎ *619/239–4500 or 800/996–3426,* FAX *619/239–4527. 416 rooms, 20 suites. 2 restaurants, bar, in-room modem lines, pool, outdoor hot tub, sauna, steam room, health club, shops, children's programs, concierge, business services, convention center, parking (fee). AE, D, DC, MC, V.*

$$–$$$$ 🏨 **Balboa Park Inn.** Directly across the street from Balboa Park, this all-suites B&B is housed in four Spanish colonial–style 1915 residences connected by courtyards. Prices are reasonable for the romantic one- and two-bedroom suites. Each has a different flavor, including contemporary versions of Italian, French, Spanish, or early Californian; some have fireplaces, wet bars, whirlpool tubs, patios, and kitchens. Continental breakfast and a newspaper are delivered to guests every morning. ✉ *3402 Park Blvd., 92103,* ☎ *619/298–0823 or 800/938–8181,* FAX *619/294–8070. 26 suites. AE, D, DC, MC, V.*

$$–$$$$ 🏨 **Horton Grand Hotel.** A Victorian confection in the heart of the historic Gaslamp District, the Horton Grand comprises two 1880s hotels moved brick by brick from nearby locations. Its delightfully retro rooms are furnished with period antiques, ceiling fans, and gas-burning fireplaces. The choicest rooms overlook a garden courtyard that twinkles with miniature lights each night. The hotel is a charmer, but service can be erratic. ✉ *311 Island Ave., 92101,* ☎ *619/544–1886 or 800/542–1886,* FAX *619/239–3823. 105 rooms, 24 suites. Restaurant, bar, business services, meeting rooms, airport shuttle, parking (fee). AE, D, DC, MC, V.*

$$$ 🏨 **Holiday Inn on the Bay.** On the Embarcadero and overlooking San Diego Bay, this high-rise hotel is convenient for vacationers and business travelers. Rooms are unsurprising but spacious and comfortable, and views from the balconies are hard to beat. ✉ *1355 N. Harbor Dr., 92101,* ☎ *619/232–3861 or 800/877–8920 for central reservations,* FAX *619/232–4924. 600 rooms, 17 suites. Restaurant, bar, in-room modem lines, pool, exercise room, shops, coin laundry, business services, meeting rooms, airport and Amtrak shuttle, parking (fee). AE, D, DC, MC, V.*

$$$ 🏨 **Westin Hotel San Diego–Horton Plaza.** Although it is fronted by a startling lighted blue obelisk, this high-rise, formerly the Doubletree, is all understated marble and brass. The spacious rooms are in pastels of coral blue and pale orange. With its prime downtown location, the hotel attracts many business travelers. The lobby lounge is packed every night with local financiers and weary shoppers from the adjacent Horton Plaza. ✉ *910 Broadway Circle, 92101,* ☎ *619/239–2200 or 800/528–0444 for central reservations,* FAX *619/239–0509. 450 rooms, 14 suites. Restaurant, lobby lounge, sports bar, in-room modem lines, room service, pool, outdoor hot tub, sauna, 2 tennis courts, health club, business services, parking (fee). AE, D, DC, MC, V.*

$$–$$$ 🏨 **Gaslamp Plaza Suites.** Listed on the National Register of Historic Places, this 11-story structure just a block from Horton Plaza was built in 1913 as San Diego's first "skyscraper." Elegant public areas have old marble, brass, and mosaics. Guests can enjoy the view and a complimentary Continental breakfast on the rooftop terrace. Book ahead if you're visiting in high season. ✉ *520 E St., 92101,* ☎ *619/232–9500 or 800/874–8770,* FAX *619/238–9945. 52 suites. Restaurant, bar, parking (fee). AE, D, DC, MC, V.*

$–$$ 🏨 **Rodeway Inn.** On one of the better streets downtown, this property is clean, comfortable, and nicely decorated. Continental breakfast is included in the room rate. ✉ *833 Ash St., 92101,* ☎ *619/239–2285, 800/228–2000 for central reservations, 800/522–1528 in CA,* FAX *619/235–6951. 45 rooms. In-room modem lines, hot tub, sauna, coin* *laundry, business services, meeting rooms, free parking. AE, D, DC, MC, V.*

$ 🔧 **La Pensione.** Rooms at this downtown budget hotel are modern, clean, and well designed, with good working areas and kitchenettes. The hotel is near the Old Town trolley line and convenient to the restaurants of the city's version of Little Italy. The café downstairs is a place to linger over a cappuccino or provolone and prosciutto sandwich. ⊠ *1700 India St., 92101,* ☎ *619/236–8000 or 800/232–4683,* 𝔽𝔸𝕏 *619/ 236–8088. 80 rooms. Café, kitchenettes, coin laundry, free parking. AE, D, DC, MC, V.*

$ 🔧 **Super 8 Bayview.** This motel's location is less noisy than those of other low-cost establishments. The accommodations are nondescript but clean, and some have refrigerators. Room rates include Continental breakfast. ⊠ *1835 Columbia St., 92101,* ☎ *619/544–0164 or 800/ 537–9902,* 𝔽𝔸𝕏 *619/237–9940. 101 rooms. Pool, coin laundry, airport and Amtrak shuttle, free parking. AE, DC, MC, V.*

Harbor Island, Shelter Island, and Point Loma

Two man-made peninsulas between downtown and the community of Point Loma, Harbor Island and Shelter Island both hold grassy parks, tree-lined paths, lavish hotels, and good restaurants. Harbor Island is closest to the downtown area and less than five minutes from the airport. Narrower Shelter Island is nearer to Point Loma. Both locations command views of the bay and the downtown skyline. Not all the lodgings listed here are on the islands themselves, but all are in the vicinity.

$$$$ 🔧 **Sheraton San Diego Hotel & Marina.** Of this property's two high-rises, the smaller, more intimate West Tower has larger rooms with separate areas suitable for business entertaining. The East Tower has the better sports facilities. Rooms throughout are California-style spiffy. Views from the upper floors of both sections are superb, but because the West Tower is closer to the water it has fine outlooks from the lower floors, too. ⊠ *1380 Harbor Island Dr., 92101,* ☎ *619/291–2900 or 800/325–3535 for central reservations,* 𝔽𝔸𝕏 *619/692–2337. 1,050 rooms. 3 restaurants, 2 bars, deli, patisserie, in-room modem lines, room service, 3 pools, wading pool, 2 outdoor hot tubs, massage, 4 tennis courts, health club, jogging, beach, boating, bicycles, pro shop, playground, airport shuttle, parking (fee). AE, D, DC, MC, V.*

$$$–$$$$ 🔧 **Bay Club Hotel & Marina.** Rooms in this appealing low-rise Shelter Island property are large, light, and furnished with rattan tables and chairs and Polynesian tapestries; all have refrigerators and views of either the bay or the marina from outside terraces. A buffet breakfast and limo service to the airport or Amtrak are included in the room rate. ⊠ *2131 Shelter Island Dr., 92106,* ☎ *619/224–8888 or 800/672–0800,* 𝔽𝔸𝕏 *619/225–1604. 95 rooms, 10 suites. Restaurant, bar, room service, pool, outdoor hot tub, exercise room, bicycles, concierge, business services, meeting rooms, free parking. AE, D, DC, MC, V.*

$$$–$$$$ 🔧 **Travelodge Hotel Harbor Island.** Lodgers here get the views and amenities of more expensive hotels for less, with such perks as in-room coffeemakers and local phone calls. Those staying on the two executive floors also get a free buffet breakfast. The public areas and guest rooms are bright and airy. The Waterfront Cafe & Club overlooks the marina, and (Gen-Xers take note) actress/singer Florence Henderson has been known to pull her boat into a slip here and join in the karaoke evenings on Friday and Saturday nights. ⊠ *1960 Harbor Island Dr., 92101,* ☎ *619/291–6700 or 800/578–7878 for central reservations,* 𝔽𝔸𝕏 *619/293–0694. 201 rooms, 6 suites. Restaurant, bar, in-room modem lines, pool, outdoor hot tub, exercise room, jogging, shops, laun-*

dry service, meeting rooms, airport shuttle, free parking. AE, D, DC, MC, V.

$$–$$$$ ⊞ **Humphrey's Half Moon Inn.** This sprawling South Seas–style resort has grassy open areas with palm trees and tiki torches. Rooms, some with kitchens and some with harbor or marine views, have modern furnishings. Locals throng to Humphrey's, the on-premises seafood restaurant, and to the jazz lounge; the hotel also hosts outdoor jazz concerts June–October. ⊠ *2303 Shelter Island Dr., 92106,* ☎ *619/224–3411 or 800/345–9995 for reservations,* FAX *619/224–3478. 128 rooms, 54 suites. Restaurant, bar, in-room modem lines, room service, pool, hot tub, putting green, croquet, Ping-Pong, boating, bicycles, airport and Amtrak shuttle, coin laundry, business services, meeting rooms, free parking. AE, D, DC, MC, V.*

$$–$$$$ ⊞ **Kona Kai Continental Plaza Resort and Marina.** Though the Kona Kai name may suggest a Polynesian theme, this 11-acre property has been refurbished in a mixture of Mexican and Mediterranean styles. The spacious and light-filled lobby, with its Maya sculptures and terra-cotta tiles, opens onto a lush esplanade that overlooks the hotel's marina. The rooms are well appointed, if a bit small, and most look out onto either the marina or San Diego Bay. ⊠ *1551 Shelter Island Dr., 92106,* ☎ *619/221–8000 or 800/566–2524,* FAX *619/221–5953. 168 rooms, 38 suites. Restaurant, bar, room service, 2 pools, 2 hot tubs, 2 saunas, 2 tennis courts, jogging, health club, volleyball, beach, airport and Amtrak shuttle, free parking. AE, D, DC, MC, V.*

$$–$$$ ⊞ **Best Western Island Palms Hotel & Marina.** This waterfront inn, with an airy skylit lobby, is a good choice if you have a boat to dock; the adjacent marina has guest slips. Both harbor- and marina-view rooms are available. Standard accommodations are fairly small; if you're traveling with family or more than one friend, the two-bedroom suite with an eat-in kitchen is a good deal. ⊠ *2051 Shelter Island Dr., 92106,* ☎ *619/222–0561 or 800/922–2336,* FAX *619/222–9760. 68 rooms, 29 suites. Restaurant, bar, in-room modem lines, pool, outdoor hot tub, business services, meeting rooms, free parking. AE, D, DC, MC, V.*

$–$$ ⊞ **Best Western Posada Inn.** Many of the rooms at this comfortable if plain inn have harbor views. Point Loma's seafood restaurants are within walking distance. ⊠ *5005 N. Harbor Dr., 92106,* ☎ *619/224–3254 or 800/231–3811,* FAX *619/224–2186. 112 rooms. Pool, outdoor hot tub, exercise room, airport shuttle, free parking. AE, D, DC, MC, V.*

$ ⊞ **Outrigger Motel.** A short walk along the bay from the Outrigger leads to Harbor and Shelter islands, and across the street from the motel are fishing docks and the Point Loma Sea Foods Market and Restaurant. Some rooms show signs of wear (such as water stains on the bathroom wallpaper), but the operators' gradual upgrade of the premises will bring new carpeting and kitchen appliances. Pets are permitted ($25 fee). ⊠ *1370 Scott St., 92106,* ☎ *619/223–7105 or 800/232–1212,* FAX *619/223–8672. 36 rooms. Kitchens, pool, laundry service, free parking. AE, D, DC, MC, V.*

$ ⊞ **Ramada Limited Point Loma.** Recent renovations make this motel nicer than its next door neighbor the Outrigger, but there are no kitchen units. The location is convenient, though on a busy street, and the rooms with bay views are quite a deal. This establishment serves complimentary Continental breakfast and has a heated pool and a bayview bar with billiards. ⊠ *1403 Rosecrans St., 92106,* ☎ *619/225–9461,* FAX *619/225–1163. 86 rooms. Bar, breakfast room, pool, free parking. AE, D, DC, MC, V.*

$ 🖭 **Travelodge Point Loma.** For far less money, you'll get the same view
here as at the higher-priced hotels. Of course, there are fewer amenities and the neighborhood (near the navy base) isn't as serene, but the
rooms—all with coffeemakers—are adequate and clean. ⊠ *5102 N.
Harbor Dr., 92106,* ☎ *619/223–8171 or 800/578–7878 for central
reservations,* FAX *619/222–7330. 45 rooms. Pool, free parking. AE, D,
DC, MC, V.*

Hotel Circle, Mission Valley, and Old Town

Lining both sides of the stretch of I–8 that lies between Old Town and
Mission Valley are a number of moderately priced accommodations
that constitute the so-called Hotel Circle. A car is an absolute necessity here. Although not particularly scenic, this location is convenient
to Balboa Park, the zoo, downtown, the beaches, the shops of Mission Valley, and Old Town. Mission Valley hotels, near movie theaters
and restaurants as well as shops, are more upscale than those of Hotel
Circle but generally less expensive than comparable properties at the
beaches. Old Town itself has a few picturesque lodgings and some mod-
estly priced chain hotels near I–5; when you're making reservations,
request a room that doesn't face the freeway.

$$$–$$$$ 🖭 **Doubletree Hotel San Mission Valley.** Across from Fashion Valley
Mall and adjacent to the Hazard Center, the Doubletree is also con-
venient to Highway 163. Public areas are light-filled and comfortable,
well suited to this hotel's large business clientele. Spacious rooms dec-
orated in contemporary pastels have ample desk space and built-in
modem hook-ups on every phone; complimentary coffee, irons, and
ironing boards are also provided. ⊠ *7450 Hazard Center Dr., 92108,*
☎ *619/297–5466 or 800/547–8010 for central reservations,* FAX *619/
297–5499. 294 rooms, 6 suites. Restaurant, 2 bars, in-room modem
lines, room service, 2 pools, outdoor hot tub, sauna, 2 tennis courts,
shops, nightclub, business services, convention center, airport shuttle,
free parking. AE, D, DC, MC, V.*

$$$–$$$$ 🖭 **San Diego Marriott Mission Valley.** This high-rise sits in the middle
★   of the San Diego River valley near San Diego Jack Murphy Stadium
and the Rio Vista Plaza shopping center and minutes from the Mis-
sion Valley and Fashion Valley malls. The hotel is well equipped for
business travelers—the front desk provides 24-hour fax and photocopy
services, and rooms come with desks, computer modem hook-ups, and
private voice mail—but the Marriott also caters to vacationers with
comfortable rooms (with individual balconies), a friendly staff, and free
transportation to the malls. ⊠ *8757 Rio San Diego Dr., 92108,* ☎ *619/
692–3800 or 800/228–9290 for central reservations,* FAX *619/692–0769.
347 rooms, 6 suites. Restaurant, sports bar, in-room modem lines, room
service, pool, outdoor hot tub, sauna, tennis court, exercise room, coin
laundry, business services, free parking. AE, D, DC, MC, V.*

$$$–$$$$ 🖭 **San Diego Mission Valley Hilton.** Directly fronting I–8, this prop-
erty has soundproof rooms decorated in a colorful contemporary style.
The stylish public areas and lush greenery in the back will make you
forget this hotel's proximity to the freeway. Although geared toward
business travelers—the hotel has a business center and guests are al-
lowed complimentary use of an IBM personal computer—children
stay free, and small pets are accepted ($25). ⊠ *901 Camino del Rio
S, 92108,* ☎ *619/543–9000, 800/733–2332, or 800/445–8667;* FAX
*619/543–9358. 342 rooms, 8 suites. Restaurant, bar, sports bar, in-
room modem lines, pool, outdoor hot tub, exercise room, free park-
ing. AE, D, DC, MC, V.*

$$–$$$$ ⊠ **Heritage Park Bed & Breakfast Inn.** The beautifully restored man-
★   sions in Old Town's Heritage Park include this romantic 1889 Queen
Anne. Rooms range from smallish to ample, and most are bright and
cheery. A two-bedroom suite is decorated with period antiques. Break-
fast and afternoon tea are included in the room rate. ⊠ *2470 Heritage
Park Row, 92110,* ☎ *619/299–6832 or 800/995–2470,* FAX *619/299–
9465. 10 rooms, 1 suite. In-room modem lines. AE, MC, V.*

$$–$$$ ⊡ **Best Western Hacienda Hotel Old Town.** Pretty and white, with bal-
conies and Spanish-tile roofs, the Hacienda is in a quiet part of Old
Town, away from the freeway and the main retail bustle. The layout
is somewhat confusing, and accommodations are not large enough to
earn the "suite" label the hotel gives them, but they're decorated in
tasteful southwestern style and equipped with microwaves, coffeemakers,
mini-refrigerators, clock radios, and VCRs. ⊠ *4041 Harney St., 92110,*
☎ *619/298–4707 or 800/888–1991,* FAX *619/298–4771. 159 rooms.
Restaurant, bar, pool, outdoor hot tub, exercise room, concierge, free
parking. AE, D, DC, MC, V.*

$$–$$$ ⊡ **Best Western Hanalei Hotel.** As its name suggests, the theme of this
friendly Hotel Circle property is Hawaiian: Palm trees, waterfalls, koi
ponds, and tiki torches abound. Rooms are decorated in tropical
prints. What used to be a golf course next door has been restored to
a bird sanctuary. Free transportation is provided to local malls and Old
Town. The hotel is virtually surrounded by heavy traffic, which can
make for a noisy stay. ⊠ *2270 Hotel Circle N, 92108,* ☎ *619/297–
1101 or 800/882–0858,* FAX *619/297–6049. 416 rooms. 2 restaurants,
bar, in-room modem lines, pool, hot tub, free parking. AE, D, DC, MC,
V.*

$$–$$$ ⊡ **Ramada Plaza Hotel Old Town.** The hacienda-style Ramada has Span-
ish colonial–style fountains, courtyards, and painted tiles, and south-
western decor in the rooms. Breakfast, cocktail reception, and transfers
to the airport, bus, and Amtrak are all complimentary. Business-class
rooms have modem lines and other amenities. ⊠ *2435 Jefferson St.,
92110,* ☎ *619/260–8500 or 800/272–6232 for central reservations,*
FAX *619/297–2078. 152 rooms. Restaurant, pool, outdoor hot tub, ex-
ercise room, airport and Amtrak shuttle, free parking. AE, D, DC, MC,
V.*

$–$$ ⊡ **Days Inn Hotel Circle.** Rooms in this large complex are par for a chain
motel but have the bonus of Nintendo for the kids and irons and
boards; some units also have kitchenettes. Airport, Amtrak, zoo, and
Sea World shuttles are provided. ⊠ *543 Hotel Circle S, 92108,* ☎ *619/
297–8800, 800/227–4743 on weekdays 8–4:30, 800/325–2525 for
central reservations;* FAX *619/298–6029. 280 rooms. Restaurant, refrigerators, pool, hot tub, barbershop, beauty salon, coin laundry, airport and Amtrak shuttle, free parking. AE, D, DC, MC, V.*

$–$$ ⊡ **Vacation Inn.** Already an excellent value for Old Town, this cheer-
★   ful property further pleases its guests by throwing in such perks as garage
parking, Continental breakfast, and afternoon snacks. You'll find all
of today's conveniences—coffeemakers, microwave ovens, and refrigerators—but rustic colors and reproduction furnishings lend rooms an
old-country-inn feel. Families and tourists will appreciate the proximity
to Old Town attractions and restaurants, along with the heated pool
off the shaded courtyard. ⊠ *3900 Old Town Ave.,* ☎ *619/299–7400
or 800/451–9846,* FAX *619/299–1619. 125 rooms. In-room modem lines,
refrigerators, pool, outdoor hot tub, coin laundry, business services,
meeting rooms, airport shuttle, free parking. AE, D, DC, MC, V.*

La Jolla

Million-dollar homes line the beaches and hillsides of La Jolla, one of the world's most beautiful, prestigious communities. The village—the heart of La Jolla—is chockablock with expensive boutiques, galleries, and restaurants. Don't despair, however, if you're not old money or even nouveau riche; this popular vacation spot has sufficient lodging choices for every pocket.

$$$$ ⊡ **Sheraton Grande Torrey Pines.** The low-rise, high-class Sheraton
★   Grande blends discreetly into the Torrey Pines clifftop, looking almost insignificant until you step inside the luxurious lobby and gaze through native and subtropical foliage at the Pacific Ocean and the 18th hole of the Torrey Pines golf course. Amenities include complimentary butler service and free town-car service to La Jolla and Del Mar. The oversize accommodations are simple but elegant; most have balconies or terraces. In addition to easy access to the Torrey Pines course, guests also have privileges ($7.50) next door at the fine health club–sports center at the Scripps Clinic. The fare at the hotel's spiffy-chic Torreyana Grille changes with seasons. Caesar salad and filet mignon are menu stalwarts, but you're likely to find lobster pot stickers and coffee-lacquered duck breast as well. The well-selected wine list showcases California vintages. ⊠ *10950 N. Torrey Pines Rd., 92037,* ☎ *619/ 558–1500 or 800/325–3535 for central reservations,* FAX *619/450–4584. 392 rooms, 17 suites. Restaurant, 2 bars, in-room modem lines, in-room safes, minibars, room service, pool, outdoor hot tub, sauna, 2 tennis courts, exercise room, putting green, aerobics, croquet, volleyball, bicycles, concierge, business services, meeting rooms, parking (fee). AE, D, DC, MC, V.*

$$$–$$$$ ⊡ **Hyatt Regency La Jolla.** The Hyatt is in La Jolla's Golden Triangle,
★   about 10 minutes from the beach and the village. The postmodern design elements of architect Michael Graves's striking lobby continue in the spacious rooms, where warm cherry-wood furnishings contrast with austere grey closets. Fluffy down comforters and cushy chairs and couches make you feel right at home, though, and business travelers will appreciate the endless array of office and in-room services. The hotel's four trendy restaurants include Cafe Japengo (☞ Pacific Rim *in* Chapter 4). Rates are lower here on weekends. ⊠ *Aventine Center, 3777 La Jolla Village Dr., 92122,* ☎ *619/552–1234 or 800/233–1234 for central reservations,* FAX *619/552–6066. 400 rooms, 25 suites. 4 restaurants, bar, pool, outdoor hot tub, beauty salon, massage, 2 tennis courts, aerobics, basketball, health club, jogging, business services, meeting rooms, parking (fee). AE, D, DC, MC, V.*

$$$–$$$$ ⊡ **La Valencia.** This pink Spanish-Mediterranean confection drew film
★   stars down from Hollywood in the 1930s and '40s for its setting and views of La Jolla Cove. Many rooms have a genteel European look, with antique pieces and richly colored rugs. The personal attention provided by the staff, as well as in-room features such as plush robes and grand bathrooms, make the stay even more pleasurable. The hotel is near the shops and restaurants of La Jolla Village and what is arguably the prettiest beach in San Diego. Rates are lower if you're willing to look out on the village. Be sure to take a stroll around the back tiered gardens. ⊠ *1132 Prospect St., 92037,* ☎ *619/454–0771 or 800/451– 0772,* FAX *619/456–3921. 100 rooms. 3 restaurants, bar, pool, outdoor hot tub, health club, shuffleboard, business services, meeting rooms, parking (fee). AE, D, DC, MC, V.*

$$$–$$$$ ⊡ **Scripps Inn.** You'd be wise to make reservations well in advance for this small, quiet inn tucked away on Coast Boulevard; its popularity with repeat visitors ensures that it is booked year-round. Kitchen fa-

cilities and lower weekly and monthly rates (not available in summer) make it attractive to long-term guests. All accommodations have ocean views and minirefrigerators, and two have fireplaces. Continental breakfast (included in the room rate) is served in the lobby each morning. ⊠ *555 S. Coast Blvd.,* ☎ *619/454–3391,* ℻ *619/456–0389. 13 rooms. AE, D, MC, V.*

$$$–$$$$ ⌨ **Sea Lodge.** Palm trees, fountains, red-tile roofs, and Mexican tile work lend a Spanish flavor to this low-lying compound on La Jolla Shores beach. Rooms, a few with kitchenettes, have rattan furniture and floral-print bedspreads; all have hair dryers, coffeemakers, and irons as well as wooden balconies that overlook lush landscaping and the sea. ⊠ *8110 Camino del Oro, 92037,* ☎ *619/459–8271 or 800/237–5211,* ℻ *619/456–9346. 128 rooms. Restaurant, bar, in-room modem lines, room service, pool, outdoor hot tub, sauna, 2 tennis courts, exercise room, Ping-Pong, beach, coin laundry, business services, meeting rooms, free parking. AE, D, DC, MC, V.*

$$–$$$$ ⌨ **Bed & Breakfast Inn at La Jolla.** Noted architect Irving Gill designed this B&B in a quiet section of La Jolla across the street from the Museum of Contemporary Art and one block from the beach. Rooms are of various sizes and styles—some are done in Laura Ashley prints, others have wicker or rattan furnishings—but all are pretty. Nice touches include complimentary full breakfast and fresh fruit, sherry, and terry robes. The gardens in the back were planned by Kate Sessions, who was instrumental in landscaping Balboa Park. ⊠ *7753 Draper Ave., 92037,* ☎ *619/456–2066 or 800/582–2466,* ℻ *619/456–1510. 16 rooms, 15 with bath. MC, V.*

$$–$$$$ ⌨ **Colonial Inn.** A tastefully restored Victorian-era building, this is the oldest hotel in La Jolla. In keeping with the period, rooms are formal (some could use new carpets and furniture coverings). Ocean views cost more than village views. The inn is on one of La Jolla's main thoroughfares, near boutiques, restaurants, and La Jolla Cove. ⊠ *910 Prospect St., 92037,* ☎ *619/454–2181 or 800/832–5525, 800/826–1278 in CA,* ℻ *619/454–5679. 74 rooms. Restaurant, bar, refrigerators, pool, business services, meeting rooms, parking (fee). AE, DC, MC, V.*

$$–$$$$ ⌨ **La Jolla Cove Suites.** It may lack the charm of some of the older properties of this exclusive area, but this motel with studios and suites (some with spacious oceanfront balconies) gives its guests the same first-class views of La Jolla Cove at much lower rates. Snorkelers and divers can take advantage of lockers and outdoor showers. A Continental breakfast is served in the sunroom. The free underground lot is also a bonus in a section of town where a parking spot is a prime commodity. ⊠ *1155 S. Coast Blvd., 92037,* ☎ *619/459–2621 or 800/248–2683,* ℻ *619/454–3522. 96 rooms. Kitchenettes, pool, hot tub, putting green, coin laundry, business services, meeting rooms, free parking. AE, D, DC, MC, V.*

$$–$$$$ ⌨ **Prospect Park Inn.** One block from the beach and near some of the
★ best shops and restaurants, this European-style inn with a delightful staff sits in a prime spot in La Jolla Village. Many rooms (some with kitchenettes) have sweeping ocean views from their balconies; one spectacular penthouse suite faces the ocean, another the village. An upstairs sundeck with fantastic views is a great spot to enjoy the delicious Continental breakfast (included in the room rates). There is no smoking on the premises. ⊠ *1110 Prospect St., 92037,* ☎ *619/454–0133 or 800/433–1609,* ℻ *619/454–2056. 20 rooms, 2 suites. In-room modem lines, library, business services, free parking. AE, D, DC, MC, V.*

$$–$$$ ☷ **Best Western Inn by the Sea.** In a quiet section of La Jolla Village, within five blocks of the beach, the five-story Inn by the Sea has all the modern amenities at reasonable rates for La Jolla. Rooms are done in pastel tones and have private balconies with views of either the sea or the village. Continental breakfast, the morning newspaper, and La Jolla phone calls are on the house. ⊠ *7830 Fay Ave., 92037,* ☎ *619/ 459–4461 or 800/462–9732, 800/526–4545 in CA and Canada,* FAX *619/456–2578. 150 rooms. In-room modem lines, pool, outdoor hot tub, coin laundry, business services, meeting rooms, free parking. AE, D, DC, MC, V.*

$$ ☷ **Holiday Inn Express.** Many rooms at this modest property in the southern section of La Jolla are remarkably large, with huge closets; some have kitchenettes, and three suites have separate eat-in kitchens. The decor is nothing to write home about, but this is a good value for families who want to stay in La Jolla and still have a few dollars left over for shopping and dining. Complimentary Continental breakfast is included in the room rates. ⊠ *6705 La Jolla Blvd., 92037,* ☎ *619/ 454–7101 or 800/451–0358,* FAX *619/454–6957. 58 rooms, 3 suites. Pool, outdoor hot tub, billiards, coin laundry, free parking. AE, D, DC, MC, V.*

$$ ☷ **Lodge at Torrey Pines.** On a bluff between La Jolla and Del Mar,
★ the lodge commands a view of miles and miles of coastline. The public Torrey Pines Golf Course is adjacent, and scenic Torrey Pines State Beach and nature reserve are close by; the village of La Jolla is a 10-minute drive away. Most rooms have dark wood furnishings and contemporary fabrics. One drawback: the building is old; walls between units are thin, and the plumbing can be noisy. Still, the service here is excellent and the lodge is a good value, especially for golfers. ⊠ *11480 N. Torrey Pines Rd., 92037,* ☎ *619/453–4420 or 800/995–4507,* FAX *619/453–0691. 74 rooms. 2 restaurants, bar, coffee shop, lobby lounge, pool, golf privileges, free parking. AE, D, DC, MC, V.*

Mission Bay and the Beaches

Mission Bay Park, with its beaches, bike trails, boat-launching ramps, golf course, and grassy parks, is a hotel haven. Mission and Pacific beaches have many small hotels and motels. The coastal areas have a casual atmosphere and a busy thoroughfare that provides endless shopping, dining, and nightlife possibilities. You can't go wrong with any of these locations, as long as the frenzy of hundreds at play doesn't bother you.

$$$–$$$$ ☷ **Catamaran Resort Hotel.** Resident birds are often poised on a perch
★ in the lush lobby of this appealing hotel, set between Mission Bay and Pacific Beach. The grounds are similarly tropical, and tiki torches light the way for guests staying at one of the six two-story buildings or the 14-story high-rise. The room decor—dark wicker furniture and tropical prints—echoes the Polynesian theme. The popular Cannibal Bar hosts rock bands; a classical or jazz pianist tickles the ivories at the Moray Bar. Though the Catamaran is couples-oriented, children 18 or under stay free. ⊠ *3999 Mission Blvd., 92109,* ☎ *619/488–1081 or 800/288–0770, 800/233–8172 in Canada,* FAX *619/488–1387 for reservations, 619/488–1619 for front desk. 320 rooms. Restaurant, bar, piano bar, pool, hot tub, exercise room, nightclub, bicycles, parking (fee). AE, D, DC, MC, V.*

$$$–$$$$ ☷ **Crystal Pier Motel.** A landmark since the 1930s, this place is no longer the bargain it once was, nor does it have the amenities of the other properties in its price category. You're paying for character and proximity to the ocean—the blue-and-white cottages here are literally on the pier.

The units sleep four but cost the same no matter what the occupancy. Call four to six weeks in advance for reservations. The minimum stay permitted is three nights from mid-June through mid-September, two nights the rest of the year. ✉ *4500 Ocean Blvd.,* ☎ *619/483–6983 or 800/748–5894,* ℻ *619/483–6811. 29 cottages. Kitchenettes, free parking. D, MC, V.*

$$$–$$$$ 🏨 **San Diego Hilton Beach and Tennis Resort.** Trees, Japanese bridges, and ponds surround the bungalow accommodations at this deluxe resort; rooms and suites in a high-rise building have views of Mission Bay Park. Most of the well-appointed rooms have wet bars, spacious bathrooms, and patios or terraces. There's complimentary day care for children over age five (daily during the summer, on weekends the rest of the year), and the sports facilities are excellent. Aquatic sports equipment is available for rent at the nearby marina. ✉ *1775 E. Mission Bay Dr., 92109,* ☎ *619/276–4010 or 800/445–8667 for central reservations,* ℻ *619/275–7991. 337 rooms, 20 suites. 2 restaurants, bar, coffee shop, in-room modem lines, pool, wading pool, 2 hot tubs, 4 putting greens, 5 tennis courts, exercise room, boating, bicycles, playground, car rental, free parking. AE, D, DC, MC, V.*

$$$–$$$$ 🏨 **San Diego Princess Resort.** This 44-acre resort is so beautifully landscaped that it's been the setting for a number of movies, and it provides a wide range of recreational activities as well as access to a marina. Bright fabrics and plush carpets make for a cheery ambience; unfortunately, the walls here are motel-thin. All rooms have private patios and coffeemakers, and a number have kitchens. Of the resort's various eateries, the Barefoot Bar and Grill is the most fun; guests and visitors come here to kick off their shoes and boogie in a sand-filled, strobe-lit setting. ✉ *1404 W. Vacation Rd., 92109,* ☎ *619/274–4630 or 800/344–2626,* ℻ *619/581–5929. 462 cottages. 3 restaurants, 2 bars, room service, 5 pools, outdoor hot tub, sauna, 19-hole putting golf course, 6 tennis courts, croquet, health club, jogging, volleyball, boating, bicycles, free parking. AE, D, DC, MC, V.*

$$$ 🏨 **Bahia Hotel.** This huge complex on a 14-acre peninsula in Mission Bay Park has furnished studios and suites with kitchens; many have wood-beam ceilings and tropical decor. The hotel's *Bahia Belle* cruises Mission Bay at sunset, and guests can return for yuks at the on-premises Comedy Isle club. Rates are reasonable for a place so well located—within walking distance of the ocean—and with so many amenities, including use of the facilities at the Catamaran Hotel. ✉ *998 W. Mission Bay Dr., 92109,* ☎ *619/488–0551 or 800/288–0770, 800/233–8172 in Canada,* ℻ *619/488–7055 or 619/488–1387 for reservations. 321 rooms. Restaurant, bar, piano bar, pool, outdoor hot tub, 2 tennis courts, bicycles, rollerblading, free parking. AE, D, DC, MC, V.*

$$$ 🏨 **Best Western Blue Sea Lodge.** Many of the rooms at this Pacific Beach low-rise have balconies and ocean views; some have kitchenettes. A shopping center with restaurants and boutiques is nearby. ✉ *707 Pacific Beach Dr., 92109,* ☎ *619/488–4700 or 800/258–3732,* ℻ *619/488–7276. 100 rooms. In-room safes, pool, hot tub. AE, D, DC, MC, V.*

$$$ 🏨 **Hyatt Islandia.** Its location in appealing Mission Bay Park is one of the many pluses of this property, which has rooms in several low-level lanai-style units, as well as marina suites and rooms in a high-rise building. Many of the modern accommodations overlook the hotel's gardens and koi fish pond; others have dramatic views of the bay area. This hotel is famous for its lavish Sunday champagne brunch. In winter, whale-watching expeditions depart from the Islandia's marina. ✉ *1441 Quivira Rd., 92109,* ☎ *619/224–1234 or 800/233–1234 for central reservations,* ℻ *619/224–0348. 346 rooms, 76 suites. 2 restau-*

rants, in-room modem lines, pool, outdoor hot tub, exercise room, marina, boating, laundry service, meeting rooms, free parking. AE, D, DC, MC, V.

$$–$$$ ⊡ **Dana Inn & Marina.** This hotel with an adjoining marina is a bargain. Recent renovations have improved the rooms with bright pastels, and the new lobby includes a fun aquarium. High ceilings in the second-floor rooms give a welcome sense of space, and some even have a view of the inn's marina. Many sports facilities are on the premises, and Sea World and the beach are within walking distance. ⊠ *1710 W. Mission Bay Dr., 92109,* ☎ *619/222–6440 or 800/445–3339,* FAX *619/222–5916. 196 rooms. Restaurant, bar, room service, pool, outdoor hot tub, 2 tennis courts, Ping-Pong, shuffleboard, boating, bicycles, coin laundry, business services, free parking. AE, D, DC, MC, V.*

$$ ⊡ **Pacific Shores Inn.** One of the better motels in the Mission Bay area, this property is less than a half-block from the beach. Rooms, some of them spacious, are decorated in a simple contemporary style. Kitchen units with multiple beds are available at reasonable rates; your pet (under 20 lbs.) can stay for an extra $25. Continental breakfast is included in the room rate, and all rooms have minirefrigerators. ⊠ *4802 Mission Blvd., 92109,* ☎ *619/483–6300 or 800/826–0715,* FAX *619/483–9276. 55 rooms. Refrigerators, pool, coin laundry, free parking. AE, D, DC, MC, V.*

$–$$ ⊡ **Mission Bay Motel.** A half block from the beach and right on the local main street, this motel has modest units, some with kitchenettes. Great restaurants and nightlife are within walking distance, but you may find the area a bit noisy. ⊠ *4221 Mission Blvd., 92109,* ☎ *619/483–6440. 50 rooms. Pool, free parking. D, MC, V.*

$–$$ ⊡ **Ocean Manor Apartment Hotel.** Some folks have been returning for years to this Sunset Cliffs hotel, which rents units by the day (three-day minimum for ones with kitchens), week, or month in winter; you'll need to reserve well in advance. Though the beach below has long since washed away, other beaches are within walking distance. The comfortable studios and one- and two-bedroom suites are furnished plainly in the style of the 1950s—which is when the amiable owners took over the place. There is no maid service, but fresh towels are always provided. ⊠ *1370 Sunset Cliffs Blvd., 92107,* ☎ *619/222–7901 or 619/224–1379 for guest calls. 25 units. Pool, Ping-Pong, shuffleboard, free parking. MC, V.*

Hostels

Banana Bungalow San Diego (⊠ 707 Reed Ave., Mission Beach 92109, ☎ 619/273–3060 or 800/546–7835).

HI–The Metropolitan Hostel–Downtown San Diego (⊠ 521 Market St., San Diego 92101, ☎ 619/525–1531 or 800/909–4776, code #43, FAX 619/338–0129).

HI–Point Loma Hostel (⊠ 3790 Udall St., San Diego 92107, ☎ 619/223–4778).

Grand Pacific Hostel (⊠ 437 J. St., 92101, ☎ 619/232–3100 or 800/438–8622).

Ocean Beach International Backpacker Hostel (⊠ 4961 Newport Ave., 92107, ☎ 619/223–7873 or 800/339–7263, FAX 619/223–7881).

6 Nightlife and the Arts

People come to San Diego for the sand and surf, but the fun in this coastal community doesn't end when the sun goes down. Musical hot spots span the spectrum from jazz to disco to garage-band grunge to country-western. Downtown, especially in and around the Gaslamp Quarter, bustles with cultural events—symphony, theater, opera. Baritones and ballads can also be heard from the pristine stages of La Jolla. Head to the beaches for a traditional So-Cal party scene.

NIGHTLIFE

By Dan Janeck

Updated by
Kate Deely

Music at local pop-music clubs ranges from easy-on-the-ears rock to alternative fare from San Diego's finest up-and-coming groups. Dance clubs and bars in the Gaslamp Quarter and at Pacific and Mission beaches tend to be the most crowded spots in the county on the weekends, but don't let that discourage you from visiting these quintessential San Diego hangouts. Authentic country-western music is also an option for those willing to go a bit farther afield. Should your tastes run to softer music, there are plenty of piano bars in which to unfrazzle and unwind. The coffeehouse culture here has become so lively that java joints, especially those along Hillcrest's Coffeehouse Row and scattered along the beach communities, have become legitimate nightlife destinations in themselves.

Check the free weekly *Reader* for band information or *San Diego* magazine's "Restaurant & Nightlife Guide" for the full slate of after-dark possibilities. Call the **SRH Info Hotline** (☎ 619/973–9269) to locate hip to downright bizarre one-night events.

California law prohibits the sale of alcoholic beverages after 2 AM; last call is usually at about 1:40. You must be 21 to purchase and consume alcohol, and most places will insist on current identification. Be aware that California also has some of the most stringent drunk-driving laws in the United States; roadblocks are not an uncommon sight.

Bars and Nightclubs

Aero Club (✉ 3365 India St., Middletown, ☎ 619/297–7211), named for its proximity to the airport, is practically a landmark in its Middletown neighborhood. The familiar crowd, friendly bartenders, and first-rate selection of beer have made this small, one-time dive thrive.

Bitter End (✉ 770 5th Ave., Gaslamp Quarter, ☎ 619/338–9300) is a sophisticated martini bar (above) and a hip dance club (below). With its variety of beverage, music, and atmosphere, this dual-level hot spot in the heart of downtown will please the most finicky of cosmopolitans.

Blue Tattoo (✉ 835 5th Ave., Gaslamp Quarter, ☎ 619/238–7191) is a popular destination for San Diego's young professionals, who often wait in long lines to get in. A strict dress code is enforced (no jeans, T-shirts, hats, sweat shirts, or tennis shoes) on Friday and Saturday nights. Entertainment varies nightly, and there is a nominal cover charge.

Cannibal Bar (✉ 3999 Mission Blvd., Pacific Beach, ☎ 619/488–1081) customers devour the oldies, contemporary jazz, blues, and swing music performed by local bands such as The Steely Damned. Because of its beach location, this tropical-theme nightclub in the Catamaran Resort Hotel attracts locals and visitors of all ages.

Club 66 (✉ 901 5th Ave., downtown, ☎ 619/234–4166), under the restaurant Dakota's, takes the old Route 66 as its inspiration, with stainless-steel decor and gas-station memorabilia. Dance to disco, high energy, and Top 40.

Daily Planet (✉ 1200 Garnet Ave., Pacific Beach, ☎ 619/272–6066), painted in neon purple, yellow, and green, is sure to catch your eye. The crowd is fun-loving and unpretentious.

E Street Alley (✉ 919 4th Ave., downtown, ☎ 619/231–9200), hardly for the Bruce Springsteen groupie, is a treat for the senses. The Blue

Room, with its scattered plush couches and pool tables, serves up live jazz on Thursday and blues the rest of the week. Club E is a smartly designed, spacious dance club with a DJ spinning Top 40 tunes. Chino's is an exquisite restaurant featuring American cuisine with a Southeast Asian flair. The club is on E Street between 4th and 5th avenues.

Hurricane's Bar and Grill (⌧ 315 Ocean Front Walk, Mission Beach, ☎ 619/488–1870) has taken Mission Beach by storm. Noise from the waterfront property carries all the way to the breaking waves as talented rock bands perform nightly for a lively crowd.

Jimmy Love's (⌧ 672 5th Ave., Gaslamp Quarter, ☎ 619/595–0123) combines a dance club, a sports bar, and a restaurant all into one venue. Rock and jazz bands alternate for nightly entertainment.

Karl Strauss' Old Columbia Brewery & Grill (⌧ 1157 Columbia St., downtown, ☎ 619/234–2739) was the first microbrewery in San Diego. It draws an after-work downtown crowd and later fills with beer connoisseurs from all walks of life.

Moose McGillycuddy's (⌧ 1165 Garnet Ave., Pacific Beach, ☎ 619/274–2323), a major pick-up palace, is also a great place to go with friends or hang out with the locals. Fun music powers the dance floor, and the staff serves up drinks and Mexican food.

O'Hungrys (⌧ 2547 San Diego Ave., Old Town, ☎ 619/298–0133) is famous for its yard-long beers and barwide sing-alongs. Be sure to drink up quickly though—this landmark saloon closes at midnight.

Pacific Beach Bar and Grill (⌧ 860 Garnet Ave., Pacific Beach, ☎ 619/272–4745) is just a stumbling block away from the beach. The popular nightspot has a huge outdoor patio so you can enjoy star-filled skies as you party with locals and visitors. There is plenty to see and do, from billiards and satellite sports to an interactive trivia game.

Coffeehouses

Like the rest of the country, San Diego has gotten into cafés and coffeehouses in a big way. If you're up for caffeine-hopping, the Hillcrest intersection of 5th and University avenues is abuzz with options—all of them grinding a variety of elixirs and proffering everything from full meals to light pastries. Most open their doors by 7 AM and continue serving until midnight or later. The crowds are diverse, ranging from lesbian and gay fashion plates to bookish college students to yuppies.

Brockton Villa (⌧ 1235 Coast Blvd., La Jolla, ☎ 619/454–7393), a palatial café overlooking La Jolla Cove, has indoor and outdoor seating, as well as scrumptious desserts and coffee drinks. It closes at 10 PM.

Café Crema (⌧ 1001 Garnet Ave., Pacific Beach, ☎ 619/273–3558) is a meeting spot for the pre- and post-bar crowd. It's easy to lose track of time here.

Euphoria (⌧ 1045 University Ave., Hillcrest, ☎ 619/295–1769) has a Gen-X feel and is a great place to meet friends before dinner or barhopping. For many people, it's an alternative to bars.

Gelato Vero (⌧ 3753 India St., Middletown, ☎ 619/295–9269) is where a predominately young crowd gathers for some fine desserts and a second-floor view of the downtown skyline. The place is usually occupied by regulars who stay for hours at a time.

Pannikin (⌧ 523 University Ave., ☎ 619/295–1600) is a bright coffeehouse which tends to draw folks who've been shopping at the several good Hillcrest bookstores. There are two rooms, one relatively sedate, the other more lively.

The Study (✉ 401-A University Ave., Hillcrest, ☎ 619/296–4847) attracts those who value seclusion—private conversation or study is made easier with the cubicle-like seating areas.

Twiggs Tea and Coffee Co. (✉ 4590 Park Blvd., University Heights, ☎ 619/296–0616), a peaceful neighborhood establishment, has outdoor seating. The adjacent green room hosts poetry readings and, on occasion, music.

Zanzibar Coffee Bar and Gallery (✉ 976 Garnet Ave., Pacific Beach, ☎ 619/272–4762), a cozy, dimly lit spot along Pacific Beach's main strip, is a great place to mellow out.

Comedy and Cabaret

Comedy Isle (✉ Bahia Hotel, 998 W. Mission Bay Dr., Mission Bay, ☎ 619/488–6872) serves up the latest laughs from local and national talent.

Comedy Store (✉ 916 Pearl St., La Jolla, ☎ 619/454–9176), just like its sister establishment in Hollywood, hosts some of the best national touring and local talent.

Tidbits (✉ 3838 5th Ave., Hillcrest, ☎ 619/543–0300) showcases the best of southern California's female impersonators in hilarious nightly cabaret and comedy "tidbits," with charity benefit shows on Sunday.

Country-Western

Big Stone Lodge (✉ 12237 Old Pomerado Rd., Poway, ☎ 760/748–1135), a former Pony Express station turned dance hall, showcases the two-steppin' tunes of the owners' band. If you don't know country-western dances, don't fret; free lessons are given some nights.

The Country Club (✉ 1121 3rd Ave., Chula Vista, ☎ 619/426–2977) presents live country bands on Wednesday, Friday, and Saturday; there are jam sessions Sunday.

In Cahootz (✉ 5373 Mission Center Rd., Mission Valley, ☎ 619/291–8635), with its great sound system, large dance floor, and occasional big-name performers, is the destination of choice for cowgirls and -boys and city slickers alike. Free dance lessons are given every day except Wednesday, when seasoned two-steppers strut their stuff. Happy hour seven days a week is one of this bar's many lures.

Leo's Little Bit O' Country (✉ 680 W. San Marcos Blvd., San Marcos, ☎ 760/744–4120), with one the largest country-western dance floors in the county, is another fun place to hoof it and take free dance lessons.

Magnolia Mulvaney's (✉ 8861 N. Magnolia Ave., Santee, ☎ 619/448–8550) serves as country-music headquarters for East County residents.

Zoo Country (✉ 1340 Broadway, El Cajon, ☎ 619/442–9900) attracts herds of line-dancin', two-steppin' cowpersons. There is live music Friday through Sunday and a DJ seven nights a week. Free dance lessons are given Friday, Saturday, and Sunday.

Dance Clubs

Club Emerald City (✉ 945 Garnet Ave., Pacific Beach, ☎ 619/483–9920) attracts an uninhibited clientele for loud alternative dance music.

This beach-town spot is unpredictable and worth a visit for the adventurous.

Green Circle Bar (✉ 827 F St., Gaslamp Quarter, ☎ 619/232–8080) is frequented by a mostly under-30 Euro-type crowd that grooves to anything from acid jazz to blues and soul. Live bands perform on Wednesday and Thursday nights.

Johnny M's (✉ 801 4th St., Gaslamp Quarter, ☎ 619/233–1131) patrons get down and boogie to '70s and '80s dance music at this huge disco. A blues room is open Wednesday, Friday, and Saturday from 10 PM to 1:30 AM.

Olé Madrid (✉ 755 5th Ave., Gaslamp Quarter, ☎ 619/557–0146) is not for the meek or mild. Leave the squares at street level and head straight to the basement for deep house grooves and tribal rhythms spun by celebrated DJs from near and far. Between songs, sip a tangy sangria.

Romperoom (✉ 505 Market St., Gaslamp Quarter, no phone), an alcohol-free Saturday-night-only club, lets night owls dance until dawn to house grooves and techno.

Taxxi (✉ 1025 Prospect St., La Jolla, ☎ 619/551–5230) is for serious nightclubbers. On the busy bar and restaurant strand in La Jolla, this dance club lures Hollywood club-types who dance to disco, funk, and house music.

Gay and Lesbian Nightlife

Gay Male Bars

Bourbon Street (✉ 4612 Park Blvd., University Heights, ☎ 619/291–0173), resembling its New Orleans' namesake with its relaxing surroundings and courtyard, is a piano bar with live entertainment nightly.

Brass Rail (✉ 3796 5th Ave., Hillcrest, ☎ 619/298–2233), a Hillcrest fixture since the early '60s, is the oldest gay bar in San Diego. The club hosts dancing nightly and go-go boys on the weekends.

Flicks (✉ 1017 University Ave., Hillcrest, ☎ 619/297–2056), one of few local video bars, plays music and comedy videos on four big screens. Drink specials and video formats vary each night.

Kickers (✉ 308 University Ave., Hillcrest, ☎ 619/491–0400) rounds up country-music cowboys to do the latest line dance. Free lessons are given weeknights from 7 to 8:30. If you're hungry after all that dancing, Hamburger Mary's on the premises serves until 11 PM on weekends.

Numbers (✉ 3811 Park Blvd., North Park, ☎ 619/294–9005) has a giant-screen video, six pool tables, darts, and daily drink specials.

Rich's San Diego (✉ 1051 University Ave., Hillcrest, ☎ 619/497–4588), a popular dance club, has nightly male revues. Thursday night's Club Hedonism spotlights groove house and tribal rhythms.

Wolf's (✉ 3404 30th St., North Park, ☎ 619/291–3730) is a Levi's-leather bar that's open late every night.

Lesbian Bars

Club Bombay (✉ 3175 India St., Middletown, ☎ 619/296–6789) occasionally has live entertainment and always attracts a dancing crowd. It also hosts Sunday barbecues.

The Flame (✉ 3780 Park Blvd., Hillcrest, ☎ 619/295–4163), a San Diego institution, is a friendly dance club that caters to lesbians most of the week. On Tuesday, the DJ spins for the popular Boys' Night.

Jazz

Croce's (✉ 802 5th Ave., Gaslamp Quarter, ☎ 619/233–4355), the intimate jazz cave of restaurateur Ingrid Croce (singer-songwriter Jim Croce's widow), books superb acoustic-jazz musicians. Next door, Croce's Top Hat puts on live R&B nightly from 9 until 2. Musician A.J. Croce, son of Jim and Ingrid, often headlines at both clubs.

Elario's (✉ 7955 La Jolla Shores Dr., La Jolla, ☎ 619/459–0541), perched on the top floor of the Summer House Inn, delivers an ocean view and a lineup of internationally acclaimed jazz musicians.

Humphrey's by the Bay (✉ 2241 Shelter Island Dr., Shelter Island, ☎ 619/523–1010 for concert information), surrounded by water, is the summer stomping grounds for musical legends such as Harry Belafonte and Three Dog Night. From June to September, this dining and drinking oasis hosts the city's best outdoor jazz, folk, and light-rock concert series. The rest of the year the music moves indoors to Humphrey's Lounge for some first-rate jazz most Sunday, Monday, and Tuesday nights, with piano-bar and other music on other nights.

Pal Joey's (✉ 5147 Waring Rd., Allied Gardens, near San Diego State University, ☎ 619/286–7873) is a smoky neighborhood bar with a loyal clientele that enjoys dancing Friday and Saturday nights to authentic jazz and blues with a lot of soul.

Piano Bars/Mellow

Hotel Del Coronado (✉ 1500 Orange Ave., Coronado, ☎ 619/435–6611), the famous fairy-tale hostelry, has piano music in its Crown Room and Palm Court. The Ocean Terrace Lounge has live bands nightly from 9 PM to 1 AM.

Top O' the Cove (✉ 1216 Prospect St., La Jolla, ☎ 619/454–7779) pianists play show tunes and standards from the '40s to the '80s at this magnificent Continental restaurant.

Westgate Hotel (✉ 1055 2nd Ave., downtown, ☎ 619/238–1818), one of the most elegant settings in San Diego, has piano music in the Plaza Bar.

Rock, Pop, Folk, Reggae, and Blues

Belly Up Tavern (✉ 143 S. Cedros Ave., Solana Beach, ☎ 760/481–9022), an eclectic live-concert venue located in converted Quonset huts, hosts critically acclaimed artists who play everything from reggae, rock, new wave, Motown, and folk to—well, you name it. Always a fun choice, the Belly Up attracts people of all ages. Sunday nights are usually free and spotlight local R&B artists.

Blind Melons (✉ 710 Garnet Ave., Pacific Beach, ☎ 619/483–7844) is frequented by the local beach and college crowd. This bustling bar features rock, blues, and reggae bands every night of the week.

Bodie's (✉ 528 F St., Gaslamp Quarter, ☎ 619/236–8988) presents the best rock and blues bands in San Diego, as well as up-and-coming bands from out of town.

Brick by Brick (✉ 1130 Buenos Ave., Bay Park, near Mission Bay, ☎ 619/275–5483) is always abuzz with the music of San Diego's top alternative and experimental rock groups.

Casbah (✉ 2501 Kettner Blvd., near the airport, ☎ 619/232–4355), a small club, showcases rock, reggae, funk, and every other kind of band—except Top 40.

Livewire (✉ 2103 El Cajon Blvd., North Park, ☎ 619/291–7450), an underground twenty-something hole-in-the-wall, has plenty of character; there are usually more tattoos and pierced body parts than people.

Patrick's II (✉ 428 F St., downtown, ☎ 619/233–3077) serves up live New Orleans–style jazz, blues, and rock in an Irish setting.

Therapy at Ministry (✉ 3595 Sports Arena Blvd., directly across from the Sports Arena, ☎ 619/223–5598), presented every Friday night, is one of the few Industrial Gothic regular-basis "happenings." You'll enjoy yourself immensely if you're into serious industrial music and like hanging out with "vampires" and alternative types.

Winston's Beach Club (✉ 1921 Bacon St., Ocean Beach, ☎ 619/222–6822), a bowling alley turned rock club, hosts local bands, reggae groups, and occasionally '60s rockers bands. The crowd, mostly locals, can get rowdy.

Singles Bars

Barefoot Bar and Grill (✉ San Diego Princess Resort, 1404 W. Vacation Rd., ☎ 619/274–4630), a beachfront bar, attracts flocks of singles, especially on spring and summer Sunday nights. Live music and happy-hour specials fill the joint up early, making for long latecomer lines.

Dick's Last Resort (✉ 345 4th Ave., downtown, ☎ 619/231–9100) is not for Emily Post adherents. The surly waitstaff and abrasive service are part of the gimmick. The rudeness notwithstanding, fun-loving party people pile into this barnlike restaurant and bar. Dick's has live music and one of the most extensive beer lists in San Diego.

Jose's (✉ 1037 Prospect St., La Jolla, ☎ 619/454–7655) is a hit with yuppies from La Jolla and other neighboring beach communities. This small but clean hole-in-the-wall's lack of space gives suave singles an excuse to get up close and personal.

Old Bonita Store & Bonita Beach Club (✉ 4014 Bonita Rd., Bonita, ☎ 619/479–3537), a South Bay hangout, has a DJ spinning retro house music.

U. S. Grant Hotel (✉ 326 Broadway, downtown, ☎ 619/232–3121) is the classiest spot in town for meeting fellow travelers while relaxing with a Scotch or a martini at the mahogany bar. The best local Latin, jazz, and blues bands alternate appearances. It's definitely for the over-30 business set.

THE ARTS

National touring companies perform regularly at the Civic Theatre and Golden Hall, and in Escondido at the California Center for the Arts. Programs at San Diego State University, the University of California at San Diego, private universities, and community colleges host a range of artists, from well-known professionals to students. The daily *San Diego Union-Tribune* lists current attractions and complete movie schedules. The weekly *Reader* devotes an entire section to upcoming cultural events. *San Diego* magazine publishes monthly listings and reviews. Those "in the know" rely on San Diego's many community micromags found in most coffeehouses in La Jolla, Pacific Beach, downtown, and Hillcrest.

It is best to book tickets well in advance, preferably at the same time you make hotel reservations. Outlets exist for last-minute tickets, though you risk either paying top rates or getting less-than-choice seats—or both.

Half-price tickets to most theater, music, and dance events can be bought on the day of performance at the **Times Arts Tix** (✉ Horton Plaza, ☎ 619/497–5000). Only cash is accepted. Advance full-price tickets may also be purchased through Times Arts Tix.

Visa and MasterCard holders may buy tickets for many scheduled performances through **TicketMaster** (☎ 619/220–8497). Service charges vary according to the event, and most tickets are nonrefundable.

Dance

California Ballet Company (☎ 619/560–5676 or 619/560–6741) performs high-quality contemporary and traditional works, from story ballets to Balanchine, September to May. The *Nutcracker* is staged annually at the Civic Theatre (✉ 202 C St., downtown); other ballets are presented at the Lyceum (✉ 79 Horton Plaza), the Poway Center for the Performing Arts (✉ 15500 Espola Rd., Poway), and other locations.

Issacs, McCaleb & Dancers (☎ 619/296–9523) stages interpretative dance presentations, incorporating live music, at major theaters and concert halls around San Diego County.

Film

Science, space-documentary, observation-of-motion, and sometimes psychedelic films are shown on the Omnimax screen at the **Reuben H. Fleet Space Theater** (✉ Balboa Park, 1875 El Prado, ☎ 619/238–1233).

Landmark Theatres, known for first-run foreign, art, American independent, and documentary offerings, operates five theaters in the San Diego area: the **Cove** (✉ 7730 Girard Ave., La Jolla, ☎ 619/459–5404); the **Guild Theatre** (✉ 3827 5th Ave., Hillcrest, ☎ 619/295–2000); the **Hillcrest Cinemas** (✉ 3965 5th Ave., ☎ 619/299–2100), a posh new multiplex; the **Ken Cinema** (✉ 4061 Adams Ave., ☎ 619/283–5909), which plays a roster of art/revival films that changes almost every night (many programs are double bills), along with *The Rocky Horror Picture Show* every Saturday at midnight; and the **Park** (✉ 3812 Park Blvd., Hillcrest, ☎ 619/294–9264).

Sherwood Auditorium (✉ 700 Prospect St., La Jolla, ☎ 619/454–2594) regularly hosts foreign and classic film series and special cinema events, including the wildly popular Festival of Animation, January to March.

Music

La Jolla Chamber Music Society (☎ 619/459–3724) presents internationally acclaimed chamber ensembles, orchestras, and soloists at Sherwood Auditorium (☞ *below*) and the Civic Theatre.

Open-Air Theatre (✉ San Diego State University, ☎ 619/594–6947) presents top-name rock, reggae, and popular artists in summer concerts under the stars.

San Diego Chamber Orchestra (☎ 760/753–6402), a 35-member ensemble, performs once a month October through April.

San Diego Opera (✉ Civic Theatre, 202 C St., downtown, ☎ 619/232–7636 or 619/236–6510) draws international artists. Its season of five operas runs January–April in the 3,000-seat Civic Theatre.

San Diego Sports Arena (✉ 3500 Sports Arena Blvd., ☎ 619/224–4176) holds 14,000-plus fans for big-name rock concerts.

San Diego State University School of Music and Dance (✉ SDSU, various venues, 5500 Campanile Dr., ☎ 619/594–6884) presents concerts in many genres, including jazz, classical, and world music.

Sherwood Auditorium (✉ 700 Prospect St., La Jolla, ☎ 619/454–2594), a 550-seat venue in the Museum of Contemporary Art, hosts classical and jazz events.

Spreckels Organ Pavilion (✉ Balboa Park, ☎ 619/226–0819) holds a giant outdoor pipe organ dedicated in 1915 by sugar magnate Adolph Spreckels. Robert Plimpton performs at 2 on most Sunday afternoons and on most Monday evenings in summer. On summer evenings, local military bands, gospel groups, and barbershop quartets also perform here.

Spreckels Theatre (✉ 121 Broadway, ☎ 619/235–9500), a designated-landmark theater erected more than 80 years ago, hosts musical events—everything from Mostly Mozart to small rock concerts. Ballets and theatrical productions are also held here. Its good acoustics and historical status make this an appealing site.

Theater

California Center for the Arts (✉ 340 N. Escondido, ☎ 760/738–4100) presents mainstream theatrical productions such as *Grease* and *The Odd Couple.*

Coronado Playhouse (✉ 1775 Strand Way, Coronado, ☎ 619/435–4856), a cabaret-type theater near the Hotel Del Coronado, stages regular dramatic and musical performances. Friday and Saturday dinner packages are available.

Diversionary Theatre (✉ 4545 Park Blvd., University Heights, ☎ 619/220–0097) is San Diego's premier gay and lesbian company.

Gaslamp Quarter Theatre Company (✉ Hahn Cosmopolitan Theatre, 444 4th Ave., downtown, ☎ 619/234–9583) stages comedies, dramas, mysteries, and musicals at a 250-seat venue.

La Jolla Playhouse (✉ Mandell Weiss Center for the Performing Arts, University of California at San Diego, 2910 La Jolla Village Dr., ☎ 619/550–1010) crafts exciting and innovative productions, from May to November, under the artistic direction of Michael Greif. Many Broadway shows, such as *Tommy* and *How to Succeed in Business Without Really Trying,* have previewed here before heading for the East Coast.

La Jolla Stage Company (✉ Parker Auditorium, 750 Nautilus St., La Jolla, ☎ 619/459–7773) presents lavish productions of Broadway favorites and popular comedies year-round on the La Jolla High School campus.

Old Globe Theatre (✉ Simon Edison Centre for the Performing Arts, Balboa Park, 1363 Old Globe Way, ☎ 619/239–2255) is the oldest professional theater in California, performing classics, contemporary dramas, and experimental works. It produces the famous summer

Shakespeare Festival at the Old Globe and its sister theaters, the Cassius Carter Centre Stage and the Lowell Davies Festival Theatre.

Poway Center for the Performing Arts (⊠ 15498 Espola Rd., Poway, ☎ 760/748–0505), an ambitious theater outside San Diego, presents musical comedy and other lighthearted fare.

San Diego Comic Opera Company (⊠ Casa del Prado Theatre, Balboa Park, ☎ 619/231–5714) presents four different productions of Gilbert and Sullivan and similar works from October through July.

San Diego Junior Theater (⊠ Casa del Prado Theatre, Balboa Park, ☎ 619/239–8355) is a highly regarded school where children ages 6–18 perform and run productions Friday at 7 PM and weekends at 2 and 7 PM.

San Diego Repertory Theatre (⊠ Lyceum, 79 Horton Plaza, ☎ 619/235–8025), San Diego's first resident acting company, performs contemporary works year-round.

San Diego State University Drama Department (⊠ Don Powell Theatre and elsewhere on SDSU campus, 5500 Campanile Dr., ☎ 619/594–6884) presents contemporary and classic dramas.

Sledgehammer Theatre (⊠ 1620 6th Ave., ☎ 619/544–1484), one of San Diego's cutting-edge theaters, stages avant-garde pieces in St. Cecilia's church.

Starlight Musical Theatre (⊠ Starlight Bowl, Balboa Park, ☎ 619/544–7800, phone disconnected off-season), a local summertime favorite, is a series of musicals performed in an outdoor amphitheater from mid-June through early September. Because of the theater's proximity to the airport, actors are often forced to freeze mid-scene while a plane flies over.

Sushi Performance and Visual Art (⊠ 320 11th Ave., ☎ 619/235–8466), a nationally acclaimed group, provides an opportunity for well-known performance artists to do their thing.

The Theater in Old Town (⊠ 4040 Twiggs St., Old Town, ☎ 619/688–2494) presents punchy revues and occasional classics. Shows like *Forbidden Broadway, Ruthless, Gilligan's Island,* and *Forbidden Hollywood* have made this a popular place.

UCSD Theatre (⊠ Mandell Weiss Center for the Performing Arts, University of California at San Diego campus, La Jolla Village Dr. and Expedition Way, La Jolla, ☎ 619/534–4574) presents productions mounted by students of the university's theater department, from September to May.

Welk Resort Theatre (⊠ 8860 Lawrence Welk Dr., Escondido, ☎ 760/749–3448 or 800/932–9355), a famed dinner theater about a 45-minute drive from downtown, puts on polished Broadway-style productions.

7 Outdoor Activities and Sports

At least one stereotype of San Diego is true—it is an active, outdoors-oriented community. People recreate more than spectate. It's hard not to, with the variety of choices available, from boccie and ballooning to golf, surfing, sailing, and volleyball.

BEACHES

San Diego's beaches are among its greatest natural attractions. In some places, the shorefront is wide and sandy; in others, it's narrow and rocky or backed by impressive sandstone cliffs. You'll find beaches awhirl with activity and deserted spots for romantic sunset walks. For a surf and weather report, call 619/221–8884. For a general beach and weather report, call 619/289–1212. Pollution, which has long been a problem near the Mexican border, has lately inched northward as well. The weather page of the *San Diego Union-Tribune* includes pollution reports along with listings of surfing and diving conditions.

Overnight camping is not allowed on any San Diego city beaches, but there are campgrounds at some state beaches throughout the county (☎ 800/444–7275 for reservations). Lifeguards are stationed at city beaches from Sunset Cliffs up to Black's Beach in the summertime, but coverage in winter is provided by roving patrols only. Dogs are permitted on most San Diego beaches and adjacent parks on a leash between 6 PM and 9 AM; they can run unleashed anytime at Dog Beach at the north end of Ocean Beach and at Rivermouth in Del Mar. It is rarely a problem, however, to bring your pet to isolated beaches during the winter.

Pay attention to signs listing illegal activities; undercover police often patrol the beaches, carrying their ticket books in coolers. Glass is prohibited on all beaches, and fires are allowed only in fire rings or elevated barbecues. Alcoholic beverages—including beer—are completely banned on some city beaches; others allow you to partake between 8 AM and 8 PM. Check out the signs posted at the parking lots and lifeguard towers before you hit the shore with a six-pack or some wine coolers. Imbibing in beach parking lots, on boardwalks, and in landscaped areas is always illegal.

The beaches below are listed from south to north, starting just above the Mexican border.

South Bay

Border Field State Beach. The southernmost San Diego beach is different from the majority of California beaches. It is a marshy area with wide chaparrals and wildflowers, a favorite among horse riders and hikers. The beach is usually open from 9 AM to sunset, Thursday through Sunday, in summer. However, swimming is prohibited, and the beach is often closed in winter because of sewage contamination from Tijuana. Parking is plentiful, and there are rest rooms. ⊠ *Exit I–5 at Dairy Mart Rd. and head west along Monument Rd.*

Imperial Beach. In July, this classic southern California beach is the site of one of the nation's largest sand-castle competitions. The surf here is often excellent, but sewage contamination can be a problem. There are summertime lifeguards, rest rooms, parking, and nearby food vendors. ⊠ *Take Palm Ave. west from I–5 until it hits water.*

Coronado

Silver Strand State Beach. This quiet Coronado beach is ideal for families. The water is relatively calm, lifeguards and rangers are on duty year-round, and there are places to rollerblade or ride bikes. Four parking lots provide room for more than 1,500 cars. Sites at a campground ($12–$16 per night) for self-contained RVs are available on a first-come, first-served basis; stays are limited to seven nights. ⊠ *From San Diego–Coronado Bay Bridge, turn left onto Orange Ave., which*

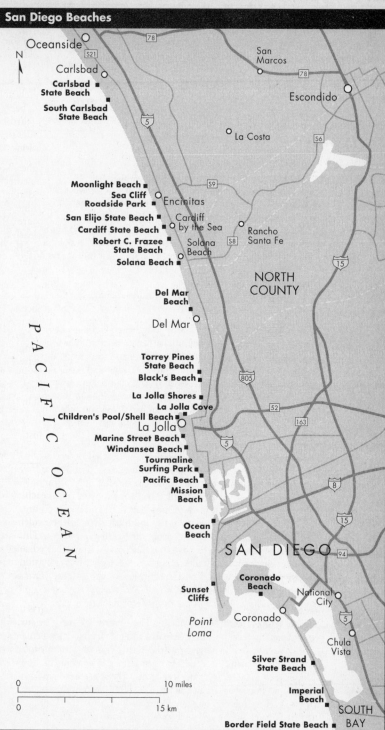

becomes Hwy. 75, and follow signs, ☎ *619/435–5184.* 🚗 *Parking $4, but not always collected Labor Day–Feb.*

Coronado Beach. With the famous Hotel Del Coronado as a backdrop, this stretch of sandy beach is one of San Diego County's largest and most picturesque. It's perfect for sunbathing or games of Frisbee. Parking can be difficult on the busiest days, but there are plenty of rest rooms and service facilities, as well as fire rings. ✉ *From the bridge turn left on Orange Ave. and follow signs.*

Point Loma

Sunset Cliffs. Beneath the jagged cliffs on the west side of the Point Loma peninsula is one of the more secluded beaches in the area. It's popular with surfers and locals. At the south end of the peninsula, near Cabrillo Point, tidal pools teeming with small sea creatures are revealed at low tide. Farther north, the waves lure surfers and the lonely coves attract sunbathers. Stairs at the foot of Bermuda and Santa Cruz avenues provide beach access, as do some (treacherous at points) cliff trails. There are no facilities. A visit here is more enjoyable at low tide; check the local newspaper for tide schedules. ✉ *Take I–8 west to Sunset Cliffs Blvd. and head south.*

San Diego

Ocean Beach. Much of this mile-long beach is a haven for volleyball players, sunbathers, and swimmers. The area around the municipal pier at the south end is a hangout for surfers and transients; the pier itself is open to the public for fishing and walking and has a restaurant at the end. The beach is just south of the channel entrance to Mission Bay. You'll find food vendors and fire rings; limited parking is available. Swimmers should beware of unusually vicious rip currents here. ✉ *Take I–8 west to Sunset Cliffs Blvd. and head south. Turn right on Santa Monica Ave.*

Mission Beach. San Diego's most popular beach, known locally as the Strand, draws huge crowds on hot summer days. The 2-mile-long continuous stretch extends from the north entrance of Mission Bay to Pacific Beach. A narrow boardwalk paralleling the beach is popular with walkers, roller skaters, bladers, and bicyclists. Surfers, swimmers, and volleyball players congregate at the south end. Toward the north end, near the Belmont Park roller coaster, the beach narrows and the water becomes rougher. The crowds grow thicker and somewhat rougher as well. Parking can be a challenge, but there are plenty of rest rooms and restaurants in the area. For a description of the bayside activities at Mission Bay, *see* Chapter 2. ✉ *Exit I–5 at Garnet Ave. and head west to Mission Blvd. Turn south and look for parking.*

Pacific Beach/North Pacific Beach. The boardwalk turns into a sidewalk here, but there are still bike paths and picnic tables along the beachfront. Pacific Beach runs from the north end of Mission Beach to Crystal Pier. North Pacific Beach extends from the pier north. The scene here is particularly lively on weekends. There are designated surfing areas, and fire rings are available. On-street parking is your best bet, or you can try the big lot at Belmont Park near the south end. ✉ *Exit I–5 at Garnet Ave. and head west to Mission Blvd. Turn north and look for parking.*

La Jolla

The beaches of La Jolla combine unusual beau___
scuba diving, and surfing. On the down side, they a___
have limited parking facilities. Don't think about bringing yo___
dogs aren't even allowed on the sidewalks above some beaches here.

Tourmaline Surfing Park. This is one of the area's most popular beaches for surfing and sailboarding year-round. There is a 175-space parking lot at the foot of Tourmaline Street, but it normally fills to capacity by midday. ⊠ *Take Mission Blvd. north (it turns into La Jolla Blvd.) and turn west on Tourmaline St.*

Windansea Beach. If the scenery here seems familiar, it's because Windansea and its habitués were the inspiration for Tom Wolfe's satirical novel *The Pump House Gang,* about a group of surfers who protect their surf-turf from outsiders. The beach's towering waves (caused by an underwater reef) are truly world-class. With its incredible views and secluded sunbathing spots set among sandstone rocks, Windansea is also one of the most romantic of West Coast beaches, especially at sunset. ⊠ *Take Mission Blvd. north (it turns into La Jolla Blvd.) and turn west on Nautilus St.*

Marine Street Beach. Wide and sandy, this strand of beach often teems with sunbathers, swimmers, walkers, and joggers. The water is good for surfing and bodyboarding, though you'll need to watch out for riptides. ⊠ *Accessible from Marine St., off La Jolla Blvd.*

Children's Pool. In addition to panoramic views of ocean and coastline this shallow lagoon, protected by a seawall, has small waves and no riptide. The pool is popular with scuba divers who explore the offshore reef when the surf is low. It's also a good place to watch marine mammals—seals and sea lions frequent the cove. ⊠ *Follow La Jolla Blvd. north. When it forks, take the left, Coast Blvd.*

Shell Beach. Just north of the Children's Pool is a small cove, accessible by stairs, with a relatively secluded beach. The exposed rocks just off the coast have been designated a protected habitat for seals; you can watch them sun themselves and frolic in the water. ⊠ *Continue along Coast Blvd. north from the Children's Pool.*

✳ **La Jolla Cove.** This is one of the prettiest spots in the world. A palm-tree-lined park sits on top of cliffs formed by the incessant pounding of the waves. At low tide the tidal pools and cliff caves provide a destination for explorers. Divers and snorkelers can explore the underwater delights of the San Diego–La Jolla Underwater Ecological Reserve. The cove is also a favorite of rough-water swimmers for whom buoys mark distances. ⊠ *Follow Coast Blvd. north to signs, or take the La Jolla Village Dr. exit from I–5, head west to Torrey Pines Rd., turn left, and drive down hill to Girard Ave. Turn right and follow signs.*

La Jolla Shores. On summer holidays, all access routes are usually closed to one of San Diego's most popular beaches. The lures here are a wide sandy beach and the most gentle wave action in San Diego, with fun surf for boogie-boarders, bodysurfers, and regular surfers. A concrete boardwalk parallels the beach. Arrive early to get a parking spot in the lot at the foot of Calle Frescota. ⊠ *From I–5 take La Jolla Village Dr. west and turn left onto La Jolla Shores Dr. Head west to Camino del Oro or Vallecitos St. Turn right and look for parking.*

Black's Beach. The powerful waves at this beach, officially known as Torrey Pines City Park Beach, attract surfers, and its relative isolation appeals to nudist nature lovers (though by law nudity is prohibited).

Access to parts of the shore coincides with low tides. There are no life-guards on duty, and strong ebb tides are common: only experienced swimmers should take the plunge. Storms have weakened the cliffs over the past few years; they're dangerous to climb and should be avoided. ⊠ *Take Genesee Ave. west from I–5 and follow signs to Glider Port; easier access, via a paved path, available on La Jolla Farms Rd., but parking limited to 2 hrs.*

Del Mar

Torrey Pines State Beach/State Reserve. One of San Diego's best beaches contains 1,700 acres of bluffs, bird-filled marshes, and sandy shoreline. A network of trails leads through rare pine trees to the coast below. The large parking lot is rarely full. Lifeguards are on duty weekends (weather permitting) from Easter until Memorial Day, daily from then until Labor Day, and again on weekends through September. Torrey Pines tends to get crowded during the summer, but more isolated spots under the cliffs are a short walk in either direction. ⊠ *Take the Carmel Valley Rd. exit west from I–5,* ☏ *619/755–2063.* ▦ *Parking $4.*

Del Mar Beach. The numbered streets of Del Mar, from 15th to 29th, end at a wide beach popular with volleyball players, surfers, and sun-bathers. Parking can be a problem on nice summer days, but access is relatively easy. The portions of Del Mar south of 15th Street are lined with cliffs and are rarely crowded. Leashed dogs are permitted on most sections of Del Mar Beach year-round; between October and May dogs may run free at Rivermouth, Del Mar's northernmost beach. During the annual summer meeting of the Del Mar Thoroughbred Club, horse bettors can be seen sitting on the beach in the morning working on the *Daily Racing Form* before heading across the street to the track. ⊠ *Take the Via de la Valle exit from I–5 west to Old Hwy. 101 (also known as Camino del Mar in Del Mar) and turn left.*

Solana Beach

Most of the beaches of this little city are nestled under cliffs, and access is limited to private stairways. However, at the west end of Lomas Santa Fe Drive (at an area known as Pill Box because of the bunker-like structures on top of the cliffs), you'll find access to a small beach, known locally as Fletcher Cove. Also here are rest rooms and a large parking lot. During low tide, it's an easy walk under the cliffs to nearby beaches. ⊠ *From I–5 take Lomas Santa Fe Dr. west to its end.*

Cardiff-by-the-Sea

Cardiff State Beach. This beach begins at the parking lot immediately north of the cliffs at Solana Beach. A reef break draws surfers, though this area otherwise is not particularly appealing. ⊠ *From I–5, turn west on Lomas Santa Fe Dr. to S21 (Old Hwy. 101) and turn right.* ☏ *760/753–5091.* ▦ *Parking $4.*

San Elijo State Beach. There are campsites (☏ 800/444–7275 for reservations) atop a scenic bluff at this park, which also has a store and shower facilities plus beach access for swimmers and surfers. Sites run $17–$23. ⊠ *From I–5, turn west on Lomas Santa Fe Dr. to S21 (Old Hwy. 101) and turn right.* ☏ *760/753–5091.* ▦ *Parking $4.*

Encinitas

Sea Cliff Roadside Park. Palm trees and the golden domes of the nearby Self Realization Fellowship earned this picturesque beach its local nickname, Swami's. The beach is also a top surfing spot; the only access is by a long stairway leading down from the clifftop park. ⊠ *Follow S21 (Old Hwy. 101) north from Cardiff, or exit I–5 at Encinitas Blvd., go west to S21, and turn left.*

Moonlight Beach. Large parking areas and full facilities make this beach, tucked into a break in the cliffs, a pleasant stop. ⊠ *Take the Encinitas Blvd. exit from I–5 and head west until you hit the Moonlight parking lot.*

Carlsbad

Carlsbad State Beach, South Carlsbad State Beach. Erosion from winter storms has made the southern Carlsbad beaches rockier than most beaches in southern California. This is particularly true of South Carlsbad, a stretch of which is named in honor of Robert C. Frazee, a local politician and civic booster. Still, it's a good swimming spot, there are fine street- and beach-level promenades just outside of downtown Carlsbad, and there is overnight camping for self-contained RVs (☎ 800/444–7275). No overnight camping is allowed at Carlsbad State Beach, farther to the north, but there is a fishing area and a parking lot. ⊠ *Exit I–5 at La Costa Ave. and head west to S21. Turn north and follow coastline,* ☎ 760/438–3143. ☞ *Free at Carlsbad State Beach; $4 (parking fee per car) at South Carlsbad State Beach.*

Oceanside

Swimmers, surfers, and marines (from nearby Camp Pendleton) often come to play on Oceanside's beaches. The surf is good around the Oceanside Pier at the foot of 6th Avenue and on either side of the two jetties. ⊠ *Take Vista Way west from I–5 to Hill St. (Old Hwy. 101) and turn right. Best access points are from Cassidy St. and the Oceanside Harbor area.*

PARTICIPANT SPORTS

Ballooning

Enjoy the views of the Pacific Ocean, the mountains, and the coastline south to Mexico and north to San Clemente from a hot-air balloon at sunrise or sunset. The conditions are perfect: necessary winds and wide-open spaces. Ballooning companies operating in the San Diego area include **California Dreamin'** (⊠ 162 S. Rancho Santa Fe Rd. Suite F10, Encinitas, ☎ 760/438–9550 or 800/373–3359), **Pacific Horizon Balloon Tours** (⊠ 1342 Camino del Mar, Del Mar, ☎ 619/481–6225 or 800/244–1790), and **Skysurfer Balloon Company** (⊠ 1221 Camino del Mar, Del Mar, ☎ 619/481–6800 or 800/660–6809 in CA).

Bicycling

On any given summer day Highway S21 from La Jolla to Oceanside looks like a freeway for cyclists. Never straying more than a quarter mile from the beach, it is easily the most popular and scenic bike route around. Experienced cyclists follow Lomas Santa Fe Drive in Solana Beach east into Rancho Santa Fe, perhaps even continuing east on Del Dios Highway, past Lake Hodges, to Escondido. These roads can be narrow and winding in spots, but for more leisurely rides, Mission Bay, San Diego Harbor, and the Mission Beach boardwalk are all flat and scenic. San Diego also has a velodrome (☎ 619/296–3345) in Balboa Park. Local bookstores and camping stores sell guides to some challenging mountain-bike trails in outer San Diego County. A free comprehensive map of all county bike paths is available from the local office of the **California Department of Transportation** (✉ 2829 Juan St., San Diego 92110, ☎ 619/688–6699).

Bicycle Barn in Pacific Beach (✉ 746 Emerald St., ☎ 619/581–3665) and **Hamel's Action Sports Center** in Mission Beach (✉ 704 Ventura Pl., ☎ 619/488–5050) are among the places that rent bikes.

Boccie Ball

The Italian version of lawn bowling is played on Monday, Wednesday, and Friday, from 1 to 5, on courts in the Morley Field section of Balboa Park (☎ 619/692–4919). The games are open to the public, and there are usually boccie balls at the courts.

Diving

Enthusiasts the world over flock to San Diego to skin-dive and scuba-dive off La Jolla and Point Loma. At La Jolla Cove, you'll find the **San Diego–La Jolla Underwater Ecological Park.** Farther north, off the south end of Black's Beach, the rim of **Scripps Canyon** lies in about 60 ft of water. The canyon plummets to more than 900 feet in some sections. Another popular diving spot is **Sunset Cliffs** in Point Loma, where the sea life and flora are relatively close to shore. Strong rip currents make it an area best enjoyed by experienced divers. It is illegal to take any wildlife from the ecological preserves in La Jolla or near Cabrillo Point. Spearfishing requires a license (available at most dive stores), and it is illegal to take out-of-season lobster and game fish out of the water.

Diving equipment and boat trips can be arranged through **San Diego Divers Supply** (✉ 4004 Sports Arena Blvd., ☎ 619/224–3439), **Ocean Enterprises** (✉ 7710 Balboa Ave., Clairemont, ☎ 619/565–6054), **Del Mar Ocean Sports** (✉ 12271 Camino Del Mar, ☎ 619/792–1903), or at the **Diving Locker** (✉ 1020 Grand Ave., Pacific Beach, ☎ 619/272–1120; ✉ 405 N. Highway 101, Solana Beach, ☎ 619/755–6822). For recorded diving information, contact the San Diego City Lifeguards Office (☎ 619/221–8884).

Fishing

The Pacific Ocean is full of corbina, croaker, and halibut. No license is required to fish from a public pier, such as the Ocean Beach pier. A fishing license from the state **Department of Fish and Game** (✉ 4949 Viewridge Ave., San Diego 92123, ☎ 619/467–4201), available at most bait-and-tackle stores, is required for fishing from the shoreline. Children under 15 do not need a license.

Lake Jennings, Lake Sutherland, and Lake San Vicente in the East County are popular spots for catching trout and bass. Lake Morena and Lake Jennings have both fishing and camping facilities. For information about city-operated lakes, call 619/465–3474. Three freshwater lakes—Dixon, Hodges, and Wohlford—surround the North County city of Escondido. Camping is allowed at Wohlford at the Oakvale R.V. Park (☎ 760/749–2895) and at Lyle's at Dixon Lake (☎ 760/741–3328 or 760/741–4680 for ranger station). Boats can be rented at all the above-mentioned lakes; a state fishing license is required.

Several companies conduct half-day, full-day, or multiday fishing expeditions in search of marlin, tuna, albacore, and other deep-water fish. **Fisherman's Landing** (✉ 2838 Garrison St., Point Loma, ☎ 619/221–8500), **H&M Landing** (✉ 2803 Emerson St., Point Loma, ☎ 619/222–

1144), and **Seaforth Boat Rental** (⊠ 1641 Quivira Rd., West Mission Bay, ☎ 619/223–1681) are among the companies operating from San Diego. **Helgren's Sportfishing** (⊠ 315 Harbor Dr. S, Oceanside, ☎ 760/722–2133) has trips from Oceanside Harbor.

Fitness

Most major hotels have full health clubs, with at least weight machines, stationary bicycles, and spas. Several hotels with elaborate spas offer one-day spa-and-fitness programs for nonguests. **Le Meridien Spa & Clarins Institut de Beaute** (⊠ 2000 2nd St., Coronado, ☎ 619/435–3000) has four pampering packages that include the use of fitness facilities and admission to exercise classes. A package at the **Rancho Bernardo Inn** (⊠ 17550 Bernardo Oaks Dr., Rancho Bernardo, ☎ 619/675–8500) includes massage, a facial, and use of the fitness center. Day-spa packages at the **Rancho Valencia Resort** (⊠ 5921 Valencia Circle, Rancho Santa Fe, ☎ 619/756–1123) include massage, aromatherapy, and use of fitness facilities.

Frog's Mission Valley Health Club (⊠ 901 Hotel Circle S, ☎ 619/291–3500) has a weight room, saunas, and tennis and racquetball courts. Visitors can use the splendid facilities at the **Sporting Club at Aventine** (⊠ 8930 University Center La., La Jolla, ☎ 619/552–8000). The **24 Hour Fitness Centers** in the area (⊠ 5885 Rancho Mission Rd., Mission Valley, ☎ 619/281–5543; ⊠ 3675 Midway Dr., Sports Arena–Point Loma area, ☎ 619/224–2902; ⊠ 4405 La Jolla Village Dr., Golden Triangle/UTC, ☎ 619/457–3930) allow nonmembers to use the facilities for a small fee. **Gold's Gym** (⊠ 2949 Garnet Ave., Mission Beach, ☎ 619/272–3400) allows drop-ins. **Bodyworks Health & Fitness** (⊠ 1130 7th Ave., downtown, ☎ 619/232–5500) allows nonmembers to use the facilities for a small fee. **Athletic Center** (⊠ 1747 Hancock St., ☎ 619/299–2639) has a low daily rate for visitors.

Frisbee Golf

This is just like golf, except that it's played with Frisbees. A course, laid out at Morley Field in Balboa Park, is open seven days a week from dawn to dusk, and there is no charge to play. Rules are posted. Directions to the field are available from the Balboa Park Visitors Center (☎ 619/239–0512).

Golf

It would be difficult to find a better place to play golf year-round than San Diego. The climate—generally sunny, without a lot of wind—is perfect for the sport, and there are courses in the area to suit every level of expertise. Experienced golfers can play the same greens as PGA-tournament participants, and beginners or rusty players can book a week at a golf resort and benefit from expert instruction. You'd also be hard pressed to find a locale that has more scenic courses—everything from sweeping views of the ocean to verdant hills inland.

As you might expect, these advantages make San Diego popular with golfers; during busy vacation seasons, it can be difficult to get a good tee-off time. Call in advance to see if it's possible to make a reservation. You don't necessarily have to stay at a resort to play its course; check if the one you're interested in is open to nonguests. Most public courses in the area provide an inexpensive current list of fees and charges for all San Diego courses. The **Southern California Golf Association** (☎ 818/980–3630) publishes an annual directory with detailed and valuable information on all clubs. Another good resource for golfers is the **Southern California Public Links Golf Association** (☎ 714/994–4747).

The following is not intended to be a comprehensive list but provides suggestions for some of the best places to play in the area. The greens fee is included for each course; carts (in some cases mandatory), instruction, and other costs are additional.

Courses

Carmel Mountain Ranch Country Club (✉ 14050 Carmel Ridge Rd., San Diego, ☎ 619/487–9224) has 18 holes, a driving range, and equipment rentals. A challenging course with many difficult holes, Carmel Mountain Ranch is not particularly scenic: it's in a suburban area and runs through a housing development. Greens fee: $60–$70.

Coronado Municipal Golf Course (✉ 2000 Visalia Row, Coronado, ☎ 619/435–3121) has 18 holes, a driving range, equipment rentals, and a snack bar. Views of San Diego Bay and the Coronado Bridge from the back 9 holes on this good walking course make it popular—and rather difficult to get on. Greens fee: $20–$30.

Eastlake Country Club (✉ 2375 Clubhouse Dr., Chula Vista, ☎ 619/482–5757) has 18 holes, a driving range, equipment rentals, and a snack bar. A fun course for golfers of almost all levels of expertise, it's not overly difficult, though features such as water hazards provide a challenge. Greens fee: $44–$59.

Mission Bay Golf Center (✉ 2702 N. Mission Bay Dr., San Diego, ☎ 619/490–3370) has 18 holes, a driving range, equipment rentals, and a restaurant. A not-very-challenging executive (par 3 and 4) course, Mission Bay is lit for night play. Greens fee: $14–$16.50.

Mt. Woodson Country Club (✉ 16422 N. Woodson Dr., Ramona, ☎ 760/788–3555) has 18 holes, equipment rentals, a golf shop, and a snack bar. This heavily wooded course in the mountains outside San Diego has scenic views and interesting wooden cart bridges. Greens fee: $42.50–$60.

Rancho San Diego Golf Course (✉ 3121 Willow Glen Rd., El Cajon, ☎ 619/442–9891) has 36 holes, a driving range, and equipment rentals. A good walking course, Rancho San Diego has nice practice putting greens and lots of cottonwood trees. Greens fee: $21–$35.

Singing Hills Country Club (✉ 3007 Dehesa Rd., El Cajon, ☎ 619/442–3425) has 54 holes, a driving range, equipment rentals, and a restaurant. The lush course, set in a canyon, has many water hazards. One of *Golf Digest*'s favorites, Singing Hills comes highly recommended by everyone who's played it. Hackers will love the executive par-3 course; seasoned golfers can play the championship courses. Greens fee: $30–$35.

Steele Canyon Golf Course (✉ 3199 Stonefield Dr., Jamul, ☎ 619/441–6900) has 27 holes, a driving range, a golf shop, and a snack bar. Carts are a necessity at this hilly Gary Player–designed course with fine views. Greens fee: $48–$65.

Torrey Pines Municipal Golf Course (✉ 11480 N. Torrey Pines Rd., La Jolla, ☎ 619/452–3226) has 36 holes, a driving range, and equipment rentals. One of the best public golf courses in the United States, Torrey Pines has views of the Pacific from every hole and is sufficiently challenging to host the Buick Invitational in February. It's not easy to get a good tee time here; out-of-towners are better off booking the in-

In case you want to see the world.

At American Express, we're here to make your journey a smooth one. So we have over 1,700 travel service locations in over 120 countries ready to help. What else would you expect from the world's largest travel agency?

do more

AMERICAN
EXPRESS

http://www.americanexpress.com/travel

Travel

In case you want to be welcomed there.

We're here to see that you're always welcomed at establishments everywhere. That's why millions of people carry the American Express® Card – for peace of mind, confidence, and security, around the world or just around the corner.

do more

AMERICAN
EXPRESS

Cards

And just in case.

We're here with American Express® Travelers Cheques and Cheques *for Two*.® They're the safest way to carry money on your vacation and the surest way to get a refund, practically anywhere, anytime.
Another way we help you...

do more

AMERICAN
EXPRESS

Travelers
Cheques

structional Golf Playing Package, which includes cart, greens fee, and a golf-pro escort for the first three holes. Greens fee: $45–$50.

Resorts

Aviara Golf Club (✉ 7447 Batiquitos Dr., Carlsbad, ☎ 760/929–0077) has 18 holes (designed by Arnold Palmer), a driving range, equipment rentals, and views of the protected adjacent Batiquitos Lagoon and the Pacific Ocean. Greens fee: $105–$125.

Carlton Oaks Lodge and Country Club (✉ 9200 Inwood Dr., Santee, ☎ 619/448–4242) has 18 holes, a driving range, equipment rentals, a clubhouse, a restaurant, and a bar. Many local qualifying tournaments are held at this difficult Pete Dye–designed course with lots of trees and water hazards. Greens fee: $65–$75.

Carmel Highland Doubletree Golf and Tennis Resort (✉ 14455 Penasquitos Dr., San Diego, ☎ 619/672–9100), a fairly hilly, well-maintained course, has 18 holes, a driving range, equipment rentals, and a clubhouse with restaurant. Greens fee: $42–$55.

La Costa Resort and Spa (✉ Costa del Mar Rd., Carlsbad, ☎ 760/438–9111 or 800/854–5000) has two 18-hole PGA-rated courses, a driving range, a clubhouse, equipment rentals, an excellent golf school, and a pro shop. One of the premier golf resorts in southern California, La Costa hosts the Mercedes Championships in January. All this doesn't come cheap, but then again, how many courses will send a limo to pick you up at the airport? Greens fee: $130–$170.

Morgan Run Resort and Club (✉ 5690 Cancha de Golf, Rancho Santa Fe, ☎ 619/756–2471), a very popular walking course near polo grounds and stables, has 27 holes, a driving range, equipment rentals, and a pro shop. Greens fee: $50–$60.

Pala Mesa Resort (✉ 2001 Old Hwy. 395, Fallbrook, ☎ 760/728–5881) has 18 holes, a driving range, and equipment rentals. Narrow fairways help make this a challenging course, but it's well maintained and has views of the inland mountains. Greens fee: $55–$70.

Rancho Bernardo Inn and Country Club (✉ 17550 Bernardo Oaks Dr., Rancho Bernardo, ☎ 619/675–8470, ext. 1) has 45 holes on-site, a driving range, equipment rentals, and a restaurant. Guests can play three other golf courses at company-operated resorts: Mt. Woodson, Temecula Creek, and Twin Oaks. Ken Blanchard's Golf University of San Diego, based here, is world famous. Rancho Bernardo Inn lays out one of the best Sunday brunches in the county. Greens fee: $65–$80.

Redhawk (✉ 45100 Redhawk Parkway, Temecula, ☎ 909/695–1424 or 800/451–4295) has 18 holes in an arboretum-like setting, a driving range, putting green, and snack bar. The par-72 course offers enough challenges to earn a top-ten ranking from *California Golf Magazine.* Greens fee: $48–$75.

Hang Gliding

The **Torrey Pines Glider Port** (✉ 2800 Torrey Pines Scenic Dr., La Jolla), perched on the cliffs overlooking the ocean just north of La Jolla, is one of the most spectacular—and easiest—spots to hang glide in the world. However, it is definitely for experienced pilots only. Hang-gliding lessons and tandem rides for inexperienced hang gliders are available from the **Hang Gliding Center** (☎ 619/452–9858) based here.

Hiking and Nature Trails

Guided hikes are conducted regularly through Los Penasquitos Canyon Preserve and the Torrey Pines State Reserve (☞ La Jolla *in* Chapter 2), the San Dieguito River Valley Regional Open Space (⊠ 21 mi north of San Diego on I–5 to Lomas Santa Fe Dr. east 1 mi to Sun Valley Rd. north into park, ☎ 619/235–5440), and the Tijuana Estuary (☎ 619/575–3613). A list of scheduled walks appears in the Night and Day section of the Thursday *San Diego Union-Tribune*.

Mission Trails Regional Parks (⊠ 1 Father Junípero Serra Tr., San Diego 92119, ☎ 619/668–3275), which encompasses nearly 6,000 acres of mountains, wooded hillsides, lakes, and riparian streams, is just 8 mi from downtown San Diego. Trails here range from easy to difficult; they include one with a superb city view from Cowles Mountain and another along a historic missionary path.

Horseback Riding

Holidays on Horseback (☎ 619/445–3997), in the East County town of Descanso, leads rides ranging from one to nine hours in the Cuyamaca Mountains and rents easy-to-ride fox trotters to beginners. **Bright Valley Farm** (⊠ 11990 Campo Rd., Spring Valley, ☎ 619/670–1861) is a wonderful place to ride. **Sandi's Rental Stables** (⊠ 2060 Hollister St., Imperial Beach, ☎ 619/424–3124) leads rides through Border Field State Park.

Ice Skating

These two facilities have skate rentals, public sessions, and lessons: **Ice Capades Chalet** (⊠ University Towne Centre, 4545 La Jolla Village Dr., ☎ 619/452–9110) and **San Diego Ice Arena** (⊠ 11048 Ice Skate Pl., Mira Mesa, ☎ 619/530–1825).

Jet Skiing

Waveless Mission Bay and the small Snug Harbor Marina (☎ 760/434–3089), just east of the intersection of Tamarack Avenue and I–5 in Carlsbad, are favorite spots. Jet Skis can be launched from most beaches, although they need to be ridden beyond surf lines, and some beaches have special regulations governing their use. **California Water Sports** (☎ 760/434–3089) has information about equipment rentals and purchases. **Seaforth Boat Rentals** (☎ 619/223–1681) rents Jet Skis for use in the South Bay Marina in Coronado, and they are also available at Snug Harbor in Carlsbad.

Jogging

From downtown, the most popular run is along the Embarcadero, which stretches around the bay. There are uncongested sidewalks all through the area. The alternative for downtown visitors is to head east to Balboa Park, where trails snake through the canyons. Mission Bay is renowned among joggers for its wide sidewalks and basically flat landscape. Trails head west around Fiesta Island from Mission Bay, providing distance as well as a scenic route. Del Mar has the finest running trails along the bluff; park your car near 15th Street and run south along the cliffs for a gorgeous view of the ocean. Organized runs occur almost every weekend. They're listed in *Competitor* magazine (☎ 619/793–2711), which is available free at bike and running shops, or by calling the **San Diego Track Club** (☎ 800/450–7382). **The Sports Authority** (⊠ 8550 Rio San Diego Dr., Mission Valley, ☎ 619/295–

1682) has all the supplies and information you'll need for running in San Diego. Some tips: Don't run in bike lanes, and check the local newspaper's tide charts before heading to the beach.

Off-Road Driving

The 40,000-acre **Ocotillo Wells State Vehicular Recreation Area** (☎ 760/767–5391) provides plenty of room to ride around in dune buggies, motorcycles, and three-wheel vehicles. It can be reached by following Highway 78 east from Julian.

Rollerblading and Roller Skating

The sidewalks at Mission Bay are perfect for rollerblading and skating; you can admire the sailboats and kites while you get some exercise. Rent in-line skates at **Hamel's Action Sports Center** in Mission Beach (⊠ 704 Ventura Pl., ☎ 619/488–5050). **Bicycle Barn** in Pacific Beach (⊠ 746 Emerald St., ☎ 619/581–3665) also rents blades. **Skateworld** (⊠ 6900 Linda Vista Rd., Linda Vista, ☎ 619/560–9349) has several public sessions daily.

Sailing and Boating

Winds in San Diego are consistent, especially during the winter. If you're bringing your boat here, there are several marinas that rent slips to the public, including the **Best Western Island Palms Hotel & Marina** (⊠ 2051 Shelter Island Dr., ☎ 619/222–0561); the **Dana Inn and Marina** (⊠ 1710 W. Mission Bay Dr., ☎ 619/222–6440); **Hyatt Islandia** (⊠ 1441 Quivira Rd., ☎ 619/224–1234); the **Kona Kai Club** (⊠ 1551 Shelter Island Dr., ☎ 619/222–1191); the **San Diego Marriott Hotel and Marina** (⊠ 333 W. Harbor Dr., ☎ 619/234–1500); and the **Sunroad Resort Marina** (⊠ 955 Harbor Island Dr., ☎ 619/574–0736). Both the **San Diego Yacht Club** (⊠ 1011 Anchorage La., ☎ 619/222–1103) and the **Southwestern Yacht Club** (⊠ 2702 Qualtrough St., ☎ 619/222–0438) have reciprocal arrangements with other yacht clubs.

Vessels of various sizes and shapes—from small paddleboats to sleek 12-meters—can be rented from the **Bahia Hotel** (⊠ 998 W. Mission Bay Dr., ☎ 619/488–0551); the **Catamaran Resort Hotel** (⊠ 3999 Mission Blvd., ☎ 619/488–1081); **Harbor Sailboats** (⊠ 2040 Harbor Island Dr., Suite 104, ☎ 619/291–9570); the **Hotel Del Coronado** (⊠ 1500 Orange Ave., Coronado, ☎ 619/435–6611); the **Hyatt Islandia** (⊠ 1441 Quivira Rd., ☎ 619/224–1234); the **Mission Bay Sports Center** (⊠ 1010 Santa Clara Pl., ☎ 619/488–1004); and **Seaforth Boat Rental** (⊠ 1641 Quivira Rd., ☎ 619/223–1681).

Sail and power boat charters and cruises can be arranged through the **Charter Connection** (⊠ 1715 Strand Way, Coronado, ☎ 619/437–8877); **Fraser Charters, Inc.** (⊠ 2353 Shelter Island Dr., ☎ 800/228–6779); **Hornblower Dining Yachts** (⊠ 2825 5th Ave., ☎ 619/238–1686), which operates sunset cocktail and dining cruises; and **Classic Sailing Adventures** (⊠ Shelter Island Marina, ☎ 619/224–0800), which has champagne sunset cruises. For information, including tips on overnight anchoring, contact the **Harbor Police** (☎ 619/686–6200).

Surfing

If you're a beginner, consider paddling out at Mission, Pacific, Tourmaline, La Jolla Shores, Del Mar, or Oceanside Beach. More experienced surfers usually head for Sunset Cliffs, the La Jolla reef breaks, Black's Beach, or Sea Cliff Roadside Park in Encinitas. *See* Beaches, *above,* for descriptions. **Kahuna Bob's Surf School** (☎ 760/438–4845) conducts two-hour lessons seven days a week; all equipment is supplied.

Many local surf shops rent boards, including **Star Surfing Company** (☎ 619/273–7827) in Pacific Beach and **La Jolla Surf Systems** (☎ 619/456–2777) and **Hansen's** (☎ 760/753–6595) in Encinitas.

Swimming

The most spectacular pool in town is Belmont Park's 58-yard-long **Plunge** (✉ 3115 Ocean Front Walk, Mission Bay, ☎ 619/488–3110). The **Copley Family YMCA** (✉ 3901 Landis St., City Heights, ☎ 619/283–2251) and **Downtown YMCA** (✉ 500 W. Broadway Ave., ☎ 619/232–7451) are centrally located. The **Magdalena Ecke YMCA** (✉ 200 Saxony Rd., Encinitas, ☎ 760/942–9622) is convenient for visitors to North County.

Tennis

Most of the more than 1,300 courts around the county are in private clubs, but there are a few public facilities. The **Balboa Tennis Club at Morley Field** (☎ 619/295–9278) in Balboa Park has 25 courts, 19 of which are lighted. Nonmembers can make reservations after paying a $4 fee. Heaviest usage is between 9 and 11 AM and after 5 PM; at other times you can usually arrive and begin playing. The **La Jolla Tennis Club** (✉ 7632 Draper Ave., ☎ 619/454–4434) has 9 free public courts near downtown La Jolla, 5 of them lighted. The 12 lighted courts at the privately owned **Peninsula Tennis Club** (✉ Rob Field, ☎ 619/226–3407) in Ocean Beach are available to the public for a $3 day-use fee.

Several San Diego resorts have top-notch tennis programs staffed by big-name professional instructors. **Rancho Bernardo Inn** (✉ 17550 Bernardo Oaks Dr., Rancho Bernardo, ☎ 619/675–8500) has 12 tennis courts and packages that include instruction, accommodations, and meals. **Rancho Valencia Resort** (✉ 5921 Valencia Circle, Rancho Santa Fe, ☎ 619/756–1123), which is among the top tennis resorts in the nation, has 18 hard courts and a variety of instruction programs. **La Costa Resort and Spa** (✉ Costa Del Mar Rd., Carlsbad, ☎ 760/438–9111), home to the annual Toshiba Tennis Classic, has 21 courts including two Wimbledon-quality grass courts, professional instruction, clinics, and workouts.

Volleyball

Ocean Beach, South Mission Beach, Del Mar Beach, Moonlight Beach, and the western edge of Balboa Park are major congregating points for volleyball enthusiasts.

Waterskiing

Mission Bay is one of the most popular waterskiing areas in southern California. It is best to get out early when the water is smooth and the crowds are thin. Boats and equipment can be rented from **Seaforth Boat Rentals** (✉ 1641 Quivira Rd., near Mission Bay, ☎ 619/223–1681). The private **San Diego and Mission Bay Boat and Ski Club** (✉ 2606 N. Mission Bay Dr., ☎ 619/276–0830) operates a slalom course and ski jump in Mission Bay's Hidden Anchorage. Permission from the club or the Mission Bay Harbor Patrol (☎ 619/221–8985) is required.

Windsurfing

Also known as sailboarding, windsurfing is a sport best practiced on smooth waters, such as Mission Bay or the Snug Harbor Marina at the intersection of I–5 and Tamarack Avenue in Carlsbad. Rentals and instruction are available at the **Bahia Hotel** (✉ 998 W. Mission Bay Dr., ☎ 619/488–0551); the **Catamaran Resort Hotel** (✉ 3999 Mission Blvd., ☎ 619/488–1081); **Mission Bay Sportcenter** (✉ 1010 Santa Clara Pl., ☎ 619/488–1004); and **Windsport** (✉ 844 W. Mission Bay Dr., ☎ 619/488–4642), all in the Mission Bay area. The **Snug Harbor Marina** (✉ 4215 Harrison St., Carlsbad, ☎ 760/434–3089) has rentals and instruction. More experienced windsurfers will enjoy taking a board out on the ocean. Wave jumping is especially popular at the Tourmaline Surfing Park in La Jolla and in the Del Mar area.

SPECTATOR SPORTS

Qualcomm Stadium (✉ 9449 Friars Rd., ☎ 619/525–8282), formerly San Diego Jack Murphy Stadium, is at the intersection of I–8 and I–805. To get to the **San Diego Sports Arena** (✉ 3500 Sports Arena Blvd., ☎ 619/224–4171), take the Rosecrans exit off I–5 and turn right onto Sports Arena Boulevard. The **ARCO Training Center** at Otay Lake (✉ 1750 Wueste Rd., Chula Vista, ☎ 619/482–6222) has free daily (9–5) tours of soccer, tennis, track and field, and other Olympic training facilities.

Baseball

The **San Diego Padres** (☎ 619/283–4494) slug it out for bragging rights in the National League West from April into October. Games with such rivals as the Los Angeles Dodgers and the San Francisco Giants are usually the highlights of the home season at Qualcomm Stadium. Tickets are usually available on game day.

Basketball

The **San Diego State University Aztecs** (☎ 619/283–7378) compete in the Western Athletic Conference with such powers as Utah State and Brigham Young University. The Aztecs play December–March at Peterson Gym on the San Diego State campus (☎ 619/594–6947).

The **University of San Diego Toreros** (☎ 619/260–4600) compete in the West Coast Athletic Conference against Pepperdine, the University of San Francisco, the University of California at Santa Barbara, and other teams.

Football

The **San Diego Chargers** (☎ 619/280–2111) of the National Football League fill Qualcomm Stadium from August through December. Games with AFC West rivals the Oakland Raiders and Denver Broncos are particularly intense.

The **San Diego State University Aztecs** compete in the Western Athletic Conference. The biggest game of the year is always a showdown with Brigham Young University. The winner of the WAC plays in the **Holiday Bowl** (☎ 619/283–5808), around the end of December in Qualcomm Stadium. The Aztecs play their home games at Qualcomm.

Golf

The La Costa Resort and Spa (☎ 760/438–9111) hosts the prestigious **Mercedes Championships** in January, featuring the winners of the previous year's tournaments. The **Buick Invitational** brings the pros to the Torrey Pines Municipal Golf Course in February (☎ 619/452–3226).

Horse Racing

The annual summer meeting of the **Del Mar Thoroughbred Club** (☎ 619/755–1141) on the Del Mar Fairgrounds attracts the best horses and jockeys in the country. Racing begins in July and continues through early September, every day except Tuesday. The Del Mar Fairgrounds also serves as a satellite-wagering facility (☎ 619/755–1167) with TV coverage of betting on races from tracks throughout California. Take I–5 north to the Via de la Valle exit.

Ice Hockey

The **San Diego Gulls** (☎ 619/224–4625) of the West Coast Hockey League take to the ice from late October to March at the San Diego Sports Arena (☎ 619/224–4171).

Over-the-Line

As much a giant beach party as a sport, this game is a form of beach softball played with three-person teams. Every July, the world championships are held on Fiesta Island, with two weekends of wild beer drinking and partying. Some good athletes take part in the games, too. Admission is free, but parking is impossible and traffic around Mission Bay can become unbearable. Call the Old Mission Beach Athletic Club (☎ 619/688–0817) for more information.

Soccer

The popular **San Diego Sockers** (☎ 619/224–4625) team—whose games can be raucous fun—compete in the Continental Indoor Soccer League from June through September at the San Diego Sports Arena (☎ 619/224–4171).

8 Shopping

San Diego's shopping areas are a mélange of self-contained megamalls, historic districts, homey villages, funky neighborhoods, and chic suburbs. You could literally spend a whole day at some of them—in addition to stores, restaurants, and amusements, Horton Plaza, for instance, even has live theater. In the beach towns, cruising the shops provides a break from the surf and sun. There are bargains to be had all over the city, in thrift stores and at outlet stores and several swap meets.

AN DIEGO'S MANY SHOPS are so spread out that the city can feel like one big mall, especially since so many national retailers and so much mass-produced merchandise are represented. You have to poke around some of the smaller neighborhoods—Hillcrest, La Jolla's Prospect Street and Girard Avenue, parts of Old Town, and the farm trails of inland San Diego North County among them—to find more offbeat and homegrown items, but it's worth the effort.

By Marael Johnson

Updated by Bobbi Zane

Most establishments are open daily 10–6; department stores and shops within the larger malls stay open until 9 PM on weekdays. Sales are advertised in the daily *San Diego Union-Tribune* and in the *Reader,* a free weekly that comes out on Thursday.

Shopping Districts

Coronado

Orange Avenue, in the center of town, has six blocks of ritzy boutiques and galleries.

The elegant **Hotel Del Coronado** (✉ 1500 Orange Ave.) houses 28 exclusive specialty shops on its Galleria level. **Sue Tushingham McNary Art Gallery** (✉ Hotel Del Coronado, ☎ 619/435–1819) specializes in painting, lithographs, and miniatures. **Opals and Gems of Australia** (✉ Hotel Del Coronado, ☎ 619/435–1184) sells opal jewelry and watches.

Ferry Landing Marketplace (✉ 1201 1st St., at B Ave.) has many boutiques and shops. **Coronado Holidays** (✉ Ferry Landing Marketplace, ☎ 619/435–6097) is a year-round Christmas shop. **Men's Island Sportswear** (✉ Ferry Landing Marketplace, ☎ 619/437–4696) has hats, sportswear, and accessories. Sterling silver jewelry can be found at the **Silver Designer** (✉ Ferry Landing Marketplace, ☎ 619/437–1428).

Downtown

Horton Plaza, bordered by Broadway, 1st Avenue, G Street, and 4th Avenue, is a shopper's Disneyland, with one-of-a-kind shops, multilevel department stores—including **Macy's** (☎ 619/231–4747) and **Nordstrom** (☎ 619/239–1700)—fast-food counters, classy restaurants, live theater, and cinemas. Among the center's 140 shops are **F.A.O. Schwarz** (☎ 619/702–7500) for children's toys; the largest **Sam Goody** (☎ 619/233–0890) music and video store in the country; **Warner Bros. Studio Store** (☎ 619/233–3058) for movie memorabilia; **Gnarley's for Surf** (☎ 619/236–1750); and **Bath & Body Works** (☎ 619/702–5719).

Victorian buildings and renovated warehouses in the historic **Gaslamp Quarter** along 4th and 5th avenues house art galleries, antiques, and specialty shops. **International Gallery** (✉ 643 G St., ☎ 619/235–8255) sells gifts, crafts, and folk, primitive, and native art from around the world. **Cuban Cigar Factory** (✉ 551 5th Ave., ☎ 619/238–2429) sells hand-rolled cigars. **Lulu Boutique** (✉ 762 5th Ave., ☎ 619/238–5673) has designer clothing and accessories for men and women. **Le Travel Store** (✉ 745 4th Ave., ☎ 619/544–0005) stocks luggage, totes, travel packs, luggage carts, and travel accessories. Adjacent to the Gaslamp Quarter, **Unicorn Company Arts & Antiques Mall** (✉ 704 J St., ☎ 619/232–1696) is the largest antiques complex in San Diego.

The Paladion (✉ 777 Front St., ☎ 619/232–1685) is San Diego's answer to Rodeo Drive. This posh complex's upscale boutiques include Cartier, Tiffany & Co., Gianni Versace, Bernini, and Salvatore Ferragamo.

Golden Triangle

University Towne Centre (✉ La Jolla Village Dr. between I–5 and I–805, ☎ 619/546–8858), a megamall several miles east of coastal La Jolla, has 160 specialty shops, department stores, cinemas, and restaurants, plus an Ice Chalet (☎ 619/452–9110) skating rink. **Nordstrom** (☎ 619/457–4575) and **Robinsons-May** (☎ 619/455–5650) are UTC's anchor department stores. UTC specialty shops include **Ann Taylor** (☎ 619/450–6550); **Banana Republic** (☎ 619/554–0180); **Bebe** (☎ 619/623–0374); and **Ben Bridge Jeweler** (☎ 619/453–9996).

The **Costa Verde Shopping Center** (✉ Genesee Ave. and La Jolla Village Dr.) is an enormous strip mall of convenience stores and inexpensive eateries. **Distinctions** (✉ 8650 Genesee Ave., ☎ 619/550–1776) specializes in women's fashions in sizes 10 and up; styles range from dresses and sportswear to swimwear and accessories.

Inland Farm Trails

Despite its urbanization, much of San Diego County remains rural; inland valleys and mountains support boutique farms that supply gourmet ingredients to the nation's finest restaurants. Summer visitors to **Dowle's San Pasqual Valley Produce** (✉ 15665 San Pasqual Valley Rd., Escondido, ☎ 760/789–7201) near Wild Animal Park pick vegetables directly from the fields. **The Farm Stand** (✉ San Pasqual Valley Rd., 2 ¾ mi w. of Wild Animal Park, ☎ 760/432–8912) sells fresh produce daily. **Bates Nut Farm** (✉ 15954 Woods Valley Rd., Valley Center, ☎ 760/749–3333) sells nuts and has a petting zoo. Closer to the coast, the **Vegetable Shop** (✉ 6123 Calzada del Bosque, Rancho Santa Fe, ☎ 619/756–3184) grows premium fruits and vegetables for many of San Diego's upscale restaurants, as well as famed California eateries such as Berkeley's Chez Panisse and Spago in Los Angeles.

Kensington, Hillcrest, and North Park

Though their boundaries blur, each of these three established neighborhoods north and northeast of downtown contains a distinct urban village with shops, cafés, and entertainment venues.

More than 20 dealers in the **Adams Avenue** area of Kensington sell everything from postcards and kitchen utensils to cut glass and porcelain.

Gay and funky **Hillcrest,** north of Balboa Park, is home to many gift, book, and music stores. **International Male** (✉ 3964 5th Ave., ☎ 619/294–8600) sells contemporary men's fashions at reasonable prices. **Obelisk** (✉ 1029 University Ave., ☎ 619/297–4171), in a busy area between bars and a coffeehouse, holds a bounty of gay and lesbian literature, cards, and gifts. **John's Fifth Avenue Luggage** (✉ 3833 4th Ave., ☎ 619/298–0993) has a large selection of travel accessories. Other shops in Hillcrest include clothing boutiques, among them **California Man** and **London Underground.** Don't miss **Babette Schwartz,** a zany pop-culture store.

The **Uptown District,** an open-air shopping center on University Avenue, houses several furniture, gift, and specialty shops. **Trader Joe's** (✉ Uptown District, 1090 University Ave., ☎ 619/296–3122) stocks an affordable and eclectic selection of gourmet foods and wines from around the world.

Retro rules in North Park. "Nostalgia" shops along **Park Boulevard** and **University Avenue at 30th Street** carry clothing, accessories, furnishings, wigs, and bric-a-brac of the 1920s–'60s. **Auntie Helen's** (✉ 4028 30th St., ☎ 619/584–8438), a nonprofit thrift emporium, sells heirlooms, collectibles, seasonal items, furniture, and brand-name clothing. Proceeds provide medical equipment, clothing, and laundry service to people living with AIDS. Head to **Henry's Marketplace** (⊠ 4175 Park Blvd., ☎ 619/291–8287) for fresh produce, bin grains, nuts, snacks, dried fruits, and health foods and ingredients.

La Jolla

High-end and trendy boutiques line Girard Avenue and Prospect Street. Shopping hours vary widely in La Jolla, so it's wise to call specific stores in advance.

The **Green Dragon Colony** (⊠ Prospect St., near Ivanhoe St.), La Jolla's historic shopping area, dates back to 1895, when the first structure was built by Anna Held, who was governess for Ulysses S. Grant Jr. Perched on a bluff overlooking La Jolla Cove, the Green Dragon and adjacent **Coast Walk Plaza** contain 22 shops and three restaurants.

CLOTHING

Custom Shirts of La Jolla (⊠ 7643 Girard Ave., ☎ 619/459–6147) stocks men's slacks, jackets, and sportswear, and makes custom-fitted shirts. **Gentleman's Quarter** (⊠ 1224 Prospect St., ☎ 619/459–3351) specializes in European-designed suits, shirts, and sportswear. **La Jolla Surf Systems** (⊠ 2132 Avenida de la Playa, ☎ 619/456–2777) carries swimsuits and other resort wear for men and women.

Capriccio (⊠ 6919 La Jolla Blvd., ☎ 619/459–4189) is a *Women's Wear Daily* recommendation for high-end designer ensembles and elegant evening wear. **Red** (⊠ 1298 Prospect St., ☎ 619/456–3934) sells trendy women's clothing. **Sigi Boutique** (⊠ 7888 Girard Ave., ☎ 619/ 454–7244) displays a range of European clothing and accessories for women. **Studio E** (⊠ 1262½ Prospect St., ☎ 619/551–1126) specializes in casual and elegant women's wear.

CRAFTS, FINE ART, JEWELRY

Africa and Beyond (⊠ 1250 Prospect St., ☎ 619/454–9983) carries ethnic art, crafts, masks, jewelry, and beads. **The Collector** (⊠ 1274 Prospect St., ☎ 619/454–9763) is a world-renowned source for colored gemstones and contemporary pieces designed by international jewelers and resident goldsmiths. **Fogel's Antique Beads** (⊠ 1128 Wall St., ☎ 619/456–2696) has European precious beads, including dazzling Austrian and Czech crystal beads; restringing is done here. **La Jolla Cove and Shell Shop** (⊠ 1325 Coast Blvd., ☎ 619/454–6080) stocks specimen and decorative shells, coral, and nautical gifts.

Lamano Gifts (⊠ 1260½ Prospect St., ☎ 619/454–7732) sells Mardi Gras–style papier mâché masks made in Venice. **Pomegranate** (⊠ 1152 Prospect St., ☎ 619/459–0629) sells accessories and exceptional antique jewelry. **Prospect Place Fine Art** (⊠ 1268 Prospect St., ☎ 619/ 459–1978) displays the works of Mexican artists. **Mark Reuven Gallery** (⊠ 1298 Prospect St., ☎ 619/459–8914) hangs photos of celebrities and sports figures. **Tasende Gallery** (⊠ 820 Prospect St., ☎ 619/454– 3691) specializes in modern European painting and sculpture.

Mission Valley/Hotel Circle

The Mission Valley/Hotel Circle area, northeast of downtown near I– 8 and Highway 163, has four major shopping centers. **Fashion Valley** (⊠ 452 Fashion Valley), **Hazard Center** (⊠ 7676 Hazard Center Dr.), **Mission Valley Center** (⊠ 1640 Camino del Rio N), and **Rio Vista Shopping Center** (⊠ Rio San Diego Dr., Stadium Way exit off I–8) contain hundreds of shops, as well as restaurants, cinemas, and branches of almost every San Diego department store.

Recently renovated Fashion Valley, an outdoor mall with lush landscaping and a contemporary mission theme, is San Diego's upscale shopping area, with more than 200 shops and restaurants. The mall operates shuttles to and from major hotels and has Spanish-speaking sales associates in every store. The major department stores here are **Neiman Marcus** (☎ 619/692–9100); **Nordstrom** (☎ 619/295–4441); **Saks Fifth Avenue** (☎ 619/260–0030); and **Robinsons-May** (☎ 619/291–5800). Specialty shops include **Origins** (☎ 619/295–9681), which carries organic personal-care products. **St. Croix Shop** (☎ 619/291–0441) has a large selection of hand-crafted sweaters, knits, and outerwear. **Smith & Hawken** (☎ 619/298–0441) stocks fancy gardening supplies, plants, and gifts.

Mission Valley Center's department-store lineup includes **Macy's Home & Furniture** (☎ 619/299–9811); **Robinsons-May** (☎ 619/297–2511); and **Montgomery Ward** (☎ 800/950–0345). The center's **Nordstrom Rack** (☎ 619/296–0143) has 50% reductions on top-of-the-line end-of-season collections from the Nordstrom department store. **Loehmann's** (☎ 619/2966–7776) is known for low prices on quality women's apparel. **Oshman's Sporting Goods** (☎ 619/299–0701) has all types of athletic and camping equipment.

North County

Del Mar Plaza (⌧ 15th St. and Camino Del Mar, ☎ 619/792–1555) has a Mediterranean ambience, flower-filled courtyards and fountains, a spectacular view of the Pacific, and some fine restaurants. Among the shops of interest here, **Black Market** (☎ 619/794–0355) carries classic clothing only in basic black. The **White House** (☎ 619/794–4038) sells stylish apparel only in white. **Silver Goose West Gifts** (☎ 619/755–4810) specializes in gifts and collectibles. **Neroli** (☎ 619/792–2883) has exquisite European lingerie.

Del Mar locals appreciate the relaxed atmosphere of **Flower Hill Mall** (⌧ 2710 Via de la Valle, east of I–5, ☎ 619/481–7131). **Russell Charles** (⌧ 2650 Via de la Valle, ☎ 619/794–8447) in the mall specializes in men's casual and active wear and has a tailor on premises. **Thinker Things** (⌧ 2670 Via de la Valle, ☎ 619/755–4488) carries an extensive collection of dolls and puppets in addition to its toys, crafts, and games.

Casual Solana Beach recently began polishing its image with development of the **Cedros Design District,** a collection of 50 shops specializing in interior design and gifts. David Turner, owner of **Elements Furniture and Gifts** (⌧ 118 S. Cedros Ave., ☎ 619/792–7773), who designs furnishings for TV's *Single Guy, Ellen,* and *Seinfeld,* sells copies of the chairs, sofas, and accessories you see on those shows. **Cedros Trading Co.** (⌧ 307 S. Cedros Ave., ☎ 619/794–9016) has a selection of imported items.

Farther north in Encinitas is the **Lumberyard** (⌧ 1st St. and Old Hwy. 1), an upscale strip mall where you'll find everything from yogurt shops and stationery to sportswear and sushi. **Hansen's** (⌧ 1105 1st St., ☎ 760/753–6595), a block or so south of the Lumberyard center, is one of San Diego's oldest surfboard manufacturers. The store also stocks a full line of recreational clothing and casual wear.

Ocean Beach/Mission Beach/Pacific Beach

Among the T-shirt shops, yogurt stands, and eateries that line the coast within San Diego proper are a few stores worthy of a browse. **Pilar's Beach Wear** (⌧ 3745 Mission Blvd., Mission Beach, ☎ 619/488–3056) has one of California's largest selections of major-label swimsuits. **Gary Gilmore Goldsmith** (⌧ 4919 Newport Ave., Ocean Beach, ☎ 619/225–1137) carries elegant, simple jewelry crafted by the owner. **Mallory's OB Attic** (⌧ 4921 Newport Ave., Ocean Beach, ☎ 619/

223–5048) sells collectibles and antique and used furniture. **Trader Joe's** (✉ 1211 Garnet Ave., Pacific Beach, ☎ 619/272–7235) stocks affordable gourmet items, wines and cheeses, and dried fruits and nuts.

Old Town

North of downtown, off I–5, the colorful Old Town historic district recalls a Mexican marketplace. Adobe architecture, flower-filled plazas, fountains, and courtyards decorate the shopping areas of **Bazaar del Mundo, La Esplanade,** and **Old Town Mercado,** where you'll find international goods, toys, souvenirs, and arts and crafts.

Bazaar del Mundo (✉ 2754 Calhoun St., ☎ 619/296–3161) is Old Town's most colorful shopping complex. The boutiques here sell designer items, crafts, fine arts, and fashions from around the world. **Ariana** (☎ 619/296–4989) and the **Guatemala Shop** (☎ 619/296–3161) in the Bazaar del Mundo carry ethnic and contemporary clothing. **Pottery Maker** (☎ 619/294–2028) sells hand-thrown pots and ceramic treasures.

Maidhof Bros. (✉ 1891 San Diego Ave., ☎ 619/574–1891) is one of California's oldest and largest dealers in nautical and brass items. **Dodson's Corner Shops** (✉ 2611 San Diego Ave., ☎ 619/293–4885) houses a collection of Old West Indian shops. The **Mexico Shop** (✉ 2783 San Diego Ave., ☎ 619/298–9167) carries silver, fans, mantillas, and ceramics.

Not far from Old Town is the home of San Diego's premier flea market. Bargain shoppers spend their weekend mornings at **Kobey's Swap Meet** (✉ San Diego Sports Arena parking lot, 3500 Sports Arena Blvd., ☎ 619/226–0650). The open-air event seems to expand every week, with sellers displaying everything from futons to fresh strawberries. The back section with second-hand goods is a bargain hunter's delight. The swap meet is open Thursday–Sunday, 7 AM–3 PM; admission is $1.

Seaport Village

Seaport Village (✉ West Harbor Dr., at Kettner Blvd.) is a waterfront complex of shops and restaurants, just northwest of the Convention Center. **Seaport Village Shell Company** (☎ 619/234–1004) carries shells, coral, and jewelry. **Seasick Giraffe** (☎ 619/236–8383) has yachting, travel, and safari wear. **Magic Shop and Southpaw** (☎ 619/236–1556) specializes in magic, games, gifts, and tools for left-handed people.

The **Olde Cracker Factory** (✉ 448 W. Market St., ☎ 619/233–1669) near Seaport Village contains three floors of specialty shops in a converted brick warehouse.

9 Side Trips

San Diego County sprawls from the
Pacific Ocean to suburban communities
that seem to sprout overnight on
canyons and cliffs. The Cleveland
National Forest and Anza-Borrego
Desert mark the county's eastern
boundaries; the busiest international
border in the United States is its
southern line. To the north, the marines
at Camp Pendleton practice land, sea,
and air maneuvers in southern
California's largest coastal greenbelt,
the demarcation zone between
congested Orange and Los Angeles
counties and mellower San Diego.

AN DIEGO PROPER HAS MORE OPEN SPACE than most
cities its size, but even its residents like to repair occasionally to the less-congested (though rapidly

By Bobbi Zane   growing) North County and Anza-Borrego Desert. North County attractions continue to multiply as the 1990s draw to a close—the expected 1999 opening of a Lego theme park in Carlsbad will only
increase tourism to the area, whose major stops already include San
Diego Wild Animal Park, the mountain town of Julian, and miles of
shoreline.

Pleasures and Pastimes

Beaches

The easily accessible beaches of San Diego North County are popular
with locals, many of whom stake out their favorite sunning, surfing,
body-boarding, and walking territories at Del Mar, Solana Beach,
Encinitas, Carlsbad, or Oceanside. *See* Chapter 7 for descriptions of
area beaches.

Desert Adventures

Anza-Borrego Desert State Park encompasses more than 600,000 acres
of desert, most of it wilderness. Springtime, when the wildflowers are
in full bloom, is a good season to visit. In sandstone canyons, you can
walk in the footsteps of prehistoric camels, zebras, and giant ground
sloths.

Dining

With the North County's clutch of wealthy communities, it shouldn't
come as a surprise that some prominent chefs have opened chic restaurants here. By contrast, casual dining is the rule in the beach towns,
inland mountain towns, and desert communities.

CATEGORY	COST*
$$$$	over $50
$$$	$30–$50
$$	$20–$30
$	under $20

per person for a three-course meal, excluding drinks, service, and 7.75% tax

Flowers

The North County is a prolific flower-growing region. Nurseries, some
open to the public, line the hillsides on both sides of I–5 in Encinitas,
Leucadia, and Carlsbad. During the winter most of the poinsettias sold
in the United States are shipped from here. Quail Botanical Gardens
in Encinitas displays plants year-round.

Lodging

If you stay overnight in the North County, your choices are diverse,
from hotels providing courtly, Old World service to basic motels catering to the beach crowd. Tennis and golf resorts and health-oriented
spas abound, and some fine bed-and-breakfast inns have sprung up in
Julian and other inland towns.

CATEGORY	COST*
$$$$	over $175
$$$	$120–$175
$$	$80–$120
$	under $80

All prices are for a standard double room, excluding 8%–10% tax.

THE SAN DIEGO NORTH COAST
From Del Mar to Oceanside

To say the north-coast area of San Diego County is different from the city of San Diego is a vast understatement. From the northern tip of La Jolla to Oceanside, a half-dozen small communities developed separately from urban San Diego—and from one another. The rich and famous were drawn to Del Mar, for example, because of its wide beaches and Thoroughbred horse-racing facility. Up the road, agriculture, not paparazzi, played a major role in the development of Solana Beach and Encinitas. Carlsbad still reveals its ties to the old Mexican rancheros and the entrepreneurial instinct of John Frazier, who told people the area's water could cure common ailments. In the late 19th century, not far from the current site of the posh La Costa Hotel and Spa, Frazier attempted to turn the area into a massive replica of a German mineral-springs resort.

An explosion of development that began in the 1980s and continued into the 1990s has intensified the suburbanization of the north coast. Once lovely hillsides have been bulldozed and leveled to make room for bedroom communities in Oceanside, Carlsbad, and even such high-priced areas as Rancho Santa Fe and La Jolla.

Highway S21 (known locally as Old Highway 101) connects beach towns going north: Del Mar, Solana Beach, Encinitas, Cardiff-by-the-Sea, Leucadia, Carlsbad, and Oceanside; the road changes its name each time it enters a new town.

Numbers in the margin correspond to points of interest on the San Diego North County map.

Del Mar

23 mi north of downtown San Diego on I–5, 9 mi north of La Jolla on S21.

Del Mar is best known for its race track, chic shopping strip, celebrity visitors, and wide beaches. Along with its collection of shops, **Del Mar Plaza** (⊠ 15th St., at S21—a.k.a. Camino del Mar) also contains outstanding restaurants and landscaped plazas and gardens with Pacific views. Del Mar has become headquarters for romantic balloon excursions; the late afternoon is the best time to spot the colorful balloons as they float over the hills and coastline. *See* Ballooning *in* Chapter 7 for a list of operators.

Access to Del Mar's beaches is from the streets that run east–west off Coast Boulevard. Summer evening concerts take place at **Seagrove Park** (⊠ 15th St., west end), a small stretch of grass overlooking the ocean.

❶ The **Del Mar Fairgrounds** is home to the **Del Mar Thoroughbred Club** (⊠ 2260 Jimmy Durante Blvd., ☎ 619/755–1141). Crooner Bing Crosby and his Hollywood buddies—Pat O'Brien, Gary Cooper, and Oliver Hardy, among others—organized the club in the '30s, primarily because Crosby thought it would be fun to have a track near his Rancho Santa Fe home. Del Mar soon developed into a regular stop for the stars of stage and screen. Even now the racing season here (usually July–September, post time Wednesday–Monday at 2 PM) is one of the most fashionable in California. During the off-season, horse players can still gamble at the fairgrounds, thanks to a satellite wagering facility that televises races from other California tracks. Times vary,

San Diego North County

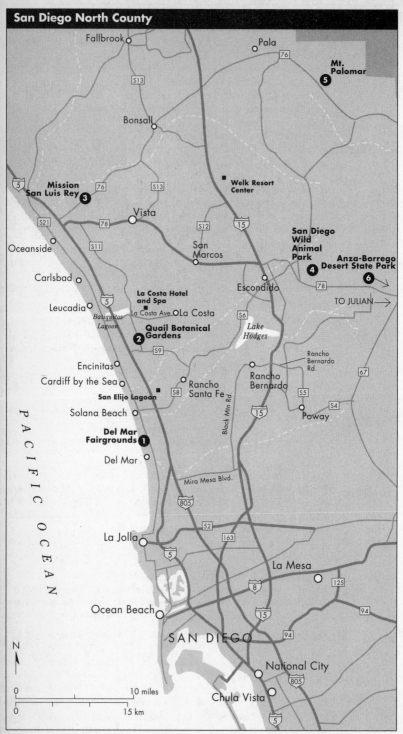

depending on which tracks in the state are operating. Del Mar Fairgrounds hosts more than 100 different events each year, including the San Diego County Fair. ⊠ *Head west at I–5's Via de la Valle Rd. exit,* ☎ *619/755–1161.*

🖐 **Freeflight,** a small exotic-bird training facility adjacent to the Del Mar Fairgrounds, is open to the public. Visitors are allowed to handle the birds—a guaranteed child pleaser. ⊠ *2132 Jimmy Durante Blvd.,* ☎ *619/481–3148.* 🎟 *$1.* ⊙ *Daily 10–4.*

Dining and Lodging

$$–$$$ ✕ **Cilantros.** Seafood enchiladas, portobello mushroom fajitas, and spit-roasted chicken with a mild chili sauce are among the subtly spiced Southwest-style dishes served at this Del Mar favorite. The inexpensive tapas menu, with such delicacies as duck quesadillas, Dungeness crab corn cakes, and soft tacos of smoked chicken with tropical-fruit salsa, is a little easier on the wallet. For a quick lunch, try the "gourmet wrapps"—rice and other ingredients wrapped in a spinach or tomato tortilla. ⊠ *3702 Via de la Valle,* ☎ *619/259–8777. AE, DC, MC, V.*

$$ ✕ **Epazote.** The menu changes seasonally at this relative of Cilantros that also serves Southwest-style cuisine. The salads are ample and tasty, the tacos imaginative, the fish dishes satisfying, and the margaritas superb. There's an ocean view from the patio, which gets busy on weekend nights and during the Sunday champagne brunch. ⊠ *1555 Camino del Mar, Suite 322,* ☎ *619/259–9966. AE, DC, MC, V.*

$$ ✕ **Il Fornaio.** Come here for good homemade pastas and crispy pizza, served in the Italianate dining room or on the terrace. The grilled meats can be dry, but the fish and pasta dishes are generally quite good. Il Fornaio also operates a wine bar in the adjacent outdoor piazza, where oenophiles can sit under an umbrella and enjoy the ocean view. ⊠ *1555 Camino del Mar, Suite 301,* ☎ *619/755–8876. AE, DC, MC, V.*

$$ ✕ **Pacifica Del Mar.** The ocean view alone would lure crowds to this
★ contemporary restaurant, which emphasizes Pacific Rim cuisine. The least-complicated dishes are generally the most successful. Try the "tacoshimi" appetizer, the barbecued king salmon, and the various stir-fries. The crème brûlée dessert is justifiably famous. ⊠ *1555 Camino del Mar, Suite 321,* ☎ *619/792–0476. AE, D, DC, MC, V.*

$$ ✕ **Spices Thai Cafe.** One of the North County's most stylish ethnic restaurants serves beautiful dishes, some of the best Thai cuisine in town. The traditional *pad Thai*—noodles with shrimp, bean sprouts, and egg—is a colorful feast, and the seafood selections and salads are also highly recommended. ⊠ *Piazza Carmel Shopping Center, 3810 Valley Centre Dr., Suite 903,* ☎ *619/259–0889;* ⊠ *16441 Bernardo Center Dr., Rancho Bernardo,* ☎ *619/674–4665. AE, D, DC, MC, V.*

$$ ✕ **Torrey Pines Cafe.** Locals flock to this reasonably priced sister to the Bird Rock Cafe in La Jolla to enjoy an eclectic menu of home-style cooking. The dishes are categorized according to size, inviting diners to mix, match, and share. The menu changes seasonally—the simplest dishes, such as the tasty osso buco, are generally the best bets. The wine list is good, and there's microbrewed beer on tap. ⊠ *2334 Carmel Valley Rd.,* ☎ *619/259–5878. AE, D, DC, MC, V.*

$$$–$$$$ ✕🏨 **L'Auberge Del Mar Resort and Spa.** L'Auberge is modeled on the Tudor-style Hotel Del Mar, a playground for the early Hollywood elite that was demolished in 1969. The inn is filled with dark-wood antiques, and all its spacious rooms have wet bars; many have fireplaces, full marble baths, and private balconies with garden and coastal views. The inn is home to the Center for Mind Body Medicine, presided over by antiaging guru and public-television personality Deepak Chopra. The spa specializes in aromatherapy and European herbal wraps and treat-

ments. California-Continental cuisine in the wood-paneled Dining Room includes such beautifully presented dishes as grilled salmon served with mashed potatoes and baby vegetables and roast pork with grilled fennel. The four-course specials served between 5:30 and 6:30 PM are among the best culinary bargains in San Diego. ⊠ *1540 Camino del Mar, 92014,* ☎ *619/259–1515 or 800/553–1336,* ℻ *619/755–4940. 120 rooms. 2 restaurants, bar, 2 pools, outdoor hot tub, beauty salon, spa, 2 tennis courts, health club, meeting rooms. AE, D, DC, MC, V.*

$$–$$$ 🖭 **Stratford Inn.** Rooms at this inn three blocks from the ocean are large, with ample closet space and dressing areas; some have views of the water. Suites with kitchenettes are available. Room rates include Continental breakfast. ⊠ *710 Camino del Mar, 92014,* ☎ *619/755–1501 or 800/446–7229,* ℻ *619/755–4704. 93 rooms. 2 pools. AE, D, DC, MC, V.*

Solana Beach

1 mi north of Del Mar on S21, 25 mi north of downtown San Diego on I–5 to Lomas Santa Fe Dr. west.

Once-quiet Solana Beach is quickly developing a reputation as *the* place to look for antiques, collectibles, and contemporary fashions and artworks. The Cedros Design District, occupying a long block near the new Amtrak station, contains shops, galleries, designers' studios, and restaurants. You can have high tea and browse the stores at **Cedros Trading Co.** (⊠ 307 S. Cedros Ave., ☎ 619/794–9016), which is open Thursday, Friday, and Sunday from noon to 4 PM.

Dining

$$$–$$$$ ✕ **Pamplemousse Grill.** A notable newcomer to North County's fine-
★   dining scene, the "Grapefruit Grill" achieves the elegant simplicity of a French country inn. The grilled meats and fish are perfectly prepared. Other menu items include an excellent lamb stew, a seafood stew with lobster, some colorful salads, and good crab cakes. Grapefruit sorbet clears the palate between courses, and the desserts are as tasty as they are eye-catching. The service is attentive at this restaurant on the Del Mar border, though the kitchen can be slow. ⊠ *514 Via de la Valle,* ☎ *619/792–9090. AE, D, DC, MC, V. Call for Mon. hrs; no lunch weekends.*

$–$$ ✕ **California Pizza Kitchen.** Bright, noisy, and cheerful, this family restaurant in the Beachwalk shopping center produces designer pizzas in its wood-fired oven, ranging from the conventional to the outlandish: five-cheese and tomato, mixed-grill vegetarian, rosemary chicken potato, and moo-shu-chicken calzone. Pasta dishes and salads are large. ⊠ *437 S. Hwy. 101,* ☎ *619/793–0999. AE, D, DC, MC, V.*

$ ✕ **Fidel's.** A particular favorite on its block of neighborhood Mexican eateries, Fidel's serves good renditions of traditional south-of-the-border dishes in a low-key atmosphere. The restaurant's outdoor patio draws a lively crowd. ⊠ *607 Valley Ave.,* ☎ *619/755–5292. MC, V.*

$ ✕ **Zinc Cafe.** Solana Beach's most popular sidewalk cafe lies at the head of Cedros Avenue's trendy Design District. Sit at one of the outdoor tables and enjoy the vegetarian breakfast and lunch selections or some truly decadent desserts. You can't go wrong with the veggie "Zinc burger," the black-bean chili, or the always-superb soup of the day. *Huevos rancheros* (eggs served on a tortilla with black beans and mango salsa) and delectable pastries are among the breakfast options.

✉ *132 S. Cedros Ave.,* ☎ *619/793–5436. No credit cards. No dinner. Closed Mon. at noon.*

Rancho Santa Fe

4 mi east of Solana Beach on S8 (Lomas Santa Fe Dr.), 29 mi north of downtown San Diego on I–5 to S8 east.

Groves of huge, drooping eucalyptus trees cover the hills and valleys of exclusive Rancho Santa Fe, which achieved unwanted notoriety in 1997 when members of the Heaven's Gate cult committed suicide at a mansion here. Rancho Santa Fe, east of I–5 on Via de la Valle Road, is horse country. It's common to see entire families riding the many trails that crisscross the hillsides.

Lillian Rice, one of the first women to graduate with a degree in architecture from the University of California, designed the town, modeling it after villages in Spain. Her first structure, a 12-room house built in 1922, evolved into the Inn at Rancho Santa Fe, which became a gathering spot for celebrities such as Bette Davis, Errol Flynn, and Bing Crosby. The challenging Rancho Santa Fe Golf Course, the original site of the Bing Crosby Pro-Am and considered one of the best courses in southern California, is open only to members of the Rancho Santa Fe community and guests of the inn.

Dining and Lodging

$$$$ ✕ **Mille Fleurs.** The recent winner of a *Gourmet* magazine "top tables"
★ award, this gem of a French auberge has a setting that is as romantic as its contemporary French cuisine is exquisite. The menu, which changes daily, might include first courses such as rabbit in aspic or shrimp bisque with cognac and asparagus flan, followed by entrées of poached pike quenelles with saffron sauce on spinach or confit of duck with braised Belgian endive, wild-blueberry sauce, and new potatoes. Mille Fleurs is near Chino's, the county's most famous vegetable farm, where the chef shops daily. ✉ *6009 Paseo Delicias,* ☎ *619/756–3085. Reservations essential. AE, DC, MC, V. No lunch weekends.*

$$$$ ✕▥ **Rancho Valencia Resort.** One of southern California's hidden
★ treasures has luxurious accommodations in Spanish-style casitas scattered among landscaped grounds. Gardens yield a year-round profusion of flowers. Many of the spacious suites have corner fireplaces that can be seen from the bed. Each suite also has a private patio and wet bar. Rancho Valencia is adjacent to three well-designed golf courses and is one of the top tennis resorts in the country. The inn's first-rate restaurant has earned raves for its California cuisine. The dinner menu changes seasonally and includes such dishes as sautéed sea scallops with sweet-pepper coulis and duck foie gras with turnip confit. ✉ *5921 Valencia Circle, 92067,* ☎ *619/756–1123 or 800/548–3664,* 𝔽𝔸𝕏 *619/756–0165. 43 suites. Restaurant, bar, 2 pools, 2 outdoor hot tubs, 18 tennis courts, croquet, health club, hiking, bicycles. AE, DC, MC, V.*

$$–$$$$ ✕▥ **Inn at Rancho Santa Fe.** Understated elegance is the theme of this genteel old resort in the heart of the village. This is the sort of place where people don their "whites" and play croquet on the lawn Sunday afternoons. Most accommodations are in red-tile-roof cottages scattered about the property's parklike 20 acres. Some cottages have two bedrooms, private patios, fireplaces, and hot tubs. The inn also maintains a beach house at Del Mar for guest use and has membership at the exclusive Rancho Santa Fe Golf Club. ✉ *5951 Linea del Cielo, 92067,* ☎ *619/756–1131 or 800/654–2928,* 𝔽𝔸𝕏 *619/759–1604. 90* *rooms. 3 dining rooms, bar, room service, pool, golf privileges, 3 tennis courts, croquet, exercise room, meeting rooms. AE, DC, M, V.*

Encinitas

6 mi north of Solana Beach on S21, 7 mi west of Rancho Santa Fe on S9, 28 mi north of downtown San Diego on I–5.

Flower breeding and growing is the major industry in Encinitas. The city, which encompasses the coastal towns of Cardiff-by-the-Sea and Leucadia as well as inland Olivehain, is home to Paul Ecke Poinsettias, the largest producer (open only to the trade) of the crimson Christmas blossom. During the spring bloom season, some commercial nurseries near I–5 are open to the public. The palm trees of Sea Cliff Roadside Park (☞ Beaches *in* Chapter 7) and the golden domes of the Self-Realization Fellowship mark the southern entrance to downtown Encinitas.

The **San Elijo Lagoon Ecological Reserve,** east of east of S21 just north of Solana Beach, is the most complex of the estuary systems in San Diego North County. A network of trails surrounds the area, which is home to more than 300 species of plants and many fish and migrating birds. ⊠ *From S21, head east at Chesterfield Dr., cross the train tracks, and head south at San Elijo Ave., which becomes Manchester Ave. Lagoon entrance is 8/10 mi from S21 and Chesterfield.*

The **Self-Realization Fellowship** (Swami's to the locals) was built at the turn of the century and is a retreat and place of worship for the followers of a religious sect that holds weekly services, group meditations, and other activities. Its beautiful gardens, containing koi ponds and seasonal flowers, are open to the public. ⊠ *939 2nd St.,* ☎ *760/436–7220.* ⊙ *Tues.–Sun. 11 AM–5 PM.*

An example of the Encinitas area's dedication to horticulture can be found at the **Quail Botanical Gardens,** home to thousands of different varieties of plants, especially drought-tolerant species. Individual displays include Central American, Himalayan, Australian, and African tropical gardens; a California native plant display; an old-fashioned demonstration garden; and plantings of subtropical fruit. ⊠ *230 Quail Gardens Dr.,* ☎ *760/436–3036.* ✑ *$3.* ⊙ *Daily 9–5.*

Dining and Lodging

$–$$ ✕ **El Callejon.** This festive Mexican café tucked away in a minimall spills over onto several patios. Many tables are outdoors, where heaters provide warmth, but the indoor tables can be drafty in chilly weather. The extensive menu highlights regional dishes not available at most restaurants, such as shrimp or beef in cilantro sauce and chicken in chipotle sauce. The bar pours several dozen tequilas, making the margarita combinations virtually endless. ⊠ *Moonlight Plaza Shopping Center, 345 1st St. (Hwy. 101),* ☎ *760/634–2793. AE, D, MC. V.*

$–$$ ✕ **Vigilucci's Pizzeria.** Combining the breezy openness of a beach café with the ambience of a traditional Italian trattoria-pizzeria, this casual restaurant has a wood-burning oven that turns out thin, chewy pizzas, light on the toppings. Among the tasty pastas is one baked with eggplant. This is a sister restaurant to Vigilucci's Trattoria in downtown Encinitas, but the food here is better and the heated patio has an ocean view. ⊠ *1933 San Elijo Ave., Cardiff-by-the-Sea,* ☎ *760/634–2335. AE, D, DC, MC, V.*

$ ✕ **George's.** Surfboards dangle from the ceiling and surfer memorabilia adorns a wall at this funky reminder of Encinitas's days as the quintessential North County beach town. Overstuffed omelets, good burgers, grilled sandwiches (named after local surfing beaches), and thick shakes hark back to the days before anyone had heard the word "cholesterol." You can order a salad instead of a burger or ask for fruit rather than fries with your sandwich, but who are you kidding? ✉ *641 1st St.,* ☎ *760/942–9549. MC, V.*

$$ 🖭 **Radisson Inn Encinitas.** This low-rise blends into an Encinitas hillside just east of Old Highway 101. Rooms have richly colored rugs and comfy upholstered chairs; some have kitchenettes and some have ocean views. Continental breakfast is complimentary. ✉ *85 Encinitas Blvd., 92024,* ☎ *760/942–7455 or 800/333–3333,* FAX *760/632–9481. 90 rooms. Restaurant, bar, pool, outdoor hot tub. AE, D, DC, MC, V.*

$ 🖭 **Moonlight Beach Motel.** Folksy and laid-back, this motel is the closest to the beach at Encinitas. Rooms are basic but spacious and clean. Some have ocean views. Weekly rates are available. ✉ *233 2nd St., 92024,* ☎ *760/753–0623,* FAX *760/944–9827. 24 rooms. Kitchenettes. AE, DC, MC, V.*

En Route The oceanside community of **Leucadia,** named after a famous Greek promontory, was incorporated into Encinitas in 1986. Its main street, a few miles north of Encinitas, contains art galleries and other shops as well as some commercial flower nurseries that are open to the public. The narrow, rocky stretch of beach in Leucadia—a steep, stone staircase leads down to one portion of it—is popular with surfers.

Carlsbad

6 mi from Encinitas on S21, 36 mi north of downtown San Diego on I–5.

Carlsbad owes its name and Bavarian look to John Frazier, who lured people to the area a century ago with talk of the healing powers of mineral water bubbling from a coastal well. The water was found to have the same properties as water from the German mineral wells of Karlsbad—hence the name of the new community. Remnants from this era, including the original well and a monument to Frazier, are found at the **Alt Karlsbad Haus** (✉ 2802A Carlsbad Blvd.).

Carlsbad is expanding: The Four Seasons Resort Aviara opened in 1997, and Lego Family Park, a theme park based on the children's building sets, should be completed by 1999.

Development has destroyed many of the lagoon and salt marsh wildlife habitats that punctuated the North County coastline, but **Batiquitos Lagoon** is being restored to support large fish and bird populations. A short interpretive trail leads from the visitor center. ✉ *Batiquitos Dr. south (east of I–5's Poinsettia La. exit),* ☎ *760/431–2019.*

In spring, you can walk through the **Flower Fields at Carlsbad Ranch,** where the hillsides are abloom with thousands of ranunculuses from March through April. During the winter holidays, these same fields are ablaze with scarlet poinsettias from the nearby Ecke Nursery. ✉ *Palomar Airport Rd., east of I–5,* ☎ *760/431–0352.*

Dining and Lodging

$$$$ ✕🖭 **La Costa Hotel and Spa.** Don't expect glitz and glamour at this famous resort; it's surprisingly low-key, with low-slung buildings and vaguely Southwest contemporary–style rooms. Although many guests come for La Costa's tranquil setting, the resort has one of the most

comprehensive sports programs in the area. There are two championship golf courses and a golf school, plus a large tennis center. The spa is world-famous, with services ranging from massages to nutritional counseling; spa cuisine is available in three restaurants. The complex includes Pisces Delicacies of the Sea restaurant, long one of San Diego's top seafood venues. ⊠ *2100 Costa del Mar Rd., 92009,* ☎ *760/438–9111 or 800/854–5000,* FAX *760/931–7569. 478 rooms. 5 restaurants, 2 lounges, in-room modem lines, room service, pool, beauty salon, spa, 2 18-hole golf courses, 21 tennis courts, health club, hiking, jogging, conference center, car rental. AE, D, DC, MC, V.*

$$$$ 🖬 **Four Seasons Resort Aviara.** This new hilltop luxury resort sits on 30 acres overlooking Batiquitos Lagoon and an Arnold Palmer–designed golf course. The large rooms at the Spanish Colonial–style property are opulently appointed; all have private balconies or landscaped terrace sitting areas, and marble bathrooms with deep soaking tubs. ⊠ *7100 Four Seasons Point, 92009,* ☎ *760/931–6672 or 800/332–3442,* FAX *760/931–0390. 331 rooms. 4 restaurants, 3 lounges, pool, beauty salon, spa, 18-hole golf course, 8 tennis courts, health club, hiking, bicycles, meeting rooms, car rental. AE, DC, MC, V.*

$$$–$$$$ 🖬 **Carlsbad Inn.** Gabled roofs, half-timbered walls, and stone supports are among the architectural elements of note at this sprawling European-style inn and time-share condominium complex in the heart of Carlsbad village. Rooms, which range from large to cramped, are furnished in Old World fashion, including pencil-post beds and wall sconces. Many have ocean views and kitchenettes; some also have fireplaces and hot tubs. ⊠ *3075 Carlsbad Blvd., 92008,* ☎ *760/434–7020 or 800/235–3939,* FAX *760/729–4853. 60 rooms. Pool, outdoor hot tub, sauna, exercise room, coin laundry, meeting rooms. AE, D, DC, MC, V.*

$$–$$$ 🖬 **Best Western Beach View Lodge.** Reservations are essential at this reasonably priced Mediterranean-style low-rise near the beach. Despite the name, few rooms have a beach view. Functional rooms have lightwood or whitewashed furnishings; some have fireplaces and balconies. Room rates include complimentary Continental breakfast. The Best Western Beach Terrace Inn on the water—better views, higher prices—is under the same ownership. ⊠ *3180 Carlsbad Blvd., 92008,* ☎ *760/729–1151 or 800/433–5415,* FAX *760/729–1151. 41 rooms. Kitchenettes, pool, outdoor hot tub. AE, D, DC, MC, V.*

Oceanside

8 mi north of Carlsbad on S21, 37 mi north of downtown San Diego on I–5.

With 900 slips, **Oceanside Harbor** (☎ 760/966–4570) is the north coast's center for fishing, sailing, and ocean-water sports. Oceanside Pier, the longest on the West Coast, has shops and restaurants. **Camp Pendleton,** encompassing 17 mi of Pacific shoreline, is the nation's largest amphibious military training facility. It's not unusual to see herds of tanks and flocks of helicopters maneuvering through the dunes and brush alongside I–5.

★ ❸   **Mission San Luis Rey** was built by Franciscan friars in 1798 under the direction of Father Fermin Lasuen to help educate and convert local Native Americans. The well-preserved San Luis Rey was the 18th and largest of the California missions. The sala (parlor), a friar's bedroom, a weaving room, the kitchen, and a collection of religious art convey much about early mission life. Retreats are still held here, but a picnic area, a gift shop, and a museum (which has the most extensive collection of old Spanish vestments in the United States) are also on the grounds. Self-guided tours are available. The mission is on Highway 76, which becomes Mission Avenue inland from S21 (from the ocean, continue east on Highway 76 approximately 4 mi, past the Mission Avenue business district area and I–5). ⊠ *4050 Mission Ave.,* ☎ *760/ 757–3651.* ⬚ *$3.* ⊙ *Mon.–Sat. 10–4:30, Sun. 11:30–4:30.*

Lodging

$$–$$$$ ⬚ **Oceanside Marina Inn.** Of all the oceanfront lodgings in North County towns, this motel occupies the best location—a spit of land surrounded by water on all sides. All rooms have either ocean or harbor views. The inn was purchased by the City of Oceanside in 1994 with the intent of transforming it into a luxury resort. It's not there yet, but the rooms are unusually large and many contain fully equipped kitchens, fireplaces, and expansive ocean-view balconies. Room rates include Continental breakfast. A free bus shuttles guests to the beach. ⊠ *2008 Harbor Dr. N, 92054,* ☎ *760/722–1561 or 800/252–2033,* ℻ *760/ 439–9758. 64 rooms. Kitchenettes, pool, outdoor hot tub, sauna, coin laundry. AE, MC, V.*

San Diego North Coast Essentials

Arriving and Departing

BY BUS

The San Diego Transit District (☎ 619/233–3004) covers the city of San Diego up to Del Mar. The **North County Transit District** (☎ 760/743– 6283) serves San Diego County from Del Mar north.

BY CAR

Interstate 5, the main freeway artery connecting San Diego to Los Angeles, follows the coastline. To the west, running parallel to it, is S21 (known locally, but not signed, as Old Highway 101, and at points signed as Highway 101), which never strays too far from the ocean. Watch the signs, because the road has a different name as it passes through each community.

BY PLANE

McClellan Palomar Airport (⊠ 2198 Palomar Airport Rd., Carlsbad, ☎ 760/431–4646) is a general-aviation airport run by the county of San Diego and open to the public. Commuter airlines sometimes have flights from Palomar to Orange County and Los Angeles.

BY TRAIN

Amtrak (☎ 760/722–4622 in Oceanside, or 800/872–7245) operates trains daily between Los Angeles, Orange County, and San Diego, with stops in Solana Beach and Oceanside. The last train leaves San Diego at approximately 7 each night (9 on Friday; the last arrival is at approximately midnight). **Coaster** (Coast Express Regional Rail Service, ☎ 760/722–6283 or 800/262–7837) operates commuter rail service between San Diego and Oceanside with weekday-only service to San Diego, Old Town, Sorrento Valley, Solana Beach, Encinitas, Carlsbad Poinsettia Station, Carlsbad Village Station, and Oceanside.

Guided Tours

Civic Helicopters (⊠ 2192 Palomar Airport Rd., ☎ 760/438–8424) gives whirlybird tours of the area. The tours run about $70 per person per half hour and go along the beaches to the Del Mar racetrack. **Barnstorming Adventures** (☎ 760/438–7680 or 800/759–5667) conducts open-cockpit vintage biplane and Piper Cub excursions from McClellan Palomar Airport. Tours of varying lengths and amenities start at $110 per couple.

Visitor Information

Carlsbad Convention and Visitors Bureau (✉ Box 1246, Carlsbad 92008, ☎ 760/434–6093). **Greater Del Mar Chamber of Commerce** (✉ 1101 Camino del Mar, 92014, ☎ 619/793–5292). **Oceanside Chamber of Commerce** (✉ 928 North Coast Hwy., 92054, ☎ 760/722–1534). **San Diego North County Convention and Visitors Bureau** (✉ 720 N. Broadway, Escondido 92025, ☎ 760/745–4741).

INLAND NORTH COUNTY

Rancho Bernardo, Escondido, Fallbrook, and Temecula

Even though the coast is only a short drive away, the beach communities seem far removed from the quiet lakes of Escondido, the avocado-growing country surrounding Fallbrook, or, north of the county, the vineyards of Temecula. Home to old missions, San Diego Wild Animal Park, the Welk Resort Center, and innumerable three-generation California families, the inland area of North County is the quiet rural sister to the rest of San Diego County.

Numbers in the margin correspond to points of interest on the San Diego North County map.

Rancho Bernardo

23 mi northeast of downtown San Diego on I–15.

Rancho Bernardo straddles a stretch of I–15 between San Diego and Escondido. Primarily a suburban community, it is the location of the Rancho Bernardo Inn, a resort complex with golf, tennis, and spa facilities. The town is also the home base of Ken Blanchard's Golf University of San Diego.

Dining and Lodging

$$$ ✕ **French Market Grill.** The old-world ambience of the Grill's stylish dark-wood dining room and the twinkling lights in the patio seating area will help you forget that you're eating in a shopping center. Pasta dishes and salads give an Italo-Californian accent to a menu whose dominant note is French. The fare changes with the seasons, but you can always count on expertly prepared fish, chicken, and meat dishes. Lamb is a specialty: Try the succulent lamb shank served with homemade artichoke ravioli or roasted lamb loin with porcini mushrooms. Desserts are luxurious, the service is cheerful and attentive, and the California and French wines are reasonably priced. ✉ *Ralph's Shopping Center, 15717 Bernardo Heights Pkwy.,* ☎ *619/485–8055. AE, DC, MC, V.*

$$–$$$ ✕ **Bernard'O.** You'll find eclectic seasonal California-European cuisine at this comfortable if sparse dining room. Appetizers include escargots and a grilled portobello mushroom served on sautéed spinach. Pastas are homemade—try the "ravioli of the day." Light sauces accompany the fresh fish; filet mignon comes with a richer brandy and green-peppercorn sauce. ✉ *Rancho Bernardo Village Shopping Center, 12457 Rancho Bernardo Rd.,* ☎ *619/487–7171. AE, D, DC, MC, V. No lunch weekends; closed Mon.*

$ ✕ **Chiêu-Anh.** Vietnam has developed one of the world's great cuisines, which you may sample in fine form here. Try the spring rolls, the rice noodles with charbroiled shrimp, one of the clay-pot dishes, or the shrimp on sugarcane. ⊠ *16769 Bernardo Center Dr., Suite 10 (behind Block-buster),* ☎ *619/485–1231. AE, DC, MC, V. No lunch weekends.*

$$$$ ✕⊓ **Rancho Bernardo Inn.** Red-roof buildings surround tile court-
★ yards with Italian fountains at this 265-acre resort with a decidedly
Mediterranean ambience. Golf is a top priority—a championship golf
course is on site and guests have access to four neighboring links.
Many of the spacious rooms are furnished with Mexican and Italian
antiques. The inn's dining room, El Bizcocho (dinner only, plus a fine
Sunday brunch; jacket and tie) has earned a reputation throughout San
Diego County for consistently superb Continental cuisine. ⊠ *17550
Bernardo Oaks Dr., 92128,* ☎ *619/487–1611 or 800/542–6096,* FAX
*619/675–8501. 287 rooms. 2 restaurants, 2 bars, in-room modem lines,
room service, 2 pools, 8 outdoor hot tubs, massage, sauna, spa, steam
room, driving range, 18-hole golf course, putting green, 12 tennis
courts, health club, volleyball, bicycles, shops, children's programs,
concierge, business services, meeting rooms. AE, D, DC, MC, V.*

Escondido

*8 mi north of Rancho Bernardo on I–15, 31 mi northeast of down-
town San Diego on I–15.*

Escondido is a thriving, rapidly expanding residential and commercial
city of more than 80,000 people and the center of a variety of attrac-
tions.

The **California Center for the Arts,** an entertainment complex with two
theaters, an art museum, and a conference center, presents operas, mu-
sicals, plays, dance performances, and symphony and chamber-music
concerts. The museum's focus is 20th-century California art. ⊠ *340
N. Escondido Blvd.,* ☎ *760/738–4100.* ⊟ *Museum $4.* ☉ *Tues.–Sat.
10–5, Sun. noon–5.*

Deer Park Vintage Cars and Wine is a branch of the award-winning
Napa Valley Deer Park Winery. Outside are select models from a col-
lection of more than 120 vintage convertibles. There is also a gift
shop–delicatessen and a picnic area. ⊠ *29013 Champagne Blvd., 15
mi north of Escondido,* ☎ *760/749–1666.* ☉ *Daily 10–5.*

Orfila Vineyards holds tours and tastings. The Rose Arbor has a pic-
nic area. ⊠ *13455 San Pasqual Valley Rd.,* ☎ *760/738–6500.*

★ ⚲ ❹ **San Diego Wild Animal Park** is an extension of the San Diego Zoo. The
2,200-acre preserve in the San Pasqual Valley is designed to protect
endangered species of animals from around the world. Five exhibit areas
have been carved out of the dry, dusty canyons and mesas to represent
the animals' natural habitats in North Africa, South Africa, East Africa,
Asian swamps, and Asian plains.

The best way to see these preserves is on the 50-minute, 5-mi Wgasa
Bushline Monorail ride (included in the price of admission). As you
pass in front of the large, naturally landscaped enclosures, you'll see
animals bounding through prairies and mesas as they would in the wild.
More than 3,000 animals of 450 species roam or fly through the ex-
pansive grounds. Enemy species are separated from each other by deep
moats, but only the tigers, lions, and cheetahs are kept in isolation.
Photographers with zoom lenses can get spectacular shots of zebras,
gazelles, and rhinos (a seat on the right-hand side of the monorail is
best for viewing the majority of the animals). The trip is especially en-
joyable in the early evening, when the heat has subsided and the ani-

mals are active and feeding. On summer nights, the monorail travels through the park after dark, and soft amber sodium-vapor lamps highlight the animals in action.

The park is as much a botanical garden as a zoo, and botanists collect rare and endangered plants for preservation. The 5-ft-tall desert cypress found here is native to the Sahara; only 16 such trees are still in existence there.

The 1¼-mi-long **Kilimanjaro Safari Walk** winds through some of the park's hilliest terrain in the East Africa section, with observation decks overlooking the elephants and lions. A 70-ft suspension bridge, made of Douglas fir poles, spans a steep ravine, leading to the final observation point and a panorama of the San Pasqual Valley and the Wild Animal Park.

The ticket booths at **Nairobi Village,** the park's center, are designed to resemble the tomb of an ancient king of Uganda. Animals in the **Petting Kraal** affectionately tolerate tugs and pats and are quite adept at posing for pictures with toddlers. At the **Congo River Fishing Village,** 10,000 gallons of water pour each minute over a huge waterfall into a large lagoon. **Hidden Jungle,** an 8,800-square-ft glass house, features creatures that creep, flutter, or just hang out in a tropical habitat: Gigantic cockroaches and bird-eating spiders share the turf with colorful butterflies and hummingbirds and oh-so-slow-moving two-toed sloths. **Lorikeet Landing** holds 75 loud and colorful lorikeets—you can buy a cup of nectar at the aviary entrance to induce the small parrots to land on your hand. **Heart of Africa,** a 1997 exhibit, contains several simulated environments, from fringe forest to savanna, plus a waterhole and a working research station.

Ravens, vultures, hawks, and a great horned owl perform throughout the day at the **Bird Show Amphitheater.** All the park's animal shows are entertainingly educational. The gift shops stock African crafts and animal-oriented souvenirs, and free-loan cameras are available. Serious shutterbugs might consider joining one of the park's special photo caravans ($65–$89, including admission). ⊠ *Take I–15 north to Via Rancho Pkwy. and follow signs (6 mi),* ☎ *760/480–0100.* ⊡ *$18.95, includes all shows and monorail tour; a combination pass ($28.50) grants entry, within 5 days of purchase, to both the San Diego Zoo and the San Diego Wild Animal Park; parking $3. AE, D, MC, V.* ☺ *Daily from 9 AM; closing hrs vary with season (call ahead).*

San Pasqual Battlefield State Historic Park and Museum commemorates an important moment in the Mexican-American War. On December 6, 1846, a contingent of Americans, including famous frontier scout Kit Carson, was defeated by a group of Californios (Spanish-Mexican residents of California). This was the Californios' most notable success during the war, but the Americans, with support from Commodore Stockton in San Diego, regained control of the region. ⊠ *15808 San Pasqual Valley Rd.,* ☎ *760/489–0076.* ⊡ *Free.* ☺ *Weekends only 10–5.*

Dining and Lodging

$$–$$$　✕ **Sirino's.** Here's an excellent choice for pre-concert dining close to the California Center for the Arts. The simpler French or Italian dishes are particularly recommended; homemade bread accompanies them. The wine list is serious, as are the desserts. The service is friendly and attentive. ⊠ *113 W. Grand Ave.,* ☎ *760/745–3835. Reservations essential. AE, D, DC, MC, V. Closed Sun.–Mon. No lunch Sat.*

$$ ✕ **150 Grand Cafe.** The seasonal menu of this pretty restaurant show-cases California-style dishes prepared with a European flair. It's within walking distance of the California Center for the Arts. ⊠ *150 W. Grand Ave.,* ☎ *760/738–6868. AE, DC, MC, V. Closed Sun.–Mon. except performance nights.*

$$–$$$$ 🏨 **Welk Resort Center.** This sprawling resort, built by bandleader Lawrence Welk in the 1960s, includes a hotel, time-share condomini-ums, and residences. A museum displays Welk memorabilia, a theater presents Broadway-style musicals year-round, and there are many shops on the premises. Hotel rooms have a Southwest flavor. ⊠ *8860 Lawrence Welk Dr., 92026,* ☎ *760/749–3000 or 800/932–9355,* FAX *760/749–6182. 132 rooms. Restaurant, deli, 3 pools, 3 outdoor hot tubs, 3 18-hole golf courses, 3 tennis courts, theater, children's pro-grams, meeting rooms. AE, D, DC, MC, V.*

Mount Palomar

❺ *35 mi northeast of Escondido on I–15 to Hwy. 76 to S6, 66 mi north-east of downtown San Diego on Hwy. 163 to I–15 to Hwy. 76 to S6.*

Palomar Observatory, atop Mount Palomar and home to the 200-inch Hale Telescope, is the site of some of the most important astronomi-cal discoveries of the 20th century. The small museum at the observa-tory contains photos of some of these discoveries and presents informative videos. A park with picnic areas surrounds the observatory. ⊠ *Hwy. S6, at the end of Hwy. 76, east of I–15,* ☎ *760/742–2119.* 🎫 *Free.* ☉ *Observatory for self-guided tours: daily 9–4.*

Visitors to Mount Palomar can take the scenic way down the 6,140-ft mountain by way of the **Palomar Plunge,** an 18-mi bike ride to the bottom (no pedaling required) conducted by Gravity Activated Sports (⊠ *16220 Hwy. 76,* ☎ *760/742–2294).*

Mission San Antonio de Pala, built in 1816, is a living remnant of the mission era that serves the local Native American community. Displays in a small museum include artifacts from the original mission. ⊠ *Hwy. 76, 6 mi east of I–15,* ☎ *760/742–3317.* 🎫 *$2.* ☉ *Museum and gift shop: Tues.–Sun. 10–3.*

Fallbrook

19 mi northwest of Escondido on I–15 to Mission Rd. (S13) to Mis-sion Dr.

With 6,000 hillside acres planted, Fallbrook bills itself as the Avocado Capital of the World. But citrus and macadamia nuts are also grown in the region. Historic Old Main Street, a few antiques malls, and agri-culture are the attractions here; walking is the best way to explore.

Shopping

Coyote Hill Farms (⊠ 1517 Macadamia Dr., ☎ 760/723–3564) sells avocados, citrus fruit, and gift baskets. **Ruthy's Antique and Curio Mall** (⊠ 205 N. Main St., ☎ 760/723–8043) specializes in estate-sale items, collectibles, and original autographs of famous people. **The Westerner** (⊠ 110 N. Main St., ☎ 760/728–1462) is an old-fashioned dry-goods store specializing in western wear, complete with a cashiers' cage and a jar of penny candy.

Temecula

29 mi from Escondido, 60 mi from San Diego on I–15 north to Rancho California Rd. east.

Once an important stop on the Butterfield Overland Stagecoach route and a market town for the huge cattle ranches occupying the surrounding hillsides, Temecula (pronounced teh-*mec*-cyoo-la) is southern California's only developed wine region. Premium wineries, most of which allow tasting for a small fee, can be found along Rancho California Road as it snakes through oak-studded rolling hills. Temecula draws thousands of visitors to its Balloon and Wine Festival held in April or May. Hot-air-balloon excursions are a good choice year-round; **Sunrise Balloons** (☎ 800/548–9912) has morning flights.

Thornton Winery (✉ 32575 Rancho California Rd., ☎ 909/699–0099) produces several varieties of wine, including Culbertson champagne; it offers weekend tours and daily tastings. **Callaway Vineyard & Winery** (✉ 32720 Rancho California Rd., ☎ 909/676–4001) is best known for its Callalees chardonnay. Tastings, tours, and theme dinners and luncheons are all available, and there's a gift shop. **Maurice Car'rie Vineyard & Winery** (✉ 34225 Rancho California Rd., ☎ 909/676–1711) has a tasting room, a gift shop, and a picnic area.

Once a hangout for cowboys, **Old Town Temecula** still looks the part. Park on Front Street and walk along the six-block stretch past the large 19th-century wooden buildings that line the streets; several antiques shops here specialize in local and Old West memorabilia.

Temecula Historic Museum adjacent to Sam Hicks Park displays Native American and farming memorabilia. Guided walking tours of Old Temecula are conducted from here by appointment (donations appreciated). ✉ *41905 Marino Dr., off Front St.,* ☎ *909/676–0021.* 🎟 *Free.* ☉ *Wed.–Sun. 11–4.*

The **Santa Rosa Plateau Ecological Reserve** provides a glimpse of what this countryside was like before the developers took over. Trails wind through oak forests past vernal pools and rolling grassland. A visitor and operations center that opened in 1997 has interpretive displays and maps; some of the reserve's hiking trails begin here. ✉ *Take I–15's Clinton Keith Rd. exit and head west 5 mi,* ☎ *909/677–6951.* 🎟 *$2.* ☉ *Sunrise–sunset.*

Dining and Lodging

$$–$$$ ✕ **Cafe Champagne.** The Thornton Winery's airy country restaurant, whose big windows overlook the vineyards, serves light California cuisine with an emphasis on pasta, chicken, and fish dishes. The house champagne is a fitting complement to the fine cuisine. ✉ *32575 Rancho California Rd.,* ☎ *909/699–0099. AE, D, DC, MC, V. No dinner Mon.*

$–$$ ✕ **Baily Wine Country Cafe.** Tucked in the back of a shopping center, this pleasant café with a patio dining area serves soups, sandwiches, and tasty California cuisine with light sauces. Picnics can be ordered 24 hours in advance. The wine list is varied and good. ✉ *27644 Ynez Rd.,* ☎ *909/676–9567. AE, DC, MC, V.*

$$$$ 🏨 **Temecula Creek Inn.** The upscale golf resort occupies a collection of low-slung red-roof buildings on a hillside a short distance from the wine-touring area. ✉ *44501 Rainbow Canyon Rd.,* ☎ *909/694–1000 or 800/962–7335,* FAX *909/676–3422. 80 rooms. Restaurant, refrig-*

erators, pool, outdoor hot tub, driving range, 27-hole golf course, putting green, 2 tennis courts, meeting rooms. AE, D, DC, MC, V.

$$–$$$ ⌂ **Loma Vista Bed and Breakfast.** The only overnight accommodation within the Temecula wine country, a Mission-style bed-and-breakfast inn, has tranquil views of vineyards, citrus groves, and gardens. ⌂ *3350 La Serena Way,* ☎ *909/676–7047. 6 rooms. Outdoor hot tub. D, MC, V.*

Inland North County Essentials

Arriving and Departing

BY BUS

North County Transit District (☎ 760/743–6283) routes crisscross the Escondido area.

BY CAR

Escondido sits at the intersection of Highway 78, which heads east from Oceanside, and I–15, the inland freeway connecting San Diego to Riverside, 30 minutes north of Escondido. Del Dios Highway winds from Rancho Santa Fe through the hills past Lake Hodges to Escondido. Highway 76, which connects with I–15 a above Escondido, veers east to Mount Palomar. I–15 continues north to Fallbrook and Temecula.

Visitor Information

Escondido Chamber of Commerce (⌂ 720 N. Broadway, ☎ 760/745–2125). **Fallbrook Chamber of Commerce** (⌂ Dept. CTP, 233 E. Mission Rd., Suite A, 92028, ☎ 760/728–5845). **Rancho Bernardo Chamber of Commerce** (⌂ 11650 Iberia St., Suite 220, ☎ 760/487–1767). **San Diego North County Convention and Visitors Bureau** (⌂ 720 N. Broadway, Escondido 92025, ☎ 760/745–4741). **Temecula Valley Chamber of Commerce** (⌂ 27450 Ynez Rd., ☎ 909/676–5090).

THE BACKCOUNTRY AND JULIAN

The Cuyamaca and Laguna mountains to the east of Escondido—sometimes referred to as the backcountry by county residents—is a favorite weekend destinations for hikers, nature lovers, and apple-pie fanatics. Most of the last group head to Julian, a historic mining town that is now better known for apples than for the gold that once was extracted from its hills. Nearby Cuyamaca Rancho State Park is full of well-maintained trails and picnic and camping areas.

The **Sunrise National Scenic Byway Highway** is the most dramatic approach to Julian—its turns and curves reveal amazing views of the desert from the Salton Sea all the way to Mexico. You can spend an entire day roaming these mountains; an early-morning hike to the top of Garnet Peak (mile marker 27.8) is the best way to catch the view. Springtime wildflower displays are spectacular, particularly along Big Laguna Trail from Laguna Campground. There are picnic areas along the highway at Desert View and Pioneer Mail.

An alternate route into the mountains is through **Cuyamaca Rancho State Park** (⌂ Hwy. 79, 9 mi east of I–8, ☎ 760/765–0755). The park spreads over 24,677 acres of open meadows, forested mountains, and oak woodlands. Several peaks rise above 6,000 ft. Oak and pine trees adorn the park's hills; small streams and meadows provide a quiet escape for nature lovers. There are 120 mi of hiking and nature trails, campgrounds, a small museum, and along the road you may spot the remains of a now-closed gold mine.

Julian and Santa Ysabel

62 mi from San Diego (to Julian), east on I–8 and north on Hwy. 79.

Gold was discovered in the Julian area in 1869 and quartz was unearthed a year later. More than $15 million worth of gold was taken from local mines in the 1870s. Today, this mountain town retains some historic false-front buildings from its mining days. When gold and quartz became scarce, the locals turned to growing apples and pears. The pears are harvested in September, the apples in October. During the harvest season you can buy fruit, sip cider, eat apple pie, and shop for antiques and collectibles. But spring is equally enchanting (and less congested with visitors), as the hillsides explode with wildflowers, lilacs, and peonies. Artists and craftspeople have long maintained studios in the hillsides surrounding Julian; their work is frequently on display in local shops and galleries.

Hour-long tours of an authentic Julian gold mine are given by the **Eagle Mining Company.** A small rock shop and gold-mining museum are also on the premises. ⊠ *C St., 5 blocks east from center of town,* ☎ *760/765–0036.* ⌘ *$7.* ☉ *Daily 10–3, weather permitting.*

The 1.2-mi trail through **Volcan Mountain Wilderness Preserve** passes through orchards, groves of oak, and native manzanita to a panoramic viewpoint extending north all the way to Mount Palomar. At the entrance you pass through gates designed by local artist James Hubbell, who is known for his ironwork, wood carving, and stained glass. ⊠ *From Julian, take Farmer Rd. to Wyonla Rd.; go east a few yards, and then north on Farmer Rd.,* ☎ *760/765–0824.* ⌘ *Free.* ☉ *24 hrs.*

Three Native American tribes called the Santa Ysabel Valley home. The village of **Santa Ysabel,** 7 mi west of Julian, holds several interesting shops. People come from miles around to buy bread at **Dudley's Bakery** (⊠ 30218 Hwy. 78, ☎ 760/765–0488), open Wednesday through Sunday. The **Santa Ysabel Gallery** (⊠ 30352 Hwy. 78, ☎ 760/765–1676), also open Wednesday through Sunday, specializes in the work of local artists. **Weaving Works Fiber Art Gallery** (⊠ 30352 Hwy. 78, ☎ 760/765–1986), open Thursday through Sunday 11 to 4, sells handwoven clothing and novelty items by local craftspeople.

Tiny **Mission Santa Ysabel** (⊠ Hwy. 79, west of town of Santa Ysabel, ☎ 760/765–0810) is a late-19th-century adobe mission that continues to cater to several local Native American communities.

Dining and Lodging

$$ ✕ **Julian Grille.** The menu at this casual restaurant inside a historic home appeals to a variety of tastes, including vegetarian. Chicken dishes are popular, as are steaks and the smoked pork chops served with apple sauce. Lunch options include good burgers, whopping sandwiches, and soups. The requisite apple pies are made by the Julian Pie Co. across the street. ⊠ *2224 Main St.,* ☎ *760/765–0173. AE, MC, V. No dinner Mon.*

$–$$ ✕ **Bailey Barbecue.** The ribs, sausages, and chicken at this backwoods barbecue joint are slowly smoked over a live-oak fire and served with a tangy, not-too-sweet sauce. Everything on the menu is available for take-out. ⊠ *2307 Main St.,* ☎ *760/765–9957. MC, V. Closed Tues.–Wed.*

$$$-$$$$ 🏨 **Orchard Hill Country Inn.** Perched on a hill above town, this inn with
★ a sweeping view of the surrounding countryside sets a new standard
for luxury among backcountry accommodations. All rooms are dec-
orated with antiques and handcrafted quilts. Five Craftsman-style cot-
tages contain luxury suites with fireplaces, double whirlpool tubs, and
wet bars. Additional rooms in the lodge are less opulent but are spa-
cious and comfortable. Room rates include breakfast. Dinner is avail-
able to guests on weekends, when a minimum stay of two nights is
required. ⊠ *Washington St., Julian 92036,* ☎ *760/765–1700. 22
rooms. Meeting rooms. AE, MC, V.*

$-$$ 🏨 **Julian Lodge.** This bed-and-breakfast near the center of town is a
replica of a late-19th-century Julian hotel. The rooms and public spaces
are furnished with antiques; on chilly days, guests can warm themselves
at the large stove in the lobby. Room rates include a buffet-style Continental breakfast. ⊠ *4th and C Sts., Julian 92036,* ☎ *760/765–1420
or 800/542–1420. 23 rooms. AE, D, MC, V.*

The Backcountry and Julian Essentials

Arriving and Departing

BY BUS

See The Desert Essentials, *below.*

BY CAR

A loop drive beginning and ending in San Diego is a good way to explore this area. You can take the Sunrise National Scenic Byway Highway (sometimes icy in winter) from I–8 to Highway 79 and return
through Cuyamaca to I–8. If you're only going to Julian, take either
the Sunrise Highway or Highway 79, and return to San Diego via Highway 78 past Santa Ysabel to Ramona and Highway 67; from here, I–
8 heads west to downtown.

Visitor Information

Julian Chamber of Commerce (⊠ 2129 Main St., 92036, ☎ 760/765–
1857)

THE DESERT

Every spring, the stark desert landscape east of the Cuyamaca Mountains explodes with colorful wildflowers. The beauty of this spectacle,
as well as the natural quiet and blazing climate, lures many tourists
and natives each year to Anza-Borrego Desert State Park, less than a
two-hour drive from central San Diego.

For hundreds of years, the only humans to linger in the area were Native Americans from the San Dieguito, Kamia, and Cahuilla tribes, but
the extreme temperature eventually forced them to leave, too. It was-
n't until 1774, when Mexican explorer Captain Juan Bautista de Anza
first blazed a trail through the area as a shortcut from Sonora, Mexico, to San Francisco, that modern civilization had its first glimpse of
the oddly enchanting terrain.

The desert is best visited between October and May to avoid the extreme summer temperatures. Winter temperatures are comfortable, but
nights (and sometimes days) are cold, so bring a warm jacket.

*Numbers in the margin correspond to points of interest on the San Diego
North County map.*

Anza-Borrego Desert State Park

❻ *88 mi from downtown San Diego (to park border due west of Bor-rego Springs), east on I-8, north on Hwy. 67, east on S4 and Hwy. 78, north on Hwy. 79, and east on S2 and S22.*

Today, more than 600,000 acres of desert are included in the Anza-Borrego Desert State Park, making it the largest state park in the contiguous 48 states. It is also one of the few parks in the country where people can camp anywhere. No campsite is necessary; just follow the trails and pitch a tent wherever you like. Rangers and displays at an excellent underground **Visitor Information Center** (✉ Palm Canyon Dr., Borrego Springs, ☎ 760/767-4205) can point you in the right direction.

The Anza-Borrego Desert State Park is too vast even to consider exploring in its entirety. Five hundred miles of paved and dirt roads traverse the park, and visitors are required to stay on them so as not to disturb the ecological balance. However, 28,000 acres have been set aside in the eastern part of the desert near Ocotillo Wells for off-road enthusiasts. General George S. Patton conducted field training in the Ocotillo area to prepare for the World War II invasion of North Africa, and the area hasn't been the same since.

Many of the Anza-Borrego Desert's sites can be seen from paved roads, but some require driving on dirt roads. Rangers recommend using four-wheel-drive vehicles when traversing dirt roads. Carry the appropriate supplies: shovel and other tools, flares, blankets, and plenty of water. Canyons are susceptible to flash flooding; inquire about weather conditions before entering.

Narrows Earth Trail is a short walk off Highway 78, east of Tamarisk Grove, that reveals the many geologic processes involved in forming the canyons of the Anza-Borrego Desert. Water, wind, and faulting created the commanding vistas along **Erosion Road,** a self-guided 18-mi auto tour along county road S22. The **Southern Emigrant Trail** follows the route of the Butterfield Stage Overland Mail through the desert.

At **Borrego Palm Canyon,** just a few minutes west of the Anza-Borrego Visitor Information Center, a 1½-mi trail leads to a small oasis with a waterfall and palm trees. The Borrego Palm Canyon campground is one of only two developed campgrounds with flush toilets and showers in the park. (The other is Tamarisk Grove Campground, at the intersection of Highway 78 and Yaqui Pass Road; sites at both run $15-$16.)

Geology students from all over the world visit the Fish Creek area of Anza-Borrego to explore a famous canyon known as **Split Mountain** (✉ Split Mountain Rd., south from Hwy. 78 at Ocotillo Wells), a narrow gorge with 600-ft perpendicular walls that was formed by an ancestral stream. Fossils in this area have led geologists to think that a sea covered the desert floor at one time. A 2-mi nature trail just west of Split Mountain rewards a hiker with a good view of shallow caves created by erosion. Another trail in the Split Mountain area leads to one of two stands of **elephant trees** in the park. ✉ *Park headquarters: 200 Palm Canyon Dr., Borrego Springs 92004, ☎ 760/767-5311. ☎ $5. ☉ Park year-round 24 hrs; visitor center Oct.-May daily 9-5, June-Sept. weekends and holidays 9-5.*

Pick up the phone.
Pick up the miles.

1-800-FLY-FREE

Is this a great time, or what? :-)

Now when you sign up with MCI you can receive up to 8,000 bonus frequent flyer miles on one of seven major airlines.

Then earn another 5 miles for every dollar you spend on a variety of MCI services, including MCI Card® calls from virtually anywhere in the world.*

You're going to use these services anyway. Why not rack up the miles while you're doing it?

Urban planning.

CITYPACKS

The ultimate guide to the city—a complete pocket guide plus a full-size color map.

Borrego Springs

31 mi from Julian, east on Hwy. 78 and north on S3.

If you're not interested in communing with the desert without a shower and pool nearby, Borrego Springs has several hotels and restaurants. There is little to do in this oasis besides lie or recreate in the sun.

Lodging

$$–$$$$ 🏨 **La Casa del Zorro.** You need walk only a few hundred yards from this low-key resort to be alone under the sky, and you may well see roadrunners crossing the highway. Accommodations are set in comfortable one- to three-bedroom ranch-style houses complete with living rooms and kitchens; some three-bedroom suites have private pools. The elegant Continental restaurant puts on a good Sunday brunch. ⊠ *3845 Yaqui Pass Rd., 92004,* ☎ *760/767–5323 or 800/824–1884,* FAX *760/767–4782. 77 rooms, including 42 suites and 19 casitas. Restaurant, bar, 3 pools, outdoor hot tubs, beauty salon, 6 tennis courts, health club, bicycles, children's programs, meeting rooms. AE, D, DC, MC, V.*

$–$$$ 🏨 **Palm Canyon Resort.** One of the largest properties around Anza-Borrego Desert State Park includes a hotel (¼ mi from the visitor center), an RV park, a restaurant, and recreational facilities. More upscale rooms have wet bars, refrigerators, ceiling fans, and balconies or patios. ⊠ *221 Palm Canyon Dr., 92004,* ☎ *760/767–5341 or 800/242–0044,* FAX *760/767–4073. 60 rooms. Restaurant, 2 pools, 2 outdoor hot tubs, coin laundry, meeting rooms. AE, D, DC, MC, V.*

Outdoor Activities and Sports

The 18-hole **Rams Hill Country Club** (☎ 760/767–5124) course is open to the public. The greens fee is $85, which includes a mandatory cart. **Borrego Roadrunner Club** (☎ 760/767–5374) has an 18-hole golf course. The greens fee is $15. An optional cart costs $10. Courts at **Borrego Resorts International Tennis** (☎ 760/767–9748) are open to the public.

OFF THE BEATEN PATH **OCOTILLO WELLS STATE VEHICULAR RECREATION AREA –** The sand dunes and rock formations at this haven for off-road enthusiasts are fun and challenging. Camping is permitted throughout the area, but water is not available. The only facilities are in the small town (really no more than a corner) of Ocotillo Wells. ⊠ *Hwy. 78, east from Borrego Springs Rd.,* ☎ *760/767–5391.*

Salton Sea

85 mi (to park headquarters) from Borrego Springs, Hwy. 78E to Hwy. 111N.

The Salton Sea, due east of Anza-Borrego Desert State Park, was created in 1905–07, when the Colorado River flooded north through canals meant to irrigate the Imperial Valley. The water is extremely salty, even saltier than the Pacific Ocean, and it is primarily a draw for fishermen seeking corbina, croaker, and tilapia. Some boaters and swimmers also use the lake. The state runs a park, **Salton Sea State Recreation Area** (⊠ Hwy. 111N, at northeast edge of Salton Sea, ☎ 760/393–3059), with sites for recreational vehicles, and primitive camping.

A hiking trail and an observation tower at the **Salton Sea National Wildlife Refuge** make it easy to spot the dozens of varieties of migratory birds that stop at the Salton Sea. ⊠ *Off Hwy. 86, south end of Salton Sea,* ☎ *760/348–5278.*

The Desert Essentials

Arriving and Departing

BY BUS

The **Northeast Rural Bus System** (NERBS, ☎ 760/767–4287) connects Julian, Borrego Springs, Oak Grove, Ocotillo Wells, Agua Caliente, Ramona, and many other small communities with El Cajon, 15 mi east of downtown San Diego, and the East County line of the San Diego trolley, with stops at Grossmont shopping center and North County Fair. Service is by reservation, and buses do not run on Sunday and on some holidays.

BY CAR

From downtown San Diego, take I–8 east to Highway 67 north, to Highway 78 east, to Highway 79 north, to S2 and S22 east.

Visitor Information

Anza-Borrego Desert State Park (✉ Box 299, Borrego Springs 92004, ☎ 760/767–5311). **Borrego Springs Chamber of Commerce** (✉ 622 Palm Canyon Dr., Borrego Springs 92004, ☎ 760/767–5555). **Destinet** (☎ 800/444–7275), for campsite reservations. **Wildflower hotline** (☎ 760/767–4684), during spring blooming season only.

10 Tijuana, Rosarito Beach, and Ensenada

Since you've come as far as the southwesternmost city in the continental United States, take advantage of the opportunity and go "un poquito mas allá" (just a bit farther) and experience Mexico. Just 18 mi south of San Diego lies Baja California, a 1,000-mi-long stretch of beaches, desert, and hills that has long been a refuge for Californians with an urge to swim, surf, fish, and relax in a country unlike their own.

By Maribeth
Mellin

Updated by
Edie Jarolim

TIJUANA, AT THE INTERNATIONAL BORDER, is the most popular destination for day-trippers from San Diego, who come for the souvenir shopping, sports events, and sophisticated Mexican dining. Rosarito Beach, 18 mi south of Tijuana on the Pacific coast, attracts travelers in search of a more laidback Mexico. Ensenada, a major port, combines many elements of Tijuana and Rosarito but also retains its own character.

It is possible to visit Tijuana, Rosarito Beach, and Ensenada in a long, busy day. Begin by bypassing Tijuana and heading straight for the toll road to Rosarito Beach, about a 40-mi drive south. Once in Rosarito, stop at the Rosarito Beach Hotel for breakfast, take a short walk on the beach in front of the hotel, and check out a few of the shops on Boulevard Juárez. Return to the toll road just south of the hotel and continue south for 45 mi to Ensenada. Take your time along this stretch of road, and exit at Salsipuedes and El Mirador to admire the view.

In Ensenada, park at the Plaza Marina on the waterfront and do your exploring on foot. Spend an hour or two wandering along Avenida López Mateos and its side streets, where you may find bargains on leather goods and jewelry in high-quality shops. Hussong's bar is an essential stop for rowdy types; culture-seekers should tour the Riviera del Pacifico, a former gambling palace built in the 1920s. Return to the waterfront for a quick run through the fish market and a snack of fish tacos, and try to be back on the road by early afternoon—and to save room for a lobster lunch at Puerto Nuevo, about 10 mi south of Rosarito.

If you finish lunch by mid-afternoon, you'll be able to reach Tijuana before nightfall. Once in the city, park in a lot by Calle 2A, the road that ties the highway to the border; walk up Calle 2A to Avenida Revolución, finish your souvenir shopping, and have dinner at a restaurant on the way back to your car. It's smart to wait until after 7 PM to cross the border, when rush-hour traffic has diminished.

A more leisurely tour would include an overnight stay in Rosarito Beach. By doing so, you can spend the morning in Tijuana seeing the sights and pricing possible purchases. Check into your hotel in Rosarito in the early afternoon, and then visit the beach or the shops. Dine in Rosarito or Puerto Nuevo, get to bed early, and start off to Ensenada in the morning. Spend a half-day there, and then head back to Tijuana, where you can pick up that last tacky souvenir from a salesman along the border traffic lines.

Pleasures and Pastimes

Dining

Baja's cuisine reflects its natural setting, highlighting food from the sea. Fresh fish, lobster, and shrimp are the dining draws here, along with abalone and quail. Restaurants as a rule are low-key, except in Tijuana and Ensenada, where dining options range from *taquerías* (taco stands) to upscale Continental palaces. Dress is accordingly casual at nearly all Baja restaurants, and reservations are not required unless otherwise noted. Some restaurants add a 15% service charge to the bill.

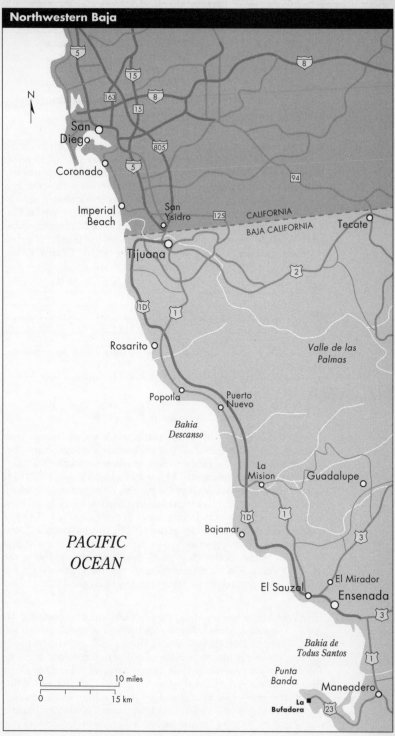

N

San Diego

Coronado

Imperial Beach

San Ysidro

Tijuana

CALIFORNIA

BAJA CALIFORNIA

Tecate

Rosarito

Valle de las Palmas

Popotla

Puerto Nuevo

Bahia Descanso

La Mision

Guadalupe

PACIFIC OCEAN

Bajamar

El Sauzal

El Mirador

Ensenada

Bahia de Todus Santos

Punta Banda

Maneadero

La Bufadora

0   10 miles

0   15 km

CATEGORY	COST*
$$$	over $20
$$	$10–$20
$	under $10

*per person for a three-course meal, excluding drinks and service

Golf

Baja is becoming a great destination for golfers, with championship courses in Tijuana and nearby Rosarito Beach.

Lodging

Lodgings throughout Baja are mostly low-key, and great deals can found at some small hostelries. A few of the out-of-the-way and budget-priced hotels do not accept credit cards; some of the more lavish places add a 10%–20% service charge to your bill. Most properties also raise their rates for the December–April high season. Rates here are based on high-season standards. Expect to pay 25% less during the off-season. Several agencies in the United States book reservations at Baja hotels, condos, and time-share resorts, which may actually cost less than hotel rooms if you are traveling with a group of four or more (☞ Tijuana, Rosarito Beach, and Ensenada A to Z, *below,* for details).

CATEGORY	COST*
$$$$	over $160
$$$	$90–$160
$$	$40–$90
$	under $40

*All prices are for a standard double room, excluding service charge and sales tax (10%).

TIJUANA

29 km (18 mi) south of San Diego on I–5 or I–805.

Tijuana is the only part of Mexico many people see, and it gives both a distorted and an accurate view of the country's many cultures. Before the city became a gigantic recreation center for southern Californians, it was a ranch populated by a few hundred Mexicans. In 1911, a group of Americans who invaded the area and attempted to set up an independent republic were quickly driven out by Mexican soldiers. When Prohibition hit the United States in the 1920s and the Agua Caliente Racetrack and Casino opened (1929), Tijuana boomed. Americans seeking alcohol, gambling, and more fun than they could find back home flocked across the border, spending freely and fueling the region's growth. Tijuana became the entry port for what some termed a "sinful, steamy playground," frequented by Hollywood stars and the idle rich.

Then Prohibition was repealed, Mexico outlawed gambling, and Tijuana's fortunes dwindled. But though the flow of travelers from the north slowed to a trickle for a while, Tijuana still captivated those in search of the sort of fun that was illegal or just frowned upon at home. The ever-growing numbers of servicemen stationed in San Diego kept Tijuana's sordid reputation alive, and southern Californians continued to cross the border to explore the foreign culture and landscape. Drivers headed into Baja's wilderness drove through downtown Tijuana, stopping along Avenida Revolución and its side streets for supplies and souvenirs.

When the toll highway to Ensenada was finished in 1967, travelers bypassed the city and tourism dropped again. But Tijuana began attracting residents from throughout Latin America. The city's population mushroomed from a mere 300,000 in 1970 to more than 2 million today. The city has spread into canyons and dry riverbeds, over hillsides, and onto ocean cliffs. As the government struggles to keep up with the growth and demand for services, thousands live without electricity, running water, and adequate housing in squatters villages along the border.

City leaders, realizing that tourism creates jobs and bolsters Tijuana's fragile economy, are working hard to attract visitors. The city has an international airport; a fine cultural center that presents professional music, dance, and theater groups from throughout the world; and deluxe high-rise hotels. Park benches and shade trees on brick paths winding away from the traffic encourage visitors to linger. Still, although it's no longer considered just a bawdy border town, the city remains best known as a place for an intense, somewhat exotic daylong adventure.

Tijuana's tourist attractions have remained much the same through-out the century. The impressive El Palacio Frontón (Jai Alai Palace), where betting is allowed, draws crowds of cheering fans to its fast-paced matches. Some of Mexico's greatest bullfighters appear at the ocean-front and downtown bullrings, and there are an extraordinary num-ber of places in town that provide good food and drinks.

And then, of course, there's shopping. From the moment you cross the border, people will approach you or call out and insist that you look at their wares. If you drive, workers will run out from auto-body shops to place bids on new paint or upholstery for your car. All along Avenida Revolución and its side streets, shops sell everything from tequila to Tiffany lamps; serious shoppers can spend a full day searching and bargaining for their items of choice. If you intend to buy food in Mex-ico, get the U.S. customs list of articles that are illegal to bring back so that your purchases won't be confiscated.

Numbers in the margin correspond to points of interest on the Tijuana map.

❶ At the **San Ysidro Border Crossing,** locals and tourists jostle each other along the pedestrian walkway through the Viva Tijuana dining and shop-ping center and into the center of town. Artisans' stands line the walk-way and adjoining streets, providing a quick overview of the wares to be found all over town.

❷ An unusual perspective on Mexico's culture can be found at the **Mex-itlán.** The combination museum and entertainment-shopping complex designed by architect Pedro Ramírez Vásquez has scale models of all the major architectural and cultural landmarks throughout Mexico; unfortunately, the place has not been well maintained and has lost its festive air. ✉ *Av. Ocampo between Calles 2 and 3,* ☎ *66/38–41–01.* ▨ *$2.50.* ☉ *Wed.–Sun. 9–5.*

❸ Tijuana's main tourism zone has long been the raffish **Avenida Rev-olución,** lined with a cacophonous array of shops and restaurants, all catering to uninhibited tourists. Shopkeepers call out from their door-ways, offering low prices for an odd assortment of garish souvenirs. Many shopping arcades open onto Avenida Revolución; inside the front doors are mazes of small stands with low-priced pottery and other hand-icrafts.

❹ The Moorish-style **El Palacio Frontón** (Jai Alai Palace) is a magnificent building and an exciting place for watching and betting on fast-paced jai alai games. Next door, at a large branch of the Caliente Race Book, bettors can wager on horse races and sports events broadcast from Cal-ifornia via satellite TV (☞ Outdoor Activities and Sports, *below*).

152

Avenida
Revolución, **3**

Centro
Cultural, **9**

El Palacio
Frontón (Jai
Alai Palace), **4**

L.A. Cetto
Winery, **5**

Mexitlán, **2**

Mundo
Divertido, **6**

Playas
Tijuana, **11**

Plaza de Toros
Monumental,
12

Plaza Río
Tijuana, **10**

Pueblo
Amigo, **7**

Rió Tijuana, **8**

San Ysidro
Border
Crossing, **1**

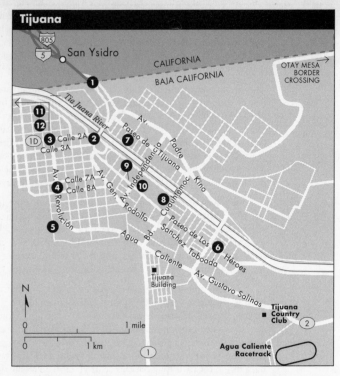

Most of Baja's legendary wineries are in the Ensenada region, but Tijuana now has a branch of the **L.A. Cetto Winery.** Visitors are invited to tour the bottling plant, sample the wines, and spend as long as they'd like in the gift and wine shop. ⊠ *Cañon Johnson 8151, at Av. Constitución,* ☎ *66/85–30–31.* 🎫 *$1; $2 with wine tasting.* ☉ *Tues.–Sun. 10–5.*

6 Mundo Divertido is a popular family attraction in the Río zone. The amusement park includes a miniature golf course, batting cages, an exciting roller coaster, and a video-game parlor with more than 130 games. The park has a food court with hot dogs and burgers along with tacos and corn on the cob. Admission is free, and it costs just a few pesos to hop on the rides. ⊠ *Paseo de los Héroes, at Calle Velasco, no phone.* ☉ *Weekdays noon–9, weekends 11–10.*

7 Pueblo Amigo contains enough distractions to be a destination unto itself. This entertainment center is built to resemble a colonial Mexican village, with stuccoed buildings painted soft yellow, blue, and rose and tree-lined pathways leading to a gazebo with a brick dome. The complex includes the fanciest hotel near downtown, several restaurants and clubs, a huge grocery store, and a large branch of the Caliente Race Book, where gambling on televised races and sporting events is legal. ⊠ *Paseo Tijuana, between Puente Mexico and Av. Independencia.*

8 The **Río Tijuana** area—as the section that runs along Avenida Paseo de los Héroes parallel to the dry Tia Juana River is called—is one of the city's main thoroughfares, with large statues of historical figures, including one of Abraham Lincoln, in the center of the *glorietas* (traffic circles). With its impressive Cultural Center, several shopping complexes, fine restaurants, and fashionable discos, this part of town rivals Avenida Revolución for the tourists' and locals' attention. ⊠ *Between Blvd. Agua Caliente and border.*

❾ The **Centro Cultural** was designed by architects Manuel Rosen and Pedro Ramírez Vásquez, who also created Mexico City's famous Museum of Anthropology. The center's exhibits of Mexican history are a good introduction for those visitors whose first taste of Mexico is at the border. The Omnimax Theater, with its curving 180-degree screen, shows films on a rotating schedule, often coinciding with temporary exhibits. Usually one English-language film is shown daily. Temporary exhibits on art and culture change frequently. The center's bookstore has a selection of Mexican history, culture, and arts in both Spanish and English. ⊠ *Paseo de los Héroes and Av. Independencia,* ☎ *66/84–11–11.* 🎟 *Museum $2, museum and Omnimax Theater $3.50.* ⊙ *Daily 9–8.*

❿ **Plaza Río Tijuana,** the area's largest shopping complex, is enormous, with good restaurants, department stores, hundreds of shops, and a multiplex theater where at least one English-language film is usually shown. The plaza has become a central square of sorts, where holiday fiestas are held. The area has been landscaped with shade trees and flowers, and there are long, wide sidewalks leading from the shopping complex to the Cultural Center. ⊠ *Paseo de los Héroes, across from the Centro Cultural.*

⓫ **Playas Tijuana,** along the oceanfront, is a mix of modest and expensive residential neighborhoods, with a few restaurants and hotels. The long, isolated beaches are visited mostly by residents.

⓬ **Plaza de Toros Monumental,** the "Bullring by the Sea," sits at the northwest corner of the beach area, right by the border (☞ Outdoor Activities and Sports, *below*). The bullring is occasionally used for summer concerts as well.

Dining and Lodging

$$ ✕ **El Faro de Mazatlán.** Fresh fish simply prepared is the hallmark of one of Tijuana's best seafood restaurants. This is the place to try seviche, abalone, squid, and lobster without spending a fortune. Meals start with a savory soup and crusty rolls. The dining room, frequented by professionals from nearby offices, is a peaceful spot for a long, leisurely lunch. Appetizers and soup are included in the price of the meal. ⊠ *Blvd. Sanchez Taboada 9542,* ☎ *66/84–88–82. MC, V.*

$$ ✕ **La Fonda de Roberto.** Roberto's is by far the best restaurant in Tijuana for traditional cuisine from the many culinary regions of Mexico. Try the *chiles en nogada* (chilies stuffed with raisins and meat and topped with cream and pomegranate seeds), meats with spicy *achiote* (a blend of spices) sauce, and many varieties of *mole* (a blend of spices and bitter chocolate). Portions are small, so order liberally and share samples of many dishes. ⊠ *La Siesta Motel, Old Ensenada Hwy. (also called Calle 16 de Septiembre) near Blvd. Agua Caliente,* ☎ *66/86–16–01. MC, V.*

$$ ✕ **La Taberna Española.** The mainstay of Plaza Fiesta's multiethnic cafés, this Spanish tapas (appetizers) bar attracts a youthful, sophisticated crowd. The menu is printed only in Spanish, but with a bit of imagination you should be able to select a representative sampling, such as octopus in its own ink, spicy sausages, Spanish tortilla with potatoes and eggs, and fava beans. Inside the café, it's smoky, fragrant, and invariably crowded; sit at the outdoor tables for a view of the folks waiting in line. ⊠ *Plaza Fiesta, Paseo de los Héroes 10001,* ☎ *66/84–94–01. No credit cards.*

$$ ✕ **Tia Juana Tilly's.** Popular with both tourists and locals looking for revelry and generous portions of Mexican specialties, this is one of the few places where you can get *cochinita píbil* (a Yucatecan dish made of roast pig, red onions, and bitter oranges) or the traditionally bitter and savory chicken mole. Part of the same chain is Tilly's Fifth Ave., catercorner to the original on Avenida Revolución. ✉ *Av. Revolución, at Calle 7,* ☎ *66/85–60–24. AE, MC, V.*

$ ✕ **Carnitas Uruapan.** You'll need to take a cab to this large, noisy restaurant, where patrons mingle at long wood tables, toasting one another with chilled *cervezas* (beer). The main attraction here is *carnitas* (marinated pork roasted over an open pit), sold by weight and served with homemade tortillas, salsa, cilantro, guacamole, and onions. ✉ *Blvd. Díaz Ordaz 550,* ☎ *66/81–61–81;* ✉ *Paseo de los Héroes at Av. Rodríguez, no phone. No credit cards.*

$ ✕ **La Especial.** At the foot of the stairs leading to an underground shopping arcade, this restaurant attracts diners in search of home-style
★ Mexican cooking at low prices. The gruff, efficient waiters, decked out in black slacks and vests, shuttle platters of *carne asada* (grilled strips of marinated meat), enchiladas, and burritos, all with a distinctive flavor found nowhere but in this busy, cavernous basement dining room. ✉ *Av. Revolución 718,* ☎ *66/85–66–54. No credit cards.*

$ ✕ **Señor Frog's.** Heaping plates of barbecued chicken and ribs and buckets of ice-cold bottles of cerveza are the mainstay at this fun and festive formula eatery, one of many in the Carlos Anderson chain. The loud music and laughter make for a raucous atmosphere, and the food is consistently good. ✉ *In Pueblo Amigo Center, Paseo Tijuana,* ☎ *66/82–49–58. AE, MC, V.*

$$$ 🏨 **Camino Real.** Elegant and fashionable, this branch of one of Mexico's best hotel chains opened in 1996 near the Cultural Center. The location is ideal for walking to most attractions, and the plush rooms have faxes and direct-dial phones. The Fouquet's de Paris restaurant specializes in French haute cuisine, and has a garden café; Azulejos is more informal. ✉ *Paseo de los Héroes 10305, 22320,* ☎ *66/33–40–00 or 800/722–6466,* 🖷 *66/33–40–01. 250 rooms and suites. 2 restaurants, 2 bars, room service, laundry service. AE, MC, V.*

$$$ 🏨 **Holiday Inn Pueblo Amigo.** The only thoroughly modern hotel in the center of Tijuana's tourist zone, the bright, white Holiday Inn has several sizes of rooms decorated in green, beige, and peach, with cable TV, minibars, and direct-dial long-distance telephones. The indoor pool, sauna, and gym are popular with business travelers, who also have use of meeting facilities and a business center. Ask about special rates. ✉ *Via Oriente 9211, at Pueblo Amigo, 22450,* ☎ *66/83–50–30 or 800/465–4329,* 🖷 *66/83–50–32. 108 rooms and suites. Restaurant, indoor pool, beauty salon, sauna, exercise room. AE, MC, V.*

$$ 🏨 **Gran Hotel.** The two mirrored towers of the hotel are Tijuana's most
★ ostentatious landmarks. The atrium restaurant is a favorite lunch and Sunday brunch spot. The rooms used to be the nicest in town, but new hotels have upped the standards. Still, it's a good spot for golfers, business travelers, and those who want moderately priced luxury. ✉ *Blvd. Agua Caliente 4558, 22420,* ☎ *66/81–70–00 or 800/472–6385,* 🖷 *66/81–70–16. 422 rooms. Restaurant, pool, 2 tennis courts, exercise room, nightclub, travel services. AE, MC, V.*

$$ 🏨 **Otay Bugambilias.** Proximity to the Tijuana airport and the Otay Mesa manufacturing plants makes this modest hotel a great find. The pink three-story building has motel-like rooms; suites have kitchenettes. ✉ *Blvd. Industrial, at Carretera Aeropuerto, 22450,* ☎ 🖷 *66/*

23–76–00 or 800/472–1153. 129 rooms. Restaurant, bar, pool, exercise room, meeting rooms, airport shuttle. AE, MC, V.

$ 🏨 **La Villa de Zaragoza.** This brown stucco motel is such a success that the management keeps adding rooms—the newest have kitchenettes, and all have air-conditioning and cable TV. The location, near the Jai Alai Palace and one block from Revolución, is ideal. The neighborhood can be noisy, however, so it's best to choose a room at the back. The guarded parking lot is a major plus. The motel is used by tour groups, so book ahead for holidays and weekends. Discounts are available for extended stays. ✉ *Av. Madero 1120, 22000,* ☎ *66/85–18–32,* FAX *66/85–18–37. 66 rooms. Restaurant. MC, V.*

Nightlife and the Arts

Tijuana has toned down its Sin City image; much of the nighttime action now takes place at the **El Palacio Frontón** and the racetrack. Several hotels, especially the **Holiday Inn Pueblo Amigo** and **Gran Hotel,** have live entertainment. Tijuana's discos usually have strict dress codes, with no T-shirts, jeans, or sandals allowed.

The **Hard Rock Cafe** (✉ Av. Revolución 520 between Calles 1 and 2, ☎ 66/85–02–06) has the same menu and decor as the chain's other branches. **Como Que No** (✉ Av. Sanchez Taboada 95, ☎ 66/84–27–91) is popular with the sophisticated disco set, while the adjacent **Dime Que Si** (☎ 66/84–27–91) is a romantic piano bar. **Baby Rock** (✉ Calle Diego Rivera 1482, ☎ 66/88–04–40), an offshoot of a popular Acapulco disco, attracts a young, hip crowd.

Outdoor Activities and Sports

BULLFIGHTS

Skilled matadors from throughout Mexico and Spain battle *el toro* at **El Toreo de Tijuana** (✉ Av. Agua Caliente outside downtown, ☎ 66/85–22–10) on Sunday at 4, May through October. In July and August you can also see fights at the **Plaza de Toros Monumental** (✉ Playas Tijuana area, Ensenada Hwy., ☎ 66/85–22–10) on Sunday at 4. Admission to bullfights varies, depending on the fame of the matador and the location of your seat.

GOLF

The **Tijuana Country Club** (✉ Blvd. Agua Caliente, east of downtown, ☎ 66/81–78–55) is open to Gran Hotel guests; other hotels can set up golf for their guests, too. It provides rental clubs, electric and hand carts, and caddies for the 18-hole course.

GREYHOUND RACES

At the **Hipódromo de Agua Caliente,** horse racing was phased out in 1993, but greyhounds race nightly at 7:45 and afternoons at 2 on Saturday and Sunday. In the Foreign Book area, gamblers can bet on races taking place in California and shown at Caliente on TV monitors. ✉ *Blvd. Agua Caliente, at Salinas,* ☎ *66/81–78–11; 619/231–1919 in San Diego, CA.*

JAI ALAI

This ancient Basque sport, in some ways similar to handball but using a large, scooped-out paddle called a *frontón,* is played in the Moorish-style **El Palacio Frontón,** or Jai Alai Palace. Matinee games start at noon on Monday and Friday; night games start at 8 PM from Tuesday through Saturday. General admission is $5. ✉ *Av. Revolución and Calle 8,* ☎ *66/85–25–24 or 619/231–1919 in San Diego, CA.*

Shopping

The Avenida Revolución shopping area spreads down Calle 1 to the pedestrian walkway leading from the border. Begin by checking out the stands along the border-crossing walkway, comparing prices as you travel toward Avenida Revolución. You may find that the best bargains are closer to the border; you can pick up your piñatas and serapes on your way out of town. The traditional shopping strip is Avenida Revolución, between Calles 1 and 8; it's lined with shops and arcades that display a wide range of crafts and curios. Bargaining is expected on the streets and in the arcades, but not in the finer shops.

The shops in **Plaza Revolución,** at the corner of Calle 1 and Avenida Revolución, stock quality crafts. **La Piel** (⊠ Av. Revolución between Calle 4 and 5, ☎ 66/87–23–98) carries leather jackets, backpacks, and luggage. **Ralph Lauren Polo Outlet** (⊠ Viva Tijuana Center, ☎ 66/88–76–98) is a licensed outlet for the designer's sportswear. **Sanborns** (⊠ Av. Revolución, at Calle 8, ☎ 66/88–14–62) has beautiful crafts from throughout Mexico, an excellent bakery, and chocolates from Mexico City. **Sara's** (⊠ Av. Revolución, at Calle 4, ☎ 66/88–29–32), one of the best department stores in Tijuana, sells imported perfumes and fine clothing. The finest folk-art store, **Tolan** (⊠ Av. Revolución between Calles 7 and 8, ☎ 66/88–36–37), carries everything from antique carved wooden doors to tiny ceramic miniature village scenes.

MARKET

The **Mercado Hidalgo** (⊠ Av. Independencia, at Av. Sanchez Taboada, 2 blocks south of Paseo de los Héroes) is Tijuana's municipal market, with rows of fresh produce, grains, herbs, some souvenirs, and the best selection of piñatas in Baja.

SHOPPING CENTERS

Plaza Fiesta, on Paseo de los Héroes across from Plaza Río Tijuana, has a collection of boutiques, jewelry stores, and stained-glass shops. You can find great buys on fashionable clothing and shoes at **Plaza Río Tijuana** on Paseo de los Héroes. **Pueblo Amigo,** also on Paseo de los Héroes, has a few small folk-art shops and Ley, a gourmet grocery that sells salad by the pint and hard-to-find Mexican delicacies such as fresh mole sauce and pickled carrots and cauliflower.

ROSARITO BEACH

29 km (18 mi) south of Tijuana on Hwy. 1.

Not so very long ago, Playas de Rosarito (Rosarito Beach) was a small seaside community with virtually no tourist trade. It was part of the municipality of Tijuana, an overlooked suburb on the way to the port city of Ensenada. But as the roads improved, and particularly after Baja's Transpeninsular Highway was completed in 1973, Rosarito Beach began to flower. In 1995, it became its own municipality, with a government separate from that of Tijuana. Rosarito's population, about 110,000, is growing steadily.

Rosarito's main street, alternately known as the Old Ensenada Highway and Boulevard Benito Juárez, reflects the unrestrained growth and speculation that have both helped and harmed the city. The street is packed with restaurants, bars, and shops in a jarring juxtaposition of architectural styles, with some of the largest developments halted midway for lack of investors.

It nevertheless remains a relaxing place to visit. Southern Californians have practically made Rosarito a weekend suburb. Surfers, swimmers, and sunbathers come here to enjoy the beach, one of the longest in northern Baja: It's an uninterrupted stretch of sand from the power plant at the far north end of town to below the Rosarito Beach Hotel, about 8 km (5 mi) south. Horseback riding, jogging, and strolling are popular along this strand. Whales pass not far from shore on their winter migration; dolphins and sea lions sun on rocks jutting out from the sea. Rosarito has always attracted a varied crowd, and today's group is no exception—an assemblage of prosperous young Californians building villas in vacation developments, retired Americans and Canadians homesteading in trailer parks, and travelers of all ages from all over the world.

Hedonism and health get equal billing in Rosarito. One of the area's major draws is its seafood, especially lobster, shrimp, and abalone. The visiting Americans act as if they've been dry for months—margaritas and beer are the favored thirst quenchers. People throw off their inhibitions here, at least to the degree permitted by the local constables. A typical Rosarito day might begin with a breakfast of eggs, refried beans, and tortillas, followed by a few hours of horseback riding on the beach. Lying in the sun or strolling through the shops takes care of midday. Siestas are imperative and are usually followed by more shopping, strolling, or sunbathing before dinner, dancing, and sleep.

Rosarito Beach has few historic or cultural attractions, beaches and bars being the main draws. Sightseeing consists of strolling along the beach or down **Boulevard Benito Juárez,** which runs parallel to it.

An immense PEMEX gasoline installation and electric plant anchor the northern end of Boulevard Juárez, which then runs along a collection of new shopping arcades, restaurants, and motels. The eight-story Quinta Del Mar condo and hotel complex is the first major landmark, followed by the **Quinta Plaza** shopping center, which contains a car wash, pharmacy, bakery, specialty shops, and restaurants, as well as the tourism office and the Centro de Convenciones, a 1,000-seat convention center. The **Festival Plaza** hotel and shopping center, with its distinctive roller coaster–like facade, sits just south of Quinta Plaza on Boulevard Juárez. Just beyond Festival Plaza is the **Rosarito Beach Hotel,** which marks the end of the strip. The hotel's glassed-in bar is the best place for absorbing the local ambience.

Dining and Lodging

$$ ✕ **Azteca.** The enormous dining room at the Rosarito Beach Hotel has a view of the pool and beach area. Many visitors come here exclusively for the Sunday brunch; expect to wait in line on holiday weekends. Both Mexican and American dishes are served, and the size of the portions makes up for the erratic quality of the food. The hotel has a Mexican buffet and fiesta here on Friday nights. ⊠ *Rosarito Beach Hotel, Blvd. Juárez,* ☎ *661/2–01–44. MC, V.*

$$ ✕ **Calafia.** Though not in Rosarito proper, this unusual restaurant and trailer park are worth a visit (it's a 10-minute car or cab ride south). The owners have added a historic element to their property by filling the public spaces with photos and artifacts from Baja's early days. But most visitors are drawn to Calafia's dining room, where tables are scattered on small terraces down the cliffside to the crashing sea. The food is standard Mexican fare, but it all tastes great when combined with the fresh salt air and sea breezes. Calafia has an outdoor dance floor at the base of the cliffs, where live bands sometimes perform. ⊠ *Km 35.5 Old Ensenada Hwy., 22710,* ☎ *661/2–15–81 or 800/225–2342,* FAX *661/2–15–80. MC, V.*

$$ ✕ **Dragon del Mar.** A miniature waterfall greets guests in the marble foyer of this Chinese restaurant, where a pianist plays relaxing music. Carved wooden partitions in the expansive dining room help create an intimate dining experience. The food is well prepared. ⊠ *Blvd. Juárez 283,* ☎ *661/2–06–04. MC, V.*

$$ ✗ **El Nido.** A dark, wood-paneled restaurant with leather booths and a large central fireplace, this is one of the oldest eateries in Rosarito. Diners unimpressed with the newer, fancier establishments come here for the good mesquite-grilled steaks and for grilled quail from the owner's farm in the Baja wine country. ⊠ *Blvd. Juárez 67,* ☎ *661/2–14–30. MC, V.*

$$ ✗ **La Leña.** Try any of the beef dishes, especially the tender carne
★ asada with tortillas and guacamole, at this spacious and impeccably clean restaurant. ⊠ *Quinta Plaza,* ☎ *661/2–08–26. MC, V.*

$$ ✗ **Ortega's Place.** Music blares from this two-story restaurant-bar where tourists flock to inexpensive buffets. The breakfast and lunch spreads include scrambled eggs, lots of beans and rice, and basic Mexican dishes. The à la carte entrées are much more expensive, and though Ortega's is known for its lobster, you'll get a better deal elsewhere. ⊠ *Blvd. Juárez 200,* ☎ *661/2–27–91. MC, V.*

$$ ✗ **René's.** One of the oldest restaurants in Rosarito (1924), René's features chorizo (Mexican sausage), quail, frogs' legs, and lobster. There's an ocean view from the dining room, a lively bar, and mariachi music. ⊠ *Blvd. Juárez south of Rosarito Beach Hotel,* ☎ *661/2–10–20. MC, V.*

$ ✗ **La Flor de Michoacán.** Carnitas Michoacán style, served with homemade tortillas, guacamole, and salsa, are the house specialty at this Rosarito landmark. The tacos, *tortas* (sandwiches), and tostadas are great. Takeout is available. ⊠ *Blvd. Juárez 291,* ☎ *661/2–18–58. No credit cards. Closed Wed.*

$$$ 🏨 **Marriott Real Del Mar Residence Inn.** Golfers and escapists relish
★ their privacy at this all-suites hotel set on a cliff with faraway views of the sea north of Rosarito. The standard accommodations have living rooms with vaulted brick ceilings, fireplaces, kitchens, and two double beds; larger units have one or two bedrooms. The greens fee at the on-site golf course is included in packages. The hotel, 19 km (12 mi) south of the border and 10 km (6 mi) north of Rosarito, is completely removed from the action. An on-site branch of Tijuana's Pedrin's restaurant serves good seafood meals and Mexican dishes. ⊠ *Km 19.5 Ensenada toll road, 22710,* ☎ *66/31–36–70 or 800/331–3131,* 𝔽𝔸𝕏 *66/31–36–77. 66 rooms and suites. Restaurant, bar, snack bar, pool, 18-hole golf course, pro shop. AE, MC, V.*

$$ 🏨 **Brisas del Mar.** Rooms at this modern motel comfortably accommodate four persons. A few of the suites on the second story have hot tubs and views of the ocean; all have air-conditioning and TV. The motel is on the inland side of Boulevard Juárez, and traffic noise can be a problem. ⊠ *Blvd. Juárez 22, 22710,* ☎ 𝔽𝔸𝕏 *661/2–25–47; reservations in the U.S.:* ⊠ *Box 1867, Chula Vista, CA 91912,* ☎ *800/697–5223. 66 rooms. Bar, coffee shop, pool. MC, V.*

$$ 🏨 **Festival Plaza.** Designed with unrestrained fun in mind, Festival Plaza is geared toward a youthful crowd. The motel-like rooms are in an eight-story building with a facade resembling a roller coaster. The casitas (in the $$$ range) close to the beach are the quietest accommodations and have small hot tubs, separate living rooms with fold-out couches, and private garages, but no kitchen facilities. The hotel also operates a complex of 14 villas just south of Rosarito; these have full kitchens. Within the hotel complex are several bars and good restaurants (try the traditional Mexican dishes at El Patio) and the central courtyard serves as a concert stage, children's playground, and party headquarters. Discounted room rates are often available, especially in winter. ⊠ *Blvd. Juárez 11, 22710,* ☎ *661/2–08–42, 661/2–29–50, or 800/*

453–8606, FAX 661/2–01–24. *114 rooms and suites. 2 restaurants, 3 bars, pool, dance club, playground. AE, MC, V.*

$$ **Hotel Quinta Terranova.** Pretty and peaceful, this small hotel sits at the edge of the Quinta del Mar development facing a relatively quiet section of Boulevard Juárez. The green and beige rooms in a two-story, motel-like building have coffeemakers mounted on the wall, hair dryers, carpeting, and small bathrooms. The pool is set back from the street with enough plants to provide a sense of seclusion. ✉ *Blvd. Juárez 25500, 22710,* ☎ *661/2–16–44,* FAX *661/2–16–42. 84 rooms and suites. Restaurant, pool. MC, V.*

$$ **Los Pelicanos Hotel.** One of the few hotels situated directly on the beach, the Pelicanos is a favorite with Americans and Canadians who stay for weeks on end in the winter. The best rooms have oceanfront balconies, though the others—with white walls, light-wood furnishings, and large bathrooms—are nice as well. The lack of a pool is a drawback, though the sea is just a few steps away. The second-story restaurant and bar, popular sunset-watching spots, tend to attract an older, more subdued clientele feasting on steak and lobster. ✉ *Calle Cedros 115, at Calle Ebano, 22710,* ☎ *661/2–04–45,* FAX *661/2–17–57; U.S. mailing address:* ✉ *Box 433871, San Ysidro, CA 92143. 39 rooms. Restaurant, bar. AE, MC, V.*

$$ **Rosarito Beach Hotel.** Dating from the Prohibition era, this venerable hotel is Rosarito's centerpiece. It's a charmer, with huge ballrooms, tiled public rest rooms, and a glassed-in pool deck overlooking a long beach. The very plain rooms and suites in the tower are air-conditioned; some units in the original building have fans only and are very rundown. Keep in mind the noise factor when looking at rooms near the pools, playground, and side lawn where live bands play on summer afternoons. Midweek reduced rates and special packages are often available; ocean-view rooms are in the $$$ category. A refurbished 1930s mansion next door hosts the Casa Playa Spa, with massage, beauty treatments, exercise equipment, saunas, and hot tubs. ✉ *Blvd. Juárez, south end of town, 22710,* ☎ *661/2–01–44, 661/2–11–26, or 800/343–8582,* FAX *661/2–11–76. Reservations in the U.S.:* ✉ *Box 430145, San Diego, CA 92143. 275 rooms and suites. 2 restaurants, bar, 2 pools, spa, tennis court, health club, beach. MC, V.*

$ **Cupalas del Mar.** This small hotel between Boulevard Juárez and the beach is quieter than most, with sunny, clean rooms and satellite TV. ✉ *Calle Guadalupe Victoria 9, 22710,* ☎ *661/2–24–90. 39 rooms. Pool, hot tub. AE, MC, V.*

Nightlife and the Arts

The many restaurants in Rosarito Beach keep customers entertained with live music, piano bars, or *folklórico* (folk music and dance) shows; the bar scene is also active. Drinking-and-driving laws are stiff—the police will fine you no matter how little you've had. If you plan to drink, take a cab or assign a designated driver.

There's a lot going on at night at the **Rosarito Beach Hotel** (✉ Blvd. Juárez, ☎ 661/2–01–44): live music at the ocean-view Beachcomber Bar and Hugo's, a Mexican Fiesta on Friday nights, and a live band at the cavernous disco. The **Festival Plaza** (✉ Blvd. Juárez 11, ☎ 661/2–08–42) has become party central for Rosarito's youthful crowd and presents live concerts on the hotel's courtyard stage most weekends; in the hotel complex are El Museo Cantina Tequila, which serves more than 130 brands of the fiery drink. Rock & Roll Taco is a taco stand and boisterous bar all in one. **Papas and Beer** (✉ Blvd. Juárez near Rosarito Beach Hotel, ☎ 661/2–03–43) draws a young, energetic crowd.

Outdoor Activities and Sports

GOLF

The **Real del Mar Golf Club** (⊠ 18 km [12 mi] south of the border on Ensenada toll road, ☎ 66/31–34–01) has 18 holes overlooking the ocean. Golf packages are available at some Rosarito Beach hotels.

HORSEBACK RIDING

Horses can be rented at the north and south ends of Juárez and on the beach south of the Rosarito Beach Hotel for $6 per hour. In the past, some of the animals were pathetically thin and misused. Their number is now restricted and the horses are better cared for. If you're a dedicated equestrian, ask about tours into the countryside, which can be arranged with the individual owners.

SURFING

The waves are particularly good at **Popotla,** Kilometer 33; **Calafia,** Kilometer 35.5; and **Costa Baja,** Kilometer 36, on the Old Ensenada Highway. **Tony's Surf Shop** (⊠ Blvd. Juárez 312, ☎ 661/2–11–92) has surfing gear for sale or rent.

Shopping

Rosarito is a great place to shop for pottery and wood furniture. Curio stands and open-air artisans' markets line Boulevard Juárez both north and south of town, with the best pottery stands on the highway to the south. The major hotels have shopping arcades with restaurants, taco stands, and some decent crafts stores.

Interios del Rio Casa del Arte y La Madera (⊠ Quinta del Mar Plaza, ☎ 661/2–13–00) always carries an irresistible selection of Mexican folk art with a fish and sea theme, and creatively painted furnishings. **Casa la Carreta** (⊠ Km 29, Old Ensenada Hwy., ☎ 661/2–05–02), one of Rosarito's best furniture shops, is worth a visit just to see the wood-carvers create elaborate desks, dining tables, and armoires. **Casa Torres** (⊠ Rosarito Beach Hotel Shopping Center, ☎ 661/2–10–08) carries a wide array of imported perfumes. **Margarita's** (⊠ Rosarito Beach Hotel Shopping Center, no phone) has a great selection of Guatemalan textiles and clothing. The shelves of **Taxco Curios** (⊠ Quinta del Mar Plaza, ☎ 661/2–18–77) are filled with handblown glassware.

The **Calimax** grocery store on Boulevard Juárez is a good place to stock up on necessities.

En Route Vast vistas of pounding surf and solitary cliffs are interspersed with one-of-a-kind hotels and restaurants along the coastline between Rosarito Beach and Ensenada. The paved highway (Mexico Highway 1) between the two cities often cuts a path between low mountains and high oceanside cliffs; exits lead to rural roads, oceanfront campgrounds, and an ever-increasing number of resort communities. Puerto Nuevo is famous for its classic meal: grilled lobster, refried beans, rice, homemade tortillas, butter, salsa, and lime. The small fishing communities of San Miguel and El Sauzal sit off the highway to the north of Ensenada, and the Coronado Islands can be clearly seen off the coast.

ENSENADA

104 km (65 mi) south of Tijuana, 75 km (47 mi) south of Rosarito on Hwy. 1.

In 1542, Juan Rodríguez Cabrillo first discovered the seaport that Sebastián Vizcaino named Ensenada–Bahía de Todos Santos (All Saints' Bay) in 1602. Since then the town, now the third-largest city in Baja, has drawn a steady stream of "discoverers" and developers. First ranchers made their homes on large spreads along the coast and up into the mountains. Gold miners followed, turning the area into a boom-town during the late 1800s. After the mines were depleted, the area settled back into a pastoral state for a while, but the harbor gradually grew into a major port for shipping agricultural goods from the sur-rounding ranches and farms. Now, with a population of some 300,000, it is one of Mexico's largest seaports and has a thriving fishing fleet and fish-processing industry. The smell of fish from the canneries lin-ing the highway can be overpowering at times.

There are no beaches in Ensenada proper, but beaches north and south of town are satisfactory for swimming, sunning, surfing, and camp-ing. On summer and holiday weekends the population swells, but the town rarely gets overly crowded. While the hotels and resorts along the coast, especially around Rosarito Beach, attract many of the trav-elers seeking weekend escapes, Ensenada tends to draw those who want to explore a more traditional Mexican city.

In a concerted effort to attract vacationers, conventioneers, and busi-ness travelers, the waterfront area has been razed and rebuilt, with taco stands replaced by shopping centers, hotels, and the massive Plaza Ma-rina, a large shopping complex with few tenants. Several strip malls have opened in town, but many of the storefronts remain empty. Cruise ships occasionally anchor in the port, bringing day-trippers for shop-ping and dining.

Numbers in the margin correspond to points of interest on the Ensenada map.

① **Parque Revolución** (Revolution Park) is the most traditional plaza in Ensenada, with a bandstand, playground, and plenty of benches in the shade. The plaza takes on a festive feeling on Saturday and Sunday evenings, when neighbors congregate on the benches and children chase seagulls down the pathways. ✉ *Av. Juárez, at Av. Obregón.*

At the northernmost point at the water's edge sits an indoor-outdoor **②** **Fish Market,** where row after row of counters display piles of shrimp as well as tuna, dorado, marlin, snapper, and dozens of other species of fish caught off Baja's coasts. Outside, stands sell grilled or smoked fish, seafood cocktails, and fish tacos. Browsers can pick up some stan-dard souvenirs, eat well for very little money, and take some great pho-tographs. The hot-pink Plaza de Mariscos, which blocks the view of the traditional fish market from the street, is a comfortable place to eat.

The main street along the waterfront is Boulevard Costero. Fishing and **③** whale-watching tours depart from the **Sportfishing Pier** (✉ Blvd. Cos-tero, at Av. Alvarado).

④ **Plaza Cívica** (✉ Blvd. Costero, at Av. Riveroll) is a nice, small square with sculptures of Mexican heroes Benito Juárez, Miguel Hidalgo, and Venustiano Carranza.

⑤ The **Riviera del Pacífico** is a rambling, white hacienda-style mansion built in the 1920s with money raised on both sides of the border. An enormous gambling palace, hotel, restaurant and bar, the glamorous Riviera was frequented by wealthy U.S. citizens and Mexicans, par-ticularly during Prohibition. When gambling was outlawed in Mexico and Prohibition ended in the United States, the palace lost its raison d'être. During daylight, visitors can tour some of the elegant ball-rooms and halls, which host occasional art shows and civic events. Many of the rooms are locked; check at the main office to see if there is some-

162

Avenida López
Mateos, **6**

Avenida
Juárez, **7**

Fish Market, **2**

La
Bufadora, **10**

Las Bodegas de
Santo Tomás, **8**

Our Lady of
Guadalupe, **9**

Parque
Revolución, **1**

Plaza Cívica, **4**

Riviera del
Pacífico, **5**

Sportfishing
Pier, **3**

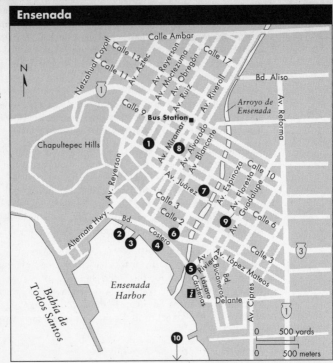

one available to show you around. The gardens alone are worth visiting, and the building now houses a museum of Baja's history. The Riviera del Pacífico is officially called the Centro Social, Cívico y Cultural de Ensenada (Social, Civic and Cultural Center of Ensenada). ⊠ *Blvd. Costero and Av. Riviera,* ☎ *61/76–43–10, 61/76–05–94 for museum.* ⊟ *Building and gardens free, museum $1.* ☉ *Daily 9–5.*

6 Ensenada's traditional tourist zone is centered along **Avenida López Mateos.** High-rise hotels, souvenir shops, restaurants, and bars line the avenue from its beginning at the foot of the Chapultepec Hills for eight blocks south to the dry channel of the Arroyo de Ensenada. Locals shop for furniture, clothing, and other necessities a few blocks inland on **7** **Avenida Juárez** in Ensenada's downtown area.

8 **Las Bodegas de Santo Tomás,** Baja's oldest winery, gives tours and tastings at its downtown winery and bottling plant. The restaurant in the winery is one of Baja's finest. The winery also operates La Esquina de Bodegas, a café, shop, and gallery in a bright blue building across Avenida Miramar. ⊠ *Av. Miramar 666,* ☎ *61/78–33–33, 619/454–7166 in the U.S.* ⊟ *$1.* ☉ *Tours Mon.–Sat. at 11 AM, 1 PM, and 3 PM; Sun. at 11 AM and 1 PM.*

9 The city's largest cathedral, **Our Lady of Guadalupe** (⊠ Av. Floresta, at Av. Juárez) is the center of processions and celebrations during religious holidays.

10 **La Bufadora** (⊠ Hwy. 23, 31 km [20 mi] south of Ensenada) is an impressive blowhole ("la bufadora" means the buffalo snort) in the coastal cliffs at Punta Banda, an isolated, mountainous point jutting into the sea. The road along Punta Banda to La Bufadora is lined with stands where growers sell locally grown olives, homemade tamales, strands of chilies and garlic, and terra-cotta planters. The drive gives short-term visitors a sampling of Baja's wilderness, and is well worth a half-day excursion. The blowhole is impressive, with seawater splashing up to 75 ft in the air with startling power, spraying sightseers standing nearby. Legend has it the blowhole is created by a whale or sea serpent trapped in an undersea cave; both these stories and the less romantic scientific facts are posted on a plaque at the side of the road. The area around the blowhole has been cleaned up, and a viewing platform and building with rest rooms have been added. Visitors now pay to park near the blowhole and file through a row of permanent vendors' stands en route to the cliff.

Dining and Lodging

$$$ ✕ **La Embotelladora Vieja.** The most elegant restaurant in Ensenada
★ is set in a converted wine-aging room at the Santo Tomás winery. The decor is classic country French, with wine bins stacked floor-to-ceiling under brick arches and crystal goblets glistening on candlelit tables. The so-called Baja French menu includes appetizers of smoked tuna and French pâté; among the most sublime entrées are the grilled lobster in cabernet sauvignon sauce, beef Montpellier with green peppercorns, and quail with sauvignon blanc sauce. Teetotalers, note: Nearly every dish is prepared with wine, though you can order some without alcohol-laden sauces. All of Baja's wineries are represented on the impressive wine list. ⊠ *Av. Miramar 666,* ☎ *61/74–08–07. MC, V. Closed Sun.*

$$ ✕ **Bronco's Steak House.** A great find near the San Nicolas Hotel, Bronco's serves exceptional steaks and Mexican specialties. Try the Boca del Rio, a New York steak stuffed with grilled onions and fiery serrano chilies. Tripe appears frequently on the menu. Brick walls, wood plank floors, and hanging spurs and chaps give the place a Wild West feel, but the mood is subdued and relaxed. ⊠ *Av. López Mateos 1525,* ☎ *61/76–49–00. MC, V.*

$$ ✕ **Casamar.** A long-standing, dependable restaurant, Casamar is known for its wide variety of excellent seafood. Lobster and shrimp are prepared in several ways but seem freshest when grilled *con mojo y ajo* (with butter and garlic). When choosing a fish dish, always ask about the catch of the day; you may luck out and get a thick steak of fresh yellowfin tuna. ⊠ *Blvd. Lázaro Cárdenas 987,* ☎ *61/74–04–17. MC, V.*

$$ ✕ **El Rey Sol.** Specialties here include French and Mexican presenta-
★ tions of fresh fish, poultry, and vegetables grown at the owner's farm in the Santo Tomás Valley. Appetizers come with the meal; the excellent pastries are baked on the premises. A side room at the front of the restaurant has been turned into a patisserie. It's a lovely spot for an afternoon espresso and sweets, or you can choose a few tasty items to go. ⊠ *Av. López Mateos 1000,* ☎ *61/78–17–33. AE, MC, V.*

$ ✕ **El Charro.** You can find less (and more) expensive rotisserie chicken,
★ beans, rice, and tortillas at other places in downtown, but El Charro still attracts a steady stream of locals and tourists. Part of the draw is the location—not far from popular bars—and the consistently good food. Hungry patrons hover over platters of chilies *rellenos* (chilies stuffed with cheese and deep-fried in batter), enchiladas, and fresh chips and guacamole at heavy wooden picnic tables under a ceiling of charred wooden beams. Other restaurants with similar names have opened on the same block; stick with the original and you won't be disappointed. ⊠ *Av. López Mateos 475,* ☎ *61/78–38–81. MC, V.*

$ ✕ **Mariscos de Bahía de Ensenada.** Red lights flicker around the front
★ door, making this popular seafood house just off the main drag easy
to spot. On weekends the upstairs and downstairs dining rooms are
packed for both lunch and dinner; tables are easier to come by on
weeknights. Clams, shrimp, lobster, red snapper, squid, and any other
sea creatures in season appear on the menu fried, baked, broiled, or
grilled, and served with a basic iceberg lettuce salad, white rice, and
tortillas made fresh at the window-front tortilleria. ✉ *Av. Riveroll 109,*
☎ *61/78–10–15. MC, V.*

$$$ ▦ **Hotel Coral & Marina.** This ambitious project is the largest resort
★ on the Baja Norte coast. A marina, long needed in Ensenada, has slips
for 600 boats and facilities for clearing customs. The rooms in two eight-
story towers are decorated in burgundy and dark green, with water-
front balconies, seating areas, cable TV, and in-room international phone
service (still a novelty in this area). Conventions, fishing and golf tour-
naments, and boat races fill the hotel on weekends; rates are often 30%–
50% lower on winter weekdays. ✉ *Mexico Hwy. 1 north of town,*
22800, ☎ *61/75–00–00 or 800/94–627–462 in Mexico, 800/862–*
9029 in U.S., ⅌ *61/75–00–05. 147 rooms and suites. Restaurant, in-*
door pool, 2 outdoor pools, 2 hot tubs, spa, 2 tennis courts, exercise
room, dive shop, boating, fishing. MC, V.

$$$ ▦ **Las Rosas.** This elegant pink palace just north of town is both inti-
★ mate and upscale; the atrium lobby features marble floors, mint green–
and–pink upholstered couches facing the sea, and a green-glass ceiling
that glows at night. All rooms face the ocean and pool; some have fireplaces and hot tubs, and even the least expensive accommodations are
lovely. The hotel is booked solid most weekends; make reservations
far in advance. ✉ *Mexico Hwy. 1 north of town, 22800,* ☎ *61/74–*
43–20, ⅌ *61/74–45–95. 32 rooms and suites. Restaurant, bar, pool,*
hot tub. AE, MC, V.

$$$ ▦ **Punta Morro.** For seclusion and the sound of crashing surf, you can't
★ beat this all-suites hotel. The three-story tan building faces the north
end of the bay. The restaurant sits on rock pilings above the waves;
you won't find a more romantic spot than at a window seat here. Enjoy
eggs Benedict or French toast in the morning, or toast the sunset with
champagne while feasting on lobster, steak, or quail. All accommodations
have terraces facing the ocean, kitchenettes, and seating areas; some
have fireplaces. Stairs lead down to a rocky beach, but the surf is usu-
ally too rough for swimming. Rates are significantly lower on week-
days. ✉ *Mexico Hwy. 1, 3 km (2 mi) north of town, Box 2891, 22800,*
☎ *61/78–35–07 or 800/526–6676,* ⅌ *61/74–44–90. Reservations*
in the U.S.: ✉ *Box 43-4263, San Ysidro, CA 92143. 30 suites. Restau-*
rant, bar, pool, hot tub, beach. MC, V.

$$ ▦ **Estero Beach Resort.** Families settle in for a week or more at this
long-standing resort on Ensenada's best beach. The rooms and suites
(some with kitchenettes) are housed in several mint-green buildings.
The best are those right by the sand; the worst (and cheapest) are in
the oldest section by the parking lot. No one expects anything fancy
here, and at times it seems all the guests are attending huge wedding
or birthday celebrations or family reunions. Guests spend their days
swimming in the ocean (a pool was under construction at press time),
fishing, riding horses, playing volleyball, and generally hanging out with
friends. Nights are spent at the casual restaurant and bar. The resort
is 10 km (6 mi) south of town. Midweek winter rates are a real bargain, and the resort feels almost deserted and peaceful at this time.
Nonguests can use the hotel's facilities for a low daily fee. ✉ *Mexico*
Hwy. 1 between Ensenada and Maneadero, 22810, ☎ *61/76–62–35,*

FAX *61/76–69–25. Reservations in the U.S.:* ⊠ *482 San Ysidro Blvd., Suite 1186, San Ysidro, CA 92173. 110 rooms. Restaurant, bar, kitchenettes, 4 tennis courts, horseback riding, volleyball, shops, playground. MC, V.*

$$ 🏨 **Hotel Mision Santa Ysabel.** The most authentically Mexican hotel right in the tourist zone, this two-story charmer has a peaceful courtyard and pool area, heavy colonial-style wood furnishings in the rooms, and lots of tile and folk art in the decor. ⊠ *Av. López Mateos (also called Calle 1) and Av. Castillo, Box 76, 22800,* ☎ *61/78–36–16,* FAX *61/78–33–45. 58 rooms and suites. 2 restaurants, pool. MC, V.*

$$ 🏨 **San Nicolás.** The suites at this massive resort have tiled hot tubs; living rooms with deep-green carpeting, mauve furnishings, and beveled-glass doors; and bedrooms with mirrored ceilings. The less extravagant rooms are comfortable and decorated with folk art. A waterfall cascades into the pool, and a good restaurant overlooks the gardens. Special rates are often available on weekdays and in the winter. ⊠ *Av. López Mateos (also called Calle 1) and Av. Guadalupe, Box 19, 22800,* ☎ *61/76–19–01,* FAX *61/76–49–30. Reservations in the U.S.:* ⊠ *Box 43706, San Diego, CA 92143,* ☎ *619/491–0682. 150 rooms and suites. 2 restaurants, bar, indoor and outdoor pools, hot tub, dance club. AE, MC, V.*

$$ 🏨 **Travelodge Ensenada.** Dependable, clean, and secure, this three-story hotel just off the main shopping street offers such comforts as in-room coffeemakers and safes and electronic door locks. The rooms, with brick ceilings and walls, feel old and dark, but carpeting and firm mattresses add warmth and comfort. ⊠ *Av. Blancarte 130, Box 1467, 22800,* ☎ *61/78–16–01, 800/578–7878 for reservations in the U.S.,* FAX *61/74–00–05. 52 rooms and suites. Restaurant, pool, hot tub, parking. MC, V.*

$ 🏨 **Corona Hotel.** One of the few in-town hotels right by the water, the Corona is a favorite for bus-tour groups. Few rooms actually have a view of the water and most suffer a bit from lack of maintenance. But there is plenty of parking, the room rates are low, and most sights are within easy walking distance. ⊠ *Blvd. Costero 1442, 22800,* ☎ *61/76–09–01,* FAX *61/76–40–23. Reservations in the U.S.:* ⊠ *482 San Ysidro Blvd., Suite 303, San Ysidro, CA 92173. 90 rooms. Restaurant, pool. MC, V.*

$ 🏨 **Hotel del Valle.** Fishermen and budget travelers frequent the clean, basic rooms in this small hotel on a relatively quiet side street. Though the rooms lack air-conditioning they do have fans, phones, and televisions (with local stations only). Guests have use of a coffeemaker in the lobby and parking spaces in front of the rooms. Ask about discounts; the rates posted behind the front desk are about 40% higher than guests in the know normally pay. ⊠ *Av. Riveroll 367, 22800,* ☎ *61/78–22–24,* FAX *61/74–04–66. 20 rooms. AE, MC, V.*

$ 🏨 **Joker Hotel.** A bizarre, brightly colored mishmash of styles makes it hard to miss this hotel, conveniently located for those traveling south of Ensenada. Spacious rooms have private balconies, satellite TV, and phones. ⊠ *Mexico Hwy. 1, Km 12.5, 22800,* ☎ FAX *61/76–72–01. 40 rooms. Pool, hot tub. MC, V.*

Nightlife and the Arts

Ensenada is a party town for college students, surfers, and other young tourists. **Hussong's Cantina** (⊠ Av. Ruíz 113, ☎ 61/78–32–10) has been an Ensenada landmark since 1892 and has changed little since then. A security guard stands by the front door to handle the often-rowdy crowd—a mix of locals and tourists of all ages over 18. The noise is usually deafening, pierced by mariachi and ranchera musicians and the whoops and hollers of the inebriated. **Papas and Beer** (⊠ Av.

Ruíz, at López Mateos, ☎ 61/78–42–31) is oriented toward the college set, who hang out the second-story windows shouting at their friends.

Outdoor Activities and Sports

BEACHES

Since the waterfront in Ensenada proper is taken up by fishing boats, boat repair yards, and commercial shipping, the best swimming beaches are south of town. **Estero Beach** is long and clean, with mild waves; the Estero Beach Hotel takes up much of the oceanfront but the beach is public. Surfers populate the beaches off Highway 1 north and south of Ensenada, particularly San Miguel, California, Tres Marías, and La Joya; scuba divers prefer Punta Banda, by La Bufadora. Lifeguards are rare; swimmers should be cautious. The tourist office in Ensenada has a map that shows safe diving and surfing beaches.

FISHING

Boats leave the **Ensenada Sportfishing Pier** regularly. The best angling is from April through November, with bottom fishing good in the winter. Charter vessels and party boats are available from several outfitters along Avenida López Mateos, Boulevard Costero, and off the sportfishing pier. Trips on group boats cost about $35 for a half day or $100 for a full day. You can book sportfishing packages including transportation, accommodations, and fishing through **Baja California Tours** (☎ 619/454–7166 in the U.S.). Licenses are available at the tourist office or from charter companies. **Ensenada Clipper Fleet** (✉ Sportfishing Pier, ☎ 61/78–21–85) has charter and group boats. **Gordo's Sportfishing** (✉ Sportfishing Pier, ☎ 61/78–35–15, FAX 61/78–23–77), one of the oldest sportfishing companies in Ensenada, has charter boats, group boats, and a smokehouse. Gordo's also operates whale-watching trips from December through February.

GOLF

The **Baja Country Club** (✉ Hwy. 1 south of Ensenada, at Maneadero, ☎ 61/73–03–03) has a secluded 18-hole course in a resort development.

Shopping

Most of the tourist shops are along Avenida López Mateos beside the hotels and restaurants. There are several two-story shopping arcades, many with empty shops. Dozens of curio shops line the street, all selling similar selections of pottery, woven blankets and serapes, embroidered dresses, and onyx chess sets.

Artes Don Quijote (✉ Av. López Mateos 503, ☎ 61/76–94–76) has carved-wood doors, huge terra-cotta pots, crafts from Oaxaca, and large brass fish and birds. **Artesanías Castillo** (✉ Av. López Mateos 656, ☎ 61/76–11–87) and **Los Castillo** (✉ Av. López Mateos 815, ☎ 61/76–11–87) both have extensive displays of silver jewelry from Taxco. **Girasoles** (✉ Av. López Mateos, no phone) stocks a great selection of dolls, pine-needle baskets, and pottery made by the Tarahumara Indians from the Copper Canyon. **La Mina de Salomón** (✉ Av. López Mateos 1000, ☎ 61/78–28–36) carries elaborate jewelry in a tiny gallery next to El Rey Sol restaurant. **Carlos Importer** (✉ Av. López Mateos, at Alvarado, ☎ 61/78–24–63) is one of the largest shops in town with high-quality pottery, tile, blown glassware, and iron furniture.

Centro Artesenal de Ensenada has a smattering of galleries and shops. The best by far is the Galería de Pérez Meillón (✉ Blvd. Costero 1094–39, ☎ 61/74–03–94), which carries museum-quality pottery and varied folk art by the indigenous peoples of northern Mexico. **La Esquina de Bodegas** (✉ Av. Miramar, at Calle 6, ☎ 61/78–35–57) is an innovative gallery, shop, and café in a century-old winery building. Baja's finest wines are sold here at reasonable prices, and an upstairs gallery features some fine glassware, pottery, and books. The small café at the back of the building serves coffees, wines, and a small menu of soups and entrées.

TIJUANA, ROSARITO BEACH, AND ENSENADA A TO Z

Arriving and Departing

By Bus

Greyhound (☎ 619/239–1288 or 800/231–2222) serves Tijuana from San Diego several times daily; the Greyhound terminal in Tijuana is at Avenida Mexico at Calle 11 (☎ 66/86–06–95). **Five Star Tours/Mexicoach** (☎ 619/232–5049) runs buses from the trolley depot on the U.S. side of the border to their depot on Avenida Revolución in Tijuana. **ABC–US** (☎ 66/26–11–46) runs buses from the San Ysidro trolley stop to downtown Tijuana, Pueblo Amigo, Plaza Rio Tijuana, and the Agua Caliente racetrack.

Buses connect all the towns in Baja Norte and are easy to use. Bus stations in northwestern Baja Norte are **Ensenada** (⊠ Av. Riveroll between Calles 10 and 11, ☎ 61/78–67–70 or 61/78–66–80) and **Tijuana** (⊠ Calzada Lázaro Cárdenas and Blvd. Arroyo Alamar, ☎ 66/21–29–82). Buses traveling to Rosarito no longer stop in town, but instead stop at the Rosarito exit on the toll road where taxis are waiting to transport passengers to town. There is no official bus station here; check at the hotels for bus schedule information.

By Car

From San Diego, I–5 and I–805 end at the border crossing into Tijuana at San Ysidro; Highway 905 leads from I–5 and I–805 to the Tijuana border crossing at Otay Mesa, near the Tijuana airport.

To head south into Baja from Tijuana, follow the signs for Ensenada Cuota, the toll road (also called Highway 1 and on newer signs the Scenic Highway) that runs south along the coast. There are two clearly marked exits for Rosarito Beach, and one for Puerto Nuevo, Bajamar, and Ensenada. The road is excellent, though it has some hair-raising curves atop the cliffs and is best driven in daylight (the stretch from Rosarito Beach to Ensenada is one of the most scenic drives in Baja). Tollbooths accept U.S. and Mexican currency; tolls are usually about $1.60. Rest rooms are available near the booths. The alternate free road— Highway 1D or Ensenada Libre—has been vastly improved, but it is difficult for the first-timer to navigate. Highway 1 continues south of Ensenada through San Quintín to Guerrero Negro at the border between Baja California and Baja Sur and on to the southernmost tip of Baja; it is no longer a toll road past Ensenada, however.

You must have Mexican auto insurance, available at agencies near the border. Note that many car-rental companies do not allow their cars to be driven into Mexico (☞ Car Rentals *in* Contacts and Resources, *below*).

By Plane

Tijuana's Aeropuerto Alberado Rodriguez is located on the eastern edge of the city, near the Otay Mesa border crossing, and is served from cities in Baja and mainland Mexico by **Mexicana** (☎ 66/83–28–50), **Aeromexico** (☎ 66/85–44–01), **AeroCalifornia** (☎ 66/84–21–00 or 66/84–28–76), and **Taesa** (☎ 66/84–84–84).

By Trolley

The **San Diego Trolley** (☎ 619/233–3004) travels from the Santa Fe Depot, at Kettner Boulevard and Broadway, to within 100 ft of the border every 15 minutes from 5 AM to midnight. The 45-minute trip costs $1.75.

Getting Around

By Bus

In **Tijuana,** the downtown station for buses within the city is at Calle 1a and Avenida Madero (☎ 66/86–95–15). Most city buses at the border will take you downtown; look for the ones marked CENTRO CAMIONERA. To catch the bus back to the border from downtown, go to Calle Benito Juárez (also called Calle 2a) between Avenidas Revolución and Constitución. **Five Star Tours/Mexicoach** (☎ 619/232–5049) runs buses from the trolley depot on the U.S. side of the border to their depot on Avenida Revolución in Tijuana. *Colectivos* (small vans usually painted white with colored stripes) cover neighborhood routes in most Baja cities and towns. The destination is usually painted on the windshield; look for them on main streets.

By Car

The best way to tour northwestern Baja is by car, though the driving can be difficult and confusing at times. If you're just visiting Tijuana, it's easiest to park on the U.S. side of the border and walk across.

The combination of overpopulation, lack of infrastructure, and heavy winter rains makes many of **Tijuana**'s streets difficult to navigate by automobile. It's always best to stick to the main thoroughfares. There are parking lots along Avenida Revolución and at most major attractions. Most of **Rosarito Beach** proper can be explored on foot, which is a good idea on weekends, when Boulevard Juárez has bumper-to-bumper traffic. To reach **Puerto Nuevo** and other points south, continue on Boulevard Juárez (also called Old Ensenada Highway and Ensenada Libre) through town. Most of **Ensenada**'s attractions are within five blocks of the waterfront; it is easy to take a long walking tour of the city. A car is necessary to reach La Bufadora and most of the beaches.

Official Requirements

Passports and Tourist Cards

U.S. citizens entering Mexico by road are required to have proof of citizenship. The only acceptable proof of citizenship is either a valid passport or an original birth certificate plus a photo ID. Tourist cards are not needed unless you are traveling south of Ensenada or are planning to stay longer than 72 hours. Tourist cards can be obtained from the information booth just inside the border. Passports are required of non-U.S. citizens for reentry at the San Ysidro or Otay Mesa border crossings.

Customs

U.S. residents may bring home duty-free up to $400 worth of foreign goods, as long as they have been out of the country for at least 48 hours. Each member of the family is entitled to the same exemption, regardless of age, and exemptions may be pooled. Included in the allowances for travelers 21 or older are one liter of alcohol, 100 cigars (non-Cuban), and 200 cigarettes. Only one bottle of perfume trademarked in the United States may be imported. There is no duty on antiques or works of art more than 100 years old. Anything exceeding these limits will be taxed at the port of entry and may be taxed in the traveler's home state.

Contacts and Resources

Car Rentals

Avis (☎ 800/331–1212) permits its cars to go from San Diego into Baja as far as 724 km (450 mi) south of the border. Cars must be returned by the renter to San Diego, and Mexican auto insurance is mandatory. Cars leased from **Courtesy Rentals** (⊠ 2975 Pacific Hwy., San Diego, CA 92101, ☎ 619/497–4800 or 800/252–9756) may be taken as far as Ensenada. **M&M Jeeps** (⊠ 2200 El Cajon Blvd., San Diego, CA 92104, ☎ 619/297–1615, FAX 619/297–1617) rents two- and four-wheel-drive vehicles with packages covering tours of the entire Baja California peninsula.

ENSENADA

Fiesta Rent-a-Car (☎ 61/76–33–44) has an office in the Hotel Corona, at Boulevard Costero. **Hertz** (☎ 61/78–29–82) is on Avenida Blancarte between Calles 1 and 2.

TIJUANA

The larger U.S. rental agencies have offices at the Tijuana International Airport. Offices in town include **Avis** (⊠ Av. Agua Caliente 3310, ☎ 66/86–40–04 or 66/86–37–18) and **Budget** (⊠ Paseo de los Héroes 77, ☎ 66/34–33–03).

Emergencies

THROUGHOUT BAJA NORTE

Police (☎ 134). **Red Cross** (☎ 132). **Fire** (☎ 136).

TIJUANA

U.S. Consulate (☎ 66/81–74–00). The **Attorney General for the Protection of Tourists Hot Line** (☎ 66/88–05–55) takes calls weekdays to help with tourist complaints and problems.

Guided Tours

Baja California Tours (⊠ 7734 Herschel Ave., Suite O, La Jolla, CA 92037, ☎ 619/454–7166, FAX 619/454–2703) operates comfortable, informative bus trips throughout Baja and can arrange special-interest tours, including shopping, culture, whale-watching and fishing trips, and tours to the wineries and La Bufadora. **San Diego Mini-Tours** (⊠ 1726 Wilson Ave., National City, CA 91950, ☎ 619/477–8687 or 800/235–5393, FAX 619/477–0705) has frequent departures throughout the day from San Diego hotels to Avenida Revolución in Tijuana and back.

Reservation Agencies

Several companies specialize in arranging hotel reservations in Baja Norte. Contact **Baja Information** (⊠ 7860 Mission Center Ct., Suite 202, San Diego, CA 92108, ☎ 619/298–4105; 800/225–2786 in the U.S., Canada, Puerto Rico; 800/522–1516 in CA, NV, AZ; FAX 619/294–7366); **Baja California Tours** (⊠ 7734 Herschel Ave., Suite O, La Jolla, CA 92037, ☎ 619/454–7166, FAX 619/454–2703); **Baja Lodging** (☎ 619/491–0682); and **Mexico Resorts International** (⊠ 4126 Bonita Rd, Bonita, CA 91902, ☎ 619/422–6900 or 800/336–5454, FAX 619/472–6778).

Travel Club

A monthly newsletter, Mexican auto insurance, Baja tours, and workshops are available through **Discover Baja Travel Club** (⊠ 3089 Clairemont Dr., San Diego, CA 92117, ☎ 619/275–4225 or 800/727–2252, FAX 619/275–1836).

Visitor Information

Regional tourist offices are usually open Monday through Friday from 9 to 7 (though some may close in early afternoon for lunch), and Saturday and Sunday from 9 to 1: **Ensenada** (✉ Blvd. Costero 1477, ☎ 617/2–30–22, FAX 61/72–30–81; ✉ Blvd. Costero, at entrance to town, ☎ 61/78–24–11), **Rosarito Beach** (✉ Blvd. Juárez, 2nd floor of Quinta Plaza shopping center, ☎ 661/2–03–96 or 661/2–30–78), **Tijuana Chamber of Commerce** (✉ Av. Revolución and Calle 1, ☎ 66/88–16–85), and the **Tijuana Convention and Tourism Bureau** (✉ Inside San Ysidro border crossing, ☎ 66/83–14–05 or 66/84–77–90; ✉ Av. Revolución between Calles 3 and 4, ☎ 66/83–05–30).

11 Portraits of San Diego

Idylling in San Diego

Books and Videos

IDYLLING IN SAN DIEGO

I'VE NEVER BEEN to Sea World; performing fish give me the willies. And during the two years I lived within striking distance of Balboa Park, I had to take visiting friends to the zoo so many times I began having nightmares about koalas. But if I came to dislike various theme-park aspects of the city, I nevertheless loved San Diego. At first sight.

A typical easterner, I went out to San Diego in the late 1970s expecting to find a smaller version of Los Angeles. The freeways were there, along with a fair share of traffic congestion, but so was an oceanscape of surprisingly pristine beauty. The first drive I took from the University of California, where I was doing graduate research, knocked me for a loop: I rounded a curve on La Jolla Shores Drive to confront a coastline that could match any on the French Riviera.

I was also taken by the distinctiveness of the many shoreline communities. For one thing, the beaches tend to get funkier as you head south from the old-money enclave of La Jolla: Pacific Beach, with its Crystal Pier, is an aging Victorian resort taken over by teenagers while transients and surfers share the turf at Ocean Beach. To the north, Del Mar has a strip of shops that rival those of Rodeo Drive, and Carlsbad and Oceanside show the democratizing influence of nearby Camp Pendleton.

Unlike Los Angeles, San Diego is still strongly defined by its relationship to the ocean—to some degree by default. During the latter half of the 19th century, the town was banking on a rail link to the east. A building boom in the 1880s was largely based on the assumption that San Diego would become the western terminus of the Santa Fe Railroad line; the city hoped to compete with Los Angeles, which was already connected by rail to San Francisco and thus to the national railroad network. The link was completed in 1885, but it proved unsuccessful for a variety of reasons, including the placement of the line through Temecula Canyon, where 30 miles of track were washed out repeatedly in winter rainstorms. The Santa Fe soon moved its West Coast offices to San Bernardino and Los Angeles, and to this day there is no direct rail service from San Diego to the eastern part of the United States.

Instead, San Diego's future was sealed in 1908, when President Theodore Roosevelt's Great White Fleet stopped here on a world tour to demonstrate U.S. naval strength. The navy, impressed during that visit by the city's excellent harbor and temperate climate, decided to build a destroyer base on San Diego Bay in the 1920s; the newly developing aircraft industry soon followed (Charles Lindbergh's plane *Spirit of St. Louis* was built here). Over the years San Diego's economy became largely dependent on the military and its attendant enterprises, which provided jobs as well as a demand for local goods and services by those stationed here.

San Diego's character—conservative where Los Angeles's is cutting edge—was formed in large part by the presence of its military installations, which now occupy more than 165,000 acres of land in the area. And the city conducts most of its financial business in a single neighborhood, the district fronting San Diego Bay, in this way resembling New York more than its economic rival up the coast. San Diego has set some of its most prestigious scientific facilities on the water—Scripps Institute of Oceanography, naturally, but also Salk Institute. Jonas Salk didn't need the Pacific marine environment for his research, but his regular morning runs along Torrey Pines Beach no doubt cleared his head.

San Diego also has the ocean to thank for its near-perfect weather. A high-pressure system from the north Pacific is responsible for the city's sunshine and dry air; moderating breezes off the sea (caused by the water warming and cooling more slowly than the land) keep the summers relatively cool and the winters warm and help clear the air of pollution. In the late spring and early summer the difference between the earth and water temperatures generates coastal fogs. This phenomenon was another of San Diego's delightful surprises: I never tired of watching the mist roll in at night, wonderfully romantic, as thick as any I'd ever seen in London and easier to enjoy in the balmy air.

If I loved San Diego from the start, I had a hard time believing in its existence. It was difficult to imagine that a functioning American city could be so attractive, that people lived and worked in such a place every day. Although I'd never considered myself a Puritan, I quickly came to realize that I'd always assumed work and leisure environments had to be separate, that one was supposed to toil in unpleasant surroundings in order to earn the time spent in idyllic settings.

I found that I could get used to working on sunny days but that it was impossible to remain unaffected by the city's physical presence. Rampant nature conspires in a variety of ways to force you to let your guard down here. In northern East Coast cities, plants are generally orderly and prim: shrubs trimmed, roses demurely draped around railings, tulips set in proper rows. Even the famed cherry blossoms of Washington, D.C., are profuse in neat columns. In San Diego, the flora, whimsical at best, sometimes border on obscenity. The ubiquitous palms come in comedic pairs: short, squat trees that look like overgrown pineapples play Mutt to the Jeff of the tall, skinny variety. The aptly named bottle-brush bushes vie for attention with bright red flame trees, beaky orange birds-of-paradise, and rich purple bougainvillea spilling out over lush green lawns. Only in Hawaii had I previously encountered anthurium, a waxy red plant with a protruding white center that seems to be sticking its tongue out at you. "We're still on the mainland," I felt like telling them all on some days: "Behave yourselves."

IRONICALLY, it was the Victorians who were largely responsible for this indecorous natural profusion. Difficult as it is to imagine now, it's the sparse brown vegetation of San Diego's undeveloped mesas that accurately reflects the climate of the region, technically a semi-arid steppe. When Spanish explorer Juan Rodríguez Cabrillo sailed into San Diego Bay in 1542, looking for a shortcut to China, he and his crew encountered a barren, desolate landscape that did not inspire them to settle here, or even stop for very long.

It wasn't until the late 19th century, when the Mediterranean in general and Italy in particular were all the rage among wealthy residents, that the vegetation now considered characteristic of southern California was introduced to San Diego. In 1889, money raised by the Ladies Annex to the Chamber of Commerce was used to plant trees in Balboa Park, and between 1892 and 1903 a wide variety of exotic foliage was brought into the city: eucalyptus, cork oak, and rubber trees, to name a few. As homeowners in the area can attest, most of the landscaped local vegetation couldn't survive if it were not watered regularly.

No doubt both the natural setting and the relentlessly fine weather help contribute to the clash of cultures that exists here. The conservative traditionalism of the military presence in town is posed against the liberal hedonism of visiting sun seekers, as well as a large local student population. Nude bathing is popular at Black's Beach in La Jolla, a spot that's reasonably private because it's fairly inaccessible. You have to hike down steep cliffs in order to get to the water. Rumor has it that every year a few navy men are killed when they lose their footing on the cliffs, so intent are they at peering through their binoculars.

But I suspect it's the rare person of any political persuasion who can confront the southern California attitude toward nudity with equanimity. I hadn't wanted to believe all the stereotypes, but the first time I went to a dinner party in town, the host asked the group if we wanted to adjourn to the hot tub after we ate. I hadn't brought my bathing suit, so I declined.

The next day, I consulted a local expert about whirlpool etiquette. "What does one do?" I asked. "Undress in front of a group of relative strangers and jump into the water with them? Does one rip off one's clothes with abandon? Fold them carefully afterward? Or go into another room and come out in the raw?" "All that's up to the individual," she answered. "Do whatever you feel comfortable with." "None of it," I asserted. "Where I come from, when people of different genders take their clothes off together, they tend to have sex." "That's optional, too," she said.

Nods to certain So-Cal conventions notwithstanding, San Diego has never come close to approaching the much-touted libertinism of Los Angeles. It has the porno theaters and sleazy clubs you'd expect in a liberty port, but little entertainment of a more sophisticated nature. Celebrities who came down from Hollywood in the 1920s and '30s sought out suites at the La Valencia Hotel and other chic La Jolla locales for the privacy, not the nightlife; the gambling they did at Del Mar racetrack to the north was of the genteel sort. Those who sought thrills—and booze during Prohibition—headed farther south, to Mexico. Raymond Chandler, who spent most of his last 13 years in La Jolla and died there in 1959, wrote a friend that the town was "a nice place . . . for old people and their parents."

FOR ALL ITS conservatism, the one thing San Diego didn't conserve was its past—in some cases because there was little to save. When Father Junípero Serra arrived in 1769 to establish the first of the California missions, he did not find the complex dwellings that characterized so many of the Native American settlements he had encountered in Mexico. Nor did his fellow Spaniards improve much upon the site during their stay; the town that the Mexicans took over in 1822 was rudimentary, consisting mostly of rough adobe huts. The mission church had been moved to a new site in 1774, and the original Spanish presidio, abandoned in the 1830s, was in ruins by the next decade; some grass-covered mounds and a giant cross built in 1913 on Presidio Hill, incorporating the tiles of the original structure, are all that's left of it.

Though a romanticized version of the city during the Mexican period (1822–49), today's Old Town district gives a rough idea of San Diego's layout at that time, when somewhat more impressive structures, such as Casa Estudillo and the Bandini House, were built. San Diego didn't really begin to flourish, however, until 1850, the year that California became a state. At that point the dominant architectural influence came from the East Coast; their enthusiasm for becoming American caused San Diegans to reject their Spanish and Mex-

ican roots as inappropriately "foreign." Thus the first brick structure in the state, the Whaley House (1856), was built in typical New England nautical style. Most of the original Old Town was destroyed by fire in 1872, and a good deal of what was left fell victim to the construction of I–5.

During the Victorian era (1880–1905), the site of the city's development moved south; entrepreneur Alonzo Horton may have miscalculated the success of the rail link to the East Coast, but when he bought up a huge lot of land in 1867 for his "Addition," he knew the city's future lay on the harbor. It was in this area, now the city's financial district, that many of the neo-Gothic structures characteristic of the period were built. Perhaps it's perversely fitting that a number of the Victorian relics in downtown San Diego were removed in conjunction with the 15-block Horton Redevelopment Project, of which the huge Horton Plaza shopping complex is the center.

San Diego finally began to reject the East Coast architectural style at the turn of the century, and at the Panama–California International Exposition of 1915 the city celebrated its Spanish roots—as well as a Moroccan and Italian past it never had—with a vengeance. The beautiful Spanish-style structures built for the occasion fit right into the Mediterranean landscape that had been cultivated in Balboa Park during the Victorian era; today these buildings house most of the city's museums. San Diego became even more thoroughly Hispanicized during the 1920s and '30s as Spanish colonial–style homes became popular in new suburbs, such as Mission Hills and Kensington, as well as in the beach communities that were developing. Downtown buildings began looking like Italian palaces and Moorish towers.

San Diego's landscape of ravines and hills is partly responsible for the city's sprawling development in the 20th century, and the popularization of the automobile in the 1930s helped ensure its continuing growth in an outward direction. The physical barriers have been overcome by an ever-expanding highway system—though not by a viable public transportation network—but the discrete, individual neighborhoods created by them remain, if their populations sometimes shift. For example, Kearny Mesa, formerly a middle-class suburban neighborhood, is now one of the many Southeast Asian communities in the city.

In some ways, as residents and visitors alike have long feared, San Diego is coming to look more like Los Angeles. Faceless developments are cropping up all over once-deserted canyons and mesas, and the huge, castlelike Mormon temple built along I–5 north of La Jolla wouldn't look out of place in Disneyland. But in the years since I lived there, San Diego has also become more like a city—that is, what easterners know to be the city in its divinely ordained form.

As recently as the early 1980s, virtually no one went downtown unless required to. It was a desolate place after dark, and people who worked there during the day never stayed around in the evening to play. Gentrification of sorts began in the mid-1970s, as the low rents attracted artists and real-estate speculators. At about the same time the city designated the formerly rough Stingaree neighborhood as the Gaslamp Quarter, but revitalization, in the form of street-level shops and art galleries, didn't really take until Horton Plaza was completed in 1985. For many years the newly installed gaslights illuminated only the homeless.

The poor and disenfranchised are still here—indeed, many lost their homes to various redevelopment projects—but now there's a concentration of good restaurants, and a serious art and theater scene is developing in the district, too. The area is also a terminus for the San Diego Trolley. This inexpensive transportation link to Mexico has, among other things, allowed Mexican artists to bring their works to a wider market and fostered a cultural as well as a touristic exchange with Tijuana, which

has cleaned up its own act considerably in recent years.

I LIKE THE INFUSION of life into downtown San Diego, and I even like Horton Plaza, which, with its odd angles and colorful banners, looks like it was designed by Alice in Wonderland's Red Queen. But maybe I miss that spot of unadulterated blight that once helped me to believe in San Diego's reality.

Reality seems to be setting in on a large scale these days. San Diego's bad neighborhoods still don't look like slums as I know them, but gang-related crime is on the increase in the southeast part of the city. In recent years, sewage spills have closed a number of southern beaches, and the problem is likely to grow, since neither San Diego nor Tijuana has enacted any large-scale programs for effective waste disposal. Friends tell me that even the weather is changing for the worse, a fact they attribute to global warming.

Would I move back to San Diego? In a minute. Like many other temporary residents, I left the city vowing to return; unlike many others, I've never managed to do more than visit. I used to think that if I had the chance I'd live in Hillcrest, a close-knit inland community with lots of ethnic restaurants and theaters that show foreign films, but I've come to realize that would only be transplanting my East Coast life into the sun. Now I think I'll wait until I'm rich and can afford to move to La Jolla; no doubt I'll be old enough by then to fit in, so I'll fully enjoy that suite in the La Valencia Hotel overlooking the cove.

— Edie Jarolim

BOOKS AND VIDEOS

Books

There is no better way to establish the mood for your visit to Old Town San Diego than by reading Helen Hunt Jackson's 19th-century romantic novel, *Ramona,* a best-seller for more than 50 years and still readily available. The Casa de Estudillo in Old Town has been known for many years as Ramona's Marriage Place because of its close resemblance to the house described in the novel. Richard Henry Dana Jr.'s *Two Years Before the Mast* (1869), based on the author's experiences as a merchant sailor, provides a masculine perspective on early San Diego history.

Other novels with a San Diego setting include Raymond Chandler's mystery about the waterfront, *Playback;* Wade Miller's mystery, *On Easy Street;* Eric Higgs's gothic thriller, *A Happy Man;* Tom Wolfe's satire of the La Jolla surfing scene, *The Pump House Gang;* and David Zielinski's modern-day story, *A Genuine Monster.*

Videos

Filmmakers have taken advantage of San Diego's diverse and amiable climate since the dawn of cinema. Westerns, comedy-westerns, and tales of the sea were early staples: *Cupid in Chaps, The Sagebrush Phrenologist* (how's that for a title?), the 1914 version of *The Virginian,* and Lon Chaney's *Tell It to the Marines* were among the silent films shot in the area. Easy-to-capture outdoor locales have lured many productions south from Hollywood over the years, including the following military-oriented talkies, all or part of which were shot in San Diego: James Cagney's *Here Comes the Navy* (1934), Errol Flynn's *Dive Bomber* (1941), John Wayne's *The Sands of Iwo Jima* (1949), Ronald Reagan's *Hellcats of the Navy* (1956, costarring Nancy Davis, the future First Lady), Rock Hudson's *Ice Station Zebra* (1967), Tom Cruise's *Top Gun* (1986), Sean Connery's *Hunt for Red October* and Charlie Sheen's *Navy Seals* (1990), and Danny Glover's *Flight of the Intruder* (1991). Rob Lowe did not make his infamous home videos here, but he did shoot some of *Desert Shield* (1991).

In a lighter military vein, the famous talking mule hit the high seas in *Francis Joins the Navy* (1955), in which a very young Clint Eastwood has a bit part. The Tom Hanks–Darryl Hannah hit *Splash* (1984), *Spaceballs* (1987), *Hot Shots* (1991), *Wayne's World II* (1993), and Ellen Degeneres's *Mr. Wrong* (1996) are more recent comedies with scenes filmed here. The city has a cameo role in the minihit *Flirting with Disaster* (1996), and one of the best comedies ever made, director Billy Wilder's *Some Like It Hot*—starring Marilyn Monroe, Jack Lemmon, and Tony Curtis—takes place at the famous Hotel Del Coronado (standing in for a Miami resort).

The amusingly low-budget *Attack of the Killer Tomatoes* (1976) makes good use of local scenery—and the infamous San Diego Chicken. The producers must have liked what they found in town as they returned for three sequels: *Return of the Killer Tomatoes* (1988), *Killer Tomatoes Strike Back* (1990), and—proving just how versatile the region is as a film location—*Killer Tomatoes Go to France* (1991). Unlike many films in which San Diego itself doesn't figure in the plot, the screen version of Helen Hunt Jackson's novel *Ramona* (1936), starring Loretta Young as the title character, incorporated historical settings (or replicas).

Television producers zip south for series and made-for-TV movies all the time. The alteration of San Diego's skyline in the 1980s was partially documented on the hit show *Simon & Simon.* San Diego is virtually awash in syndicated productions: *Silk Stalkings, Baywatch, High Tide,* and *Renegade* all shoot here. Reality and cop shows love the area, too: *Unsolved Mysteries, Rescue 911, America's Missing Children, Totally Hidden Video, America's Most Wanted,* and *America's Funniest People* have all taped in San Diego, making it one of the most-seen—yet often uncredited—locales in movie- and videoland.

INDEX

A

Accommodations, *xxiv*, 78–
79, 82–92
Anza-Borrego Desert, 145
*apartment and villa rentals,
xxiv, 78*
*Baja California, 150, 154–
155, 158–159, 164–165*
for children, xix, 59–61
Coronado, 78–79
downtown, 79, 82–84
family rates, 60
*Harbor Island, Point Loma,
and Shelter Island, 84–86*
home exchange, xxiv
hostels, xxvii, 92
*Hotel Circle, Mission Valley
and Old Town, 86–87*
Julian and backcountry, 143
La Jolla, 88–90
*Mission Bay and at beaches,
90–92*
*North Coast, 129–130, 131–
132, 133, 134, 135*
*North County, 126, 137, 139,
140–141*
Aero Club (bar), 94
Airport transfers, *xvii*
Air travel, *xvi–xvii*
Baja California, 167
with children, xix
cutting costs, xvi
North Coast, 135
Albert's ✗, 24
Alcazar Garden, 18
Alt Karlsbad Haus ✗, 133
American restaurants, 66–67
America's Finest City Week,
10
Amusement parks, 47, 152
Anthony's Star of the Sea
Room ✗, 75
Anza, Juan Bautista de, 143
Anza-Borrego Desert State
Park, 126, 144, 146
Apartment and villa rentals,
xxiv, 78
Aquariums. ☞ Zoos and
aquariums
Arts, 99–102
for children, 61–62
Athens Market ✗, 72
Automatic teller machines,
xxiv
Avenida López Mateos, 162
Avenida Revolución, 151
Azteca ✗, 157
Azzura Point ✗, 65

B

Baby Rock (disco), 155
Baby-sitting services, 61
Bahia Belle (paddleboat),
45–46

Bahia Hotel, *61, 91*
Bailey Barbecue ✗, 142
Baily Wine Country Cafe,
140
Baja California, *148–170*
*accommodations, 150, 154–
155, 158–159, 164–165*
beaches, 166
car rentals, 169
emergencies, 169
Ensenada, 160–167
information sources, 169
nightlife, 155, 159, 165–166
official requirements, 168
reservation agencies, 169
*restaurants, 148, 150, 153–
154, 157–158, 163–164*
Rosarito Beach, 156–160
*shopping, 155–156, 160,
166–167*
sports, 155, 160, 166
Tijuana, 150–156
tours, 169
transportation, 167–168
travel club, 169
Balboa Park, *4, 15–18, 20–
24*
children's activities, 57, 62
festivals, 10, 11
restaurants, 22, 24
walking tours, 16–17
Balboa Park Inn, 83
Ballooning, *109, 140*
Balloon tours, *xxvi*
Barefoot Bar and Grill, 99
Bars, *97–98*. ☞ Baja
California, nightlife
Baseball, *62, 117*
Basketball, *117*
Batiquitos Lagoon, 133
Battle of San Pasqual, 138
Bay Cafe, 27
Bay Club Hotel & Marina, 84
Bayou Bar and Grill, *67, 70*
Bazaar del Mundo, 51
Beaches
accommodations in, 90–92
in Baja California, 166
for children, 62
*on North Coast, 108–109,
126*
*restaurants in, 66, 67, 72–73,
74*
*in San Diego, 6, 104, 106–
109*
shopping in, 123–124
Bed & Breakfast Inn at La
Jolla, 89
Bed-and-breakfasts, *78, 83,
87, 89*
Belgian Lion ✗, 67
Bella Luna ✗, 73
Belly Up Tavern, 98
Belmont Park, 47
Bernard'O ✗, 136

Berta's Latin American
Restaurant, *73–74*
Best Western Beach View
Lodge, 134
Best Western Blue Sea Lodge
91
Best Western Hacienda Hotel
Old Town, 87
Best Western Hanalei Hotel,
87
Best Western Inn by the Sea,
90
Best Western Island Palms
Hotel & Marina, *61, 85*
Best Western Posada Inn, 85
Better Business Bureau, *xx*
Bicycling, *109–110*
tours, xxix
Big Stone Lodge (club), 96
Bitter End (bar), 94
Black's Beach, *107–108*
Blind Melon's (nightclub),
98
Blue Point Coastal Cuisine ✗,
75
Blue Tattoo (bar), 94
Boccie ball, *110*
Bodie's (rock/blues club),
98
Border Field State Beach,
104
Borrego Palm Canyon, 144
Borrego Springs, 145
Botanical Building, 18
Bourbon Street (gay bar), 97
Brass Rail (gay bar), 97
Brick by Brick (rock club),
99
Brisas del Mar ⊡, *158*
Broadway Flying Horses
Carousel, 32
Brockton Villa Restaurant,
66–67, 95
Bronco's Steak House, 163
Buick Invitational Golf
Tournament, 10
Bullfights, *155*
Buses, *xvii–xviii*
Anza-Borrego Desert, 146
Baja California, 167, 168
Julian and backcountry, 143
North Coast, 135
North County, 141
tours, xxvi

C

Cabaret, 96
Cabrillo, Juan Rodríguez, *37,
160*
Cabrillo National Monument,
37–38, 56
Café Bessom, 30
Cafe Champagne, *140*
Café Crema (coffeehouse),
95

Cafe Japengo ✕, *75*
Café Lulu, *30*
Cafe Pacifica, *76*
Cajun restaurants, *67, 70*
Calafia ✕, *157*
Calendar of events, *10–11*
California Center for the Arts, *137*
California Cuisine ✕, *70*
California-cuisine restaurants, *70*
California Pizza Kitchen ✕, *59, 130*
Camcorders, traveling with, *xviii*
Cameras, traveling with, *xviii*
Camp Pendleton, *134*
Canadian citizens
customs and duties, xx
insurance, xxiv
passports and visas, xxv
Cannibal Bar, *94*
Cardiff, *108*
Cardiff State Beach, *108*
Carlsbad, *109, 133–134*
Carlsbad Inn, *134*
Carlsbad Ranch, *133*
Carlsbad State Beach, *109*
Carnitas Uruapan ✕, *154*
Carousels, antique, *18, 32*
Car rentals, *xviii–xix, 169*
Car travel
Anza-Borrego Desert, 146
Baja California, 167, 168
driving tips, xxii
Julian, 143
North Coast, 141
North County, 141
Casa de Balboa museum complex, *18*
Casamar ✕, *163*
Casbah (rock club), *99*
Cash machines, *xxiv*
Catamaran Resort Hotel, *61, 90*
Cedros Trading Co., *130*
Centro Cultural (Tijuana), *153*
Centro Cultural de la Raza, *18*
Chevy's ✕ , *59*
Chez Loma ✕, *66*
Chicano Park, *36*
Chick's ✕, *66*
Chiêu-Anh ✕, *136–137*
Chilango's Mexico City Grill, *74*
Children, *xix, 56–63*
accommodations, 59–61
arts, 61–61
beaches, parks, and playgrounds, 62–63
dining, 59
shopping, 63
sightseeing, 56–58
Children's Museum of San Diego, *57*
Children's Pool, *43, 62, 107*

Chinese restaurant, *70*
Christmas on El Prado, *11*
Chula Vista Nature Interpretive Center, *57*
Cilantro's ✕, *129*
Cinco de Mayo Festival, *10*
Cindy Black's ✕, *71*
Clairemont-Kearny Mesa, restaurants in, *65*
Club Bombay (lesbian bar), *97*
Club Emerald City, *96–97*
Club 66, *94*
Coffeehouses, *95–96*
Colonial Inn, *89*
Comedy clubs, *96*
Comedy Isle (club), *96*
The Comedy Store (club), *96*
Como Que No (disco), *155*
Computers, traveling with, *xviii*
Concerts, *100–101*
Consumer protection, *xx*
Continental restaurants, *70–71*
Corona Hotel, *165*
Coronado Beach, *106*
Coronado Beach Historical Museum, *34*
Coronado Island, *4–5, 33–36, 56*
accommodations, 78–79
beaches, 104, 106
restaurants, 65–66, 71
shopping, 120
tour, 34
The Country Club, *96*
Country/western clubs, *96*
Creole restaurant, *67, 70*
Crest Cafe, *67*
Croce's (jazz club), *98*
Cruises, *xxvi*
Crystal Pier Motel, *90–91*
Cupalas del Mar 🖼, *159*
Customs and duties, *xx, 168*
Cuyamaca Rancho State Park, *58, 141*

D

Daily Planet (bar), *94*
Dana Inn & Marina, *92*
Dance, *100*
Dance clubs, *96–97*
Days Inn Hotel Circle, *87*
Dentists, *xxii*
Deer Park Vintage Cars and Wine, *137*
Delicatessen, *71*
Del Mar, *108, 127, 129–130*
Del Mar Beach, *62, 108*
Del Mar Fair, *10, 57–58*
Del Mar Fairgrounds, *127, 129*
Del Mar National Horse Show, *10*
Del Mar Plaza, *127*

Del Mar Thoroughbred Club, *127, 129*
Dental Museum, *54*
Dick's Last Resort (club), *99*
Dime Que Si (bar), *155*
Dining. ☞ Restaurants
Disabilities, hints for travelers with, *xx–xxi*
Discount travel, *xxi–xxii*
Diving, *110*
Dixieland Jazz Festival, *11*
Dobson's ✕, *70*
Doctors, *xxii*
Dodson's Corner, *54*
Dog racing, *155*
Doubletree Hotel San Diego Mission Valley, *86*
Downtown ArtWalk, *10*
Downtown San Diego, *5, 25–33*
accommodations, 79, 82–84
restaurants, 27, 30, 31, 66, 67, 70, 72, 73, 75–76
shopping, 120
walking tour, 26
Dragon del Mar ✕, *157*
Driving, *xxii*
Duties. ☞ Customs and duties

E

Eagle Mining Company, *142*
Elario's (jazz club), *98*
El Callejon ✕, *132*
El Campo Santo (cemetery), *51*
El Charro ✕, *163*
Elephant trees, *144*
El Faro de Mazatlán ✕, *153*
El Indio Shop ✕, *59, 74–75*
Ellen Browning Scripps Park, *43*
El Nido ✕, *158*
El Palacio Frontón (Jai Alai Palace), *151, 155*
El Rey Sol ✕, *163*
El Tecolote ✕, *74*
Embarcadero, *26–27*
Embassy Suites San Diego Bay, *61, 82*
Emerald Chinese Seafood Restaurant, *65*
Emergency information, *xxii, 169*
Encinitas, *108–109, 132–133*
Ensenada, *160–170*
Entertainment
arts, 99–102
in Baja California, 155, 159, 165–166
nightlife, 94–99
Epazote ✕, *129*
Escondido, *137–139*
Estero Beach Resort, *164–165*
E Street Alley (club), *94–95*
Euphoria (coffeehouse), *95*
Excursions from San Diego

Anza-Borrego Desert, 143–146

Julian and backcountry, 141–143

North Coast, 127, 129–136

North County, 136–141

Expresso Bar, *31*

F

Fallbrook, *139*

Family Fun Center, *58, 62*

Farm stands, *121*

Farrell's ice-cream parlor, *59*

Fast-food outlets, *59*

Ferries, *xxii, 56*

Ferry Landing Marketplace, *34–35*

Festival Plaza (hotel/shopping center), *157, 158, 159*

Festivals, *10–11*

Fidel's ✕, *130*

Fiesta Island, *47–48*

Film, *100*

Fio's ✕, *73*

Firehouse Museum, *57*

Fishing, *110–111, 166*

Fish Market (Ensenada), *161*

Fish Market ✕, *59, 76*

Fitness, *111*

The Flame (lesbian bar), *98*

Flicks (gay bar), *97*

Flowers, *126, 133*

Football, *117*

Fort Rosencrans National Cemetery, *38*

Founders Day, *11*

Four Seasons Resort Aviara 🏨, *134*

Freeflight (exotic birds), *129*

French Market Grill, *136*

French Pastry Shop, *45*

French restaurants, *71–72*

Frisbee golf, *111*

G

Gardens. ☞ Parks and gardens

Gaslamp Plaza Suites, *83*

Gaslamp Quarter, *27, 30*

Gaslamp Quarter Hot Line, *30*

Gay and lesbian travelers

hints for, *xxii–xxiii*

nightlife, *97–98*

Gelato Vero (coffeehouse), *95*

George's ✕, *132–133*

George's at the Cove ✕, *76*

Giant Dipper Roller Coaster, *58*

Glorietta Bay Inn, *35, 79*

Golden Triangle (La Jolla), *41, 121*

Golf, *xxix, 166*

Anza-Borrego Desert, 145

Baja California, 150

Ensenada, 166

miniature golf, 62

Rosarito Beach, 160

San Diego, 111–113

Tijuana, 155

tournaments, 10, 118

Gran Hotel, *154*

Greek restaurants, *72*

Green Circle Bar (dance club), *97*

Greyhound racing, *155*

Guided tours. ☞ Tours and sightseeing

H

Hang gliding, *113*

Harbor excursion, *xxvi, 56*

Harbor Island, *38, 84–86*

Hard Rock Cafe, *59, 67, 155*

Helicopter tours, *xxvi*

Heritage Park, *51*

Heritage Park Bed & Breakfast Inn, *87*

Hiking, *114*

Hillcrest, *24, 121*

Hillcrest Cityfest Street Fair, *10*

Historic sites

Cabrillo National Monument, 37–38, 56

Coronado, 35

Gaslamp Quarter, 27, 30

North County, 138

Old Town, 51, 52–53

Hob Nob Hill ✕, *59, 67*

Holiday Bowl, *117*

Holiday Inn Express, *61, 90*

Holiday Inn on the Bay, *61, 83*

Holiday Inn Pueblo Amigo, *154*

Home exchange, *xxiv*

Horseback riding, *xxix, 114, 160*

Horse racing, *118*

Horton, Alonzo, *25*

Horton Grand Hotel, *30, 83*

Horton Plaza, *30–31*

Hospitality Point, *48*

Hostels, *xxvii, 92*

Hotel Circle, *86–87, 122–123*

Hotel Coral and Marina, *164*

Hotel Del Coronado, *35, 60, 78, 94*

Hotel del Valle, *165*

Hotel Mission Santa Ysabel, *165*

Hotel Quinta Terranova, *159*

Hotels. ☞ Accommodations

House of Hospitality (Balboa Park), *18*

House of Pacific Relations, *18, 20*

Humphrey's by the Bay (club), *98*

Humphrey's Half Moon Inn, *85*

Hurricane's Bar and Grill, *95*

Hussong's Cantina (bar), *165*

Hyatt Islandia 🏨, *60, 91–92*

Hyatt Regency La Jolla, *88*

Hyatt Regency San Diego, *79*

I

Ice hockey, *118*

Ice skating, *114*

Il Fornaio ✕, *129*

Imperial Beach, *104*

In Cahootz (club), *96*

Indian Fair, *10*

Indian restaurant, *72*

Information sources, *xxx*

Anza-Borrego Desert, 146

Baja California, 170

Balboa Park, 18

Coronado, 36

for gay and lesbian travelers, xxiii

Horton Plaza, 31

Julian, 143

Mission Bay, 49

North Coast, 136

North County, 141

Old Town, 50

San Diego, 31

for senior citizens, xxvi

for travelers with disabilities, xxi

for travel with children, xix

for U.K. travelers, xxx

U.S. government, xxx

Inn at Rancho Santa Fe, *131–132*

Insurance, *xxiii–xxiv*

International Visitor Information Center, *31*

Italian restaurants, *72–73*

Itinerary recommendations, *7–8*

J

Jai Alai, *155*

Jai Alai Palace (Frontón), *151, 155*

Japanese Friendship Garden, *20*

Jasmine ✕, *65*

Jazz clubs, *98*

Jet skiing, *114*

Jimmy Love's (bar), *95*

Jogging, *114–115*

Johnny M's (dance club), *97*

Joker Hotel, *165*

Jose's (bar), *99*

Julian, *58, 142–143*

Julian Grille, *142*

Julian Lodge, *143*

Junípero Serra Museum, *51*

K

Karl Strauss' Old Columbia Brewery and Grill (bar), *95*
KC's Tandoor ✕, *66, 72*
Kensington, *121*
Kickers (gay bar), *97*
Kona Kai Continental Plaza Resort and Marina, *85*
Koo Koo Roo ✕, *66*

L

La Bufadora (blowhole), *162–163*
La Casa de Bandini, *53*
La Casa de Estudillo, *53–54*
La Casa del Zorro ☒, *145*
L.A. Cetto Winery, *152*
La Costa Hotel and Spa, *133–134*
La Embotelladora Vieja ✕, *163*
La Especial ✕, *154*
La Flor de Michoacán ✕, *158*
La Fonda Roberto's ✕, *153*
La Jolla, *5, 39–45*
accommodations, 88–90
beaches, 44, 45, 107–108
festivals, 10, 11
restaurants, 43–44, 45, 66–67, 70, 71, 73, 75, 76
shopping, 122
tour, 40–41
La Jolla Caves, *41*
La Jolla Cove, *41, 43, 62, 107*
La Jolla Cove Suites, *60–61, 89*
La Jolla Shores, *62, 107*
La Leña ✕, *158*
La Panadería (bakery), *51*
La Pensione ☒, *84*
La Salsa ✕, *66*
Las Bodegas de Santo Tomás (winery), *162*
Las Rosas ☒, *164*
La Taberna Española ✕, *153*
Latin American restaurant, *73–74*
L'Auberge Del Mar Resort and Spa ✕☒ , *129–130*
Laurel ✕, *71–72*
La Valencia ☒, *43, 88*
La Villa de Zaragoza ☒, *155*
Lawrence Welk Resort ☒, *139*
Lego Construction Zone (festival), *11*
Le Meridien San Diego at Coronado ☒, *78–79*
Leo's Little Bit O'Country (club), *96*
Leucadia, *133*
Lighthouse, *37–38*
Limousines, *xxiv*
Livewire (rock club), *99*
Lodge at Torrey Pines, *90*
Lodging, *xxiv.* ☞ Accommodations

Loews Coronado Bay Resort, *60, 79*
Loma Vista Bed and Breakfast, *141*
Los Pelicanos Hotel, *159*
Luggage, what to pack, *xxv*

M

Macy's (department store), *123*
Magnolia Mulvaney's (club), *96*
Marine Room ✕, *70*
Marine Street Beach, *107*
Mariscos de Bahia Ensenada, *164*
Maritime Museum, *31, 57*
Marius ✕, *65, 71*
Marriott Real Del Mar Residence Inn, *158*
Marston House, *20*
Mason Street School, *54*
Mexican restaurants, *74–75*
Mexitlán, *151*
Mille Fleurs ✕, *131*
Mingei International Museum of World Folk Art, *20, 57*
Miniature golf, *62*
Miniature train ride, *20*
Mission Bay, *5, 45–49*
accommodations, 90–92
children's activities, 62
tour, 46
Mission Bay Motel, *92*
Mission Bay Park, *62*
Mission Beach, *106, 123–124*
Mission Cafe and Coffeehouse, *66*
Mission Coffee Cup Cafe, *67*
Mission San Antonio de Pala, *139*
Mission San Diego de Alcala, *52*
Mission San Luis Rey, *134–135*
Mission San Ysabel, *142*
Mission Valley
accommodations, 86–87
restaurants, 72, 74
shopping, 122–123
Money matters, *xxiv*
Montana's American Grill ✕, *67*
Moonlight Beach Hotel, *133*
Moonlight State Beach, *109*
Moose McGillicuddy's (bar), *95*
Morley Field Sports Complex, *20*
Mother Goose Parade, *11*
Mt. Palomar, *139*
Mount Soledad, *43*
Mundo Divertido, *152*
Museum Cafe, *43–44*
Museum of Contemporary Art, San Diego, *31–32, 43*
Museum of Photographic Arts, *20*

Museum of San Diego History, *20–21*
Museums
Balboa Park, 18, 20, 21, 22, 24
for children, 57
downtown, 30–31
La Jolla, 43, 44
North County, 138, 141
Old Town, 51, 54
Music, *10, 11, 61, 100–101*

N

National parks, passes for, *xxiv*
Nightclubs, *94–95*
Nightlife, *94–99*
Baja California, 155, 159, 165–166
Nordstrom (department store), *121, 123*
North Coast, *127, 129–136*
beaches, 108–109
guided tours, 135
shopping, 123
transportation, 135
visitor information, 136
North County, *123, 136–141*
North Park, *121–122*
Numbers (gay bar), *97*

O

Oakwood Apartments, *78*
Ocean Beach, *106, 123–124*
festivals, 10, 11
Ocean Beach Kite Festival, *10*
Ocean Manor Apartment Hotel, *92*
Oceanside, *109, 134–135*
Oceanside Marina Inn, *134*
Ocotillo Wells State Vehicular Recreation Area, *145*
Off-road vehicles, *115, 145*
O'Hungry's (bar), *95*
Old Bonita Store & Bonita Beach Club (bar), *99*
Old Globe Festival, *10–11*
Old Point Loma Lighthouse, *37–38*
Old Spaghetti Factory ✕, *59*
Old Town, *5, 49–54*
accommodations, 86–87
festivals, 10, 11
restaurants, 51, 73, 74, 76
shopping, 124
tours, 50
Old Town Mexican Café, *59, 74*
Old Town San Diego State Park, *52–53*
Olé Madrid (dance club), *97*
1 America Plaza (office tower), *32*
150 Grand Cafe ✕, *139*
Orange Avenue (Coronado), *35–36*

Orchard Hill Country Inn ☷, 143

Orfila Vineyards, 137

Organ pavilion, 24

Ortega's ✕, 158

Otay Bugambilias ☷, 154–155

Our Lady of Guadalupe (cathedral), 162

Outdoor activities, 6, 104, 106–118
Baja California, 155, 160, 166
participant sports, 109–117
spectator sports, 117–118

Outrigger Motel, 85

Over-the-Line Tournament, 10, 118

P

Pacifica Del Mar ✕, 129

Pacific Beach, 106, 123–124

Pacific Beach Bar and Grill, 95

Pacific Beach Block Party, 10

Pacific Rim restaurants, 75

Pacific Shores Inn, 92

Packages and tours, xxviii–xxix

Packing for the trip, xxv

Palenque ✕, 74

Pal Joey's (jazz club), 98

Palm Canyon Resort, 145

Palomar Mountain State Park, 58

Palomar Observatory, 58, 139

Palomar Plunge, 139

Pamplemousse Grill, 130

Panda Inn ✕, 70

Pannikin (coffeehouse), 95–96

Papas and Beer (bar; Ensenada), 165–166

Papas and Beer (bar; Rosarito Beach), 160

Parks and gardens
Anza-Borrego Desert State Park, 144
Balboa Park, 16, 18, 20
for children, 57–58, 62
Cúyamaca Rancho State Park, 58, 141
Ellen Browning Scripps Park, 43
Mission Bay, 45–49
Old Town, 54
Quail Botanical Gardens, 132
Torrey Pines State Reserve, 44

Parque Revolución, 161

Passports and visas, xxv, 168

Patrick's II (pub), 99

Peacock and Raven ✕, 24

Peohe's ✕, 65

Pho Hoa ✕, 65

Photography, xviii

Phuong Trang ✕, 65

Piano bars, 98

Piatti Ristorante ✕, 59, 73

Pirate's Cove (fun park), 58

Pizza Nova ✕, 66

Playas de Rosarito. ☞ Rosarito Beach

Playas Tijuana, 153

Playgrounds, 63

Plaza Cívica (Ensenada), 161

Plaza de Toros Monumental, 153, 155

Plaza Río Tijuana, 153

Point Loma, 5, 36–39
accommodations, 84–86
beaches, 106
restaurants, 39
tour, 36–37

Point Loma Sea Foods ✕, 39

Presidio Park, 54

Primavera Ristorante, 66

Prince of Wales Room ✕, 65–66

Prospect Park Inn, 89

Pueblo Amigo, 152

Puppet theater, 61

Q

Quail Botanical Gardens, 132

Quinta Plaza, 157

R

Radisson Inn Encinitas, 133

Rainwater's ✕, 66

Ramada Limited Point Loma, 85

Ramada Plaza Hotel Old Town, 87

Rancho Bernardo, 136–137

Rancho Bernardo Inn, 60, 137

Rancho Santa Fe, 131–132

Rancho Valencia ✕, 131

René's ✕, 158

Restaurants, 65–67, 70–76.
☞ types of cuisine
Anza-Borrego Desert, 145
Baja California, 148, 150, 153–154, 157–158, 163–164
Balboa Park, 22, 24
Beaches, 66, 67, 70, 72, 73, 75–76
for children, 59
Coronado, 65–66, 71
downtown, 66, 67, 70, 72, 73, 75–76
Embarcadero, 27
Gaslamp Quarter, 30
Horton Plaza, 31
La Jolla, 43–44, 45, 66–67, 70, 71, 73, 75, 76
Julian and backcountry, 142
Mission Bay, 48
North Coast, 126, 136–137, 139, 140
North County, 140, 142, 143

Old Town, 51, 73, 74, 76

Point Loma, 39

Seaport Village, 32

Uptown, 67, 70, 71–72, 74–75, 76

Reuben H. Fleet Space Theater and Science Center, 21, 57

Rich's San Diego (gay bar), 97

Río Tijuana, 152–153

Riviera del Pacifico, 161–162

Robinson-Rose House, 53

Rock, pop, folk, reggae, and blues clubs, 98–99

Rodeway Inn, 83–84

Rollerblading and roller skating, 115

Romperoom (dance club), 97

Rosarito Beach (Playas de Rosarito), 156–160, 167–170

Rosarito Beach Hotel, 157, 159

S

Saffron Chicken ✕, 59, 66, 76

Sailing, 115

Salk Institute, 44

Sally's ✕, 75–76

Salton Sea National Wildlife Refuge, 145

Salton Sea State Recreation Area, 145

SamSon's ✕, 59, 71

Sand Castle Days, 10

San Diego, 13–54
accommodations, xxiv, 78–79, 82–92
arts, 99–102
Balboa Park, 4, 15–18, 20–24
beaches, 6, 104, 106–109
children's activities, 56–63
Coronado, 4–5, 33–36
downtown and Embarcadero, 5, 25–33
Harbor Island, Point Loma, and Shelter Island, 5, 36–39
La Jolla, 5, 39–45
Mission Bay and Sea World, 5, 45–49
nightlife, 94–99
Old Town, 5, 49–54
restaurants, 65–67, 70–76
shopping, 120–124
sports and outdoors activities, 104–118
Torrey Pines State Reserve, 44
tours of, xxvi–xxvii
transportation, xvii
visitor information, xxx
Wild Animal Park, 56, 137–138

San Diego Actors Theatre, 61

San Diego Aerospace Museum and International Aerospace Hall of Fame, 21

San Diego Automotive Museum, 21

San Diego Chargers, 117

San Diego Children's Theater, 61

San Diego Convention Center, 27

San Diego Crew Classic, 10

San Diego Gulls, 118

San Diego Hall of Champions–Sports Museum, 21

San Diego Harbor Parade of Lights, 11

San Diego Hilton Beach and Tennis Resort, 60, 91

San Diego Junior Theatre, 61–62

San Diego Marriott Hotel and Marina, 92

San Diego Marriott Mission Valley, 86

San Diego Mission Valley Hilton ⚲, 86

San Diego Model Railroad Museum, 21, 57

San Diego Museum of Art, 21–22, 57

San Diego Museum of Man, 22

San Diego Natural History Museum, 22, 57

San Diego Padres, 117

San Diego Princess Resort, 60, 91

San Diego Railroad Museum, 58

San Diego Sockers, 118

San Diego State University Aztecs, 117

San Diego Trolley, xxvi, 168

San Diego Union Newspaper Historical Museum, 54

San Diego Wild Animal Park, 56, 137–138

San Diego Zoo, 22–24, 56

San Elijo Lagoon Ecological Reserve, 132

San Elijo State Beach, 108

San Nicolás ⚲, 165

San Pasqual Battlefield State Historic Park and Museum, 138

Santa Fe Depot, 32

Santa Rosa Plateau Ecological Reserve, 140

Santa Ysabel, 142

San Ysidro Border Crossing, 151

Scott Street (Point Loma), 39

Scripps Inn, 88–89

Sea Cliff Roadside Park, 108–109

Seafood restaurants, 75–76

Sea Lodge, 89

Seaport Village, 32, 57, 124

Seasonal events, 10–11

Sea World, 48–49, 56

Seeley Stables, 53

Self-Realization Fellowship, 132

Senior citizens, xxv–xxvi

Señor Frog's ✕, 154

Serra, Junípero, 49, 51

Shell Beach, 107

Shelter Island, 39, 84–86

Sheraton Grande Torrey Pines, 88

Sheraton San Diego Hotel & Marina, 84

Shopping, 6–7, 120–124

in Baja California, 155–156, 160

for children, 63

Silver Strand State Beach, 36, 62, 104, 106

Simon Edison Centre for the Performing Arts, 24

Singles bars, 99

Sirino's ✕, 138

Soccer, 118

Solana Beach, 108, 130–131

Solid Rock Gym, 58

South Bay, beaches in, 104

South Carlsbad State Beach, 109

Spanish Landing Park, 38

Spanish Village Art Center, 24

Spices Thai Cafe, 129

Split Mountain, 145

Sportfishing Pier, 164

Sports, 6

Anza-Borrego Desert, 145

Baja California, 155, 160, 166

for children, 62–63

participant, 109–117

seasonal events, 10–11

spectator, 117–118

Sportsmen's Sea Foods ✕, 48

Spreckels Organ Pavilion, 24

Starbucks ✕, 31

Star of India (ship), 31

Stephen Birch Aquarium-Museum, 44, 57

Stratford Inn, 130

Street fairs, 10, 11

Street Scene, 11

Students, xxvii

The Study (coffeehouse), 96

Summer Organ Festival, 10

Sunrise National Scenic Byway Highway, 141

Sunset Cliffs, 39, 106

Super 8 Bayview, 84

Surf and Turf Miniature Golf, 62

Surfing, 115–116, 160

Swimming, 116

T

Taste of Thai ✕, 76

Taxis, xxvii

Taxxi (dance club), 97

Telephones, xxvii

Temecula, 140–141

Temecula Creek Inn, 140–141

Temecula Historic Museum, 140

Tennis, 116

Thai restaurants, 76

Theater, 61–62, 101–102

Therapy at Ministry (rock club), 99

Thomas Whaley Museum, 54

Tía Juana Tilly's ✕, 154

Tidbits (club), 96

Tijuana, 150–156, 167–170

Tijuana Cultural Center, 153

Timken Museum of Art, 24

Top O' the Cove ✕, 71, 98

Torrey Pines Cafe, 129

Torrey Pines City Park (Black's Beach), 44

Torrey Pines Glider Port, 44

Torrey Pines State Beach, 108

Torrey Pines State Reserve, 44

Tosca's ✕, 72

Tourist cards, 168

Tourmaline Surfing Park, 107

Tour operators, xxvii–xxix

group tours, xxviii

packages, xxviii–xxix

senior citizens, xxvi

single travelers, xxviii

students, xxvii

theme trips, xxix

travelers with disabilities, xxi

Tours and sightseeing, xxvi–xxvii

Baja California, 169

North Coast, 135

Trains, xxix, 135

Transit Center, 32

Transportation

Anza-Borrego Desert, 146

Baja California, 167–168

Julian and backcountry, 143

North Coast, 135

North County, 141

San Diego, xvii

Trattoria Mama Anna ✕, 73

Travel agencies, xxix

gay and lesbian travelers, xxiii

travelers with disabilities, xxi

Travel gear, xxix–xxx

Travelodge Ensenada, 165

Travelodge Hotel Harbor Island, 84–85

Travelodge Point Loma, 86

Triangles ✕, 70

Trolleys, xxvi, 168

Tuna Harbor, 27

Twiggs Tea and Coffee Co. (coffeehouse), 96

U

U.K. citizens
air travel, xvi
car rental, xix
customs and duties, xx
insurance, xxiv
passports and visas, xxv
tour operators, xxix
visitor information, xxx
U. S. Grant Hotel, *32–33,
    82, 99*
**University of California at
    San Diego,** *45*
Upstart Crow & Co. ✕, *32*
Uptown District, *24*
*restaurants, 67, 70, 71–72,
    74–75, 76*

V

Vacation Inn, *87*
Vacation Isle, *49*
Vigilucci's Pizzeria ✕, *132–
    133*
Villa Montezuma, *33*

Visas. ☞ Passports and
    visas
Visitor information, *xxx.* ☞
    Information sources
Volleyball, *116*

W

Walking tours, *xxvii*
Waterfront attractions, *26–
    27*
Waterskiing, *116*
Wave Water Park, *58*
Weather, *xxx–xxxi*
Welk Resort Center 🏨, *139*
Wells Fargo Museum, *54*
Westgate Hotel, *82, 98*
**Westin Hotel San Diego-
    Horton Plaza,** *83*
Whale-watching, *xxvii,
    xxix, 38*
Wild Animal Park, *56, 137–
    138*
festival at, 11

William Heath Davis House,
    27, 30
Windansea Beach, *45, 107*
Windsurfing, *117*
Wineries, *137, 140, 152,
    162*
Winston's Beach Club (rock
    club), *99*
Wolf's (gay bar), *97*
**Wyndham Emerald Plaza
    Hotel,** *82–83*

Z

**Zanzibar Coffee Bar and
    Gallery,** *96*
Zinc Cafe, *130–131*
Zoo Country (club), *96*
Zoos and aquariums
*San Diego Wild Animal Park,
    56, 137–138*
San Diego Zoo, 22–24, 56
Sea World, 48–49, 56
*Stephen Birch Museum-
    Aquarium, 44, 57*

NOTES

NOTES

NOTES

NOTES

NOTES

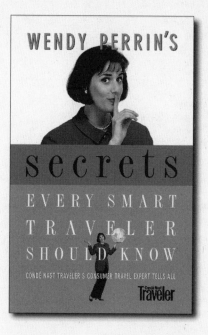

Fodor's Travel Publications

Available at bookstores everywhere, or call 1–800–533–6478, 24 hours a day.

Gold Guides

U.S.

Alaska

Arizona

Boston

California

Cape Cod, Martha's
Vineyard, Nantucket

The Carolinas &
Georgia

Chicago

Colorado

Florida

Hawai'i

Las Vegas, Reno,
Tahoe

Los Angeles

Maine, Vermont,
New Hampshire

Maui & Lāna'i

Miami & the Keys

New England

New Orleans

New York City

Pacific North Coast

Philadelphia & the
Pennsylvania Dutch
Country

The Rockies

San Diego

San Francisco

Santa Fe, Taos,
Albuquerque

Seattle & Vancouver

The South

U.S. & British Virgin
Islands

USA

Virginia & Maryland

Walt Disney World,
Universal Studios
and Orlando

Washington, D.C.

Foreign

Australia

Austria

The Bahamas

Belize & Guatemala

Bermuda

Canada

Cancún, Cozumel,
Yucatán Peninsula

Caribbean

China

Costa Rica

Cuba

The Czech Republic
& Slovakia

Eastern &
Central Europe

Europe

Florence, Tuscany
& Umbria

France

Germany

Great Britain

Greece

Hong Kong

India

Ireland

Israel

Italy

Japan

London

Madrid & Barcelona

Mexico

Montréal &
Québec City

Moscow, St.
Petersburg, Kiev

The Netherlands,
Belgium &
Luxembourg

New Zealand

Norway

Nova Scotia, New
Brunswick, Prince
Edward Island

Paris

Portugal

Provence &
the Riviera

Scandinavia

Scotland

Singapore

South Africa

South America

Southeast Asia

Spain

Sweden

Switzerland

Thailand

Toronto

Turkey

Vienna & the Danube

Special-Interest Guides

Adventures to Imagine

Alaska Ports of Call

Ballpark Vacations

Caribbean Ports
of Call

The Official Guide to
America's
National Parks

Disney Like a Pro

Europe Ports of Call

Family Adventures

Fodor's Gay Guide
to the USA

Fodor's How to Pack

Great American
Learning Vacations

Great American
Sports & Adventure
Vacations

Great American
Vacations

Great American
Vacations for
Travelers with
Disabilities

Halliday's New
Orleans Food
Explorer

Healthy Escapes

Kodak Guide to
Shooting Great
Travel Pictures

National Parks and
Seashores of the East

National Parks of
the West

Nights to Imagine

Rock & Roll Traveler
Great Britain and
Ireland

Rock & Roll Traveler
USA

Sunday in
San Francisco

Walt Disney World
for Adults

Weekends in New
York

Wendy Perrin's
Secrets Every Smart
Traveler Should
Know

Fodor's Special Series

Fodor's Best Bed & Breakfasts

America

California

The Mid-Atlantic

New England

The Pacific Northwest

The South

The Southwest

The Upper Great Lakes

Compass American Guides

Alaska

Arizona

Boston

Chicago

Colorado

Hawaii

Idaho

Hollywood

Las Vegas

Maine

Manhattan

Minnesota

Montana

New Mexico

New Orleans

Oregon

Pacific Northwest

San Francisco

Santa Fe

South Carolina

South Dakota

Southwest

Texas

Utah

Virginia

Washington

Wine Country

Wisconsin

Wyoming

Citypacks

Amsterdam

Atlanta

Berlin

Chicago

Florence

Hong Kong

London

Los Angeles

Montréal

New York City

Paris

Prague

Rome

San Francisco

Tokyo

Venice

Washington, D.C.

Exploring Guides

Australia

Boston & New England

Britain

California

Canada

Caribbean

China

Costa Rica

Egypt

Florence & Tuscany

Florida

France

Germany

Greek Islands

Hawaii

Ireland

Israel

Italy

Japan

London

Mexico

Moscow & St. Petersburg

New York City

Paris

Prague

Provence

Rome

San Francisco

Scotland

Singapore & Malaysia

South Africa

Spain

Thailand

Turkey

Venice

Flashmaps

Boston

New York

San Francisco

Washington, D.C.

Fodor's Gay Guides

Los Angeles & Southern California

New York City

Pacific Northwest

San Francisco and the Bay Area

South Florida

USA

Pocket Guides

Acapulco

Aruba

Atlanta

Barbados

Budapest

Jamaica

London

New York City

Paris

Prague

Puerto Rico

Rome

San Francisco

Washington, D.C.

Languages for Travelers *(Cassette & Phrasebook)*

French

German

Italian

Spanish

Mobil Travel Guides

America's Best Hotels & Restaurants

California and the West

Major Cities

Great Lakes

Mid-Atlantic

Northeast

Northwest and Great Plains

Southeast

Southwest and South Central

Rivages Guides

Bed and Breakfasts of Character and Charm in France

Hotels and Country Inns of Character and Charm in France

Hotels and Country Inns of Character and Charm in Italy

Hotels and Country Inns of Character and Charm in Paris

Hotels and Country Inns of Character and Charm in Portugal

Hotels and Country Inns of Character and Charm in Spain

Short Escapes

Britain

France

New England

Near New York City

Fodor's Sports

Golf Digest's Places to Play

Skiing USA

USA Today The Complete Four Sport Stadium Guide

WHEREVER YOU TRAVEL, *H*ELP IS NEVER FAR AWAY.

From planning your trip to providing travel assistance along the way, American Express® Travel Service Offices are always there to help you do more.

San Diego

American Express Travel Service
7610 Hazard Center Road
Suite 515
619/297-8101

Anderson Travel Group (R)
11828 Rancho Bernard Road
Suite 113
619/487-7722

American Express Travel Service
258 Broadway
619/234-4455

Anderson Travel Group (R)
4223 Genesee Avenue
619/292-4100

Carefree Travel (R)
2927A Canon Street
619/224-2961

Carefree Travel (R)
6940 Alvardo Road
Suite B
619/286-6200

do more
Travel

http://www.americanexpress.com/travel

American Express Travel Service Offices are located throughout California. For the office nearest you, call 1-800-AXP-3429.